HARCOURT BRACE JOVANOVICH

An exciting new approach to language arts!

Imagination

An Odyssey Through Language

Instruction that thoroughly integrates reading, writing, listening, and speaking with thinking

Literature-based learning experiences that explore universal themes, positive values, and varied cultures

Techniques that actively engage students in thinking critically, creatively, and logically as they read and respond to literature

Innovative strategies that make learning exciting and teaching enjoyable

Logical components for an integrated instructional plan

Reader's Corner
A full-color student book of literature selections with "Think and Read" and "Think and Discuss" activities—plus, for reference, Word Spot: Words, Pictures, Meanings (grade 1); Glossary (grades 2–6); and Literary Terms (grades 2–6)

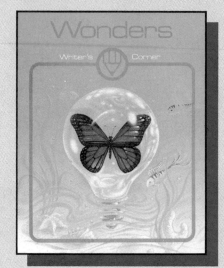

Writer's Corner
A colorful companion book that includes "Think and Write" and "Think and Extend" activities—plus Writer's Handbook (grades 1–6), Words: Alike and Different (grades 1 and 2), and Writer's Thesaurus (grades 3–6)

Activity Book
Motivating activities for each selection that allow students to analyze the writer's use of language in the context of literature

Teacher's Edition
A complete resource that contains easily usable integrated instructional plans; visual, auditory, and kinesthetic teaching models; and, in copying-master form, teacher/student resources and evaluation resources

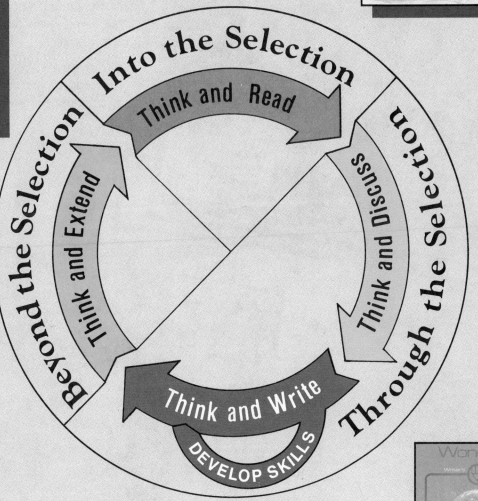

Into the Selection

Think and Read

Think and Discuss

Through the Selection

Think and Write

DEVELOP SKILLS

Beyond the Selection

Think and Extend

Quality literature—the springboard for integrating language arts!

Award-winning literature and high-interest informational selections spark active student involvement—insightful questions, lively discussions, and responsive writing.

An inviting collection of fiction and nonfiction represents the best in classic and contemporary literature.

THE THREE BEARS

An English folk tale retold in pictures by Kinuko Craft

This porridge is too hot.

Let us go for a walk. When we come back, our porridge will be ready to eat.

From Reader's Corner, Grade 1

The Garden

Story and pictures by Arnold Lobel

Frog was in his garden. Toad came walking by. "What a fine garden you have, Frog," he said. "Yes," said Frog. "It is very ni but it was hard work." "I wish I had a garden," said "Here are some flower seeds. Plant them in the ground," said F "and soon you will have a garde "How soon?" asked Toad. "Quite soon," said Frog.

From Reader's Corner, Grade 2

Universal unit themes enable students to connect ideas among selections, explore positive values in depth, and share rich multicultural experiences.

TWO OF EVERYTHING
A Chinese tale told by Li-Po
Illustrated by Jane Teiko Oka

Mr. and Mrs. Hak-Tak were rather old and rather poor. They had a small house in a village among the mountains and a tiny patch of green land on the mountain side. Here they grew the vegetables which were all they had to live on. When it was a good season and it was grown, Mr. Hak-Tak took what vegetables they could spare in a basket to the next village. There, he sold them for as much as he could get and bought some oil for their lamp, and fresh seeds. Every now and then, but not often, he bought a piece of cotton stuff to make new coats and trousers for himself and his wife. You can imagine they did not often get the chance to eat meat.

Now, one day it happened that when Mr. Hak-Tak was digging in his precious patch, he unearthed a big brass pot. He thought it strange that it should have been there for so long without his having come across it before, and he was disappointed to find it was empty. Still, he thought they wou... the pot, so when he was ready t... house in the evening he decided...

From Reader's Corner, Grade 5

48

CONNECTIONS
Dreams of Flight

Dreams of flight are woven into the myths of almost every culture. Stories tell of winged lions, dragons, and bulls. Both good and evil spirits have wings. The story of Icarus warns people not to fly too high. In another Greek myth, a hero rides Pegasus (PEG·uh·suhs), a flying horse, to glorious adventures.

For thousands of years people in Asia have flown kites. Some Asian peoples believed that flying kites over a house at night kept evil spirits away. Today kites are flown during religious festivals.

Some people's dreams of flight have reached beyond earthly skies. About 200, a Greek named Lucian of Samosata (loo·SHAHN of sam·oh·SAH·uh) wrote of people carried into space by a whirlwind. A French writer named Cyrano de Bergerac (SEE·rah·noh duh BEHR·zhuh·rak) wrote a story called "Voyage to the Moon," which was published in 1657. His voyagers traveled in a flying chariot with mechanical wings, powered by skyrockets.

A few courageous men tried to turn their dreams of flight into reality.

270

Early Dreams of Flight

Leonardo da Vinci (lee·uh·NAHR·doh dah VIN·chee), the great artist, scientist, and inventor who lived during the Italian Renaissance (REN·uh·SAHNS), knew the story of Icarus, too, dreamed of flying. In the early 1500s he made many designs of flying machines, based on careful studies of birds and bats.

Most of da Vinci's flying machines had wings that flapped, as many birds' wings do. The plan for some of his machines called for the pilot to work the wings partly with his arms and partly with his feet. However, flapping wings cannot raise a person into the air as successfully as they can lift a bird. Birds can lift their own weight in ways that people cannot. So it is unlikely that da Vinci's flapping-wing designs could have worked.

Toward the end of his life, da Vinci drew a machine in which only the outer part of the wings moved. He also built a helicopter and a pyramid-shaped parachute.

No one knows if da Vinci ever tried to fly one of his machines. There is some evidence that he did—unsuccessfully. He may have tried from a hill called "Swan Mountain," near Florence, Italy; for he wrote, "The great bird will first take flight from the back of the great swan, filling the universe with amazement."

More than a hundred years later, two French brothers did what Leonardo da Vinci had dreamed was possible.

Leonardo da Vinci
(1452–1519)

271

From Reader's Corner, Grade 6

Learning strategies that promote understanding and sharing ideas

Into the Selection

Preceding each selection, **Think and Read** helps students

▶ activate prior knowledge

▶ make predictions

▶ set a purpose for reading

Focusing on "Just the Thing for Geraldine"

Think and Read

▶ Talk about the different kinds of lessons you might take. Ask your classmates questions.

▶ Look at the title and the pictures on pages 30–39. Think about lessons you know about.
  • Who do you think is the main character?
  • What kind of lessons are being given? What makes you think as you do?
  • What might happen in this story?

▶ Get ready to read a story about a possum named Geraldine. As you read, think about what Geraldine is good at doing. Notice what she is not so good at doing. Think about what to add to this chart.

What Geraldine Is Good at Doing	What Geraldine Is Not So Good at Doing

Now turn the page and read "Just the Thing for Geraldine." Then you will talk about talents.

29

From Reader's Corner, Grade 3

Sample pages are reduced. Actual sizes are 7½"x 9" (Reader's Corner).

Through the Selection

Following each selection, **Think and Discuss** guides students through a range of thinking processes and encourages them to ask questions.

Think and Discuss

Think about the story. Copy the chart on page 29. Fill in the information. Then answer the questions.

1. Use your chart. What is Geraldine not so good at doing? Why do you think this is so?

2. Why do you think Geraldine's parents want her to learn ballet and sculpture?

3. Why does Geraldine not want to take singing lessons?

4. Think about Geraldine's brother Randolph. What do you think his special talent might be? Tell why. Tell how you think he might use his talent.

5. Geraldine opens a juggling school. How else might she use her talent for juggling?

6. Why is this story in a unit about things that are one of a kind?

WORK IN A GROUP

Tell what having a talent means to you. Ask questions about what your classmates say. Talk about the answers.

50

From Reader's Corner, Grade 3

Responding to literature through the writing process

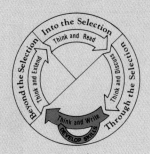

Through the Selection

Using the literary selection as a springboard, **Think and Write** focuses on a specific type of writing and guides students through the writing process.

Focusing on "Just the Thing for Geraldine"

Think and Write

A Friendly Letter About a Talent

Choose one thing that you do well. Write a letter to your teacher.

Prewriting

- Think. Why am I writing? Who will read what I write?

- Finish this chart. Think about what you do well. Think about why your talent is important.

What I Do Well	Why It Is Important

- Talk over your ideas with your classmates.

Drafting

- Use your chart for ideas. Write a letter to your teacher. Tell what you do well.

- Remember to use the five parts of a letter.

- Remember why you are writing. Remember for whom you are writing.

12

From Writer's Corner, Grade 3

Sample pages are reduced. Actual sizes are 7½"x 9" (Writer's Corner).

• Do not worry about mistakes. You will have time later to make changes.

Responding

• Read your letter to yourself. Then read it to a partner. Your partner will pretend to be the teacher. Ask your partner these questions.

WORK WITH A PARTNER

1. Does my letter tell about what I do well? Tell why or why not.

2. What do you like about my letter?

3. What else would you like to know?

• Now have your classmate ask you questions about your writing.

Revising

• Think about what your partner said. Read your letter again. Then make changes.

1. Does all of your letter tell about what you do well? Each sentence should tell something about your talent.

2. Does your letter tell why what you do well is important? Try to add details to sentences. Use your prewriting chart.

13

From Writer's Corner, Grade 3

---

3. Are your ideas written in the form of a letter? Check that your letter has five parts. **page 205**

Editing

Writer's Handbook

• Make your letter ready for your teacher to read. Make changes.

Editor's Marks

☰	capitalize
⊙	make a period
∧	add something
⌃	add a comma
ᵛⱽ	add quotation marks
─ᵃ─	take something away
◯	spell correctly
¶	indent the paragraph
/	make a lowercase letter
᷉	transpose

1. Check that each sentence tells a complete thought. **page 166**

2. Check that you used capital letters for the names of people and their titles. **page 215**

3. Check that you used punctuation marks correctly. A period should follow the titles *Mr.*, *Mrs.*, and *Ms.* **page 219**

4. Use a dictionary to check your spelling.

• Make a clean copy. Write neatly and correctly.

Postwriting (Publishing)

• Address an envelope to your teacher. Put your letter in the envelope. Then hand your letter to your teacher.

◄ Thinking Back

Talk about what you did to write about your special talent.

14

From Writer's Corner, Grade 3

Skills instruction—based on students' needs!

From Writer's Corner, Grade 3

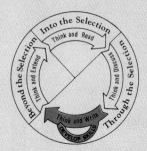

Through the Selection

The **Writer's Handbook** enables students to locate answers to their own questions about language, composition, handwriting, spelling, vocabulary, and resource skills. Conveniently located in the back of the *Writer's Corner,* it provides succinct instruction, clear examples, and immediate practice.

COMPOSITION

CLEAR SENTENCES

when • A good writer begins sentences in different ways. Sometimes a writer begins sentences with words that tell *when.*

I read about spiders <u>today</u>.
<u>Today</u> I read about spiders.

How to Change Sentence Beginnings
1. Find some sentences that begin with the same word.
2. Look for sentences that tell *when.*
3. Begin some of the sentences with words that tell *when.*

Practice

Find the word or words in each sentence that tell *when.* Then write each sentence in a different way. Begin with the word or words that tell *when.*

1. We read about spiders in class today.
2. I had read about spiders last year.
3. The teacher then showed pictures of spiders.
4. Some spiders spin webs at night.
5. I saw a spider in the garden yesterday.
6. I will bring my spider poster tomorrow.
7. Everyone in class now likes spiders.
8. I will tell my brother about spiders tonight.
9. The teacher will show us another book later.
10. I am going to read about snakes next.

From Activity Book, Grade 3

Name _____

Adjectives

Understanding Adjectives in a Story

THINK AND DISCUSS

Read the first page of the "Guess Who My Favorite Person Is" on *Reader's Corner* page 145. What are some of the things the writer tells about? What kind of words are they? How does the writer tell more about these words? A word that describes a noun is called an **adjective.** What are some other adjectives the writer uses in this story?

What does the adjective *yellow* tell about the flowers? What does the adjective *little* tell about the kid? What does the adjective *loud* tell about the sound the bees make? Adjectives tell many things about the nouns they describe. They can tell *what size, what color, how much,* and *what sound.* Sometimes they describe how something feels, tastes, or smells.

Why does the writer use adjectives in this story? Think about the adjectives the writer uses. How are they like the paints that an artist uses to paint pictures?

PRACTICE
Using Adjectives

A. Read these sentences about the story. Think of adjectives to complete the sentences. Write the sentences.

1. The ladybugs are climbing _____ flowers.

   _____

2. I see a _____ kid lying in the field.

   _____

3. What is your _____ color?

   _____

IMAGINATION, *Wonders,* "Guess Who My Favorite Person Is," pages 144–152

The **Activity Book** helps students analyze the writer's use of language in the context of literature.

Sample pages are reduced. Actual sizes are 7½"x 9" (Writer's Corner), 8¼"x10⅞" (Activity Book), and 9"x11¼" (Teacher's Edition).

Creative extension for all students

Beyond the Selection

Think and Extend activities relate literature to other curriculum areas and help students connect ideas from literature to their own experiences.

- Write facts about frogs in one circle.
- Write facts about toads in the other circle.
- Write facts that are the same for frogs and toads in the middle.

3. Plan your talk. First you may want to tell how frogs and toads are alike. Then you may want to tell how they are different.

4. Give your talk.
- Speak so everyone can hear you.
- Say your words clearly.
- Look at your classmates as you speak.

11

For the Home

The homework assignments that follow also appear on **Homework Notebook copying master 2.** You may wish to distribute the copying masters to students.

Writing Have each student dictate to a parent or older family member a story about two friends. Tell students that the stories can be about anything two friends do together and the characters can be real or imaginary.

After the parent or family member has recorded the story, the student should read it aloud. Suggest that students bring their stories to class the following day and share them with their classmates.

Reading Have students read and discuss with a parent or family member another story about friends or additional Frog and Toad stories by Arnold Lobel. The following day suggest that students share with their classmates books they especially enjoyed.

For Extended and Recreational Reading

You may wish to recommend the following books for independent reading.

Stories About Friends

May I Bring a Friend? by Beatrice S. DeRegniers. Atheneum, 1964.
What Mary Jo Shared by Janice M. Udry. Albert Whitman & Company, 1966.
Frog and Toad Together by Arnold Lobel. Harper & Row, 1972.

More Stories About Friends

Frog and Toad All Year by Arnold Lobel. Harper & Row, 1976.
Frog and Toad Are Friends by Arnold Lobel. Harper & Row, 1970.

Writer's Corner 31

From Teacher's Edition, Grade 2

Mathematics—**Writing Word Problems**

Geraldine opened a school to teach juggling. Write word problems about some things that Geraldine did.

Think and Extend

1. Geraldine sometimes juggled acorns, blackberries, pebbles, or pine cones.
   - Use the facts to write an addition problem.
   - Write the answer to the problem.

   You might write a problem like this one.

   Geraldine juggled three acorns, five blackberries, two pebbles, and one pine cone. How many things did Geraldine juggle?

2. Suppose Geraldine was juggling some blackberries. Two of the blackberries were squashed in her hand.
   - Use the facts to write a subtraction problem.
   - Write an answer to the problem.

3. Write your own word problem about Geraldine. It may be about juggling. It may be about something else in the story.
   - Write an answer to the problem.
   - Ask a classmate to solve the problem.

15

From Writer's Corner, Grade 3

The *Teacher's Edition* suggests homework assignments, provides related activities for sharing with family or friends, and includes choices for extended and recreational reading.

Teacher's Editions that make integrated language arts a pleasure to teach

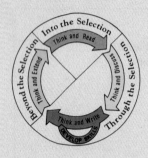

Preceding each unit, a chart for **Students with Individual Needs** suggests strategies for adapting instruction where appropriate.

A **Planning Calendar** for each selection helps teachers easily prepare lessons that integrate reading, writing, listening, and speaking with thinking.

From Teacher's Edition, Grade 2

From Teacher's Edition, Grade 2

Sample pages are reduced. Actual sizes are 9"x11¼" (Teacher's Edition).

Unit 1

Learning Center Activities

The following optional learning center activities for Unit 1 r... theme of t... activities m... completed... unit instruc... Instructions learning ce... the front o... **Edition.**

LISTENIN...
Objective:
Materials:
Procedure:
sells sea s...
directions...
Center cop...

1. Listen sounds
2. Practic twister
3. Record
4. Listen
   • Did
   • Are

PLANNING CALENDAR

		STUDENT'S EDITIONS	TEACHER'S EDITION	ACTIVITY BOOK
DAY 1 INTO THE SELECTION	**THINK AND READ**			
	Preparing to Read	■ page 7	*page 19*	
			▲ Vocabulary Notebook copying masters 2A, 2B	
	Planning a Reading Strategy	■ pages 8–19	*page 20*	
DAYS 2-4 THROUGH THE SELECTION	**THINK AND DISCUSS**			
	Remembering the Selection	■ pages 7, 20	*page 24*	
			▲ Think and Read Notebook copying master 2	
	Using the Discussion Questions	■ page 20	*page 24*	
	THINK AND WRITE			
	Making the Assignment	● page 7	*page 25*	
	Using the Writing Process	● pages 7–9	*pages 25–27*	
		● Writer's Handbook pages 170, 209, 214	▲ Response Guide copying masters 2A, 2B	
	Focusing on Language and Composition	● Writer's Handbook pages 170, 171, 209, 214	*page 28*	
	Focusing on the Writer's Use of Language		*pages 28–29*	*pages 4–6*
	Focusing on Spelling	● Writer's Handbook page 225	*pages 28–29*	
			▲ Study Steps to Learn a Word copying master	
	Focusing on Handwriting	● Writer's Handbook page 265	*page 29*	
	Focusing on Resource Skills	● Writer's Handbook page 260	*page 29*	
	Focusing on Vocabulary	● Writer's Handbook page 172	*page 29*	
DAY 5 BEYOND THE SELECTION	**THINK AND EXTEND**			
	For the Classroom	● pages 10–11	*page 30*	
	For the Home		*page 31*	
			▲ Homework Notebook copying master 2	

■ Reader's Corner   ▲ Learning Resources File
● Writer's Corner

18

Visual, Auditory, and **Kines-thetic Teaching Models** for each *Writer's Handbook* page help teachers satisfy the learning styles of a variety of students.

DEVELOPING GRAMMAR SKILLS

Use this page of the **Writer's Handbook** with students whose writing demonstrates a weakness in writing different kinds of sentences. The Teaching Models and *Practice* activity provide opportunities for students to

- identify statements, questions, and exclamations.
- identify the purpose of statements, questions, and exclamations.
- use correct end punctuation.

Note: Use this teaching strategy at the point indicated in each Teaching Model.

Use these sentences for discussion.

This flower is called a rose.
This red flower is so pretty!
Do roses come in other colors?

Ask students how the sentences are alike. You may wish to begin by modeling a possible first response.

Each sentence is alike because it tells a complete thought.

Then ask students how the sentences are different. (*Possible responses: The first sentence tells something; the second sentence shows feeling; the third sentence asks a question; each sentence ends with a different mark.*) Read aloud the definitions and example sentences on page 171. Review the three kinds of sentences.

Visual Teaching Model

Write the sentences from the teaching strategy on the chalkboard.

Follow the teaching strategy in blue.

Draw the following chart on the chalkboard. Number the left outside margin from 1–10. Tell students to copy the chart. Have them use the sentences from the *Practice* activity to fill in the chart.

	Kind of Sentence	What Sentence Does	End Mark Needed
1.			
2.			

Have volunteers explain how they filled in the chart, and fill in the chart on the chalkboard. You may wish to begin by modeling this response to item 1.

Sentence 1 is a statement. It tells about Frog. It ends with a period.

Auditory Teaching Model

Read aloud the three example sentences from the teaching strategy.

Follow the teaching strategy in blue.

Then read aloud the sentences from the *Practice* activity. Have students listen to each sentence and identify it as a statement, a question, or an exclamation. Have students explain why they answered as they did. Also, have them identify the end mark with which each sentence should end.

Note: If you choose to model a response to item 1, use the example in the Visual Teaching Model.

Kinesthetic Teaching Model

Make three sentence strips using the example statement, question, and exclamation from the teaching strategy. Have volunteers read aloud each strip.

Follow the teaching strategy in blue.

Draw a large period, question mark, and exclamation point on the chalkboard. Point to each and have volunteers match the end mark on the sentence strip with the mark on the board. Then have students draw the marks on a large sheet of paper.

Make sentence strips using the sentences from the *Practice* activity. Display and read the first sentence strip. Ask students if the sentence is a statement, a question, or an exclamation and why they think as they do.

Note: If you choose to model a response to item 1, use the example in the Visual Teaching Model.

Direct students to look at the end mark in the sentence and identify it. (*a period*) Have students trace the same mark on their papers. Then have a volunteer place the sentence strip under the period on the chalkboard. Continue with the remaining sentence strips.

Writer's Handbook/Teaching Models

GRAMMAR

KINDS OF SENTENCES

- A **statement** is a sentence that tells something. It begins with a capital letter. It ends with a **period (.)**.   statement

    Frog gives some seeds to Toad.

- A **question** is a sentence that asks something. It begins with a capital letter. It ends with a **question mark (?)**.   question

    Will Toad plant seeds?

- An **exclamation** is a sentence that shows strong feeling. It begins with a capital letter. It ends with an **exclamation point (!)**.   exclamation

    What a fine garden Frog has!

Practice

Read the sentences. Write statement for a telling sentence. Write question for an asking sentence. Write exclamation for a sentence that shows strong feeling.

1. Frog was in his garden.   statement
2. Who came walking by?   question
3. Toad stopped to look at the garden.   statement
4. What did Toad do?   question
5. Toad read a story to his seeds.   statement
6. Did Toad do anything else?   question
7. Poor Toad fell asleep in his garden!   exclamation
8. The seeds started to grow.   statement
9. What makes seeds grow?   question
10. Toad works so hard!   exclamation

171

Writer's Corner 553

From Teacher's Edition, Grade 2

Innovative strategies that make teaching and learning exciting

Imagination provides powerful teaching-learning strategies…

▶ for helping students see reading, writing, listening, and speaking as closely related language processes

▶ for teaching thinking as an integral part of all language processes

▶ for actively involving students in learning

▶ for satisfying individual learning needs and styles

▶ for teaching phonics, in the early grades, to develop fluency in reading and spelling

▶ for developing oral language proficiency

▶ for cooperative learning and reciprocal learning as alternatives for effective instruction

▶ for helping students understand the techniques they use in reading and writing successfully

▶ for activating prior knowledge, previewing reading selections, and making predictions to increase comprehension

▶ for using diagrams and charts to help students organize thinking

Useful options for assessment

In addition to tips for evaluating oral and written responses, the *Teacher's Edition* contains a wealth of copying masters for ongoing informal assessment—including checklists for evaluating listening, speaking, reading, and writing plus holistic and analytic guidelines for assessing composition.

OBSERVATION GUIDE

Name

RATING   **N:** no behavior   **B:** beginning behavior   **D:** developing behavior   **S:** secure behavior

LISTENING

	Aug.	Sept.	Oct.	Nov.	Dec.	Jan.	Feb.	Mar.	Apr.	May	June	July	Comments
• Distinguishes sounds in the environment													
• Listens to stories from books, records, films													
• Listens to new ideas													
• Listens to peers													
• Appreciates prose, poetry, rhyme													
• Listens for information													
• Comprehends facts, main ideas in discussion													

IMAGINATION, *Changes*

Observation Guide • E39

HBJ material copyrighted under notice appearing earlier in this work.

From Teacher's Edition, Grade 1

Name

WRITING 1 continued

Pretend you are Kristin. Write a letter to Nicky suggesting a business she might start to earn some money for her trip.

18 • w

Name

Writing a Letter

WRITING 1

Read this story about two good friends. After you finish, read the directions for writing about it.

After Kristin and her mom had moved to Maine from the town in Florida where they had always lived, she missed her friend, Nicky. Kristin and Nicky had promised to write to each other, but neither girl was sure that they would stick to their agreement.

After a year though, they were still writing. In each letter, Nicky told Kristin news about the people and places in the town where they had both grown up. Kristin enjoyed her new home, but reading Nicky's letters made her long to see familiar people and places.

Kristin's letters to Nicky were quite different. They told about exciting new experiences. They told of snow, sleds, skis, snowmobiles, and other winter things that were new to Kristin. Reading Kristin's letters made Nicky want to visit her badly.

Kristin surprised Nicky with a phone call one day to tell her about an idea that her mother had. She invited Nicky to visit her new home during winter vacation. She also asked if Nicky's family would let her stay with them for a few weeks in the summer.

Nicky asked her parents about what Kristin had suggested. They said it would be fine, but they wanted her to help pay for her trip by earning some of the money herself. Nicky agreed, but when she sat down to figure out her plans, she was not able to think of any ideas to earn money. She wrote to Kristin asking for ideas.

HBJ material copyrighted under notice appearing earlier in this work.

IMAGINATION, *Memories*

Writing • 17

To help formally assess instructional needs, the *Tests* booklet provides diagnostic tests of grammar, usage, mechanics, and spelling, as well as unit reading and writing tests—all in copying-master form.

Sample pages are reduced. Actual sizes are 9" × 11¼" (Teacher's Edition) and 8¼" × 10⅞" (Tests).

From Tests, Grade 4

P15

A kindergarten program for a captivating beginning

Featuring delightful children's literature, the kindergarten program of *Imagination: An Odyssey Through Language* fosters positive language experiences that integrate listening, speaking, reading, and writing with thinking.

Shared reading and writing activities help make literature meaningful for children and develop a variety of prereading and prewriting concepts.

Big Books

Quality literature, organized around appealing themes, that provides the core of kindergarten instruction and invites shared reading experiences

Activity Book

Motivating student-generated activities that focus on a variety of language concepts and skills

Storybooks

Six colorful storybooks that reproduce *Big Book* selections and offer delightful "bonus" selections for extended or recreational reading

Teacher's Edition

A kindergarten teaching resource with integrated instructional plans, a wealth of teacher/student resources in copying-master form, and bibliographies for extended and recreational reading

Exciting components for total teaching support

Teacher's ResourceBank™ (Grades K–6)

A valuable package that contains a Learning Resources File—a rich collection of student, teacher, and evaluation resources (in copying-master form) with file folders—conveniently housed in an attractive, durable case with carrying strap

Idea Book for Active Learners (Grades 1–6)

Consumable books that help students organize and record their thoughts and ideas related to each unit

Tests (Grades 1–6)

Diagnostic tests and unit reading and writing tests to help assess student progress and instructional needs

HBJ Readers' Libraries (Grades K–6)

Delightful collections of quality children's books for recreational reading, including *Beginning Readers' Library* (grade K), *Young Readers' Library* (grades 1–3), and *Junior Readers' Library* (grades 4–6)

HBJ Writer's File (Grades 1 and 2, 3–6)

A software program that helps students build language arts skills for more effective writing

Inservice Videotapes

Informative presentations that explain the philosophy and integrated instructional plan of *Imagination: An Odyssey Through Language*

Advisory Board

IMAGINATION
An Odyssey Through Language

Teacher's Edition

Happy Times!

Story Land 1 • Story Land 2

Gail Heald-Taylor
General Consultant, Language Arts

HBJ **HARCOURT BRACE JOVANOVICH, PUBLISHERS**
Orlando   San Diego   Chicago   Dallas

Acknowledgments

For permission to reprint copyrighted material, grateful acknowledgment is made to the following sources:

Alfred Publishing Co., Inc.: Music and lyrics from "Sammy," "Beautiful Day," and "This is the Way We Get Up in the Morning" in *Hap Palmer Favorites* by Hap Palmer. © Copyright MCMLXXXI by Alfred Publishing Co., Inc.

Ashton Scholastic: From pp. 41 and 97 in *The Foundations of Literacy* by Don Holdaway. Published by Ashton Scholastic, 1979.

Child's Play (International) Ltd.: Quick as a Cricket by Audrey Wood, illustrated by Don Wood. © 1982 by M. Twinn.

Dodd, Mead & Company, Inc. and The Society of Authors as the literary representative of the Estate of Rose Fyleman: "The Birthday Child" from *Round the Mulberry Bush* by Rose Fyleman. Copyright 1928 by Dodd, Mead & Company, Inc.; copyright renewed 1955 by Rose Fyleman.

Doubleday, a division of Bantam, Doubleday, Dell Publishing Group and The Society of Authors as the literary representative of the Estate of Rose Fyleman: "Mice" by Rose Fyleman from *Fifty-One New Nursery Rhymes.* Copyright 1931 by Doubleday & Company, Inc. "Singing-Time" from *The Fairy Green* by Rose Fyleman. Copyright 1923 by George H. Doran.

E. P. Dutton, a division of NAL Penguin Inc.: "Quack! Quack! Quack!" from *Hand Rhymes,* collected and illustrated by Marc Brown. Copyright © 1985 by Marc Brown.

Flint Public Library, Flint, MI: "Draw a Circle" and "Let's Go on a Bear Hunt" from *Ring a Ring O'Roses.*

Greenwillow Books, a division of William Morrow & Company, Inc.: Have You Seen My Duckling?, written and illustrated by Nancy Tafuri. Copyright © 1984 by Nancy Tafuri. *Waiting* by Nicki Weiss. Copyright © 1981 by Monica J. Weiss.

Harcourt Brace Jovanovich, Inc.: From "A Literature Curriculum" in *Literature and the Child* by Bernice E. Cullinan. Copyright © 1981

by Harcourt Brace Jovanovich, Inc. *I Love You Mouse* by John Graham, pictures by Tomie dePaola. Text copyright © 1976 by John Graham; illustrations copyright © 1976 by Tomie dePaola. "Letter Forms" from *HBJ Handwriting,* Kindergarten/Readiness, Level Yellow by Betty Kracht Johnson. Copyright © 1987 by Harcourt Brace Jovanovich, Inc.

Harper & Row, Publishers, Inc.: Abridged text and illustrations from *What Is Beyond the Hill?,* written by Ernst A. Ekker, illustrated by Hilda Heyduck-Huth. Text copyright © 1985 by Ernst A. Ekker; translation copyright © 1986 by Harper & Row, Publishers, Inc.; illustrations copyright © 1985 by Hilda Heyduck-Huth. Published by J. B. Lippincott. "At the Zoo" from *Feathered Ones and Furry* by Aileen Fisher. Copyright © 1971 by Aileen Fisher. Published by Thomas Y. Crowell. "Winter Clothes" from *The Rose on My Cake* by Karla Kuskin. Copyright © 1964 by Karla Kuskin. "Very Tall Mouse and Very Short Mouse" from *Mouse Tales,* written and illustrated by Arnold Lobel. Copyright © 1972 by Arnold Lobel. From p. 27 in *The Odyssey of Homer,* translated by Richmond Lattimore. Copyright © 1965, 1967 by Richmond Lattimore. From *Where the Wild Things Are* by Maurice Sendak. Copyright © 1963 by Maurice Sendak. From *A Tree Grows in Brooklyn* by Betty Smith. Copyright 1943, 1947 by Betty Smith. "River Winding" from *River Winding* by Charlotte Zolotow. Text copyright © 1970 by Charlotte Zolotow.

Judson Press: "Mitten Weather" and "Ten Little Chicks" from *Fingerplay Friends* by Audrey Olson Leighton. Copyright © 1984.

Bobbi Katz: From "Company" (Retitled: "Lunch for a Dinosaur") in *Upside Down and Inside Out: Poems for All Your Pockets* by Bobbi Katz. Copyright © 1973 by Bobbi Katz.

Hal Leonard Publishing Corporation: Music and lyrics from "Barnyard Song" in *Songs to Grow On,* edited by Beatrice Landeck. Copyright © 1950 by Edward B. Marks Music Corporation; copyright renewed. All rights reserved.

Lothrop, Lee & Shepard Books, a division of William Morrow & Company, Inc.: Silly Goose by Jan Ormerod. Copyright © 1986 by Jan Ormerod.

Gina Maccoby Literary Agency: "Hello and Good-by" (Retitled: "Hello and Good-bye") from *Hello and Good-by* by Mary Ann Hoberman. Copyright © 1959, renewed 1987 by Mary Ann Hoberman. Published by Little, Brown and Company.

Macmillan Publishing Company: The Chick and the Duckling by Mirra Ginsburg, illustrated by Jose Aruego. Text copyright © 1972 by Mirra Ginsburg; illustrations copyright © by Jose Aruego. From *Over, Under &Through and Other Spatial Concepts* by Tana Hoban. Copyright © 1973 by Tana Hoban. From *Changes, Changes* by Pat Hutchins. Copyright © 1971 by Pat Hutchins. "A Bear Went Over the Mountain" from *THE ROOSTER CROWS: A Book of American Rhymes and Jingles* by Maud and Miska Petersham. Copyright 1945 by Macmillan Publishing Company, renewed 1973 by Miska F. Petersham.

William Morrow & Company, Inc.: Coco Can't Wait! (Hayaku Aitaina) by Taro Gomi. Copyright © 1979 by Taro Gomi; English translation copyright © 1983 by William Morrow and Company, Inc.

Novello & Company Limited: "Mr. Lynn is very thin" from *Finger Play Fun* by A. W. Chitty. Originally published by Paxton Music Limited.

Oxford University Press: "One, two, three, four, five" from *The Oxford Dictionary of Nursery Rhymes,* edited by Iona and Peter Opie. Published by Oxford University Press, 1951. "Star Light, Star Bright" from *The Oxford Nursery Rhyme Book,* collected by Iona and Peter Opie. Published by Oxford University Press, 1955.

Pantheon Books, a division of Random House, Inc.: From *Goodbye, Hello* by Robert Welber. Copyright © 1974 by Robert Welber.

Partner Press: "A Good House," "I Can Count," and "When I Am. . ." from *Finger Frolics,* Revised, compiled by Liz Cromwell, Dixie Hibner, and John R. Faitel.

Margit M. Pendleton, Trustee: "Uno, dos, tres, cho—" from *Teaching Spanish in the Grades* by Margit MacRae. Published by Houghton Mifflin Company, 1957.

G. P. Putnam's Sons: "Hiding" from *All Together* by Dorothy Aldis. Copyright 1952 by Dorothy Aldis; copyright renewed © 1980 by Roy E. Porter.

Random House, Inc.: "The Sea" (anonymous) and "Way Down South" (anonymous) from *The Random House Book of Poetry for Children,* selected and introduced by Jack Prelutsky. Copyright © 1983 by Random House, Inc.

Marian Reiner, on behalf of Eve Merriam: From "Thumbprint" in *A Sky Full of Poems* by Eve Merriam. Copyright © 1964, 1970, 1973 by Eve Merriam. All rights reserved.

Elizabeth M. Roach, Power of Attorney for Marchette Chute: "My Dog" by Marchette Chute from *Favorite Poems Old and New,* selected by Helen Ferris.

Scholastic-TAB Publications Ltd. and Viking Penguin Inc.: From *A House Is a House for Me* by Mary Ann Hoberman. Copyright © 1978 by Mary Ann Hoberman.

Songs Music, Inc.: Music and lyrics from "The Bus Song" in *Tom Glazer's Treasury of Songs for Children.* © Songs Music, Inc., Scarborough, NY 10510.

Sterling Publishing Company, Inc., Two Park Avenue, New York, NY 10016: Music and lyrics from "Six Little Ducks" in *The Funny Songbook* by Esther L. Nelson. Copyright © 1984 by Esther L. Nelson.

Contents

Integrated Instructional Plans

Student/Teacher Resources

Evaluation Resources

Introduction to IMAGINATION, An Odyssey Through Language

Tell me, Muse, of the man of many ways, who was driven far journeys, after he had sacked Troy's sacred citadel. Many were they whose cities he saw, whose minds he learned of, many the pains he suffered in his spirit on the wide sea, struggling for his own life and the homecoming of his companions.
. . . .
. . . . Goddess, daughter of Zeus, speak, and begin our story.

The Odyssey of Homer

The "Man of Many Ways" was Odysseus — king of Ithaca in ancient Greece, hero in the war against Troy, husband of Penelope, father of Telemachus, and, in all his endeavors, a man of unusual cunning, courage, and imagination. Homer's great epic poem the *Odyssey* recounts Odysseus's long wandering journey home from the Trojan War. Three thousand years later, the *Odyssey* remains one of the enduring works of literature, and Odysseus, one of the enduring heroes.

When we hear the word *odyssey* today, however, we think of more than the epic journey of Odysseus. For as time has passed, *odyssey* has taken on other meanings: a long wandering, a series of adventurous journeys marked by many changes of fortune, an intellectual or spiritual quest. In its broadest sense, we could say that *odyssey* describes the life-long journey that all people undertake from birth.

It is that continuing human odyssey and our continuing wonder about it that are at the center of all literature. Though it is history that records our deeds, it is literature that seeks to express our thoughts, feelings, dreams, wonderings, and imaginings about the world. Since its origins in the chants and tales of unknown storytellers, literature has recorded events vividly, recalled our shared experiences, and taught us about ourselves. In doing so, it has come to us in diverse forms — both oral and written — and in divergent voices, the sum of which is our literary heritage, drawn from the past and growing into the future.

That is why literature is the natural foundation for a curriculum that integrates the teaching of listening, speaking, reading, and writing. In IMAGINATION, an integrated language program, literature provides a structure within which children are guided not only in reading a variety of selections, but also in thinking about, discussing, and responding orally and in writing to them.

As children move into, through, and beyond literature selections, they use their imaginations to make connections — to notice how selections they hear and read are linked to common themes; to incorporate into their own writing strategies that published writers use; to trace how the structure of one work is like the structure of another; to find out that people of different times and places share common feelings, experiences, and ideas; and to discover how language makes all of these connections clear.

By giving children the opportunity to use their imaginations to make these connections, IMAGINATION gives them a basis for making other connections while reading, writing, listening, and speaking. For reading, writing, listening, and speaking are integrated with thinking in a mutually enriching process.

Purposes of IMAGINATION

IMAGINATION is a carefully planned integrated language program designed to provide children with a basic literary education. The program's selections and instructional materials are all aimed toward its main objective: to provide a solid foundation of literary experiences on which students may build a lifetime of reading and writing pleasure. To reach this objective, IMAGINATION has the following goals:

- To offer students meaningful experiences that integrate listening, speaking, reading, and writing as they move into, through, and beyond literature selections
- To offer students a wide variety of pleasurable, independent reading of the highest literary quality
- To demonstrate the value of literature and to foster interest in reading
- To develop an understanding of and the ability to use the writing process: prewriting, drafting, responding, revising, editing, and postwriting (publishing, including evaluating)
- To develop the skills of reading, writing, and the other language arts, as well as logical thinking skills
- To promote cooperative and collaborative learning
- To provide models of effective strategies for listening, speaking, reading, and writing that include self questioning and critical thinking
- To encourage thoughtful, critical and creative responses to literature and to develop respect for the responses of others
- To increase understanding of literature's relationship to human experience
- To develop insights into personal thoughts, feelings, and experiences
- To promote recognition of the individual's role in the community and in society
- To develop an awareness of other people and cultures and their contributions to American life and culture as well as to world civilization
- To gain an appreciation for the literary heritage that is a legacy from one generation to another
- To develop an awareness of the meanings and nuances of language

Universal Themes and Positive Values

This chart will help you locate the **Teacher's Edition** pages on which the following universal themes and positive values are focused on in this level of IMAGINATION.

Acceptance of New Ideas

192–194

Confidence

12–14, 112–114, 288–290

Cooperation

464–466

Creativity

58–60, 64–65, 272–274, 278

Effective Communication

344–345, 350

Humor

238–239, 242, 258–260, 448–450, 490–491, 494

Positive Relationships

26–28, 32, 40–42, 47, 72–73, 76, 126–128, 132, 362–364

Responsibility

434–436

Respect for Others

176–178

Sharing

224–226

Understanding Nature

208–210, 214–215, 394–396, 400–401, 408–409, 412, 416, 476

Understanding Others

94–96, 100, 302–304, 308–309

Understanding Surroundings

140–142, 146–147, 154–155, 158, 162–163, 318–319, 322, 326–327, 380–382, 386–387

- To show the power and possibilities of language as a tool for self-expression and to develop an awareness of the persuasive power of language
- To develop an understanding of literary forms, techniques, and styles
- To demonstrate the unique artistry of individual authors and illustrators
- To develop an awareness of the relationship between literature and other subject areas

Criteria for Selections

The abundance of literature may lead us to wonder which books, of so many, children should read: Which books meet children's interests better than others do; which books best suit children's development at one stage or another; which selections offer the most pleasure, the best content, the most compelling themes; and which books pass on the important parts of our literary heritage — the classic and traditional stories, poems, and rhymes that we turn to again and again to reaffirm our common experience.

Perhaps there will never be total agreement about the literature that should comprise each child's basic literary education, but there *is* agreement that children should explore a variety of literature in order to build a foundation for a lifetime of reading pleasure.

In choosing selections for IMAGINATION, the program's developers consulted children's literature specialists,

teachers, librarians — and children and young people themselves. After potential selections were identified, they were evaluated using the following criteria:

Interest Level   Is the selection likely to interest children at this age level?

Quality   Does the selection have high literary quality?

Experience   Is the selection worthwhile, either because it brings pure enjoyment to young readers or because it fosters their personal growth?

Portrayal of Ethnic, Minority, and Special Groups   Does the selection portray all groups fairly?

Further considerations were the selections' relevance to thematic strands and their balance in such areas as content, literary type, multicultural representation, and authorship. The final choices were made after extensive classroom testing.

Organization of Literature Selections

The literature in IMAGINATION is organized thematically around strands. Beginning in kindergarten, the strands form a basis of thematic units in each textbook. The strands in the program appear in the chart on pages T10 and T11.

Thematic Strands in IMAGINATION

Level	GROWING AND CHANGING Roles, relationships, and personal growth	ADVENTURE AND SUSPENSE Real and imaginery adventures	HUMOR The humorous side of life
K	**Hello Friends!** The excitement of building friendships	**Oh, What Fun!** Fun-filled explorations and discoveries	**What a Funny Animal!** Entertaining animals and surprise endings
1	**Let's Go Together** The positive aspects of relationships with friends and family	**Far, Far Away** The call of adventure	**What a Surprise!** Humorous experiences with an element of surprise
2	**We Could Be Friends** The many aspects of friendship	**Something Is There** Mysterious happenings all around	**Tell Me Something Very Silly** The humor of comical characters and improbable events
3	**Helping Hands** Relationships based on mutual help and support	**You Can't Catch Me** Clever and resourceful escapes from danger	**One of a Kind** Unique characters and their humorous predicaments
4	**When Paths Cross** The relationships between contrasting points of view and personal growth	**Across the Land and Sea** The excitement of journeys to new lands	**What a Character!** The actions of remarkable characters in humorous situations
5	**Never Give Up** The role of perseverance in personal growth	**Facing the Unknown** Suspenseful encounters in a variety of settings	**It Must Be a Trick** Tricksters and trickery of many kinds
6	**Dream Keepers** Achievements based on individual dreams and abilities	**Expect the Unexpected** Unexpected encounters and surprise endings	**Funny Side Up** Mix-ups, mishaps and misunderstandings

FANTASY	EARTH, SEA, AND SPACE	QUEST AND HEROISM	HERITAGE
Realms of the imagination	Humans and the natural world	The many aspects of courage	Historic legacies from the past
Imagine That! Make-believe characters and imaginative adventures	**Places I Know** The security of familiar places	**Let's Go Outside** The adventure of independent exploration	
Tell Me a Story Adventures of fantasy characters	**I Wonder** The wonders of the natural world	**I'm Growing** Awareness that people and other living things grow and seek independence	
Long, Long Ago Magical beings, places, and things in a world of fantasy	**Animals All Around** Animals and their natural environments	**I Can Do It!** The courage to act independelty and assume new roles	
Would You Believe It! Cycles of life and the seasons	**There Is a Season...** Cycles of life and the seasons	**Tell Me the Name** The search for personal identity and history	
To Live with Animals Relationships between animals and humans	**To Live with Animals** Relationships between animals and humans	**Problems and Puzzles** Challenges to be met and problems to be solved	
To Live with Nature Animals and the forces of nature and their effects on human survival and the quality of life	**The Live with Nature** Animals and the forces of nature and their effects on human survival and the quality of life	**From America's Past** Heroic characters and events from American history in the 18th and 19th centuries	**America Grows Up** Heroic characters and events from American history in the 18th and 19th centuries
A Tree of Ice, A Rain of Stars Nature as a source of inspiration and beliefs	**A Tree of Ice, A Rain of Stars** Nature as a source of inspiration and beliefs	**Tests of Courage** The many forms of courage in myth, legend, and contemporary life	**Across Time, Around the World** Contributions of various cultures to world civilization

Readability in IMAGINATION

Kindergarten and Level 1 Because most kindergarten and first-grade children are not independent readers, the literature selections are intended for shared-reading experiences. For example, you might begin by reading aloud a selection such as a poem with a refrain, or a story with repetition or predictable "next sentences." Then you can invite the class to "take the next part" or to read aloud in unison. Simple plays — usually presented in the Readers Theatre format — provide still more opportunities for shared reading experiences. To promote oral language development, the selections in Kindergarten and Level One include content-rich illustrations and wordless picture stories so that children may tell or write the story they "read" in the illustrations.

Levels 2 Through 6 Throughout these levels, selections of different lengths, content, and complexity have been included for students with different interests and reading abilities. Teacher review and student testing helped determine that these selections were both interesting and accessible to students at particular grade levels. In addition, text format and organization, page format, and the use of illustration and color not only provide motivation for young readers but also support their reading efforts. Where appropriate, definitions, pronunciations, and explanations of difficult and uncommon vocabulary or foreign terms and expressions are provided on the student-book pages. At Level 6, in particular, this explanatory text often takes the form of footnotes.

Literature for a Lifetime

A literature-based, integrated language arts program requires faith in the lasting effects of teaching and learning. Such faith seems warranted. Most adults who like to read literature can describe one or a hundred rewarding contacts with books in childhood and adolescence. Many such readers might identify with Francie, the child in Betty Smith's novel *A Tree Grows in Brooklyn,* who realizes suddenly the benefits of having learned to read:

> **From that time on, the world was hers for the reading. She would never be lonely again, never miss the lack of intimate friends. Books became her friends and there was one for every mood. There was poetry for quiet companionship. There was adventure when she tired of quiet hours. There would be love stories when she came into adolescence and when she wanted to feel a closeness to someone she could read a biography. On that day when she first knew she could read, she made a vow to read one book a day as long as she lived.**

Teaching a Literature-Based Language Arts Curriculum

I hear, and I forget.
I see, and I remember.
I do, and I understand.

Chinese proverb

Many children come to school with a developing interest in literature. In their preschool years, they have become acquainted with literature in one form or another. They have responded, for instance, to the rhythms, rhymes, and repetitions of verses and songs. They have experienced the pleasure of looking at and listening to stories in books. They have followed the chain of events around a central idea or theme that forms a story.

Children's school experiences with literature, then, is an extension of this developing interest from early childhood; thus some of the goals of a literature-based, integrated language program should be to increase enjoyment and understanding — to broaden and deepen literature experience. These goals are served in two ways: first, by presenting excellent literary selections with increasing variety and complexity; and second, by encouraging and guiding oral and written response.

Ideally, response begins before a selection is read. It includes a discussion or activity to help children connect the world to be met in literature with their own experience. The reading itself invites immediate response, as do questions to elicit discussion after reading. However, children's literary experiences should not end there. It should go on to include focused activities that may make each selection special in each reader's life. The result should be self-generating: readers of literature build anticipation and skill for their next literary encounter, and they increase their desire to read literature independently for their own enjoyment.

Perhaps it goes without saying that the teacher is the key to activate experience with literature. Teachers who, themselves, love literature are priceless models of response. They inspire interest and a search for meaning in the encounter with each new story, poem, play, or work of nonfiction. They increase enjoyment and understanding through thoughtful questioning and purposeful activities — oral and written composition, interpretive reading and dramatization, music and the visual arts, and extensions of literary experiences related to the other content areas. Such teachers know that literature is a legacy to be given to children with love and enthusiasm.

The Reading Experience

PREPARING FOR READING

The preparation for reading literature can be as important as the reading experience itself. You may prepare students for reading a selection by: providing *motivation* that relates to their own experiences, by building *schema* — knowledge central to understanding the selection, and by presenting *new* terms (vocabulary). Motivation can begin with a question or an activity to show students that the selection to be read has some connection to their lives, or to their interests. For example, you might say, "Look at the picture on page 7. Have you ever known a character who did something like that? Show us by speech and action what you predict might happen next."

When students are motivated, you can then build schema by telling and showing information that will place students in the appropriate context, or set the scene for what they are to read.[1] For example, you might sketch a map to show the relative locations of the town and the river that comprise the setting of "Adam Swims the Wey" (IMAGINATION, Level 6) and elicit examples of worries that might bother Adam as he searches for his beloved lost dog, Nick.

New vocabulary and concepts — those that are key to comprehending and enjoying the selection — may also be presented as part of the preparation for reading. Present these words actively by asking students to give or elaborate upon definitions, to relate new terms to familiar related terms, and when possible to demonstrate new concepts with a quick sketch or action.

The IMAGINATION Teacher's Editions offers suggestions for all these ways to bring students to their reading with "warmed-up motors" and the confidence and knowledge they will need both to enjoy and interact with the literary work.

READING

Sharing Reading   For beginning readers, the first reading of a poem or a story is usually a shared experience, with the teacher reading aloud and the students joining in on a refrain or a predictable passage. Even fluent readers may be more confident during the reading process if they also participate in shared-reading experiences before reading silently.

Reading Silently   Some reading specialists recommend that first readings always be silent, independent readings. They point out that silent reading permits each student to read at his or her own pace. It encourages reflection and allows both time for response and time to go back and *reread* a passage before going on. Initial silent reading also helps students enjoy and interpret a selection further during a later oral reading.

Yet this recommendation for silent reading first has exceptions. Most poems should be read aloud initially. Anecdotes and funny stories beg for sharing and may lose their appeal if assigned to be read silently.

---

[1] David Rumelhart, "Schemata: The Building Blocks of Cognition," in *Theoretical Issues in Reading Comprehension,* ed. R. Spiro, B. Bruce, and W. Brewer (Hillsdale, N. J.: Erlbaum, 1980), 33–58.

Reading Orally When the content, language, or theme of a selection is complex, guided oral reading helps some students share the literary experience from the start. At no time, however, should oral reading be considered a mere exercise in "getting all the words right." Rather, it is a means to guiding understanding. Most often, this guidance is better done by (1) sharing reading before students read silently, (2) encouraging silent reading according to each student's rate and reading strategies, and (3) later having students reread all or part of a selection for a purpose — to support a point, to share excitement, or to enliven a work through oral interpretation.

POSTREADING DISCUSSION

Once a selection is read, discussion can enhance the literary experience. The main purpose of such discussion is to allow students to speak, to express their responses to the literature they are reading, and to listen to the varied responses of their classmates. Discussions can thus provide opportunities for students not only to express their own opinions but also to learn from the opinions of others. In addition, discussion can be an informal way for you to assess students' enjoyment, involvement, and understanding of what they have read. Asking a general opening question and inviting students to ask questions are good ways to begin a discussion that leads to more structured questions and activities.

General Discussion Strategies Opening discussion should be nonthreatening. It should invite immediate, pertinent response. It should, if possible, set the stage for more focused questions and activities to follow. Here are four effective ways to begin a discussion. (Consult the instructional plans in this Teacher's Edition for specific suggestions.)

1. Offer students the opportunity to retell all or part of the selection, encouraging them to add to, or elaborate upon, incidents that especially interest them. Sometimes it is a good idea to pair students for this retelling; each member of the pair tells the other a part of the selection. At other times, you may need to guide the retelling as a whole-group endeavor, using guiding questions to help students summarize, elaborate, or discover implied motives or connections between events.[2]

2. Ask what the students discovered as a result of their reading. Sometimes this may be a focusing question, based on a preparation question posed before the reading. Sometimes the question can be a more general opener ("Tell me about the story.") that invites students to share their responses, fresh from reading, without imposing a structure.

3. Ask each student to find one passage in the selection that is especially expressive or exciting to read aloud — a segment that might entice a listener to read the entire story. Subsequent discussion can begin

---

[2] John D. McNeil, *Reading Comprehension: New Directions for Classroom Practice* (Glenview, Ill.: Scott, Foresman, 1984), Chapter 1.

with a request for justification: "Why did you choose that part?"

4. Use the discussion questions that follow each selection. Students who have prepared responses to the questions will have something to contribute at once, and discussion will get off to a good start.

Early in the discussion, invite student questions: "What did you wonder about as you read the story? Did a question come to your mind as you read this poem?" Such a procedure encourages self-generated questioning as one reads, a basic strategy that good readers use constantly. (See **Strategies for Teaching Students to Generate Questions** on pages T16–T17 of this Teacher's Edition.) The end of a discussion should come when, in your judgment, the discussion has served its purpose.

Specific Questioning Strategies in the Program
In IMAGINATION, a variety of questions help you focus and extend discussions about literature, and also help provide well-rounded, unified lessons. Some of the questions are derived from the objectives for each selection. Other questions review objectives from earlier readings or seek to broaden the lesson. In each case, questions pertain to the central meaning and significance of the work, their chief purpose being to enhance students' enjoyment and understanding and to allow them to use their listening, speaking, and writing skills when responding critically and creatively.

The following are the four broad categories of questions used in the IMAGINATION program, with emphasis placed on questions that involve the higher orders of thinking skills.

1. Literal questions ask students to recall specific information presented in a story, poem, or nonfiction selection. Good literal questions do not ask for random facts. Instead, they help readers focus on what is important in the selection: main events and their sequence, main ideas and details that support them, characters' motives or traits explicitly stated in the text.

Though they are sometimes considered "low-level" thinking, answers to literal questions can help students remember, organize, and assemble a "data bank" of information. The data bank can then be accessed to help students respond to higher-level questions, to write longer responses to literature, to dramatize, or to do other related activities. With some students, the literal level needs little reinforcement. With others, it is a necessary, though insufficient, part of the literature lesson.

2. Interpretive questions ask students to respond to literature by using their own experience and reasoning. Interpretive questions are designed to help students develop thinking skills beyond the recall level. For example, the author of a poem about a winter day may present three explicit details; an interpretive question may then ask the reader to add three more details to be expected of a winter day. The author of a biography may discuss several important times in the subject's life; an interpretive question may then ask the reader to predict what happened between these events, based on the evidence given in the selection but also going beyond this evidence. After reading a fiction selection, students may be asked to interpret the "world" described there and to compare or contrast it to their own world. Some interpretive questions ask the students to use the "data bank" of specifics drawn from literature to think more broadly — to classify, deduce, and generalize.

Avid readers apply interpretive thinking skills almost automatically as they read literature. Other readers do not. In either case, interpretive questions can focus interpretation, strengthening interaction between the selection and the reader's experience. Such questions often prepare the way for interpretive activities involving the visual arts, dramatization, oral and written composition, and related reading. Interpretive questions should also enhance the reading and rereading of the selection itself. Much of the enjoyment of reading literature comes from well-focused interpretation.

3. Critical questions ask students to do something with the selection: to evaluate it as a work of literature, to apply it to a new situation, to solve a problem based on an understanding of the selection, to investigate a new area connected to the work. A fantasy, for instance, may present a world in which the law of gravity is changed. Students may evaluate the fantasy: how consistently is this change presented in the fantasy? How would our world be different if the change occurred here? How desirable or undesirable would the change be? A biography, for instance, may tell how a famous person developed a skill despite difficult circumstances. Students may then be asked to devise another plan: What other ways might the person have used to develop a skill?

In a sense, literature provides children with "free experience." The children experience not only how certain story characters perceive their problems or goals but also how these characters use thinking skills to try to solve those problems or attain those goals. Critical questions are designed to help students analyze this goal seeking and problem solving; to investigate, evaluate, and often appreciate such endeavors; and finally, to weigh the pros and cons of applying the resulting information to their own thoughts and actions. Critical questions elicit and guide judgment about a literary work itself and about its application.

4. Creative questions ask students to go beyond the selection by extending what they have read to unique situations. Based on their analysis of a literary work, students are asked to transfer their understanding to new tasks. For example, after reading a fable, students are asked to analyze the characters' actions in relation to the fable's moral. Then, based on their analysis, students are asked to generate examples of times when they might need to use the moral to solve their own problems. In doing so, students connect the theme presented in a literary work to their own experiences.

In this Teacher's Edition, the questions that follow the selections have labels identifying the levels of thinking. *Literal, Interpretive, Critical, Creative.*

Using Questions to Teach   The question types described in the preceding section are used in IMAGINATION mainly for teaching purposes, not for testing. Most questions can start a series of responses, and one question may lead to another without interrupting the main topic of discussion. The resulting pattern of discussion may not be question/answer, question/answer, as it is likely to be in testing. Instead, the pattern for the discussion of a story may be the following: a question asking for clarification of a word or phrase leads to a question involving recall of the story events, which in turn leads to a question asking for an interpretation of a character's reaction to those events.

Try applying some of the following strategies during your classroom discussions:

1. Probing   A probe can be a request for additional information to clarify or elaborate on a response, or it can be a request for other answers. Such probing questions as "Do you have any other ideas?" or "Can you tell us more about that idea?" can develop a discussion without fragmenting it. Listen to a student's response and decide whether a probe is needed.

2. Requesting verification   Ask students to return to the text in order to verify a point. Students may be asked to substantiate opinions as well as locate bases for statements of fact. At other times students may be called upon to use other sources, including their own experience, to verify a statement.

3. Providing wait time   The *wait-time,* or *think-time,* principle simply means that a time of silence comes between your question and a student's response.[3] Research shows that classes using wait time have better discussions. Responses are longer, and students show higher-level thinking than when the wait-time principle is ignored.

To apply this strategy, you might begin by saying, "Now I'm going to ask you a thought-provoking question. Take time to think about it before you tell us what you think." Ask the question, and then allow several seconds to elapse before calling for a response. *After* hearing a response, wait several seconds before commenting or asking for other responses.

4. Modeling   Recent research in reading comprehension supports a teaching strategy called *teacher modeling,* which means that you demonstrate for students your thought processes for working out the answer to a challenging question.[4] For example, you may ask an interpretive question about a scene from "The Escape," an excerpt from *Charlotte's Web* (Level 4): "What can Wilbur do the next time he gets bored?" Then you say, "This time, I'll begin the answering." Step-by-step, you talk through the thought process you use in responding to the question. That process might include **(1)** looking back through the selection to pinpoint some literal information

[3] Linda B. Gambrell, "Think-Time: Implications for Reading Instruction," *The Reading Teacher* 34 (November 1980): 143–146.

[4] David Pearson, "A Context for Instructional Research on Reading Comprehension," in *Promoting Reading Comprehension*, ed. by James Flood (Newark, Del.: International Reading Association, 1984), 1–15.

("Last time, Wilbur tried to escape from his pen when he got bored, but that didn't work for long. He'd better try something else."), **(2)** considering options ("Let's see. What do pigs do if they're bored? What do I know about that? Wilbur is a special pig — but he's still a pig. I couldn't have him read a book or play baseball."), and **(3)** coming to a conclusion ("Perhaps he could start a club. I'll explore that possibility.")

By describing your thought processes in this way, you have modeled the three steps in answering an interpretive question: **(1)** searching the literal-level "data bank" as a basis for the response; **(2)** considering alternative responses, rejecting some; and **(3)** deciding on what appears to be a good answer, and then examining it long enough to explore its value.

After you have modeled your response, discuss the modeling with students. Then pose another higher-level question and lead students through the procedure, returning to the modeling when necessary. On a subsequent question, you should observe whether students use the procedure independently. Finally, you can evaluate: Has modeling improved students' abilities to think and respond?

Teaching Students to Generate Questions   In an active, meaning-centered classroom, students are encouraged to participate in discussions by generating their own thought-provoking questions. For effective classroom discussion to occur, a climate must exist that promotes the free exchange of ideas and the taking of risks. Students must feel free to say what they think, share new ideas, give opinions, and disagree with each other.

Student-centered discussion should be encouraged, even if the noise level in the classroom is elevated. The noise produced by effective discussion is productive and a clear sign that students are active and taking responsibility for their own learning.

However, most students need to be taught how to ask questions that require more than a recall of details, or a *yes/no* response. Here are some strategies that may help you teach students how to ask thought-provoking questions.

1. Provide direct instruction in how to identify a thought-provoking question.   Begin by using the following charts to define the two types of questions: **thought questions** and **memory questions.** The charts list characteristics of both types of questions and provide key words and phrases that you can use to construct each type. You may wish to create a bulletin-board display of the charts so that during discussion, students are reminded of these key words and phrases.

2. Have students identify thought and memory questions that follow the selections, as well as questions they may find in subject-area textbooks. Ask students to verbalize the thought processes they use as they identify each question type.

3. Have students compile lists of thought questions about a discussion topic. Then have students ask each other the questions. If one student cannot answer a question, another student should attempt it. (You may want to divide into groups to compile the lists of questions. If so, a member of one group should ask a member of a different group a question.)

4. Have students distinguish between memory and thought questions.   Write the words *Memory Question* and *Thought Question* on the chalkboard. After students read a selection, have one student ask a group of classmates or the entire class questions about the selection. After each question is answered, have students identify the type of question asked. The student asking the questions should strive to ask as many thought questions as possible.

5. Have students ask questions to preview and predict.   Before they read a selection, have students preview it and write thought questions for which they hope to find answers. After they read, ask students to discuss the answers to as many questions as possible. Students may work with a partner or with a group of classmates.

THOUGHT QUESTIONS

- They ask for new ideas, new ways to use ideas, or opinions.
- They may have many good answers.
- They have answers that come from your thoughts.

Key Words and Phrases	*Examples*
What _____ ?	Imagine the best friend you can have. **What** would he or she be like?
What _____ if _____ ?	**What** would the world be like **if** people had no friends?
How do you feel about _____ ?	**How do you feel about** your best friend? Give reasons.
Can _____ ?	**Can** a pet be a friend? Tell why or why not.
How is _____ different from _____ ?	**How is** your friendship with your pet **different from** your friendship with your best friend?
How is _____ the same as _____ ?	**How is** having a best friend **the same as** reading a good book?
Why _____ ?	**Why** is it important to have friends?
In your opinion, _____ ?	**In your opinion,** what is the best quality a friend can have?

MEMORY QUESTIONS

- They ask for facts and details.
- They have only one correct answer.
- They have answers that ask you to recall information

Key Words and Phrases	Examples
Who _____ ?	**Who** are your friends?
Which one _____ ?	**Which one** have you known the longest?
Where _____ ?	**Where** did you meet your friend?
When _____ ?	**When** do you have the best times with your friend?
How many _____ ?	**How many** friends do you have?
What _____ ?	**What** did your friend do yesterday?

EVALUATING READING EXPERIENCES

To evaluate whether your literature discussions, along with prereading preparation and silent, shared, and oral reading, are of benefit to students, observe them in the following ways:

1. Notice whether students seem to seek new reading experiences and whether literature lessons are eagerly anticipated. If these reactions occur, students are attaining the goals of the reading experience, including pleasure, insight into human behavior, and appreciation for language and style.

2. Consider students' responses during discussions. Do they enter discussions enthusiastically? Do all contribute? Is there a give-and-take during the discussions that seems to produce a deepened understanding of the selection? (The importance of building enthusiasm should not be underestimated. Each new reading experience enjoyed by a child makes it less likely that he or she will become a nonreader.)

3. Consider students' answers to the questions themselves, in order to identify students' level of reading comprehension. The literal-level items (recalling details and sequence, for example) are usually easy to evaluate since they call for *convergent thinking.* This means that students will come to an agreement on a "right answer." Though suggested "correct responses" are provided in this Teacher's Edition, students' responses may vary and still be "correct."

Above-literal items (interpretive, critical, and creative) seek to develop *divergent thinking.* This means that students' answers will be different from one another since they are based on individual opinion and experience. Although examples of responses presented in this Teacher's Edition are labeled *Possible response(s),* no one can predict the range of responses that can arise from divergent thinking.

The following criteria can be used, however, in evaluating such responses:

- **Fluency** Do students contribute easily to the discussion? Are they able to produce many responses?
- **Flexibility** Are responses varied so that several *different* ideas are contributed?
- **Originality** Are some students' responses creative as well as appropriate to the question; that is, do some students demonstrate a unique ability to discern and to solve the problems posed by the question?
- **Elaboration** When probed, can students expand their responses by adding details?

4. Observe students' responses to the reading through activities such as oral or written composition, dramatization, or creative expression in the arts. If the reading experience and discussion are indeed promoting students' responses to literature, activities will help reveal and develop such responses.

Additional Readings

Cullinan, Bernice E. *Literature and the Child.* San Diego, Calif.: Harcourt Brace Jovanovich, 1981. This book is a valuable resource for any teacher using literature in the classroom.

Dillion, J. T. "Research on Questioning and Discussion." *Educational Leadership* 42 (November 1984): 50–56. Emphasis is placed on procedures that obtain results according to research on devising questions and eliciting response.

Heald-Taylor, Gail. "Predictable Literature Selections and Activities for Language Arts Instruction." *The Reading Teacher* 41 (October 1987): 6–12. This article offers practical suggestions for using predictable literature with children.

Norton, Donna E. *Through the Eyes of a Child.* Columbus, Ohio: Charles E. Merrill, 1983. This book offers excellent, specific help in devising questions for realistic fiction; see pages 420–423. The entire book stresses interaction-with-literature techniques.

Sebesta, Sam Leaton, and William J. Iverson. *Literature for Thursday's Child.* Chicago: Science Research Associates, 1975. Part III contains a plan for integrating questions and activities of different types and levels.

Torrance, E. Paul, and R. E. Myers. *Creative Learning and Teaching.* New York: Dodd, Mead, 1970. Chapters 7 through 10 contain suggestions for asking good divergent-thinking questions, with factors to consider in evaluating responses.

Notes

Ideas for Shared Reading

Ideas for Oral Reading

Ideas for Postreading Discussion

Ideas for Evaluating the Reading Experience

Other Professional Books

Other Professional Articles

The Writing Experience

FROM DISCUSSION TO COMPOSITION

Where does discussion end and composition begin? It is sometimes hard to tell. As discussion evolves from literal to interpretive to critical–creative levels, students' responses are likely to become longer and more complex, as these three sets of questions imply:

1. "What would happen if that problem occurred here instead of in the story?"
2. "Imagine that you are the cow in the story "Socks for Supper" (Level 2). Tell what you want to trade and what happened when you traded it."
3. "Suppose that you are off on a trip to see the panda in its native habitat in China ("Panda," Level 3). What would you need to know to make the trip? How could you find out? How could you put this information into a travel article for your hometown newspaper?"

How easily such critical-level questions can slide into a composition assignment! But hold back a moment. New evidence and emphasis on composition suggest that there are some intervening things to do before you say, "Take out a sheet of paper and write about it."

ORAL COMPOSITION PROCESS

Especially in the primary grades, composition should begin orally and spontaneously. For example, after reading "The Magic Porridge Pot" (Level 2) and answering questions about the story, you may ask students to suggest a list of things one would need to buy in order to make a porridge. You can then suggest that the shopping trip be turned into a story about such an event, complete with the difficulties the shopper might encounter. Accept all contributions, and encourage every member of the group to contribute something to the story. As a follow-up, some children may perform the story as a puppet show, while others illustrate the story.

Refining the Story   Gradually these spontaneous story-making sessions can be modified and enriched. After the warm-up, two or three children can choose one of the story ideas and prepare to tell it before the group. Alternatively, the entire class can continue to work on a story, but this time you might add some oral editing, skillfully and unobtrusively.

Suppose, for example, that the group has just read "The Garden," one of Arnold Lobel's "Frog and Toad" stories (Level 2). Now the group is composing a story about what happens after Toad's seeds begin to grow in his garden. A main happening has been agreed upon: The seeds will grow into such large flowers that Toad's house will be covered. One child suggests as a first sentence for the story, "The flowers got so big that Toad couldn't find his house when he came home from the store."

Now you can help extend and refine the story, "Why had Toad gone to the store in the first place?"

Student 1:   He went to buy a watering can.
Student 2:   He bought some fast-grow food he saw on television.
Student 3:   A dog on TV said, "Give your flowers a treat with Quick Grow!"
Teacher: Now let's go back and start the story.
Student 1:   The next day, Toad went to the store. He bought some plant food to make his flowers grow. Then he bought a watering can.
Student 4:   When he came back, he said, "Where's my house? All I can see are flowers!"
Student 3:   A flower said, "This is my home now! I need a big place so I can grow."
Teacher: What did the flower look like — the one that said that?
Student 3:   It was pink, and it had big green leaves.

As the story continues, you can ask questions to help students organize and amplify it. There must be a give-and-take: encouragement to take risks, to try out ideas, and to alter the story when a "better" way is discovered.

WRITTEN COMPOSITION PROCESS

Group stories first composed orally may be turned into dictated stories with the teacher writing on the chalkboard or on large charts. Eventually, written composition becomes a major feature in the interaction-with-literature process.

The Reading/Writing Connection   Before combining reading and writing, however, it is important to know *why* to encourage readers to be writers. One good reason is given by Frank Smith: "Writing can extend both our imagination and our understanding."[5] Smith also points out that writing, unlike speaking, "overcomes limitations of memory and attention." That is, the writer may stop scribbling or word-processing long enough to refresh the memory or to scratch out and revise or, simply, to go get a drink of water, play hopscotch, and try to return with a refreshed mind. The permanence of writing permits such intervals, giving a "second chance" at thinking, an opportunity to reflect and to refine thought. It is no wonder that educators are equating good writing instruction with the teaching of higher-order thinking skills.

A second reason why readers should also be writers is that writing does indeed seem to improve the reader's ability to interact with literature. The improvement takes the form of higher-level responses based on hierarchies of response to literature as well as richer composition based on a wide variety of criteria.[6,7]

---

[5] Frank Smith, *Writing and the Writer* (New York: Holt, Rinehart & Winston, 1982), 1, 34.

[6] D. Eileen Tway, *A Study of the Feasibility of Training Teachers to Use the Literature Rating Scale in Evaluating Children's Fiction Writing* (Ph. D. diss., Syracuse University, 1970).

[7] James William Calder, *The Effects of Story Structure Instruction on Third-Graders' Concept of Story, Reading Comprehension, Response to Literature, and Written Composition* (Ph. D. diss., University of Washington, 1984).

A third reason is the student's purpose, intrinsic to the composition itself. The composition, if it is ever to get off the ground, must have a valid reason for being: to settle once and for all the case for or against Rumpelstiltskin ("Rumpelstiltskin," Level 3), to find Rufus M. a well-earned list of interesting books to read ("Rufus M.", Level 3), to prepare a glossary of jargon for an aspiring baseball star ("Return of a Ball Player," Level 6), or to recall a memorable personal experience.

Stages of the Writing Process   IMAGINATION emphasizes the teaching of writing as a process of six interrelated stages: *prewriting, drafting, responding, revising, editing,* and *postwriting* (evaluating and publishing). In this ongoing, recursive process the writer actively uses knowledge, experience, and language to express ideas. Inherent in this process is the development of thinking skills, which lead to clear and effective communication. By constant exposure to speaking, listening, and literary experiences, students are provided with a language-rich environment in which to write.

Since one of the goals of IMAGINATION is to acquaint students with the process professional writers use, guidelines for the stages of the writing process are provided for each writing activity. These guidelines are intended to help students use the writing process in responding to the literature selections. The guidelines also model a process students will, we hope, internalize as they become effective, confident writers. By repeating this process, students not only learn how to write but also come to a fuller understanding, appreciation, and enjoyment of good literature and the skillful authors who have created it. We also hope that by repeating this process, students come to enjoy writing and seek opportunities to write every day. This informal writing does not need to go through all of the stages of the writing process and may include journal writing.

Prewriting   One of the most difficult obstacles a writer must surmount is getting the first few words onto paper. For that reason, carefully chosen strategies and guidelines that help stimulate thinking appear in the *Prewriting* section of each Writing activity. Students begin by considering why they are writing **(purpose)** and for whom **(audience).** Then they use the prewriting strategy to formulate and organize their ideas for writing. Students are encouraged to share their ideas with classmates before drafting.

A variety of prewriting strategies are presented in IMAGINATION. For example, students are frequently encouraged to work in pairs or small groups to **brainstorm** ideas that are relevant to a potential composition. To make a brainstorming session pay off, however, requires a few "rules" and procedures.

1. Each person should be given a fair share of time to make a contribution — no one is left out.
2. Each idea is to be accepted for the moment — no one's idea is to be scorned or ignored.
3. Someone should be designated as "recorder" to tape, write a list, or simply remember the ideas.

4. At some point, usually after three to six minutes, call a halt and have students review and evaluate what has been said.

Another prewriting strategy is a kind of visual plan called **diagramming.** In one kind of diagramming activity, students write a composition topic or theme in the center of an unlined sheet of paper, circle the word or words, and then cluster ideas related to the topic or theme around the center circle. This type of diagramming — called **clustering** — is a visual, holistic, one-page guide that helps students organize their brainstorming. For example, after reading "The Garden" (Level 2) students pretend to be Toad and write ideas that tell why Frog should win a "Friend of the Week" contest. In prewriting, students create a **cluster** of ideas that tell why Frog is a good friend. Here is an example.

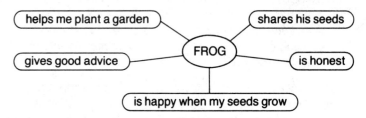

In another kind of diagramming activity — **mapping** — students create a visual representation of story elements. For example, after reading "Steal Away Home" (Level 4) students continue the story about Amos and Obie and focus on how determination helps the boys overcome problems. In prewriting, students get started by completing a map like the one that follows. Other maps in IMAGINATION help writers develop time order, characterization, and setting.

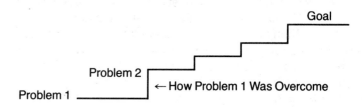

A prewriting diagram that helps facilitate narrowing a topic is the **inverted triangle.** In Level 6, after reading "Planetary Engineering," students are asked to write a research report on space exploration. Since the topic is broad, students are guided through the prewriting stage by first brainstorming topics, selecting one topic, and then completing an inverted triangle.

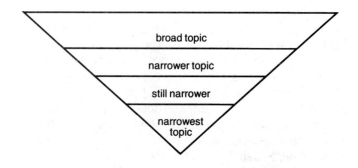

Making charts is yet another prewriting strategy in IMAGINATION that helps students begin the writing process. Like the other prewriting strategies described in this section, filling in information to complete a chart is a visual means of organizing information and ideas. The headings on the incomplete charts in all levels of IMAGINATION help stimulate students' original thoughts and ideas at the beginning of the writing process. In Level 5, after reading the play "The Homecoming," students write their own holiday play in which two characters talk excitedly about the best presents they have given someone. To begin the writing process, students make a chart that includes the following information.

```
Gift: _____
To Whom: _____
Why: _____

Gift: _____
To Whom: _____
Why: _____
```

Making lists is also included in prewriting to make the journey through the writing process more pleasant and productive for students. A prewritten word list, or **word bank**, can include nouns, verbs, adjectives, or figures of speech. Here is an example based on the poem "A House Is a House for Me" (Kindergarten). After listening to and "reading" a poem about animals and their homes, children dictate a class poem about other animals and their homes. In prewriting, children begin by suggesting various names of animals and the places in which they live.

```
          ANIMALS AND THEIR HOUSES

    bird          nest

    squirrel      tree

    frog          pond
```

During the composition process, children can draw from the word bank, selecting words that are vivid, clear, and accurate.

Sometimes, especially at the primary level, students need a sentence frame to help them generate the word bank. This frame is a fairly simple sentence that contains one or more blanks — for example, "A _____ is a house for a _____ ." Then students suggest as many appropriate words as possible to fill the blanks. The same device can be used to generate a **clause bank** — for example, "My story is about a frog that _____ ."

Quickwriting, or **freewriting,** is another prewriting activity that helps students get started: "Write down anything that comes to mind about your topic. Fill a page! Don't stop to fix it up." For example, in Level 6, after students read the photo essay "Art of the Northwest Coast Indians,"

they write a magazine article that compares two other art objects. In prewriting, students begin by selecting the art objects and quickly writing down everything they know about them. Students then review their notes and identify the thoughts on which they would like to focus.

Throughout IMAGINATION, a variety of prewriting strategies are suggested for writing activities. The strategies suggested for specific activities are just that — suggestions! Some students may wish to use other prewriting strategies modeled in the program or use original strategies to generate and organize thoughts and ideas. Since there is no "right way" to prewrite, students should be encouraged to use strategies that are most effective for them. They should also be encouraged to add to and revise thoughts and ideas generated in prewriting as they proceed through stages of the writing process.

Drafting The purpose of writing a first draft is to get the writer's ideas down on paper as quickly and fluently as possible, with no concern for correctness. Therefore, it is best never to ask that the first draft of a story, a play, a poem, or a nonfiction composition be a finished product. Drafting — creating — is a tough enough job without the added burden of correct mechanics (spelling, punctuation, capitalization, paragraphing, and neat handwriting)! Give students a feeling of the tentative nature of first-drafting. They should feel free to scratch out or scribble in. If the first draft is written on every other line, then ongoing revision and later revision will be easier, using the empty in-between lines. Revision will also be easier for students if the first draft is written on only one side of a sheet of paper.

Some students tire quickly during the first-draft stage of the written composition process. Let them take a brief break and then return to the task, reading over what they have done. Encourage them to do such reading with a "reader's eye," as if they are seeing the work for the first time — as a reader, not a writer. Explain that the ability to read one's own work from a reader's (not a writer's) viewpoint is part of an author's craft. It helps a writer make the composition interesting and clear.

If the writer gets "stuck" during the first-draft process, the writer should have a conference with the teacher, with another student, or with a group of students. During the conference, the writer should tell the purpose of his or her work and the audience for whom he or she is writing; the advisor might then suggest that a return to the prewriting diagram stage is one way to "get unstuck."

Responding This stage of the writing process can occur at almost any time. In responding, classmates read each other's work and offer suggestions for improvement while the writing process is still going on. This peer conferencing should be done, of course, at the writer's invitation. It must be guided. It should begin on a positive note — "What do you think I am saying in this composition?" — before moving to suggestions — "How might I make this composition clearer?"

The purpose of this stage is to give student writers overt contact with an audience before the time of publication so ideas and purposes can be clarified. Questions specific to each writing activity are provided for students. During the responding stage, writers should also encourage the audience to ask them questions about their writing. Model questions follow.

Questions a Writer Can Ask an Audience

- What is the part you like best?
- How can I add to my writing?
- How did you feel when . . . ?
- How can I make you feel as if you were actually there?
- Where should I add more descriptive language?
- How can I make my writing more exciting?
- Which parts don't I need?
- Which character would you like to know more about?
- Does my writing make you think that . . .? Tell why or why not.

Questions an Audience Can Ask a Writer

- Tell me more about . . . .
- Can you explain why you . . . ?
- What is going to happen next?
- How many parts do you have?
- Which part are you going to develop first? Why?
- How are you going to decide which parts to keep?
- What will you do with the parts you don't need?

Revising The trial and error of the writing process is a form of *revising* — improving content, style, tone, unity, clarity, and coherence. Some students stick to the task, revising as they go along or redrafting. Others need help early.

Generally, revising needs to be taught — and taught gradually. It is self-criticism, but criticism with a constructive purpose: to go over one's original creation with a listener's ear and a reader's eye to figure out how the content, style, and tone can be improved to communicate better with the intended audience.

Revising includes cutting unnecessary language and improving sentences and words that lack force or fail to say exactly what is intended. For example, the teacher who asked the student to describe the flower in the discussion about Toad's garden was helping the child expand, hence revise, his or her first oral draft. The child's original version, "A flower said, 'This is my home!'" might therefore become "A big, pink flower stood tall and said, 'This is my home.'" Subsequently, when the child is learning to revise written expression, the same sense of "How can I improve this?" ought to prevail.

At all levels, but with a challenging increase in complexity at intermediate grades, revising can include **sentence combining, expansion,** and **reduction.** For example, suppose a student has written three sentences: "My cat is pretty and brown. He can close his eyes. He can keep a secret." These sentences can be **combined** into one: "My pretty, brown cat can close his eyes, keeping a secret." **Sentence expansion** may include adding adjectives such as "velvety" or "furry-footed" to the description of the cat or adding a larger unit such as "My pretty brown cat with ears that turn to hear a whisper . . ."

Sentence reduction, of course, is the opposite — deleting extra words and phrases. It is well to teach students that a sentence can be too long or that trite extra words are excess baggage. Suggest that students give too-long sentences better "weight" by reducing them.

Revising suggestions in the form of questions that students may ask themselves about their writing are provided for each writing activity. Students should consider their classmates' responses as well as the suggested guidelines while revising their writing. In addition, the following questions may help some students during this stage of the writing process. You may wish to distribute copies of these questions or a simplified list, depending on grade level.

Revising Story Structure

- Does my story start in an exciting place?
- Does someone in the story have a problem or a goal?
- Is there an interesting solution or attempt at a solution of the problem?
- Does my story have an ending? Is the ending satisfying?
- Would a certain scene be more interesting if I expanded it?
- Is there a scene that is too long?
- Would some of the story be lost if the scene were shortened?
- Is the tone of the story appropriate for the purpose and audience?

Revising Conversation

- Does the dialogue "sound" like spoken language?
- Is there conversation in my story that is just "filler," serving no purpose?
- Is there a place where conversation needs to be added to increase suspense or to move the story along?

Revising Nonfiction Structure

- Can readers find the main idea(s) and supporting ideas in my writing? Should I "signal" them by underlining, by numbering, by adding headings, or by some other means?
- Is the organization clear? Does the composition have unity and coherence?
- Are connections clear? Are there places where I should add transitions and transitional phrases, such as *so, therefore, if — then, because, since, as a result?*
- Is the tone appropriate for the purpose and audience?

Revising Sentences

- Do my sentences read smoothly without making the reader stumble and have to go back to get the meaning?
- Are my sentences varied in length and complexity for added interest?
- Do my sentences flow smoothly? Have I used appropriate transitional words and expressions?
- Does each sentence have the precise words to carry its meaning?
- Can one sentence be combined with another to make the meaning clearer?

Revising Words

- Can I make my writing style more direct by striking out "empty" words such as *very* and *a lot* and by using *active* rather than *passive* voice?
- Have I chosen colorful, vivid words that carry specific meanings?
- Can I use a more specific descriptive term by finding a synonym in a thesaurus?

Editing   As part of the writing process, students are encouraged to edit their writing for grammar, usage, mechanics, and spelling. It has been suggested that teachers need to provide models for editing; otherwise, some students remain puzzled about how to begin. Sharon Fox and Virginia Allen suggest this procedure: "On the blackboard or an overhead transparency a teacher could write a composition. Insertions, crossing out, arrows leading to additional sentences written in the margins, and the sign for beginning a new paragraph could be illustrated."[8] Without such a model, some students may think that editing means that the composition must be copied over and over.

In harmony with this thinking, IMAGINATION provides guidelines for editing specific pieces of writing. Students are urged to use the guidelines and the **Writer's Handbook** to check their writing for accuracy in grammar, usage, mechanics, spelling, and handwriting. To insist that all writing be perfect in mechanics can be stultifying. Yet correct spelling, punctuation, paragraphing, and all the other rudiments of acceptable form must be taught and applied. Therefore, most authorities recommend that writers do a careful editing before preparing a *final draft* –the final copy of a written composition. This final draft, with emphasis on correct form, is prepared when the work is considered worthy by its writer. The result is a composition *product* as distinguished from the *process* that has dominated earlier drafts.

Not all composition process needs to become product, however. One authority, Donald Graves, suggests that about one out of every five compositions can be treated as product — that is, written into a final draft with correct mechanics so that it can be read easily and enjoyed by others. Editor's Marks can be used to guide this final drafting, including marking for deletion, insertion, and new paragraph. To aid spelling, students may use an alphabetized list of words frequently used but sometimes misspelled. A recent source of such a list is Robert Hillerich's *A Writing Vocabulary of Elementary Children*.[9] A class dictionary is also a useful tool.

Postwriting   In the past, evaluating writing was frequently over-emphasized to the degree that students thought the purpose of writing was correctness, instead of the communication of thoughts and ideas. It is important to keep in mind that the evaluation of student's writing should encourage, not stifle growth. Every piece of published writing contains at least one positive characteristic. The writer should be praised for what was done well, as well as be shown what needs improvement.

Should students' written products be "published?" Of course! To publish means to make public — not necessarily to be printed, bound, and sold in multiple copies across the counter. Publishing one's composition includes reading it aloud to an audience of peers, putting it on a bulletin board or in a class notebook or periodical for others to read, or sometimes binding a group of class composition products into an anthology to be placed more or less permanently in the school library. Numerous ideas for publishing are found in the program as well as in *Teaching Writing in K–8 Classrooms* by Iris M. Tiedt, et al.[10]

DEVELOP SKILLS

Recent research indicates that reading and writing skills should be taught as the need arises and in meaningful contexts. Your students' reading and writing then becomes the basis for determining which skills to teach and at which time.

At the point you identify weaknesses in your students' reading, you will want to develop vocabulary, comprehension, and when appropriate — phonics skills. For example, if you notice that a student frequently mispronounces the same homograph, you may teach a vocabulary lesson.

At the point you identify weaknesses in your students' writing, you will want to develop language and composition skills. These skills may be taught during particular stages of the writing process. For example, you may develop vocabulary skills during prewriting, sentence expansion skills during revising, and mechanics skills during editing.

As you teach specific language and composition skills, work as much as possible with the language that your students produce. Students who see how their own writing is improved by varying the sentences in their compositions or completing sentence fragments are more likely to internalize the skills taught for future use in their writing.

IMAGINATION helps students to build a solid foundation in reading and writing skills. By integrating skills development with students' reading and writing, the program offers help where it is the most effective — at the point of use.

---

[8] Sharon E. Fox and Virginia Garibaldi Allen, *The Language Arts, An Integrated Approach* (New York: Holt, Rinehart & Winston, 1983): 228.

[9] Robert L. Hillerich, *A Writing Vocabulary of Elementary Children* (Springfield, Ill.: Charles C. Thomas, 1978).

---

[10] Iris M. Tiedt et al., *Teaching Writing in K–8 Classrooms: The Time Has Come* (Englewood Cliffs, N. J.: Prentice-Hall, 1983), 196–200.

Additional Readings

Burrows, Alvina Treut, Doris C. Jackson, and Dorothy O. Saunders. *They All Want to Write.* Hamden, Conn.: Library Professional Publications, 1984. This fourth edition of a classic book, an ethnography of guiding written composition in elementary school, is a guide to the spirit as well as to technique.

Butler, Andrea and Jan Turbill. *Towards a Reading-Writing Classroom.* Portsmith, N. H.: Heineman, 1987. This book suggests effective strategies for integrating writing with reading.

Calkins, Lucy McCormick. *The Art of Teaching Writing.* Portsmith, N. H.: Heinemann, 1986. Practical guidelines for teaching writing makes this book a valuable resource.

Clay, Marie M. *What Did I Write?* Portsmith, N. H.: Heinemann, 1985. A description of the developmental stages of writing, complete with writing samples.

Freeman, Ruth H. "Poetry Writing in the Upper Elementary Grades." *The Reading Teacher* 37 (December 1983): 238–242. An ongoing poetry composition program is described, beginning with simple unrhymed forms.

Goodman, Ken. *What's Whole in Whole Language?* New York: Scholastic, 1986. A practical guide for teachers and parents interested in whole language.

Graves, Donald H. *Writing: Teachers and Children at Work.* Exeter, N. H.: Heinemann, 1983. A step-by-step account, with straightforward advice to the writing teacher, based on boundless enthusiasm and experience — a "must" for the teacher of written composition.

Graves, Donald H. and Virginia Stuart. *Write From the Start.* New York: New American Library, 1985. Suggestions for ways to tap young children's natural writing ability.

Hennings, Dorothy Grant, and Barbara Moll Grant. *Written Expression in the Language Arts: Ideas and Skills.* 2d ed. New York: Teachers College Press, 1981. Sequenced topics and activities, including a rich variety of examples, make this a most helpful guide.

Newman, Judith M., ed. *Whole Language, Theory in Use.* Portsmith, N. H.: Heinemann, 1985. The questions most often asked about whole language are answered in this book.

Temple, Charles, and Jean Wallace Gillet. *Language Arts: Learning Processes and Teaching Practices.* Boston: Little, Brown, 1984. Chapters 6 through 9 present a detailed discussion of the composition process, including the teaching of mechanics; see pages 238–249 for "Modeling and Teaching the Writing Cycle."

Tiedt, Iris M., et al. *Teaching Writing in K–8 Classrooms: The Time Has Come.* Englewood Cliffs, N. J.: Prentice-Hall, 1983. Helpful ideas to enhance the oral and written composition program are combined with theory on the process itself, including help with sentence-making, making word choices, editing, and evaluating.

Ideas for Oral Composition

Ideas for Written Composition

Interpretive Language Activities

STORYTELLING

Most educators are convinced of the benefits of telling stories daily to children of all ages. Bob Barton, a former teacher and the co-founder of the Storyteller's School of Toronto, writes about a letter he received after telling a story to a group of kindergarten children. Included in the letter the children dictated was the sentence, "When you said the words, that helped us think the pictures." Children who listen to stories develop imaginations and are able "to see the pictures" because the mechanical aspects of reading are put aside. In addition, recent research also indicates that young children who are read to will mature into better readers and more fluent users of language.[11]

Tips for Storytelling   Storytelling is more than just reading aloud a story. These tips may help you and your students become more effective, imaginative storytellers.

1. Don't retell the story word for word.   Since the personal style of the storyteller contributes to the quality of the storytelling experience, memorize only major sequences of events and key phrases. Vary the rest of the story in your own style.

2. Practice telling the story by yourself, before performing in front of an audience.   Just as a writer revises by reading aloud what he or she has written, a storyteller can make the same improvements by listening to himself or herself tell the story.

3. Prepare props, such as cut-out felt characters and costumes, only when necessary.   Instead, retell exciting stories that will excite students without the use of props.[12]

Stories recommended for storytelling are listed in *Storytelling: Art and Technique* by Augusta Baker and Elen Greene, *Handbook for Storytellers* by Caroline Feller Bauer, and *Tell Me Another* by Bob Barton.

PUPPETRY

Puppet shows hold fascination for children and adults. Students who a moment ago complained, "I can't think of what to say" are suddenly released when it is the puppets who do the talking.

Buying and Making Puppets   Durable, inexpensive puppets can often be purchased in a toy department or store. Shop for the generic kind — an all-purpose bear, a basic bird, a human face that can be decorated or manipulated to fit a specific role. Avoid puppets that promote stereotyping and the "cute" puppets that call attention to themselves but would not fit into a story.

There is an advantage in making puppets, however. The students' attention is directed to features that show character traits in a specific story, play, or poem. In order to leave time for using the puppets in a production, select one of the following easy-to-make puppets.

1. Hand puppets   A simple hand puppet may be no more than an old sock stretched over the hand and adjusted so that the curved palm of the hand opens and closes like a mouth. The face of the hand puppet can be dabbed on with tempera paint or constructed from yarn, buttons, and sewn-on shapes of cloth.

2. Stick puppets   A stick puppet may consist of a painted or cut-paper face on a flat surface such as a paper plate stapled or pasted on the end of a tongue depressor.

3. Fist puppets   A fist puppet is more elaborate than those previously mentioned. The fist puppet's head is modeled out of *papier-mâché* or other lightweight material, such as cotton or crushed paper with heavy paper covering. Features are applied with poster paint. The puppet's eyes should be larger than life to provide emphasis. A cardboard cylinder big enough to fit over the index finger is embedded at the neck of the puppet. The puppet's costume can be cloth that is cut and sewn to be gathered at the puppet's neck with sleeves that fit over the puppeteer's thumb and fifth finger.

Practice and Performance   Give students time to experiment with their newly constructed puppets — to play with voice and movement. When they are ready to perform, they may present the puppet show as Story Theater, where one or more readers read the story while puppeteers manipulate the puppets to show the action. The puppeteers may also perform the story on their own, using creative dramatics techniques to improvise dialogue and gestures. Finally, scripts may be selected or prepared. Some students may read the speeches while other students manipulate the puppets; or the puppeteers may speak the puppets' dialogue as they manipulate them.

CHORAL SPEAKING

Drawing Upon the Flow and Feel of Words   "Star light, star bright, first star I've seen tonight . . ." These simple, clear words, memory-cued by rhythm and rhyme, invite instant playback. The invitation "Now say it with me!" puts the choral-speaking mechanism in motion.

Almost every rhymed and metered poem in the primary grades can be enhanced through choral speaking. In addition, shared speaking encourages participation without risk. Shyness, fear of making mistakes, and the embarrassment of forgetting lines are all overcome as one speaks with the group.

The technique is also an aid to reading and listening skills, particularly when used in the early years. As students recite together, they may rely partly on memory, partly on listening to others, and partly on print to guide them. In this way, the "difficult" words become familiar in print.

Avoiding the Sing-Song Pitfall   In choral reading, metered poetry may begin to sound "sing-song," a mere exercise in reciting rhythm without the intended interpretation of meaning. One way to avoid this pitfall is

---

[11] Barton, Bob. *Tell Me Another* (Markam, Ontario: Pembroke Publishers Limited, 1986), 8–9.

[12] Bernice E. Cullinan, *Literature and the Child* (San Diego, Calif.: Harcourt Brace Jovanovich, 1981), 456–457.

not to confine intermediate-grade choral reading to rhymed and metered poetry. An alternative is to let the sing-song pleasure of a metered poem run half its course, and then begin to introduce variety into the reading. Another way is to concentrate on the poem's meaning. You might begin by reading a few lines of a poem and asking questions like these: "Who is saying these lines? How should the lines be said? in a puzzled voice? in a sad voice? with a laughing tone? What is happening in the poem? How can we show this feeling with our voices?" Such attention to meaning, even with nonsense poetry, will help direct the rhythm and sound away from a sing-song pattern and toward vocal variety in pace and volume.

Another way to avoid sing-song interpretations is to divide the choral reading so that not *all* speakers read *all* of the lines. Some lines can be read in unison by all speakers, but other lines will be read by a subgroup or by one speaker.

CREATIVE DRAMATICS/IMPROVISATION

Creative dramatics may begin soon after a story or a poem is read. During the discussion that follows, the teacher says, "*Show* us what you mean." A student gestures, mimes a series of actions, or speaks a line in a certain way to demonstrate a character or a description. From such a simple, brief beginning can come the activity often called *creative dramatics.* Creative dramatics is especially valuable for developing skills of inference, as students must infer the actions and motives that characters would be likely to display within the framework of the story. The inferring activity shapes and implements both action and motive. It thus goes a step beyond the more passive inference brought forward through discussion.

First Steps   Creative dramatics develops gradually. Begin by having students identify *one* crucial scene they would like to play. Then have them "try on" characters and develop gestures, facial expressions, and a manner of speech for each. Lines of dialogue may be quoted directly from the story, but memorizing should not get in the way of the playing. Instead, encourage players to *improvise* dialogue in the spirit of the story and scene.

Once the improvisation is under way, there may be a tendency for the scene to go on and on. If this happens, stop the action. (A signal from you, such as the single word "Curtain," can be used to stop the action without embarrassing anyone.) Immediately ask students to evaluate the playing: "What was strong in the playing? What seemed to be going wrong?" At this point, ask the group, players and observers alike, to reread the scene.

Insight into Character   Geraldine Siks, an expert on creative dramatics procedure, offers a further suggestion: Have each player identify first the *big purpose* of his or her character in terms of the entire story, and then the character's *little purpose* in the scene that is being played. In addition, character traits and emotions should be discussed.[13]

During this discussion, the focus should be on the characters, not the players. Say, for example: "The old man must show that he is terrified of the sea monster," not "You should act more terrified when you look at the sea monster."

Following evaluation, the scene should be replayed. Further evaluation should note any improvements in the playing.

Need for Brief but Frequent Sessions   The single-scene sessions should be brief, perhaps no longer than ten minutes in primary grades and fifteen minutes in intermediate grades. Frequent sessions, perhaps two per week, are recommended by most experts as the best way to move from creative dramatics to meaningful dramatic interpretation.

From Scene to Story   At all levels, dramatizing a single scene can lead to playing an entire story once the improvisation process runs smoothly. When an entire story is dramatized, pace and structure become more important than ever. The story must progress without having dialogue or action distract from its central focus.

Winifred Ward, perhaps the best-known expert in the field of creative dramatics in schools, advises that planners and players must "concentrate on essentials," shortening or omitting scenes that contribute to the written story but do not move the drama forward. Scenes themselves often require "tightening," which involves highlighting the essential movement and dialogue while omitting the nonessential. Ward's basic evaluation question at this point is "Did the scene move?"[14] Attention must also be directed to the clear presentation of the story's problems in an early scene and to the buildup through successive scenes to a climax and resolution.

Drama in the Content Areas   Just as creative dramatics can help make story plots come alive through activity, a similar technique called *dramatic play* can enliven the study of content areas such as social studies and mathematics.

Dramatic play begins by identifying a setting or situation and finding out as much about it as brief time permits. For example, the illustrations for "Ambassador to the Enemy," a chapter from the historical-fiction novel *Caddie Woodlawn* (Level 5), can be studied along with information about pioneer life described in the students' social studies textbook. From this information, students can compose a still-life scene of American pioneers in the mid-1800s. Each student decides on a character in the scene and describes the activity of the character, including the objects that the character may be using. At a given signal the scene comes to life. Students — playing characters — create speech, action, and interaction extemporaneously. Emphasis is on the setting and the situation — not on creating or recreating a plot.

After a brief portrayal, usually less than three minutes, the playing is stopped and evaluated: "Is it authentic?

---

[13] Geraldine Brain Siks, *Drama with Children* (New York: Harper & Row, 1977), 119.

[14] Winifred Ward, *Playmaking with Children from Kindergarten Through Junior High School,* 2d ed. (New York: Appleton-Century-Crofts, 1957), 138.

What else is needed?" Replay the scene and evaluate again. When the setting is unfamiliar — as it often is with historical periods such as those in eighteenth-century America ("To See Boston at Last," Level 6) or thirteenth-century England ("Adam Swims the Wey," Level 6) — students may seek additional information beyond the literary selection and the social studies text, all with an eye to making the scene authentic.

Dramatic play may also include acting out and solving mathematics story problems implicit in a literary selection such as "It Pays to Advertise" (Level 4). Story problems arising from this tale of a boy and his lemonade stand could include the following: "How much would you have to charge if you bought frozen lemonade and lemons at the price advertised in today's newspaper's shopping guide?" Set the scenes: the store and the lemonade stand. Then have the students "play" the problem, deciding money amounts and lemonade amounts during the enactment.

At first, dramatic play may seem difficult and a bit silly; but with persistence, it can become an effective tool for using drama to interconnect literature and the content areas. The key to its success is to emphasize authenticity: how characters in a removed setting act, what they handle, what they see, and what concerns and problems they have. In this way, it adds the glow of realism to "subject matter." As one of its greatest proponents, Dorothy Heathcote, has remarked, "Suddenly you are walking into the time of the event."[15]

INTERPRETIVE ORAL READING

Sharing Interpretations   To interpret a story or poem well requires practice and concentration. The interpretive activity should follow careful silent reading of the selection and incorporate insights gained through discussion. Interpretive oral reading usually implies an audience — one or more listeners to whom the reader presents his or her interpretation.

The key to interpretive reading is *concentration*. Readers must learn to concentrate on finding the image and the feeling they want to impart and to work steadfastly toward that goal in their oral reading. Listeners, too, must learn to concentrate their attention on the speaker in ways that make the speaker feel comfortable and show their interest and involvement. Here, then, are seven suggestions you can make to help students in your class read aloud interpretively and listen attentively:

1. **Find a selection, a stanza from a poem, or a scene from a story that you really want to read aloud to others.**

2. **Figure out why you have selected it.**   If it is funny, what makes if funny? the language? the action? the surprise? If it is scary, what makes it so? frightening words? a gradual buildup to a big scare?

3. **Now visualize the images or the pictures behind the words.**   If you "see" the pictures in your mind as you read the selection aloud, your listeners will see them too.

[15] Dorothy Heathcote, "Learning, Knowing, and Languaging in Drama," *Language Arts* 60 (September 1983): 695–701.

Sometimes it helps to tell yourself all about the pictures you imagine. Add ideas that the author did not tell you, using your imagination as you read.

4. **If the story or poem has action, try imitating the action as you practice reading.**   Then leave out the movement and try to show the action with just your voice.

5. **Practice reading until you do not have to look at the words all the time.**   Then read the selection to an empty chair approximately ten feet or more away from you. Look often at the chair as you read. If the chair were alive, could it hear you? Would it like hearing the selection the way you are reading it?

6. **For intermediate grades: Identify the purpose of each scene in a story or stanza in a poem.**   Write one phrase that tells that purpose — for example, to scare, to surprise, or to win sympathy. Then keep that purpose in mind as you read. Write the purpose on a sign and put the sign on your practice chair. Stop in the middle of your practice reading and ask yourself, "Am I reading to show that purpose?"

7. **After you have the pictures and the purpose in mind, try experimenting with the volume and pace of your voice.**   Vary your voice from almost a whisper to almost a shout, from very fast to very slow. Then use some of this variety to help your listeners get the purpose in your reading.

Improving Oral Reading   Interpretive oral reading improves with praise if the praise is specific. "You read that with a great deal of expression" is not specific enough; it does not tell the reader what he or she did effectively. A more useful comment might be, "I could hear the ghost rattling the dishes when you read that scene" or "I felt the sorrow of the man and woman when the girl told them she had to leave."

Interpretive oral reading also improves with good models. Most communities contain good models, so you may want to arrange readings by amateur or professional actors, senior citizens, or parents with time and talent for reading aloud. The request to "come and read to us" may bring surprising, pleasing results.

Improving Listening Skills   Listeners to interpretive oral-reading performances have opportunities to improve their listening skills by focusing their attention on the speaker, remaining quiet, and not providing distractions. Help students by adjusting seating and lighting to promote a good listening environment. A discussion of audience etiquette will also help.

READERS THEATRE

In Readers Theatre — the term is usually spelled that way, without an apostrophe — students read orally from scripts that are often based on selections from literature. Play scripts, then, are especially suitable for reading with this technique, since characters' speeches are already indicated. The technique is also adaptable for use with stories and poems that contain considerable direct conversation.

Specialists in the Readers Theatre technique indicate that selections may be abridged or occasionally paraphrased for script purposes. They warn, however, that scripts are to be used only for specific performance; to circulate scripts extensively or to use them for wide public performance is against the copyright law.

How It Works   Similar to actors in a play, the performers in Readers Theatre "take roles"; they speak lines assigned to characters or to one or more narrators. But unlike actors, Readers Theatre performers do not move about a stage; they hold scripts in hand or place them on music stands or desks. A few gestures and changes in position are permitted if these help the interpretation, but the real effect of the literary selection must come from the readers' oral interpretation of characters and narration. Hence the suggestions presented earlier for interpretive oral reading are appropriate for Readers Theatre practice as well.

The prospect of a Readers Theatre performance is highly motivating to students. Once roles are assigned, they do not need to be told to practice their oral reading. They will do so on their own, especially when they can practice with a partner or a "dialogue director" who can give instant feedback on whether the character is "coming through" in the reading.

Importance of the Director   The presentation can be improved by a good director who tells the readers how an audience might receive their efforts. Who should be the director? a student? the teacher? a parent volunteer? Any one of these will do if he or she can bravely but not threateningly stop the rehearsal at almost any point to offer advice: "I didn't *hear* how angry the two trolls were when Prince Lini refused them. Try that again." ("Half a Kingdom," Level 4) Of course, the director must find a balance between expecting too much in a performance and permitting flaccid, unthinking reading. Students respond to direction that asks for, but does not demand, a lively, varied interpretation.

Finally the finished production may be performed for an audience. Performers may sit or stand side by side, facing the audience, or they may position themselves so that two opposing characters face each other, the narrators off to one side and slightly closer to the audience. The audience, the performance area, and the likely arrangement of readers should be decided before final rehearsals begin so that the readers feel they are working toward a well-planned, polished performance.

STORY THEATER

Interpretive oral reading is combined with "acting out" in Story Theater. One or more students read aloud the selection, which should be a story or a poem with plenty of action. Simultaneously, a group of "players" performs the actions described in the reading. In addition, players may sometimes act as scenery. For example, several may portray a wall, a tree, or the window of a house.

How It Works   Story Theater begins with attentive reading and discussion of the story to be presented. Movement, or mime, can be encouraged as a natural extension of inference questions: "Show us how Mouse Woman pretends to be a lame mouse trying to get over a log. Show how Say-oks is surprised when the princess replaces the wooden wife at the loom." ("Mouse Woman and the Wooden Wife," Level 6) Roles are assigned or chosen by volunteers. Players develop their parts as they listen to the oral readers' rendition of the story; oral readers practice their skill until they can vary their pace to accommodate the pace of the players. The final performance, then, is a combination of oral reading and mimed action.

After its completion, the performance should be evaluated by the participants, using questions such as the following: "Which segments in the reading gave life to the story? What did the players do to make certain actions vivid? When a player was present but not specifically mentioned in a moment of action, what did he or she do? Did the player freeze, standing still so that attention was directed to the action, or did the player react to what was happening? Would a different response have been more effective?"

The critique, or evaluation, may be followed by a second performance, and students may then note improvements.

Choosing Appropriate Selections   For primary-grade children, Story Theater works well with nursery rhymes and other simple action poems. It seems especially suited to folk tales that highlight action and do not contain a great deal of dialogue. Intermediate-level students, however, may wish to experiment with Story Theater productions in which players speak lines of dialogue.

PLAY PRODUCTION

Information Presentations   In the classroom, a play script may be presented informally without scenery, costumes, or memorization, and with minimal movement. An informal presentation provides practice in characterization and timing. It also improves speaking skills, especially if readers must project their voices to an audience. The informal presentation can be enhanced if it is recorded on tape as a "radio play" with background music and sound effects. The tape may then be played for the readers' enjoyment and evaluation.

Formal Productions   Formal production based on a play script requires much more time and planning, and it deserves an audience. It may also require a budget. Still, the excitement of a formal production of a play often makes the effort worthwhile. So, too, do the other rewards: the literary learning that results from extended close work with the play script, the confidence that arises from successfully portraying characters and incidents, and the poise that comes with performing in a company before an audience.

Preparing Young Students for Play Productions
Students at the primary level need informal experience in

drama before attempting a formal play production. Both Story Theater and creative dramatics should come first. Then, when a play script is before the students and the decision is made to present it as a play, they need to become aware of its requirements. Maxine McSweeny[16] reported one group's suggestions for play performance, which the teacher wrote on the chalkboard:

- Know exactly what to say and do. (They can't make it up in front of an audience.)
- Act so the audience can see what they do.
- Speak so the audience can understand what they say.
- Make the play's story live for the audience.

Suggestions for a Successful Production   Once a class has had some experience with formal play production on a small scale, the following suggestions may help to guide more extensive productions.

1. Make sure the class has had sufficient experience in oral interpretation and movement before they try to perform a play that requires extensive dialogue and a succession of scenes.

2. Make sure the class likes the play script.   Talk it over. Ask them to explain the dramatic appeal: "What might an audience like about this play?"

3. Hold try-outs for all facets of the production, not just for acting roles.   Ask for volunteers to make scenery (drawn, painted, constructed, or hung as a backdrop), to be in charge of props, or to act as dialogue coaches. The actors themselves should be selected carefully, of course. Have them try out by improvisation rather than by reading lines. Ask pairs of students to assume the characters from the play and then to compose speeches and movements to fit a particular scene.

4. With class participation, make a schedule for rehearsals.   The first session should consist of reading lines, with attention to oral interpretation of character. The second session should begin the *blocking* of action, determining characters' movements about the stage in each scene. In general, movement must be motivated, and a character should not move while another is speaking. "Stage business" — the use of props and gestures — is included in the blocking of action. At this point actors may carry scripts, but they should also devote attention to memorizing lines. Subsequent sessions give practice, scene by scene, in dialogue and action.

5. When planning scenery, costumes, and lighting, suggest rather than strive for actuality.   Setting may be suggested by scenery sketched on wrapping paper or merely be a backdrop consisting of a curtain or drape. An item of costume, such as a hat or an appropriate jacket, can suffice to designate a character. Lighting need not require footlights or spotlights, but the playing area should be clearly visible to an audience. The playing area itself can be a cleared area in the classroom if a raised stage is not available.

6. Set aside time for a dress rehearsal, a session in which the entire production receives a run-through without interruption.   During this final rehearsal, the director keeps notes so that he or she can comment on the production afterward. The comments should be mainly positive, to encourage the players and crew to do their best. If the performance is to run smoothly, few changes should be made in the production at this point.

7. Plan to present a formal production before an audience.   Besides offering a means for appreciating the considerable efforts of the cast, crew, and director, the production of a play is intended to provide entertainment for others. Some groups plan more than one performance, for increased experiences before an audience.

A Word About Royalties   Some plays, if presented formally, require payment of royalties. Be sure to check the title and copyright pages of a play script for a royalty statement before deciding to put the script into production.

A Sense of Accomplishment   Allot time when the production is over for evaluating what was learned, what was especially satisfying, and what might be done "next time" to make the production process flow more smoothly. Teachers and other adults involved need to remember that play production in schools is for education, appreciation, and pleasure. A good question to consider is this: "Ten years from now will this play be recalled by my students with pleasure and a sense of real accomplishment?"

Also remember that theater experience with literature is *direct* experience with literature. As author Tove Jansson has a wise character say in *Moomin's Summer Madness,* "A theatre is the most important sort of house in the world, because that's where people are shown what they could be if they wanted, and what they'd like to be if they dared to, and what they really are."[17]

---

[16] Maxine McSweeny, *Creative Children's Theater for Home, School, Church, and Playground* (Cranbury, N. J.: A. S. Barnes, 1974), 131.

[17] Tove Jansson, *Moomin's Summer Madness* trans. Ernest Benn (New York: Avon Books, 1955), 105–106.

Additional Readings

Barton, Bob. *Tell Me Another.* Markam, Ontario: Pembroke Publishers Limited, 1986. The author explains techniques for using storytelling effectively in classrooms.

Coger, Lesley Irene, and Melvin R. White. *Readers Theatre Handbook: A Dramatic Approach to Literature.* 3d ed. Glenview, Ill.: Scott, Foresman, 1983. This handbook contains definitions and "rules" for successful productions, with helpful case studies of how the procedures have succeeded in schools.

McCaslin, Nellie. *Creative Drama in the Classroom,* 3d ed. New York: Longman, 1980. This edition gives reasons for using pantomime, improvisation, and creative dramatics. It is rich in examples of how to use drama in the classroom.

Provenmire, E. Kingsley. *Choral Speaking and the Verse Choir.* Cranbury, N. J.: A. S. Barnes, 1975. Definitions, procedures, and materials for verse choir are presented, with discussion focused on each age level.

Sebesta, Sam. "'Reading with More Expression' in the Elementary School." *Readers Theatre News 9* (Spring/Summer 1982): 10–11. The author explains how oral interpretation and reading as a search for meaning in literature may go hand in hand in the classroom.

Siks, Geraldine Bain. *Drama with Children.* 2d ed. New York: Harper & Row, 1983. Types of drama, including a clear definition of Story Theater, are described in Chapter 3. The book contains ample activities — procedures and goals for each, with designated age levels.

Interactive Learning

In a student-centered environment, teachers encourage students to take responsibility for their own learning. Students assume this responsibility by interacting with classmates in a variety of ways.

COOPERATIVE LEARNING

Learning cooperatively within a heterogeneous group is one way you can structure lessons to achieve learning goals. In cooperative learning, groups of students work collaboratively to achieve a common goal.

There are five basic elements of a cooperative learning group:

- **positive interdependence**   Students recognize that they can achieve their goal only if the other students in the group also achieve their goal; responsibility for each other's learning is shared. This is best achieved when membership of a group is heterogeneous in ability and personal characteristics.
- **face-to-face interaction**   Students recognize that they can achieve their goal only if there is interaction among the group members.
- **individual accountability**   Students are individually accountable for providing their share of the group's work and for mastering the material.
- **appropriate use of interpersonal and small-group skills**   To maximize learning, group members develop good working relationships.
- **group processing**   Group members assess how well they are working together and suggest ways the group can become more effective.

You play a major role in cooperative learning. Some strategies in structuring cooperative learning activities are:

- specifying the instructional objective.
- selecting the group size most appropriate to the activity; groups should have from two to six members.
- assigning students to groups; groups generally work best when students of varying ability levels are within the same group.
- explaining the task and cooperative goal; reminding students that group members will be rewarded on the basis of the quality of the group's work.
- monitoring the effectiveness of the group and intervening to improve the group's skills in working collaboratively.
- evaluating the group product and discussing the interaction of the group.

Cooperative Learning Suggestions   As you use IMAGINATION, you can set up cooperative learning groups through which students can move into, through, and beyond a literature selection. The following chart describes some general ways each integrated instructional plan can be adapted for cooperative learning. In addition, specific learning suggestions are provided within many integrated instructional plans.

Cooperative Learning Suggestions for IMAGINATION

Think and Read	**Previewing and Predicting** Have children work in groups to discuss what they think the selection they are about to listen to and "read" might be about. Each group member is responsible for making one prediction. All members should agree on one another's work before one child shares the group's predictions with the class.
Think and Discuss	**Remembering the Selection** Have children work in groups to retell the story. Each group member is responsible for retelling one part of the selection. All members should agree on one another's retelling before one child shares the group's retelling with the class. **Using the Discussion Questions** Determine the minimum number of *Think and Discuss* questions you would like each student to answer. Then divide children into groups accordingly. Each group member is responsible for answering at least one question. All group members must agree on one another's responses before one child shares the group's responses to the *Think and Discuss* questions with the class.
Think and Write	**Prewriting** Evaluate the prewriting strategy to determine if there are discrete tasks two or more group members can complete independently. If so, divide children into groups with as many members as there are tasks. Each group member is responsible for completing one section of the prewriting activity. All group members should agree on one another's work before one child shares the group's thoughts and ideas with the class.
Think and Extend	**For the Classroom** Evaluate each *Think and Extend* activity to determine if there are discrete tasks two or more group members can complete independently. If so, divide students into groups with as many members needed to complete the tasks. Each group member is responsible for completing at least one task. All group members should agree on one another's work before one student shares the group's completed product with the class.

RECIPROCAL TEACHING

Reciprocal teaching is another way students can interact with classmates and take responsibility for their own learning. In reciprocal teaching, teachers' and students' roles are interchangeable. In fact, student "teachers" eventually take some of the responsibility for teaching groups of classmates. Recent research indicates that student-led instruction during reciprocal teaching is most effective when students are grouped heterogeneously.

Before students are ready to "teach" however, you should model effective strategies and behavior. Once you observe that the strategies and behaviors have been internalized, select students to lead instruction. Your role, through the reciprocal teaching process, is to monitor the student "teachers" and provide necessary guidance. For example, you might observe that a student "teacher" is allowing a discussion to wander from the topic. To help the student get the discussion back on track, you might say:

"Remember this discussion is supposed to be about friendship." Or, after modeling effective questioning strategies, you might help the student "teacher" move the level of thinking during a discussion to a higher level by prompting the student "teacher": "What question do you think a teacher might ask at this point?"

Reciprocal Teaching Suggestions Some suggestions for adapting the integrated instructional plans in IMAGINATION to include reciprocal teaching follow.

1. In *Think and Read,* student "teachers" lead the discussion that focuses on previewing and predicting what the selection to be read might be about.

2. In *Think and Discuss,* student "teachers" lead the discussion that focuses on the selection and its theme.

3. In *Think and Write,* student "teachers" lead the discussion during the responding, revising, and editing stages.

Learning Strategies Inventory

This inventory will help you locate pages on which specific learning strategies are suggested in this *Teacher's Edition* of IMAGINATION.

Cooperative Learning

7, 12, 14, 18, 23, 26, 28, 30, 32, 37, 40, 42, 44, 46, 51, 58, 60, 64, 69, 72, 76, 78, 80, 89, 94, 96, 100, 105, 112, 114, 118, 123, 126, 128, 132, 137, 140, 142, 146, 151, 154, 158, 162, 171, 176, 178, 182, 187, 192, 194, 198, 203, 208, 210, 214, 219, 224, 226, 230, 255, 258, 260, 264, 269, 272, 274, 278, 283, 288, 290, 294, 299, 302, 304, 308, 313, 318, 322, 326, 335, 342, 344, 346, 348, 353, 362, 364, 368, 373, 380, 382, 384, 386, 391, 396, 400, 405, 408, 412, 416, 425, 434, 436, 440, 445, 448, 450, 454, 459, 462, 464, 468, 473, 476, 478, 482, 487, 490, 494, 498

Language Experience

12, 14, 26, 28, 40, 42, 60, 72, 76, 96, 112, 114, 118, 126, 128, 140, 142, 154, 156, 176, 178, 192, 194, 208, 210, 224, 226, 238, 242, 258, 260, 264, 272, 274, 278, 288, 290, 294, 302, 304, 318, 322, 342, 344, 362, 364, 380, 382, 386, 394, 396, 408, 412, 434, 436, 440, 448, 450, 453, 462, 464, 468, 476, 478, 482, 494, 496, 497

Questioning

7, 12, 15, 23, 26, 29, 37, 40, 43, 51, 58, 61, 69, 72, 77, 89, 94, 97, 105, 112, 115, 123, 126, 129, 137, 140, 143, 151, 154, 159, 171, 176, 179, 187, 192, 195, 203, 208, 211, 219, 224, 227, 235, 238, 243, 255, 258, 261, 269, 272, 275, 283, 288, 291, 299, 302, 305, 313, 318, 323, 335, 342, 362, 365, 380, 383, 394, 397, 408, 413, 434, 437, 448, 451, 462, 465, 476, 479, 490, 495

Prereading

7, 23, 37, 51, 69, 89, 105, 123, 137, 151, 169, 187, 203, 219, 235, 255, 269, 283, 299, 313, 335, 353, 373, 391, 405, 425, 445, 459, 473, 487

Prewriting

14, 28, 42, 60, 76, 96, 114, 128, 142, 158, 178, 194, 210, 226, 242, 260, 274, 290, 304, 322, 344, 364, 382, 396, 412, 436, 450, 464, 478, 494

LEARNING CENTERS

In classrooms that encourage students to take responsibility for their own learning, students also have the opportunity to make choices. Teachers who set up learning centers and encourage students to work autonomously at them provide their students with such opportunities.

That is why IMAGINATION provides ideas for listening centers, speaking centers, reading centers, and writing centers in every unit. The activities suggested relate to the theme of a particular unit and are integral to the overall integrated language arts curriculum.

Tips for Setting Up Learning Centers   Although teachers do not usually interact with students while they work at learning centers, they are responsible for establishing procedures that relate to the centers. The following general tips are intended to make using the learning-center approach to instruction an enjoyable and productive experience for you and your students.

1. Organize classroom space so learning centers are situated where students may work independently and collaboratively.   Provide individual and group work areas.

2. Introduce students to the centers so they understand what they are to do and how they are to do it.

3. Provide clear, concise directions for each activity so students are able to work without your assistance. Necessary resources such as audiovisual materials, books, or computers should be readily accessible.

4. Keep accurate records of each student's progress. Students should not only record the activities they complete, but also confer with you to discuss their perception of the interest and difficulty of the activities. Students should also be encouraged to share their work with their classmates and family members.[18]

[18] Walter McVitty, ed. *Getting It Together — Organizing the Reading–Writing Classroom* (Rozelle, NSW, Australia: Primary English Teaching Association, 1986).

Additional Readings

Berliner, David, and Ursula Casanova. "Should you try reciprocal teaching? Yes!" *Instructor* (January 1986): 12–13. Recent research findings on reciprocal teaching are reported in this article.

Brandt, Ron. "On Cooperation in Schools: A Conversation with David and Roger Johnson." *Educational Leadership* (November 1987) 14–19. David and Roger Johnson answer commonly-asked questions about cooperative learning.

Johnson, David W., Roger T. Johnson, Edythe Holubean, Patricia Roy. *Circles of Learning.* Association of Supervision and Curriculum Development, 1984. Provided in this book is a clear concise explanation of what cooperative learning is and how to use the technique effectively.

McVitty, Walter, ed. *Getting It Together — Organizing the Reading–Writing Classroom.* Rozelle, NSW, Australia: Primary English Teaching Association, 1986. Nine articles explain how to set up a classroom so students take responsibility for their own learning and naturally make the connection between reading and writing.

Other Professional Books and Articles

Ideas for Interactive Learning

Ideas for Interactive Learning

Literature and the Content Areas

TEXT STRUCTURE

There is renewed interest in the tie between literature and the content areas of the curriculum. Topics in literature overlap those in almost all subject areas — social studies, science, health, mathematics, music, and art. That fact has long been noted, but recent evidence points to the importance of another connection: *text structure* — how written communication is organized and how it delivers its message. Literature is a key to help students unlock the complexities of text structure.

Structure in Nonfiction and Fiction Informational nonfiction often is organized by patterns of logic. A stated main idea is accompanied by supporting evidence, or the evidence may be presented alone, leaving readers to infer the main idea. There are, of course, other patterns of logic — other text structures for informational nonfiction. What matters most is how clearly and consistently the patterns are followed to help the reader get the message.

Some kinds of nonfiction (a biography, a description of how things work) and nearly all works of fiction are organized by time sequence. For most young readers, text structure made up of a sequence of events is easiest to follow.[19] However, young readers still may have difficulty getting the intended messages from their reading. Connections among events, including cause–effect or effect–cause, may evade them, or they may have trouble clustering events to arrive at a generalization.

Patterns such as these are used in content-area textbooks, reference materials — and in literature; but the clarity and consistency of such patterns of text structure are most evident in literature.

Literature as Models of Structure Authors of literature are successful messengers: their text structures bear the message home to their readers. Generally, authors of literature are free to explore a structure and topic as fully as they and their readers wish. In "The Black Fox" (Level 4) author Betsy Byars devotes several pages to the main character's discoveries of the wonders of nature as he searches for the den of a black fox. Authors may also experiment, at a leisurely pace, with a combination of text structures. Janet Chenery, the author of the realistic fiction story "Wolfie" (Level 3), for example, combines time-sequence fiction about three children and their pet wolf spider with a remarkable amount of logically structured information about the wolf spider, including comparison-and-contrast diagrams.

Literature, then, affords students excellent models of text structure. When students are guided in their reading of these models, they become better able to tackle the structures of textbooks and other sources designated as content-area material. These content-area texts often are more mixed in structure and loaded with more information within a limited space than most works of fiction. Hence literature bridges the way to understanding them.

A similar case can be made in regard to sentence structure. Writers of literature are almost by definition masters of the sentence form. They shape a sentence to a point. Incidentally but effectively, they entice young readers to explore a widening variety of sentence structures.

Writers of literature also provide good models of *diction,* or word choice. Writers of stories, poetry, and literary nonfiction choose their words with care — for accurate meaning, the right shade of meaning to fit the tone and context, for connotation, rhythm, and sound. Such qualities should not be confined to "artistic" or "literary" style. They are essential to communication, especially to the fine craft of writing and reading in the content areas.

What can be done to teach these aspects of text: text structure, sentence structure, and diction? The following list provides several teaching suggestions.

   1. Provide good literary models showing structure and word choice at their best.

   2. Provide good models of text processing. "Think out loud" to show students how a skilled reader skims the titles and content of an informational selection to discover its purpose and organization. Show diagramming techniques — diagrams of content within a selection. Read rich but possibly unfamiliar sentence structures aloud to students and, at times, ask them to echo the reading to "get the taste" of new structures and terms.

   3. Give special attention to activities that teach students about text structure. Many such activites and the objectives they are designed to achieve are included in the IMAGINATION program.

USING LITERATURE SPECIFIC TO CONTENT-AREA TOPICS

The Social Studies Facts and generalizations from the social studies are seen more clearly against a tapestry of literature. For best results, bring that tapestry to students before, during, and after they encounter a social studies topic. Begin a unit with rich scheme-setting literature — the illustrated folklore of a continent to be studied, easy and exciting biographies, historical fiction that says "you are there," modern fiction that affords a visit to a distant place. Encourage deeper reading as the unit progresses. A social studies text reference to a famous historical figure, a crucial incident, or an intriguing custom can and should motivate a search for literature that tells more. When a social studies unit has been completed, related literature may keep the unit topic alive in the students' minds, to show students that there is an immediate application of their newly acquired social studies knowledge.

Interest is the prime reason for allying literature with the social studies. Social studies topics begin with the students' environment but soon extend to "expanding

---

[19] Nancy Marshall, "Discourse Analysis as a Guide for Informal Assessment of Comprehension," in *Promoting Reading Comprehension,* ed. by James Flood (Newark, Del.: International Reading Association, 1984): 79–96.

communities," increasingly distanced from readers' immediate experience. This is as it should be: Education should expand one's horizons. But these journeys to distant places and times must have relevance and excitement — hence the need for literature to help make them so. As Dorothy Grant Hennings points out, especially in regard to interest aroused by folklore as a background for social studies, readers discover "basic problems of living that human beings have struggled with from earliest times."[20]

In IMAGINATION, fiction and nonfiction selections related to social studies content at each grade level have been included, with questions and activities to help readers bridge the connection between literature and subject matter. The range of topics in the social studies is vast; to find additional literature relevant to a topic often requires use of reference sources. The annual *Subject Guide to Children's Books in Print* and *Adventuring with Books* are two good places to start.

Science

Natural science and the other sciences are provinces of literature, as both fiction and nonfiction selections in IMAGINATION attest. What can pertinent literature add to science content? First, literature supports our sense of wonder. Literature helps us explore and expand our wonderings about the world through the eyes of gifted authors and illustrators. Second, literature fosters an appreciation of accuracy and quest for accuracy. Word denotations and precise detail in literature sharpen the reader's perceptions — like a fast walk on a crisp morning. Third, literature helps us synthesize experiences. It may show, for example, how ingenuity of invention confronts natural disaster ("Changes, Changes," Kindergarten) or how human survival may be based on understanding and using the natural environment ("Bando," Level 5).

At one time there was concern that nonscientific literature might actually harm a child's development of science concepts. Hens, pigs, and spiders do not really talk — but in literature they sometimes do! Such concern has abated. Children, even at an early school age, are apparently able to see the distinction between "real" and "make-believe" — or to note the distinction when their teachers help them do so. A fascinating anecdotal article by Frances A. Smardo goes further to point out that fanciful "nonscientific" stories are just the right contrast for arousing interest in finding out "how it really is" — hence for scientific investigation.[21] By the same logic, science fiction — even when it presents a future world that may not "come true" — inspires hypothesis making and substantiated conjecture that are rooted in science.

As for informational literature devoted to science itself — there is a wealth of it. Teachers can investigate accuracy and coverage of informational science selections by reading reviews in *Science Books & Films,* published five times a year by the American Association for the Advancement of Science. A monthly column in *The Horn Book Magazine,* "Views on Science Books," discusses selections recommended on the basis of literary merit as well as scientific content.

Mathematics

Sometimes it is hard to see the relevance of a content area to one's life, even when the area is mathematics and one is preoccupied with saving money to buy a baseball glove ("It Pays to Advertise," Level 4). Some children have trouble seeing the connection between story problems in the arithmetic book and the "story problems" of real life. One study showed the superior results in mathematics problem solving when children made their own "math stories" based on their own needs.[22] Perhaps these "math stories" could even be made from the situations and characters children meet in literature; for these stories, too, may add both context and interest to mathematical problems. Many of the activities in the IMAGINATION program are based on this likelihood.

Literature also offers selections with more direct application to mathematics, ranging from simple counting rhymes to complicated literary mathematical puzzles. These connections are discovered as teachers and children explore literature; a list of 32 such items, of interest to various age levels, can be found in an article which shows their application to teaching measurement, geometric concepts, size, time, and money calculations.[23]

Health

Try a "Tasty Lit" course, as one school did: match a folklore item with a cooking item, the recipe based on the ethnic origin of the folk tale.[24] Plan a treat for Paddington to offset his penchant for sugar ("Paddington Goes to the Hospital," Level 4), or find out what Beth can do about her allergy ("An Allergy Is a Bothersome Thing," Level 4). The possibilities are wide and challenging when it comes to incorporating literature into the health curriculum. They include direct use of informational literature from the expanding list of new materials on nutrition, safety, and health maintenance. IMAGINATION selections and activities provide a start. Encourage students to pursue health-related topics further in their reading.

Art

The visual arts offer teachers and students a great variety of activities: drawing and painting, paper cutting, sculpting and modeling, constructing and printmaking. Any one of these can stir the students' imaginations and provide them with a visual means of responding to literature.

The teacher's choice of which art activity will enhance a literary experience can be guided by class discussions of a particular selection. For example, if the discussion focuses

[20] Dorothy Grant Hennings, "Reading Picture Storybooks in the Social Studies," *The Reading Teacher* 36 (December 1982): 284–289.

[21] Frances A. Smardo, "Using Children's Literature to Clarify Science Concepts in Early Childhood Programs," *The Reading Teacher* 36 (December 1982): 267–273.

[22] Robert W. Wirtz and Emily Kahn, "Another Look at Applications in Elementary School Mathematics," *Arithmetic Teacher* 30 (September 1982): 21–25.

[23] Nancy J. Smith and Karla Hawkins Wendelin, "Using Children's Books to Teach Mathematical Concepts," *Arithmetic Teacher* 29 (November 1981): 10–15.

[24] Nancy K. Cochran, "How I Teach Boys and Girls: Nutrition and World Literature," *Forecast for Home Economics* 26 (January 1981): 59.

on the *setting,* then students might sketch the setting or visualize it through collage. As they reread a description of a setting in a story or a poem, urge students to develop a mental image. Then using pencil, crayon, pastel, charcoal, or another sketching instrument, they can sketch quickly on paper the scene in their imaginations. Later, they may add details and finish the scene with tempera paint, water color, chalk, or another medium.

Characters in literature also may fire the imagination. Following a discussion of a main character's traits, invite students to model that character from clay. Encourage them to represent what the character was like and the impression that character made on the readers rather than on how the character looked. Finished clay figures, dried or baked in a kiln, can be displayed against a painted or constructed background of the story's setting. Intermediate-grade students might sculpt figures from plaster of paris blocks.

In addition to individual art projects, you may sometimes wish to encourage group projects in response to literature. For example, students could create a mural or a large map of a "journey" story, labeling each place and major event in the story. Students also could make an **accordion book** by the following method: the class identifies the main events in the story; each student sketches one of the events; the sketches are arranged in order and then connected by loose stitching or metal rings. The result is a visual display of the story sequence.

Two visual art forms, **collage** and **mobile,** add variety to the literature-and-art program. Both can help students respond to literature holistically. A **collage** is a combination of textures (cloth, foil, small flat objects) and cut-out images (news photos, parts of magazine ads, and so on) arranged on a flat surface. Its effect is to mirror and augment the tone and mood of stories and poems. A collage can also reveal a theme — not just of one selection but of many related works. For example, themes of meeting challenges, forming relationships, and relating to the natural world may all be subjects for collages.

A **mobile** is also a combination of items, but now the pieces (pictures, objects) are suspended by string or wire, and balanced so that they seem to hang in the air, turning so that the viewer sees a constantly shifting pattern. Try a mobile made of folk characters and objects important in folk tales. Use this mobile as an introduction to "folk-tale trivia" or literary allusion. Bring it out from time to time and ask students to identify each item and the folk tale from which it came.

Music The rhythms and sounds of words have their counterparts in the rhythms and sounds of music. One study shows that soft classical background music during reading aids comprehension.[25] A language arts professor comments: "With a little guidance, children can see that the composer has created an impression through rhythm and increased tempo in much the same way that a writer

may use a contrast in sentence lengths to develop a sense of quickness or calm."[26]

Poems with strong rhythms or pleasant-sounding lines can inspire song making. To create songs from poems, have students read a poem several times to bring out the rhythm, phrasing, and mood. Use choral speaking techniques to do this. Then have them investigate beat and sample melodies, progressing line by line through the poem. When the final song version is put together, tape the melody or quickly notate it above a written version of the poem.

Musical instruments can be used to create sounds that will heighten the mood for oral reading or any performance of literature. A "signature tune," for instance, may announce the entrance of each character in the telling of a folk tale. Such tunes can be composed on a homemade xylophone, recorder, or kalimba. To stress the rhythm in a poem, use rhythm sticks, various types of drums, sand blocks, and maracas. The use of musical instruments may also help establish the setting of a story or a play.

Listening to music may also enhance literary appreciation. To seek a literal tie between a literary selection and a musical selection is unnecessary. For example, no composer has written a symphony, ballet, or specific program music to accompany the Norwegian folk tale "The Three Billy Goats Gruff" (Level 1), yet children can find the troll and the setting of the drama in numerous works of the Norwegian composer Edvard Greig. Played before, during, and after the reading of a selection, such music adds impact while developing the students' listening abilities.

A "suite" of music selections (segments from works of several composers) can be collected to accompany a unit in the IMAGINATION program. The "Tell Me the Name" unit in Level 3, for instance, with a variety of moods, might stimulate a search for music that matches those moods. One such "suite" might include Mussorgsky's "Pictures at an Exhibition" to accompany J. R. R. Tolkien's poem "Oliphaunt" and Richard Strauss's "Till Eulenspiegel's Merry Pranks" to accompany the tales of "Rumpelstiltskin" (Level 3). But that's only one opinion. Let children themselves search for music that makes a "suite" connection.

A list of composers whose works can parallel the moods and structures of literature encompasses the whole history of music. Noteworthy among Western composers might be the following: Leonard Bernstein, Benjamin Britten, Cecile Louise Chaminade, Aaron Copland, Manuel de Falla, Gian Carlo Menotti, and Igar Stravinsky — as well as those in the classical tradition and modern composers of popular music. Folk music of many cultures should also be included. Students should have exposure to the composition and instrumentation of Asian music. Of special interest is the close tie between North American Indian music and the story tradition it supports. *A Cry from the Earth* by John Bierhorst (Four Winds Press, 1979) is an excellent source for this material.

[25] Colleen N. Mullikin and William A. Henk, "Using Music as a Background for Reading: An Exploratory Study," *Journal of Reading* 28 (January 1985): 353–358.

[26] Dianne Monson, "The Literature Program and the Arts," *Language Arts* 59 (March 1982): 254–258.

Content-Area Inventory

This inventory will help you locate pages in this level of IMAGINATION which extend literature to the content areas of the curriculum.

Social Studies

Story Land 1 12–13
Story Land 2 22–25, 158–163

Story Books
Hello Friends! 12–13
Oh, What Fun! 22–25
What a Funny Animal! 40–45

Teacher's Edition 18, 32, 100, 146, 278, 308, 326, 416, 440, 454, 482

Mathematics

Story Land 1 73–77, 78–79, 80–83

Story Book
Places I Know 31–35, 36–37, 38–41

Teacher's Edition 118, 132, 146, 182, 198, 246, 264, 294, 348, 440, 468, 482

Science

Story Land 2 92–109, 110–114, 115–117, 158–163

Story Books
Let's Go Outside 58–75, 76–80, 81–83
What a Funny Animal! 40–45

Teacher's Edition 18, 46, 80, 100, 118, 162, 214, 230, 246, 264, 294, 368, 386, 400, 416, 468, 498

Health

Story Land 1 115–121

Story Book
Imagine That! 29–35

Teacher's Edition 64, 132, 182, 230, 278, 348, 454, 498

Physical Education

Teacher's Edition 64, 368

Fine Arts

Teacher's Edition 32, 46, 64, 80, 162, 198, 214, 294, 308, 326, 386, 416, 468

Language Arts

Story Land 16–17

Story Book
Hello Friends! 16–17

These are only a few of the boundless opportunities to promote literary appreciation and response through the visual arts and music. Boundless, too, is the pleasure to be gained.

Additional Readings

Barron, Pamela Patrick, and Jennifer Q. Burley, eds. *Jump Over the Moon.* New York: Holt, Rinehart & Winston, 1984. Selected articles help set criteria for biography, counting and alphabet books, historical fiction and other materials pertinent to the content areas.

Davies, Rita. "How the Arts Can Be Central to Classroom Learning." *Learning* 13 (January 1985): 25–27. A teacher writes of using visual arts and music to explore a theme presented by poetry.

Dupuis, Mary M., ed. *Reading in the Content Areas: Research for Teachers.* Newark, Del.: International Reading Association Clearinghouse on Reading and Communication Skills, 1984. Experts on seven content areas (mathematics, health, science, social studies, foreign language, English, music) identify skills and strategies most pertinent to their areas. The booklet includes substantial annotated bibliographies to help teachers pursue the topics further.

Gaitskell, Charles D., and Al Hurwitz. *Children and Their Art: Methods for the Elementary School.* 4th ed. New York: Harcourt Brace Jovanovich, 1982. This book presents a synthesis of child development and art development, with examples applicable to combining visual arts and literature.

Miccinati, Jeannette Louise, Judith B. Sanford, Gene Hepner. "Teaching Reading Through the Arts: An Annotated Bibliography." *The Reading Teacher* 36 (January 1983): 412–417. Thirty-three selections, well summarized, to help the teacher bring music, art, and drama together with reading of literature.

Monson, Dianne L., and the Committee on the Elementary School Booklist. *Adventuring with Books* Urbana, Ill.: National Council of Teachers of English, 1985. Selected, annotated book lists arranged under topics relevant to the social studies, with age-level designations, make this book a most useful tool for the social studies teacher and student.

Smardo, Frances A. "Using Children's Literature as a Prelude or Finale to Music Experiences with Young Children." *The Reading Teacher* 37 (April 1984): 700–705. Research findings on this topic are accompanied by a breezily annotated list of children's literature to use with dance, singing, and musical instruments.

Taub, K. Deborah. "The Endearing, Enduring Folktale." *Instructor* XCIV (November/December 1984): 61–70. Excellent resources, including folklore selected from many regions, show how such literature augments learning (and teaching) in the content areas.

Taylor, Gail Cohen. "Music in Language Arts Instruction." *Language Arts* 58 (March 1981): 363–367. A review of recent writing on music as an aid to story enjoyment; includes a list of resources for teachers.

Other Professional Books and Articles

Literature Selections That Support the Content Areas

Activities That Support the Content Areas

Meeting the Needs of Special Students

In most classrooms today, teachers are faced with meeting the needs of students of varying backgrounds and abilities. In fact, each of the following hypothetical students may be in one classroom.

- Kim, who has recently moved to the United States, does not speak English. However, she is literate in her native language. She may be identified as a **Limited-English-Proficient Student.**
- Brian's formative years have been void of rich language experiences. He struggles with the process of listening, speaking, reading, and writing and may be identified as a **Less-Prepared Student.**
- Jack is intellectually ready for challenging work. He is highly verbal, a voracious reader, and a critical thinker. Jack may be identified as a **Gifted Student.**
- Theresa is visually impaired and Tony is hearing impaired. Both require specialized instruction and may be identified as **Special Education Students.**

Many classroom teachers are faced with the challenge and responsibility of providing a positive climate that assures that all students will succeed and learn. For that reason, in IMAGINATION suggestions for modifications of the integrated instructional plans to meet the needs of special students are provided at the beginning of each unit. It is important to remember, however, that the fundamental learning goals for these students remain the same as those for other students in the classroom. All students should be afforded the same rich, creative, experiences in listening, speaking, reading, and writing.

Additional Readings

Cummins, Jim. *Bilingualism and Minority Language Children.* Toronto: Ontario Institute for Studies in Education Press, 1981.

Cummins, Jim. *Bilingualism and Special Education: Issues in Assessment and Pedogogy.* Clevedon: Multilingual Matters Ltd., 1984.

Cummings, Jim. *Linguistic Interdependence and the Educational Development of Bilingual Children.* Los Angeles: Evaluation, Dissemination and Assessment Center, California State Universtiy, 1979.

De Avila, Edward, and Barbara Havassay. *I.Q. Tests and Minority Children.* Austin, Texas: Austin Dissemination Center for Bilingual Education, 1974.

De Avila, Edward, Barbara Havassay, and Juan Pascual-Léon. *Mexican American School Children: A Neo-Piagetian Analysis.* Washington, D. C.: Georgetown University Press, 1976.

Heald-Taylor, Gail. *Whole Language Strategies for ESL Students.* Toronto: Ontario Institute for Studies in Education Press, 1986.

Krashen, Stephen D. *Second Language Learning.* Hayward, Calif.: The Alemany Press, 1981.

Krashen, Stephen D. *Writing: Research, Theory and Applications.* London: Prentice-Hall, Ltd., 1984.

Krashen, Stephen D., and Tracy Terrell. *The Natural Approach: Language Acquisition in the Classroom.* Hayward, Calif.: The Alemany Press, 1983.

Ideas for Meeting the Needs of Special Students

Other Professional Books and Articles

A Literature Curriculum

Bernice E. Cullinan

Many children read alone before they start school. Without formal instruction, these children learn to read in a natural, developmental way. While there are many differences among them — social, economic, intellectual, racial — there are some commonalities. One is that they are paper-and-pencil kids — ones who like to make marks on paper. They use the marks to express meaning, and invent their own spellings, often using one letter to represent whole words — as in such constructions as "U R Nis." They are also children who are read to and ones for whom someone answers questions. When they ask, "What is that?" or "What does that say?" someone tells them. In sum, their learning environment is supportive, nonthreatening, noncompetitive, and one in which symbols — marks on paper — serve a function. Further, reading is experienced as a joyful sharing of interesting things that come from books.

In many cases, these children have their special books — favorites that they want read to them repeatedly. As the father of one such child said, "If I have to read *Goodnight Moon* one more time, I think I'll die!" It is only the adult who tires of the repetition in Margaret Wise Brown's book, however; for the child, the repetition is a replay of a happy experience. Children possess their favorite books in more than one way: they carry them around, pore over them, say bits and pieces of the story until they come close to approximating the text, and gradually make the language in them their own. This reading-like behavior, in which children "read" and "reread" their version of a favorite book, is a critical step — called emergent reading — in the process of attaining literacy. Don Holdaway gives an example of one child's version of a text:

TEXT	REENACTMENT
and an ocean tumbled by with a private boat for Max and he sailed off through night and day	Max stepped into his private boat and sailed off one day and one night
and in and out of weeks and almost over a year to where the wild things are. And when he came to the place where the wild things are they roared their terrible roars and gnashed their terrible teeth and rolled their terrible eyes and showed their terrible claws	then when he came to where the wi — OO look at that thing — he's blowing smoke out of his nose and where the wild things are they lashed their terrible claws — *oh no!* they lashed their terrible teeth — Hrmm! — (Interviewer: 'What did they gnash?') They *lashed* their terrible claws! — showed their terrible claws and showed their terrible yellow eyes (but we've got blue eyes,)
till Max said "BE STILL!" and tamed them with a magic trick of staring into all their yellow eyes without blinking once and they were frightened and called him the most wild thing of all	till Max said, "BE STILL!" that's what he said. One of these ones have toes (turns the page to find the toed monster). Toes! (Laughs) until Max said "BE STILL!" into all the yellow eyes without blinking once. And all the wild things said, "You wild thing!" (Note the elegant transformation into direct speech.)
and made him king of all the wild things. "And now," cried Max, "let the wild rumpus start!"	And then Max said, "Let the wild rumpus start!"
No text.	That's got no words, has it!
(Picture of wild dance)	He'd better pull his tail out of the way.

Holdaway notes that the child quoted above has just turned four, has had good experiences with books, and has had Maurice Sendak's *Where the Wild Things Are* read to her four times. The most salient features of what she does in this account is to display meaning from the text continuously and to approximate the text in a way similar to the way she (and most children) approximates speech.

The lesson we need to draw from this is that children will learn to read in the same way they learn to speak if we treat reading in a similar manner. The parallels between learning to talk and learning to read are striking, and children would be far more successful at learning to read were we to treat the process the way we do learning to speak. As they are learning to speak, we surround children with continual and voluminous stimulation through our speech. There is no sequence in the speech sounds we present, and children simply take from it what they will as they begin to form speech sounds. In learning to speak, most children's efforts are met with love and enthusiasm and immediate response. There *is* reinforcement: "Say it again, say it for Daddy, tell Mommy." This tremendous flood of response and affection is worth more than 10,000 jelly beans to a child. Meaning is also necessary, for children don't practice initial sounds apart from real words; they do say "ma ma ma" and "da da da," but they say them for totally meaningful reasons. The child, then, selects from all he hears and practices what is meaningful. His oral language is self-regulated, meaning-centered, and develops naturally in a supportive environment.

So, too, will reading develop naturally if it is nurtured by a supportive environment. If a child regularly sits on a loving adult's lap or snuggles safe and warm in bed as he is read to, he associates feelings of love and joy with reading; his schema of reading includes happy associations, shared pleasures, and feelings of security. The child who has had the experience repeatedly has powerful, positive emotional underpinnings supporting his mental posture toward reading. Further, by seeing those he loves and respects enjoying the act of reading, he comes to view that act as something good to do for its own sake.

Similarly, negative feelings, especially those derived from punishment, militate *against* productive learning. A child embarrassed by the teacher for making a mistake in oral reading will avoid that type of mistake to the extent he can tell what it was. But, since he was trying to do the right thing anyway, the punishment is likely to make him avoid oral reading altogether, because *any* response may seem to him unsafe in that it can invite punishment. The greater possibility, however, is that his avoidance will spread to reading in general, to the person who embarrasses him, and to the context of the reading lesson itself. His aversion may influence him deeply, especially if the punishment is repeated often and he searches for ways to protect himself, finding defenses and developing blocks to reading.

It is abundantly clear that intellect and emotion cannot be separated in any learning task, try as we might to pretend that the cognitive and affective domains are distinct. Don Holdaway states it emphatically:

It is our way in educational matters to value the cognitive and devalue the emotional. The emotional accompaniments — or should we say, the emotional heart — of any human activity refuses to be ignored. No matter how meticulous we are about getting things intellectually right, unless things are *emotionally* right, human activity is tragically deformed.

The lesson, again, is that the introduction to literacy should be developmentally appropriate, pleasurable, and meaning-centered.

The emotional context in which anything is learned colors the learning. Each of us can recall trying to learn something new when the emotional context — anxiety, perhaps — made it impossible. Our job as teachers and parents is to accentuate the positive and make learning about literature the joyous experience it can be. It cannot be denied that seeds planted early take deep root, and as we plant the seeds of literacy, we want to plant them in soil made fertile by imagination, joy, and meaning. Literature can make that job easier.

The function of imagination should not be underestimated; it is an absolute necessity for learning. Children who have not been encouraged to imagine will have difficulty creating images when reading. This latter ability is critical in reading, since stories deal with inner feelings, intentions, and purposes — elusive abstractions for which there are few literal referents and that can be grasped only when the child evokes in his imagination some corresponding experience. Unless we can see in the mind's eye, create mental images, envision meanings, imagine possibilities, we are less than able to do our part in filling in the gaps and making meaning when interacting with a text.

Bernice E. Cullinan is Professor of Early Childhood and Elementary Education at New York University, specializing in children's literature and reading. Her publications include *Literature and the Child, Books I Read When I Was Young,* and *Literature and Young Children.* Dr. Cullinan served as a member of the 1983 Caldecott Committee of the American Library Association and as a chair of the Teacher's Choices Project for the National Council of Teachers of English. She is also a past president of the International Reading Association.

Poetry and the Teacher

Myra Cohn Livingston

I am myself,
of all my atom parts I am the sum.
And out of my blood and my brain
I make my own interior weather,
my own sun and rain.
Imprint my mark upon the world,
whatever I shall become.

Eve Merriam, "Thumbprint"

Robert Frost has written that a poem "begins in delight and ends in wisdom." The Irish poet James Stephens tells us that "What the heart knows today the head will understand tomorrow." In these words both poets suggest one of the most meaningful ways of introducing children to poetry: to infect with *delight*, stress the *joy*, approach through the *heart*, and know that wisdom and understanding will follow. It makes all the difference.

Children grow into poetry, beginning with Mother Goose. From the first time they hear rhyming verses that tell a small story, that play with words, that move along the bouncing rhythms, that stress rhyme, they are affirming a basic need to listen with both heart and movement — to respond with pleasure.

Jack be nimble,
Jack be quick,
Jack jump over
The candlestick.

Even nonsense poems allow them to test their own knowledge of what is true and what is not, to improve their self-images, and to be able to laugh both at others and at themselves:

Far and few, far and few,
Are the lands where the Jumblies live:
Their heads are green, and their hands
are blue;
And they went to sea in a sieve.

Edward Lear, "The Jumblies"

New discoveries, thoughts, dreams, and widely ranging emotions surround children as they grow up. Poetry mirrors their experiences through a more sophisticated handling of imagery, rhythm, and sound. What distinguishes poetry from other forms of literature is a rhythm that almost invites our bodies to move, our fingers to tap, our feet to dance; combinations of words that make us wish to repeat them aloud; rhymes, oftentimes, that encourage us to make up our own series of sounds; and a sort of irresistible music that engages heart, mind, and body. From the simplest folk rhyme to the ballad, from the traditional to the most experimental contemporary poem, poetry gives children room where their emotions and imaginations may run free.

DISCOVERING POETRY

The delight of poetry is in discovery: a new image, a different way of looking, the pleasure of words and rhythms used well, a humorous idea, and eccentric person, a striking metaphor. The delight is in the freedom to choose from among so many kinds of poems the ones that speak to us. The delight is in becoming familiar with riddles and limericks, haiku and counting rhymes, ballads and shape poems. The delight remains so long as children are able to come to a poem and find something of themselves and their world mirrored, extended, or even stretched. The delight allows them to act out the stories in pantomime or dance, to sculpt, to illustrate, to change the words aloud, alone or with others, to try writing poems of their own, to respond in individual ways to the poetry they hear and read.

In the IMAGINATION series, teachers will find verse and poetry to bring delight and pleasure. Here are traditional verses that have long been favorites of young readers, juxtaposed with verse by contemporary poets who write for today's young people. A mixture of light and serious verse spanning centuries and cultures has been selected within the thematic strands to afford a wide choice for both teacher and student. It may certainly happen that some of the selections will not appeal to every child or teacher. All of us hear a different tune. Some enjoy rhyming verse and ordered meter, while others prefer a freer, more open approach to poetry. Humorous verse, limericks, and riddles appeal to some; poetry with a more serious tone, a different mood, to others. Fortunately there are enough poems for all. Both teachers and students should always feel free to pick and choose what is meaningful to them as individuals.

It is here, I believe, that the wisdom and understanding of which Robert Frost and James Stephens spoke become important. Wisdom is *not* the message given by a poem to a reader; wisdom is *not* didacticism cajoling, exhorting, or instructing the reader of a poem to behave in a certain fashion; wisdom is *not* high-flown sentiments in lofty diction. Nor is wisdom achieved by tearing apart a poem to find what figures of speech, what symbolism it may contain. Rather, wisdom is acquired by knowing that as we read poetry we grow in understanding. Wisdom is found by relating our thoughts and emotions as individuals to ourselves and to others about us, to other cultures, other centuries, other places. Wisdom comes in knowing that the best poetry has something to say for each of us if we first make the commitment to find the delight. Wisdom also implies that *com*prehending is not nearly so important as *ap*prehending. As John Ciardi has pointed out, it is important that we never ask "*What* does a poem mean?" but rather "*How* does a poem mean?" For Ciardi, the skillful combination of idea, form, words, and rhythm separates real poetry from mere pleasantries put into verse form.

Most likely we will not want to speak to children about methods of delighting or wisdom and understanding. What we can do is try to show them that poetry is part of life. Poetry has something to say about the way we view ourselves, our world, and everything in that world from a drop of rain to mirrors in the Fun House to our feelings about ourselves. Poetry can be funny, it can be sad. It is not, as many believe, a unit of study we get once a year filled with iambic pentameter and some poems to memorize.

Because of the increasing number of fine poetry anthologies available, it is possible for teachers in all grades to relate poetry to almost any subject. History might be studied using some of the folk poetry of America. Numerous poems deal with science and math. The IMAGINATION Teacher's Editions offer a wide variety of suggestions for integrating poetry with other arts — painting, dancing, creative writing, and dramatics, to name just a few.

Our most difficult job as teachers today may well lie in the need to elicit imaginative responses. In a world that promotes an unusual amount of passivity, reliance on mass media, and a great deal of programmed response, teachers need to touch the imagination of each child, to encourage this individual reaction to what is heard or read. In a single classroom there may be but a handful of children who respond to a given poem, but this reaction should be praised and nurtured. What happens when a poem and the right listener, the right reader, come together can be magic.

SHARING POETRY IN THE CLASSROOM

It will come as no surprise to teachers that few children today hear nursery rhymes at home. The classroom may well be the first place children hear poetry, and the teacher may well be the first person who reads poetry to them aloud. No matter what age or level of the students, poetry should be read aloud as often as possible.

Many of the poems in IMAGINATION are suitable for individual and choral reading. Students can organize group readings of poems or memorize them for the joy of it. Many balk at the idea of memorization, but if a student especially likes a poem, the results can be wonderful! Whole classes have put on poetry programs to entertain other classes until the entire school becomes infected with the joy of performing. Again, if imagination is encouraged by the teacher, the students benefit not only from their personal response to poetry but grow with their hearts and minds to bring its enjoyment to others. Here are a few suggestions to help you get started.

1. **Choose poems you like and those you think your class will like.** Teachers cannot elicit enthusiasm for work they themselves do not enjoy. Be aware that riddles, limericks, and light verse will always be received well, but that other kinds of poetry will help young people grow in their perceptions and relationships with others.

2. **Encourage students to find verses and poems and share them with the class.**

3. **Experiment with different ways of reading the sounds and rhythms of poems.** One way to read a poem is to read each line as a separate idea followed by a pause.

Who has seen the wind? (pause)
Neither you nor I: (pause)
But when the trees blow down their
  heads (pause)
The wind is passing by.

  Christina Rosetti,
  "Who Has Seen the Wind?"

Another way is to pause at the punctuation in a line. In this stanza, then, the question mark at the end of line 1 indicates a pause, as does the colon at the end of line 2. In the third line, however, one could either pause after the word *heads* or read the last two lines as one long sentence. There is no right or wrong.

4. **Don't be afraid to make mistakes when you read poems aloud.** Everyone does. If you flub a reading, pick up and start again — this will help minimize the students' embarrassment when they make mistakes in their own readings. Both teacher and students can learn together.

5. **Read with your heart rather than your head.** If you wish to laugh as you read, do so. When a poem is sad, don't hide your sadness; let it enter your voice just as you would let happiness.

Children know what emotions are — do not underestimate their ability to know if you are reading with honesty. They would much rather have a flawed, sincere reading from you than the perfectly enunciated recitation on a tape or record.

Don't be afraid to make the leap. Leave your head in arithmetic, in history, in social studies, in science; and bring your heart and sense of delight to poetry! You may astound yourself; you will astound your students — and together you will begin a love for poetry that you may never before have imagined possible.

Myra Cohn Livingston, is Poet-in-Residence for the Beverly Hills Unified School District and a Senior Instructor at UCLA Extension. The author of more than thirty books, she has received many awards for her poetry, including the National Council of Teachers of English Award for Excellence on Poetry for Children, which was awarded her in 1980.

Bibliography

Books About Poetry

Ciardi, John. *How Does a Poem Mean?* Boston: Houghton Mifflin, 1959.
Hughes, Ted. *Poetry Is.* New York: Doubleday, 1970.
Kennedy, X. J. *An Introduction to Poetry.* 4th ed. Boston: Little, Brown, 1978.

Individual Poets

Bodecker, N. M. *Hurry, Hurry, Mary Dear! and Other Nonsense Poems.* New York: Atheneum, 1976.
Brooks, Gwendolyn. *Bronzeville Boys and Girls.* New York: Harper & Row, 1956.

Clifton, Lucille. *Everett Anderson's Year.* New York: Holt, Rinehart & Winston, 1974.

Farber, Norma. *Small Wonders.* New York: Coward, McCann & Geoghegan, 1979.

Fisher, Aileen. *Out in the Dark and Daylight.* New York: Harper & Row, 1980.

Holman, Felice. *I Hear You Smiling and Other Poems.* New York: Charles Scribner's, 1973.

Kuskin, Karla. *Dogs & Dragons, Tree & Dreams.* New York: Harper & Row, 1980.

McCord, David. *One at a Time.* Boston: Little, Brown, 1978.

Milne. A. A. *When We Were Very Young.* New York: E. P. Dutton, 1924.

Smith, William Jay. *Laughing Time: Nonsense Poems.* New York: Delacorte, 1980.

Thurman, Judith. *Flashlight and Other Poems.* New York: Atheneum, 1976.

Watson, Clyde. *Father Fox's Pennyrhymes.* New York: T. Y. Crowell, 1971.

Anthologies

Adoff, Arnold, ed. *My Black Me: A Beginning Book on Black Poetry.* New York: E. P. Dutton, 1974.

Behn, Harry, trans. *Cricket Songs.* New York: Harcourt Brace Jovanovich, 1964. Haiku attuned to young people.

Brewton, John E., and Blackburn, Lorraine A., comps. *They've Discovered a Head in the Box for the Bread and Other Laughable Limericks.* New York: Harper & Row, 1978.

Cole, William ed. *The Birds and the Beasts Were There.* Cleveland: World, 1963. Poems about animals for every reader.

De la Mare, Walter, ed. *Come Hither.* New York: Alfred A. Knopf, 1957. A favorite collection of traditional poetry.

Houston, James ed. *Songs of the Dream People: Chants and Images from the Indians and Eskimos of North America.* New York: Atheneum, 1972.

Wood, Ray, ed. *Fun in American Folk Rhymes.* Philadelphia: J. B. Lippincott, 1952.

Wordless Picture Books and the Teacher
Rosemary Salesi

> Once upon a time there lived a
> little boy and a dog. They wanted
> to catch a frog for a friend and pet.
> They started down the hill and a
> branch was in there [their] way so
> the boy cut it down and put it in
> front of him. Then he started off
> again and right before him was a
> frog. He ran towards it and triped
> [tripped] over the branch and fell
> right into the water with dog and
> all . . . .

Sarah Shubert, First Grade

Sarah Shubert's story, her own retelling of Mercer Mayer's book *A Boy, A Dog, and A Frog*[1] (Level 1), is just one example of how students can respond to a *wordless picture book,* a book in which pictures explain a concept or tell a story. Using invented spellings for some words, Sarah wrote her story after several short classroom activities: looking at the book; predicting what happened next in the story; and tell the story in sequence with the rest of the class. This lesson was in late March; for the previous three months, Sarah and her classmates kept diaries and wrote a short response paper each day. The few stories the first graders wrote, however, usually lacked a developed middle and an adequate ending; only a few were complete narratives. With the support of the plot, sequence, and characterization provided by Mercer Mayer's illustrations, well over half of the children wrote complete stories. Some, like Sarah, even observed the conventions of traditional storytelling, beginning with "Once upon a time" and ending with "And they lived happily ever after."

WHAT ARE WORDLESS PICTURE BOOKS?

For some teachers, the existence of wordless books and their use in the classroom may seem to be recent developments; but their first contemporary wordless pictures books, such as Ruth Carroll's *What Whiskers Did,*[2] appeared in the early 1930s. In the 1960s and 1970s, many illustrators resdiscovered this unique format and explored it further. They found that by using a series of sequenced illustrations with few or no words, they could introduce, develop, and eventually resolve a story problem. At this writing, over seventy-five illustrators have contributed wordless picture books to the growing body of children's literature, and each year brings more.

What is surprising about these books is their considerable variation in content, format, and style of art. There are two predominant types: *concept books,* which primarily deal with the alphabet, shapes, numbers, and such nonfiction subjects as the Apollo mission or a life cycle in nature; and *wordless stories,* which use sequenced pictures to move from an introduction of characters and problems to a climax and conclusion.[3] In a wordless story, the characters' facial expressions and actions aid the reader in deciphering the plot.

Teachers find wordless books to be an imaginative resource for promoting oral language development, storytelling, and writing skills at all grade levels. Students enjoy and think through the stories at the same time, and eventually most want to share the fun by retelling them to others.[4] Because the books call forth the children's own language, they provide opportunities for exploring concepts and creating stories.[5] The stories the children write can be used as reading material for the entire class. But perhaps most importantly, the use of wordless books can foster a positive attitude toward all books and reading.

Exposure to wordless books will benefit students now and in the future. In our visually oriented society, the ability to see the visual whole and the significance of each detail, as well as the ability to express oneself fluently, are needed by everyone.

THE TEACHER'S ROLE: GENERAL CONSIDERATIONS

Reading a wordless picture book should be an enjoyable experience for students. The student's language abilities and prior experiences, as well as the books themselves, will help determine success. In sharing these books, it is necessary to observe whether the children enjoy them. If the motivation of enjoyment is not there, avoid follow-up activities.

Except when used for lessons in making predictions, the entire book should be "read" initially without interruption. Since comprehension depends on how well the students perceive minor details and subtleties in a story, a second or third viewing, coupled with exploratory activities, will help students appreciate and respond to it more fully. Filmstrips of wordless picture books, such as those produced by Weston Woods Studios, Inc., enable large groups of students to enjoy the same story simultaneously and allow the teacher to focus attention on selected elements.

Beginning in the lower grades, wordless books can be used for step-by-step practice in describing characters and actions with words or phrases, then with one complete sentence, two or more sentences, and finally, with a number of sentences in logical order. Since many of the more

---

[1] Mercer Mayer, *A Boy, A Dog, and A Frog* (New York: Dial Press, 1967.)

[2] Ruth Carroll, *What Whiskers Did* (New York: Henry Z. Walck, 1965).

[3] Rosemary A. Salesi, "Reading, That's Easy. It's the Words That Are Tough," *Maine Reading Association Bulletin* (Spring 1973): 3–6.

[4] Rosemary A. Salesi, "Books Without Words," *New England Reading Association Journal,* 9 (1973–74): 28–30.

[5] Patricia J. Ciancolo, "Using Wordless Books to Teach Reading and Visual Literacy and to Study Literature," *Top of the News,* 29 (April 1973): 226–234.

sophisticated books can be read at either the literal or symbolic level, they work well in heterogeneous groups of students. For example, the problems that bilingual students have with books are lessened because they can label objects, describe actions, or write stories using their own languages. The books are so highly entertaining that the students may be more comfortable using their new language as they share ideas with each other.

SPECIFIC TEACHING SUGGESTIONS

The following are some ways to introduce students to wordless picture books. They may also help students gain independence for reading the books on their own.

1. Suggest that students use the title to guess what might happen in the story. This will help to prepare them for the events of the story.

2. When using a wordless picture book that tells a story, be sure the students understand that the book does tell a story. This is particularly important with preschool and early primary students.

3. If the students are to work independently, encourage them to examine the entire book first, including the cover, endpapers, title page, and dedication page. In some books, such as Peter Spier's *Noah's Ark*[6] and Diane De Groat's *Alligator's Toothache,*[7] the stories begin prior to the first page. Inferences are easier to draw when the student has examined the entire story.

4. Encourage the students to look at illustrations closely and to note details. Details in the illustrations foreshadow new events, changes in the action, or a subplot.

5. Ask questions that students should ask themselves when they read alone: What is happening? Why is it happening? What will happen next? Did I predict correctly? How do I know? What might the characters be saying to each other? What words would describe their actions and feelings?

6. Have the students examine their wordless picture books several times and talk about them with classmates. Then ask them to close the books and tell the story. If they use the book in storytelling, both children and adults tend to describe only the details in the pictures, completely ignoring the gaps that occur between them.

Storytelling becomes more natural when the book is put aside because the storyteller is more apt to fill in the missing details and feel freer to improvise. The book's content thus provides a structure around which the storyteller can fashion his or her own stories. Creative responses should be praised.

Rosemary Salesi is a widely published author of professional articles and a reading workshop leader. She is currently an associate professor of education at the University of Maine at Orono, where she teaches courses in children's literature and elementary education. She was a classroom teacher for eight years

---

Bibliography

Wordless Books for Primary Grades

Although the following selections are intended for primary grades, they need not be limited to a specific age or grade level. In most cases, students enjoy a wider range of wordless books as they mature. Children in preschool and early primary grades generally prefer realistic stories. Older, middle-school students enjoy these as well as the more sophisticated and fanciful books.

Anno, Mitsumasa. *Anno's Counting Book.* New York: T. Y. Crowell, 1977.

Briggs, Raymond. *The Snowman.* New York: Random House, 1978.

Carle, Eric. *Do You Want to Be My Friend?* New York: T. Y. Crowell, 1971.

Hoban, Tana. *Dig, Drill, Dump, Fill.* New York: Greenwillow Books, 1975.

Krahn, Fernando. *Sebastian and the Mushroom.* New York: Delacorte, 1976.

Sugita, Yutaka. *My Friend Little John and Me.* New York: McGraw-Hill, 1973.

Ueno, Noriko. *Elephant Buttons.* New York: Harper & Row, 1973.

---

[6] Peter Spier, *Noah's Ark* (Garden City, N.Y.: Doubleday, 1977).
[7] Diane De Groat, *Alligator's Toothache* (New York: Crown, 1977).

Resource Center

About the Authors and Illustrators

These notes present some information about the authors and illustrators in IMAGINATION about whom biographical material was available. You may wish to read aloud this text as you introduce the selections.

Brown, Marc   Marc Brown's wonderful sense of humor is reflected in the many books he has illustrated and written since 1969. His characters, such as Arthur, the aardvark, are modeled after real children and their everyday experiences.

Carle, Eric   Known as a successful artist and designer, Eric Carle was born in the United States but spent many years studying art in Germany. The art for his books is made from cut and layered pieces of specially prepared papers which are overprinted with crayon, tempera, and ink. *The Very Hungry Caterpillar* and *A Very Busy Spider* are some of his most famous works.

Fyleman, Rose   Born in England in 1877, Rose Fyleman was a school teacher, who later became a professional singer, voice instructor and lecturer. She founded and edited *Merry-Go-Round,* a children's magazine. In addition to these accomplishments, Rose Fyleman wrote and published her own poetry, plays and operas for children and translated French and German songs and stories for children to enjoy.

Ginsburg, Mirra   Mirra Ginsburg is a well-known translator and editor of collections and Russian and Yiddish folk tales, books, and riddles. A native of Russia, she became interested in folk tales as a child: "My childhood home in Russia was almost literally the folk tale world: pine woods and birches, wide fields and meadows rich with wild flowers closely surrounded our small town . . ."

Graham, John   Writer, editor, and college professor, John Graham became interested in children's books when he was a child. This interest was renewed when he read to his own children. Out of this experience, he began writing and creating his own stories for children. He said, "I know part of the reason I write is because I read to my children. There is a closeness at that time, a sharing of experience that plunges very deeply."

Hayes, Geoffrey   Geoffrey Hayes has written and illustrated several children's books including *The Alligator and His Uncle Tooth* and *The Secret Inside.* An artist and designer, Geoffrey Hayes also illustrated *When the Wind Blew,* a children's book by Margaret Wise Brown.

Hoban, Tana   Specializing in photography, Tana Hoban uses her talent to illustrate simple concept books for young readers. She's an award-winning photographer, film maker and television consultant and has published children's books such as *Shapes and Things, Big Ones, Little Ones* and *A Children's Zoo.*

Hoberman, Mary Ann   Mary Ann Hoberman started writing poems, songs, and stories as soon as she learned to write. After graduating from Smith College, she worked in advertising and journalism, and then began writing children's books. She has often written about insects and animals. "I like animals very much. . . . I spent a lot of time as a child sitting around watching animals, going to the zoo and looking at animals, and thinking about them. It's a great subject for poetry."

Hutchins, Pat   Pat Hutchins was born in Yorkshire, England. She was brought up in the country. She started drawing when she was quite young and designed her first children's book in her spare time after moving to New York with her husband. Upon bringing the book to a publishing company, she was asked to write her first story. She did, and the picture book *Rosie's Walk* was a success. Her philosophy about writing is contained in these words: "I try not to talk down to children. I try to keep my stories logical, even if a story is pure fantasy."

Katz, Bobbi   Author Bobbi Katz has been a fashion editor, art historian, social worker, mother, and writer for children. She has said, "I write only for children because I want to return childhood to them. I hope to join those writers and artists who delight, sensitize, and give hope to children."

Krauss, Ruth   The books of Ruth Krauss make young children feel good about themselves because they find the simple story lines easy to read. A perennial favorite among young readers is *Bears,* a wonderful verse which contains only 16 words.

Lenski, Lois   Lois Lenski is one of the best-known and loved writers of children's books. Born in a small town in Ohio, she has written books that reflect her close association with children and her interest in American life in the various regions of the United States.

Lobel, Arnold   See page 41 for the author feature about Arnold Lobel.

Ormerod, Jan   Born in Australia, Jan Ormerod has written and illustrated her own stories for children. Her book *Sunshine* won her the Mother Goose Award and the Kate Greenaway Award commendation from the Library Association in 1982.

Rossetti, Christina   Christina Rossetti was born into a family of poets and artists in London, England, in 1830. She was educated by her mother, for whom she wrote her first poem at the age of twelve. Later she helped her mother run a school. She was often painted by her brother, Dante Gabriel Rossetti, a famous poet and artist. Throughout her lifetime Christina Rossetti continued to write poetry and rhymes for children.

Samton, Sheila White   Sheila White Samton worked as a muralist and designer of wall hangings before she began writing children's books. *Beside the Bay* is her second book for children.

Spilka, Arnold   Arnold Spilka is a native of New York City. He is a renowned sculptor, painter, and writer and illustrator of children's books and has written *Whom Shall I Marry?* and a book of nonsense poems called *The Frog Went "BLAH."*

Tafuri, Nancy   Nancy Tafuri is the recipient of the 1985 Caldecott Honor Book Award for her children's book *Have You Seen My Duckling?* She has also illustrated books for authors Mirra Ginsburg and George Shannon.

Welber, Robert   Robert Welber has owned an antique shop and produced plays in New York. He is also a teacher who decided to start his own school. At his one-room elementary school in New York, the Studio on Eleventh Street, children learn from each other and, with his help, teach themselves. Robert Welber's other stories are *Frog, Frog, Frog* and *Winter Picnic.*

Wood, Audrey   In addition to owning a book import shop and teaching drama to children, Audrey Wood has written and illustrated more than a dozen books for children. In 1985, Audrey Wood and her husband Don Wood received a Caldecott Award for their book *King Bidgood's in the Bathtub.*

SAMMY

Words and Music by
HAP PALMER

Six Little Ducks

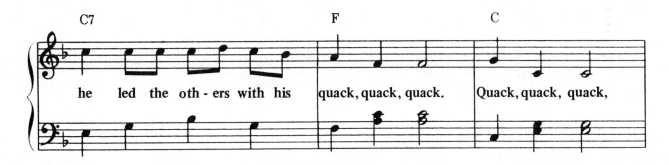

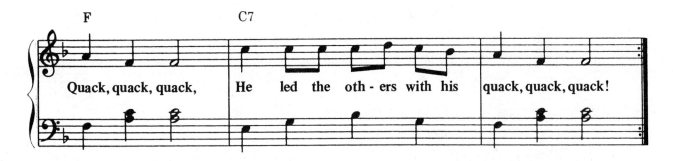

Six little ducks
That I once knew,
Fat ones, skinny ones,
Fair ones, too.
But the one little duck
With a feather on its back,
He led the others
With a quack, quack, quack.
Quack, quack, quack,
Quack, quack, quack.
He led the others
With a quack, quack, quack!

Down to the river they would go,
Wibble, wobble, wibble, wobble to and fro.
Home from the river they would come,
Wibble, wobble, wibble, wobble,
Right back home.
Quack, quack, quack,
Quack, quack, quack,
Right back home
With a quack, quack, quack!

THIS IS THE WAY WE GET UP IN THE MORNING

Words and Music by
HAP PALMER

take off our pa-ja-mas and put them a-way,___ ooh,___ ooh.___ We

slip on some clothes and start out the day,___ ooh,___ ooh.___ We

but-ton our but-tons,___ one, two, three. Tie our shoes. Now you see,

this is the way___ we get up___ in the morn-ing,___ ooh,___ ooh.

Now it's time___ to have a big break-fast, ooh,___ ooh.___ We

take our time, we don't eat too fast,___ ooh,___ ooh.___ We

start out the day by eat-ing good foods, ooh,___ ooh.___ There're

man-y yum-my things that we can choose,___ ooh,___ ooh.___ There're

eggs and ce-re-al, toast and juice, pan-cakes, cof-fee cakes, ba-con too!___

This is the way___ we get up___ in the morn-ing, ___ ooh,___ ooh.

THE BUS SONG

3. The brake on the bus goes, "Roomp, roomp, roomp!" etc.

4. The money in the bus goes, "Clink, clink, clink!" etc.

5. The wheels on the bus go 'round and around, etc.

6. There's a baby in the bus goes, "Wah, wah, wah!" etc.

7. There's a bus on the bus goes, "Bus, bus, bus!" etc.

BEAUTIFUL DAY

Words and Music by
HAP PALMER

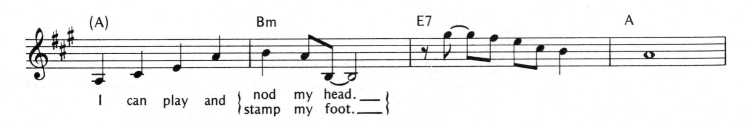

I can play and {bend my knees.___ / shake a leg.___}

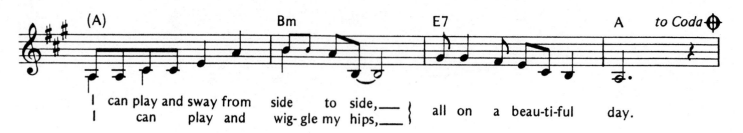

I can play and sway from side to side,___ {all on a beau-ti-ful day. / I can play and wig-gle my hips,___}

I can move and play in so man-y dif-f'rent ways;

I just cre-ate them as the mu-sic plays.___

All on a beau-ti-ful day.

BARNYARD SONG
A Kentucky folk song

1. I had a cat, and the cat pleased me, I fed my cat un-der yon-der tree. Cat goes fid-dle dee dee.____

2. I had a hen, and the hen pleased me, I fed my hen un-der yon-der tree. Hen goes chim-my chuck, chim-my chuck, Cat goes fid-dle dee dee.____

Back to %

*These measures repeated an extra time for each verse.

3. I had a duck, and the duck pleased me,
   I fed my duck under yonder tree;
   Duck goes quack, quack,
   Hen goes chimmy chuck, chimmy chuck,
   Cat goes fiddle dee dee.

4. I had a hog,
   Hog goes griffy, gruffy,
   (Repeat for Duck, Hen, Cat)

5. I had a sheep,
   Sheep goes baa, baa,
   (Repeat for Hog, Duck, Hen, Cat)

6. I had a goose,
   Goose goes swishy, swashy,

(Repeat for Sheep, Hog, Duck, Hen, Cat)

7. I had a cow,
   Cow goes moo, moo,
   (Repeat for Goose, Sheep, Hog, Duck,
   Hen, Cat)

8. I had a dog,
   Dog goes bow-wow, bow-wow,
   (Repeat for Cow, Goose, Sheep, Hog,
   Duck, Hen, Cat)

9. I had a horse,
   Horse goes neigh, neigh,
   (Repeat for Dog, Cow, Goose, Sheep,
   Hog, Duck, Hen, Cat)

Notes

**Additional Professional Books
on Reading**

**Additional Professional Articles
on Reading**

Notes

Other Songs

Activities to Use with Songs

Other Songs

Activities to Use with Songs

Unit 1
Hello Friends!

Theme: Building positive relationships with family members and friends

Reading Selections	Writing Assignments
• Goodbye, Hello	• Dictate Sentences About Things We Say Hello and Good-bye To
• Connections: Birthday Fun	• Dictate a Thank-you Note
• Story Time at School	• Dictate Sentences About School Activities
• Silly Goose	• Dictate Sentences About Actions
• Very Tall Mouse and Very Short Mouse	• Dictate Sentences About Friends

Unit Resources

As you work through the Integrated Instructional Plans in this unit, you may want to use the following resources included in the **Student/Teacher Resources** and **Evaluation Resources** sections of the *Teacher's Edition.*

Student/Teacher Resources

- Home Letters 1A, 1B, 2A, and 2B
- Extended and Recreational Reading Ideas

Evaluation Resources

- Observation and Evaluation Guides

Students With Individual Needs

	Limited-English-Proficient Students	Less-Prepared Students	Gifted Students	Special Education Students
Think and Read	• Encourage students to participate in prereading activities by discussing relevant facts about their native countries. • Explain unfamiliar vocabulary. Make words concrete by using objects, pictures, and demonstrations. • Use recordings to help students "hear" fluent language.	• Provide additional background information when personal experiences are limited. Use pictures, magazines, and filmstrips. • Emphasize strategies included in *Setting a Purpose.* Model strategies for students.	• After modeling effective prereading strategies, have students lead the discussions that focus on previewing and predicting. • After modeling effective thinking strategies, have students lead the discussions that focus on summarizing the reading process.	• Review individualized education programs (IEPs) with special education staff and discuss necessary modification of curriculum. • For visually-impaired students, provide specialized resources such as large print books, books in braille, or recordings.
Think and Discuss	• Provide students opportunities to listen to and repeat native-English speakers' language. • Pair students with native-English speakers to answer questions.	• Have students work in cooperative learning groups to answer questions. (See the suggestions at the front of this *Teacher's Edition.*) • Model by reading aloud questions and possible responses. Have students add original responses.	• During the discussions, help students focus their abstract thoughts. Model effective strategies. • Encourage students to explain complex thoughts and ideas their classmates do not understand. Model strategies for students.	• Review lesson plans with special education staff to discuss any necessary modification of curriculum. • Develop a specialized listening program for visually-impaired students.
Think and Write	• During prewriting, ask students to act out words and phrases. Help students verbalize their thoughts. • Have students dictate as you record their drafts. Read aloud their drafts before students read aloud what they have composed.	• Model the use of prewriting strategies to organize ideas. • During revising, encourage students to expand one or two sentences. Model the process for students.	• During responding, revising, and editing, help students expand complex thoughts. Model effective strategies. • Have students work in cooperative learning groups. (See the suggestions at the front of this *Teacher's Edition.*)	• Review lesson plans with special education staff to discuss any necessary modification of curriculum. • For visually-impaired students, record the directions for the stages of the writing process. Have students record their compositions.
Think and Extend	• Explain vocabulary necessary to complete the activities. Integrate appropriate lessons from science and social studies textbooks. • Have students work in cooperative learning groups. (See the suggestions at the front of this *Teacher's Edition.*)	• Have students work in cooperative learning groups. (See the suggestions for cooperative learning activities at the front of the *Teacher's Edition.*) • Encourage students to participate in *Think and Extend* activities that require speaking.	• Ask students to think of additional *Think and Extend* activities. When appropriate assign the student-generated activities instead of the activities in the *Writer's Corner.* • Have students work in cooperative learning groups. (See the suggestions at the front of this *Teacher's Edition.*)	• Review lesson plans with special education staff to discuss any necessary modification of curriculum. • For hearing-impaired students, use visual aids, such as slides and overhead projectors, to reinforce learning.

Unit 1

Introducing the Unit

Talking About the Theme To introduce children to the unit, point to and read aloud the title "Hello Friends!" Ask children to look at the picture that illustrates the opening of the unit. Begin a discussion about building relationships with family members and friends by having students answer the following questions about the picture.

1. Who do you see in the picture? (**Possible responses:** *I see a boy in the picture. There are some animals in the tree.*)
2. What is the boy doing? (**Possible responses:** *The boy is pointing to the animals in the tree. He is talking to the animals.*)
3. Do you think the boy is having a good time? Why do you think so? (**Possible responses:** *The boy is smiling. It looks like the boy is having a good time.*)
4. What would you say to the boy if you were in this picture? (**Possible responses:** *I would say to the boy, "Come play with me!" I would ask the boy if the animals are his friends.*)
5. The stories and poems in this unit go together. What do you think the stories and poems will be about? (*Accept children's responses.*)

1 Hello Friends!

1

Extending Reading The following books extend the theme of the unit. You may want to share these books as children listen to and "read" the selections in Unit 1. Have children discuss what the family members or friends in the stories do together.

Some of the Days of Everett Anderson by Lucille Clifton. Holt, Rinehart & Winston, 1975. Everett, a young boy, learns and experiences new things each day.

May I Bring a Friend? by Beatrice Schenk de Regniers. Atheneum, 1964. A little boy has a series of hilarious experiences when he and a friend visit the royal family.

George and Martha by James Marshall. Houghton Mifflin, 1972. Two hippo friends, orderly Martha and bumbling, gentle George, experience unique lives for hippos.

The Snowman by Raymond Briggs. Random House, 1978. In this wordless book, a magical snowman becomes best friends with the boy who made him.

Bulletin Board Suggestion

Make a class collage on a bulletin board, showing pictures of activities that friends do together. Have children draw or cut pictures from magazines and arrange the pictures on the bulletin board. Ask children to help you write a caption for the collage. Once the collage is completed, discuss the various activities shown.

Unit 1

Unit Activities

The following optional unit activities relate to the theme of the unit. The activities may be completed during or after unit instruction. Some of the activities are appropriate for learning centers. Instructions for setting up learning centers appear at the front of the *Teacher's Edition.*

LISTENING Corner

Objective: To listen to a story about friends.
Materials: paper, crayons, and books about family and friends that may include titles from page 3 in the *Teacher's Edition*
Procedure: Read aloud a story about two friends. Tell children that as they listen to the story, they should think about what the friends do together.

After you read the story, have children draw a picture of the friends they heard about in the story. Have children talk about their pictures and tell what they liked about the story.

SPEAKING Corner

Objective: To retell a story using puppets.
Materials: paper plates, tongue depressors, crayons, markers, and glue
Procedure: Have children make stick puppets for the story characters they read about. (Instructions for making puppets are found in the front of the *Teacher's Edition.*)

Ask children to work with a partner. Have them use the stick puppets to retell the story they listened to. Encourage children to ask each other questions.

READING Corner

Objective: To read about building relationships with family and friends.
Materials: books about family and friends that may include titles from page 3 in the *Teacher's Edition*
Procedure: Ask children to select a book. You may wish to read it aloud to a group of children.
Encourage children to share the book with each other and tell the story to each other.

WRITING Corner

Objective: To make a booklet showing activities done with family, with friends, and by oneself.
Materials: paper and crayons or markers
Procedure: Ask children to think about the many different things they like to do with family members, with friends, and by themselves.

- On one sheet of paper, have them draw a picture of something they like to do with a friend.
- On a second piece of paper, have them draw a picture of something they like to do with someone at home.
- Then, have them draw a picture of something they enjoy doing by themselves.

You may wish to have children dictate sentences or action words for the pictures. Staple the pages together to form a booklet called "All the Things I Can Do."

Note: Some children will prefer to dictate their sentences as you write. Others will want to write on their own. Accept their writing regardless of its stage of development. Allow them to draw, scribble, or write using their own spelling.

Focusing on "Good-bye, Hello"

While **listening** to and **reading** the selection, children will focus on trying new experiences. Children will also use **writing, listening,** and **speaking** skills as they respond to the selection. They will use higher-level **thinking** throughout the lesson.

OBJECTIVE

WRITING/THINKING

- To dictate a response to literature using the writing process.
- To write in the narrative/imaginative domain.
- To use words that name people.
- To use words that name animals.
- To write about a personal experience.

READING/THINKING

- To compare characters.
- To interpret how a character feels.
- To evaluate the placement of a poem in a thematic unit.
- To recognize patterns in selection.
- To discriminate between big and small.
- To recognize initial correspondences. (/g/g)

SPEAKING/THINKING

- To discuss personal experiences before reading a selection.
- To participate in shared reading.
- To participate in group discussions.
- To dictate a response to literature.

LISTENING/THINKING

- To listen to the oral reading of a selection.
- To listen to and analyze responses to opinions about a selection.
- To listen for rhyming words.
- To listen for initial sounds. (/g/)

LEARNING STRATEGIES

- Brainstorming ideas related to children's own experiences.
- Previewing the selection and making predictions about the content.
- Completing a chart to help comprehension.
- Completing a chart to help organize writing.
- Analyzing the writer's use of language.

Summary

A child observes young animals as they leave their mothers to go out and learn about the world. The child follows the same pattern as she leaves her mother to go to school.

INDIVIDUAL NEEDS

Suggestions for teaching children with special needs are provided on *Teacher's Edition* page 1.

- The blue objectives may require direct instruction.

PLANNING CALENDAR

			STUDENT'S EDITIONS	TEACHER'S EDITION	ACTIVITY BOOK
DAY 1 **INTO THE SELECTION**	**THINK AND READ**				
	Preparing to Read		● *pages 2–11* ■ *pages 2–11*	*page 7*	
	Planning a Reading Strategy		● *pages 2–11* ■ *pages 2–11*	*page 8*	
DAYS 2-4 **THROUGH THE SELECTION**	**THINK AND DISCUSS**				
	Remembering the Selection		● *pages 2–11* ■ *pages 2–11*	*page 12*	
	Discussing the Selection		● *pages 2–11* ■ *pages 2–11*	*page 13*	
	THINK AND WRITE				
	Making the Assignment			*page 14*	
	Using the Writing Process			*pages 14–15*	
	Develop Skills				
	Focusing on Language			*page 16*	*pages 1–2*
	Focusing on Composition			*page 17*	
	Focusing on Auditory Discrimination			*page 17*	
	Focusing on Visual Discrimination			*page 17*	
	Focusing on Sound-Letter Correspondences			*page 17*	*page 3*
	Focusing on the Writer's Use of Language			*page 16*	
DAY 5 **BEYOND THE SELECTION**	**THINK AND EXTEND**				
	For the Classroom			*page 18*	
	For the Home			*page 19*	
				▲ Homework Notebook copying master 1	

● *Happy Times! Story Land 1*   ▲ *Learning*
■ *Hello Friends! Storybook*   *Resources File*

Cooperative Learning

Cooperative learning suggestions for *Think and Read* appear at the beginning of the *Teacher's Edition.*

Preparing to Read

▶**Relating to Children's Experiences**   Ask children to recall to whom they say good-bye each day and to whom they say hello. Also have them discuss appropriate times to say good-bye and hello.

After the discussion, have children listen as you read aloud the poem "Hello and Good-bye" and ask children to name the things to which the poet says good-bye and hello.

Hello and Good-bye
by Mary Ann Hoberman

Hello and good-bye
Hello and good-bye
When I'm in a swing
Swinging low and then high,
Good-bye to the ground
Hello to the sky.

Hello to the rain
Good-bye to the sun,
Then hello again sun
When the rain is all done.

In blows the winter,
Away the birds fly.

Notes for Cooperative Learning

Notes for Preparing to Read

Good-bye and hello
Hello and good-bye.

▶**Previewing and Predicting** Point to the title of the poem and read it to the children. Then ask them to look at each of the five sets of pictures and identify who or what may be saying good-bye or hello. You may wish to model a response.

I see one cat and three kittens in the first picture. One kitten is away from its mother. The kitten is looking at a bug. I think the kitten is saying good-bye to its mother and hello to the bug because the title is "Goodbye, Hello."

▶**Setting a Purpose** Tell children that as they listen to "Good-bye , Hello" they should think about the thing that happens the same in every verse.

Planning a Reading Strategy

Sharing Reading Read aloud the poem several times, sharing the illustrations and pointing to the text. Draw attention to the words *Good-bye, Mother,* and *Hello* that are repeated throughout the lesson.

Encourage children to react spontaneously with comments and questions after you have read the story. You may wish to have children pantomime the actions of the characters in the story and wave good-bye and hello at the appropriate times.

Reading Orally Read aloud the story. Encourage students to join in reciting the words that repeat, such as Good-bye, Mother, Hello, _____.

Reading Silently Give children the opportunity to "read" the poem independently. Explain that the illustrations will help them remember what is happening in the poem.

From Good-bye, Hello

A story in verse by Robert Welber

Pictures by June Goldsborough

A kitten goes creeping
Away from the rug.

2

Good-bye, Mother.
Hello, bug.

3

8

A mouse goes out
To climb and see.

4

Good-bye, Mother.
Hello, tree.

5

A bird begins
To try to fly.

6

Good-bye, Mother.
Hello, sky.

7

A squirrel comes running
Down the tree.

8

Good-bye, Mother.
Hello, bee.

9

A child is watching
Each little creature.

10

Good-bye, Mother.
Hello, teacher.

11

Notes

Ideas for Cooperative Learning

Ideas for Meeting the Needs of Individual Students

Questioning Strategies

Think and Discuss

Cooperative Learning

Cooperative learning suggestions for *Think and Discuss* appear at the beginning of the **Teacher's Edition.**

Remembering the Selection

Ask children to recall the story and identify

- each character who says good-bye and hello.
- to whom each character says good-bye.
- to whom each character says hello.

Encourage children to look at the poems illustrations to help themselves recall the information. You may wish to create a class chart to record children's responses.

Goodbye, Mother.
Hello, bug.

Good-bye, Mother.
Hello, tree.

Good-bye, Mother.
Hello, sky.

Goodbye, Mother.
Hello, bee.

Good-bye, Mother.
Hello, teacher.

Notes for Cooperative Learning

Notes for Remembering the Selection

Discussing the Selection

The following questions focus on trying new experiences on your own. As children respond to the questions, ask them to support their answers with examples from the poem. Encourage children to agree or disagree with their classmates' responses and to substantiate their opinions.

Remind children to speak clearly and loudly enough so they can be heard and understood.

1. What does each animal in the poem do that is the same? (**Possible response:** *Each animal says good-bye to its mother and hello to something new.*) *(Literal)*

2. What does the girl in the story do? (**Possible response:** *The girl watches the animals and then says good-bye to her mother and hello to her teacher.*) *(Literal)*

3. How do you think the girl feels about saying good-bye to her mother and hello to her teacher? (**Possible response:** *The girl feels a little frightened, but she also feels excited.*) *(Interpretive)*

4. How did you feel the first day of school? (**Possible response:** *I felt lonely because I did not know anyone.*) *(Creative)*

5. How do you think the little girl in the story is growing and changing? (**Possible response:** *The girl in the*

story is growing up because she is doing new things by herself.) *(Critical)*

During the discussion, children will need to

- **compare** the actions of the animals in the poem and tell what they do that is the same.
- **recall** what the girl in the poem does.
- **interpret** how the girl in the poem feels.
- **relate** how they themselves felt on their first day of school.
- **evaluate** why the poem belongs in the thematic unit.

You may wish to model responses to the questions. Use the possible responses given.

Tips for Evaluating the Oral Response

- Children should speak clearly and at the appropriate volume.
- Children should respond in complete thoughts.
- Children should ask relevant questions.

Additional Discussion Questions

Notes for Evaluating the Oral Response

Think and Write

Cooperative Learning

Cooperative learning suggestions for *Think and Write* appear at the beginning of the *Teacher's Edition*.

Making the Assignment

Review that children say good-bye and hello to people, places, and things every day. Tell them that now they are going to write about the people and things they say good-bye and hello to each day. They will make a class book of their writing.

Using the Writing Process

Prewriting Ask children to name people, animals, places, and things they say good-bye and hello to during the day. List their responses on the chalkboard or on chart paper. Point to and read each word after you write it. A sample chart follows.

Good-bye and Hello			
People	Animals	Things	Places
Dad Grandma bus driver kindergarten class	pet kitten fish	bicycle teddy bear	school house

Notes for Cooperative Learning

Notes for Making the Assignment

Drafting Have children dictate sentences to you that tell to whom or what they say good-bye and hello. Begin by modeling a response and writing it on the chalkboard or on chart paper. An example follows.

> Goodbye, Sarah.
> Hello, kindergarten class.

Write each child's dictated sentences at the bottom of a piece of paper. Then follow this procedure.

- Read the sentences to the child.
- Read the sentences with the child.
- Have the child read the sentences.
- Have the child illustrate the sentences.

Responding/Revising/Editing After each child has dictated sentences and illustrated them, reread the sentences you wrote. Draw attention to conventions of writing such as beginning sentences with a capital letter, leaving spaces between words, ending sentences with a period, and following left-to-right progression.

Postwriting (Sharing) Compile children's papers in a class book entitled "Good-bye, Hello." Display the book in the reading corner for children to read independently or with each other.

Notes for Using the Writing Process

Notes for Evaluating the Written Response

Develop Skills

Strategies for developing concepts and skills related to "Good-bye, Hello" are included in this section. Select appropriate activities to teach to the whole class, small groups or individual children.

Developing Concepts and Skills

Language:	Naming Words
Composition:	Story
Auditory Discrimination:	Rhyming Words
Visual Discrimination:	Big and Small
Sound-Letter Correspondences:	Initial Correspondence /g/g

Focusing on Language

Using Words that Name People   Tell children that there are many different kinds of words and that some words name people. Then ask them to listen for words that name people as you reread the story "Good-bye, Hello."

After rereading the poem, ask children to name the words that name people. Write each word on the chalkboard and read it aloud.

Use *Activity Book* page 1 with children. Have them identify the pictures of people at the top of the page. As each is identified, have them find the word, run their fingers under it, and say it aloud. Have each child draw a picture of a person and dictate to you a word that names the person he or she drew. Write the naming word on the writing rule for the child. You may wish to have some children copy the word.

Using Words that Name Animals   Explain that some words name animals. Follow the procedure in Using Words that Name People to list words that name animals. Then use *Activity Book* page 2 with children.

Focusing on the Writer's Use of Language

If you haven't done so, point out the writer's name (Robert Welber) on the first page of the selection. Ask children to identify the words the writer used over and over again in the poem. (**Possible responses:** *Good-bye, Mother, Hello*)

Discuss why the writer may have decided to repeat these words. (**Possible responses:** *The words used over and over again make the poem sound better when it is read aloud. The words used over and ober again help you know what will happen next.*)

Focusing on Composition

Note: Through observing and evaluating children's writing in a variety of situations and at different times, you can gather data that will help you understand and support individual children's writing development. Use the *Checklist for Observing and Evaluating Writing* in the **Evaluation Resources** section of the *Teacher's Edition*.

Writing About a Personal Experience Ask children to think about how they felt on their first day of school and then to write about the experience.

Accept their writing regardless of its stage of development. Many children will draw pictures while others scribble, write letters, and use invented spelling. Have children share their writing by reading it aloud to you to a group of classmates, or to family members.

Focusing on Auditory Discrimination

Listening for Rhyming Words Read aloud **Story Land 1** pages 8–9. Then repeat the words *tree* and *bee.* Ask children to tell how the words are the same. (**Possible response:** *They both have the same ending sounds.*) Then ask children to name other words that have the same ending sound they hear in *tree* and *bee.* Tell children that words that end with the same ending sound are called **rhyming words.**

Reread "Good-bye, Hello" two pages at a time. Ask children to name the rhyming words they hear. Discuss why the writer used rhyming words in the poem.

Focusing on Visual Discrimination

Noticing the Difference Between Big and Small Review with children that in "Good-bye, Hello" young animals left their mothers for the first time. Have children look at the picture on *Story Land 1* pages 2–3 and identify the mother cat and the baby kittens. Discuss the fact that the mother cat is big and the kittens are small. Then ask children to identify the big and small things in the remaining illustrations.

Focusing on Sound-Letter Correspondences

Recognizing Initial /g/g Ask children to listen for the word *good-bye* as you read aloud the writing they did for *Think and Write.* After reading the class book, write on the chalkboard the word *good-bye.* Have children say the word. Then circle the first letter of *good-bye* and explain that the word begins with the letter *g.*

Use **Activity Book** page 3 with children. Have them repeat the word *good-bye* as they finger-trace the uppercase *G* and the lowercase *g.*

Have children identify the pictures at the top of the page. As each is identified, have them find the word, run their fingers under it, and say it aloud. Explain that each picture begins with the same sound they hear at the beginning of *good-bye.* Then have children listen for the /g/ sound as you say the words *gold, garden, goose.*

Have children name other words that begin with the same sound they hear at the beginning of *good-bye, girl,* and *gate.* Then ask each child to draw a picture of something whose name begins with the same sound and to dictate to you a word that names the picture. Write the word on the writing rule for the child. You may wish to have some children copy the word.

Activity Book: Language

Activity Book: Language

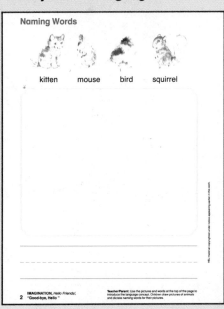

Activity Book: Sound/Letter

Think and Extend

Cooperative Learning

Cooperative learning suggestions for *Think and Extend* appear at the beginning of the *Teacher's Edition.*

For the Classroom

Science—Identifying Big and Small Animals

Discuss how animals vary in size, ranging from tiny insects to huge elephants. Have children cut out magazine pictures of animals and group them according to whether they are big or small. After the pictures have been grouped, help children identify the animals and have them suggest additional ways they are the same and different.

 Cooperative Learning

This *Think and Extend* activity can be used for cooperative learning. Have children work in pairs. Ask one child to cut out pictures of small animals and the second child to cut out pictures of big animals. Have partners share their pictures with each other. Both partners must agree on each others' work before one child shares the pictures with the class.

Social Studies—Learning About People Who Work in the School

Ask children to name people who work in the school. Their list may include: the principal, the school nurse, the secretary, the crossing guard, the librarian and the teachers.

Invite as many school workers as possible to visit the class and discuss their jobs with the class. After the visit, have children dictate a language experience story telling what they learned about the workers.

Notes for Cooperative Learning

Additional Classroom Activities

For the Home

The homework assignment that follows also appears on **Homework Notebook copying master 1.** You may wish to distribute the copying masters to the children.

Writing Have children dictate to an older family member stories about new experiences. Encourage family members to follow this procedure after taking the child's dictation.

- Read the story to the child.
- Read the story with the child.
- Have the child read the story.
- Have the child illustrate the story.

Suggest that children share their stories with classmates the following day.

Reading Have older family members read and discuss with children rhymes or stories that tell about new experiences. Suggest that they discuss new experiences the child may have had.

For Extended and Recreational Reading

You may wish to recommend the following books about new experiences for children to share with family members. Encourage family members to visit the public library with children to select the books to be read.

Books About New Experiences

Madeline by Ludwig Bemelmans. Viking, 1939.

And To Think That I Saw It on Mulberry Street by Dr. Seuss. Vanguard, 1939.

Look What I Can Do by Jose Aruego. Scribner, 1971.

Mr. Grumpy's Outing by John Burningham. Holt, Rinehart & Winston, 1971.

Poems and Rhymes About Animals

Animal poems for children selected by DeWitt Conyers. Children's Press, 1982.

A Bug in a Jug and Other Funny Rhymes by Gloria Patrick. Carolrhoda Books, 1970.

Father Fox's Pennyrhymes by Clyde Watson. Scholastic Book Services, 1971, by arrangement with T. Y. Crowell.

Additional Home Activities

Additional Books for Extended and Recreational Reading

Notes

Ideas for Cooperative Learning

Ideas for Meeting the Needs of Individual Students

Questioning Strategies

Focusing on "Birthday Fun"

While **listening** to and **reading** the selection, children will focus on family activity. Children will also use **writing, listening,** and **speaking** skills as they respond to the selection. They will use higher-level **thinking** skills throughout the lesson.

OBJECTIVES

WRITING/THINKING

- To dictate a response to literature using the writing process.
- To write in the practical/informative domain.
- To use familial names.
- To write about a personal experience.

READING/THINKING

- To recognize the main character in a wordless story.
- To evaluate the placement of a story in a thematic unit.
- To recognize the use of photographs to tell a story.
- To discriminate between big and small, young and old.
- To recognize initial correspondences. (/f/f)

SPEAKING/THINKING

- To discuss personal experiences before reading a selection.
- To participate in shared reading.
- To participate in group discussions.
- To dictate a response to literature.
- To narrate a story while classmates pantomime the actions.

LISTENING/THINKING

- To listen to an oral interpretation of a wordless story.
- To listen to and analyze responses to opinions about a selection.
- To listen for the names of people in a family.
- To listen for initial sounds. (/f/)

LEARNING STRATEGIES

- Brainstorming ideas related to children's own experiences.
- Previewing the selection and making predictions about the content.
- Completing a drawing to help comprehension.
- Completing a chart to help organize writing.
- Analyzing the writer's use of language.

Summary

A young boy celebrates his birthday at a family party. A birthday cake, presents, and noisemakers make the celebration very special. Family members gathered together make the party fun.

INDIVIDUAL NEEDS

Suggestions for teaching children with special needs are provided on *Teacher's Edition* page 1.

- The blue objectives may require direct instruction.

PLANNING CALENDAR

		STUDENT'S EDITIONS	TEACHER'S EDITION	ACTIVITY BOOK
DAY 1 **INTO THE SELECTION**	**THINK AND READ**			
	Preparing to Read	● *pages 12–15* ■ *pages 12–15*	*page 23*	
	Planning a Reading Strategy	● *pages 12–15* ■ *pages 12–15*	*page 24*	
DAYS 2-4 **THROUGH THE SELECTION**	**THINK AND DISCUSS**			
	Remembering the Selection	● *pages 12–15* ■ *pages 12–15*	*page 26*	
	Discussing the Selection	● *pages 12–15* ■ *pages 12–15*	*page 27*	
	THINK AND WRITE			
	Making the Assignment		*page 28*	
	Using the Writing Process		*pages 28–29*	
	Develop Skills			
	Focusing on Language		*page 30*	*pages 4–5*
	Focusing on Composition		*pages 30–31*	
	Focusing on Auditory Discrimination		*page 31*	
	Focusing on Visual Discrimination		*page 31*	
	Focusing on Sound-Letter Correspondences		*page 31*	*page 6*
	Focusing on the Writer's Use of Language		*page 30*	
DAY 5 **BEYOND THE SELECTION**	**THINK AND EXTEND**			
	For the Classroom		*page 32*	
	For the Home		*page 33*	
			▲ Homework Notebook copying Master 2	

● ***Happy Times! Story Land 1*** ▲ *Learning*
■ ***Hello Friends!*** Storybook *Resources File*

Note: Through observing and evaluating children's reading in a variety of situations and at different times, you can gather data which can help you understand and support individual children's reading development. Use the *Checklist for Observing and Evaluating Reading* in the **Evaluation Resources** section of the *Teacher's Edition.*

Cooperative Learning

Cooperative learning suggestions for *Think and Read* appear at the beginning of the **Teacher's Edition.**

Preparing to Read

▶**Relating to Children's Experiences** Collect items such as a wrapped present, a party hat, a balloon, a noisemaker, and a party paper plate and cup. Show these to children and ask them to tell about experiences they have had with such items.

After the discussion, have each child tell when his or her birthday is. Record these dates on a special calendar. Then have children listen as you read aloud "The Birthday Child." Ask them to think about what is special about a birthday child.

The Birthday Child
by Rose Fyleman

Everything's been different
  All the day long,
Lovely things have happened,
  Nothing has gone wrong.

Nobody has scolded me,
  Everyone has smiled.
Isn't it delicious
  To be a birthday child?

Notes for Cooperative Learning

Notes for Preparing to Read

▶**Previewing and Predicting**   Point to the title of the information story and read it aloud to the children. Have them think about what the story might be about. Ask them to share their ideas. You may wish to model a response.

I think the story will be about someone's birthday because I see a cake with candles.

▶**Setting a Purpose**   Tell children that the story is wordless. As they look at the photographs that tell the story, they should think about the things the people do to make a birthday fun.

Planning a Reading Strategy

Sharing Reading   Allow children to take turns telling the story in their own words. Encourage them to point to the details in the photographs as their stories are told.

Encourage children to react spontaneously with comments and questions after the stories have been told.

Reading Silently   Have children carefully examine the photographs in the wordless story. Tell them to think about who is in each photograph and what the people are doing and saying.

Reading Orally   Ask volunteers to perform the roles of the family members by pantomiming the actions suggested by each photograph. Ask additional volunteers to give a narration as children pantomime.

Think and Discuss

Note: Through observing and evaluating children's oral language (listening and speaking) in a variety of situations and at different times, you can gather data which can help you understand and support individual children's oral development. Use the *Checklist for Evaluating Oral Language* on page 00 of the *Teacher's Edition* to gather data.

 Cooperative Learning

Cooperative learning suggestions for *Think and Discuss* appear at the beginning of the *Teacher's Edition.*

Remembering the Selection

Ask children to recall in sequential order each event that occurs during the party. Encourage them to look at the photographs to help themselves recall this information. You may wish to create a class drawing to record children's responses.

Birthday Fun

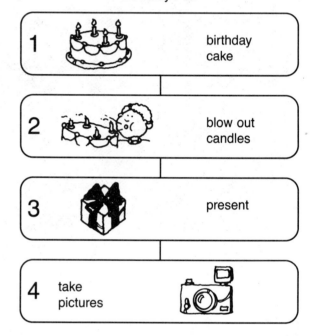

1 — birthday cake

2 — blow out candles

3 — present

4 take pictures

Notes for Cooperative Learning

Notes for Remembering the Selection

26

Discussing the Selection

The following questions focus on family activity. As children respond to the questions, ask them to support their answers with examples from the story. Encourage children to agree or disagree with their classmates' responses and to substantiate their opinions.

Remind children to speak clearly and loudly enough so they can be heard and understood.

1. Who is celebrating a birthday? How do you know? (**Possible responses:** *The boy is celebrating his birthday. I know because he blows out the candles and everyone gives him gifts.*) *(Literal)*

2. How do you think the boy feels about his birthday party? (**Possible response:** *I think the boy is having a lot of fun at his party because he looks very happy and excited.*) *(Inferential)*

3. What are the different family members doing to make the birthday party fun? (**Possible responses:** *Mother brings in a cake with lighted candles. Everyone claps when the candles are blown out. His grandparents give him a gift.*) *(Inferential)*

4. If you could add one more photograph to the story, what would it show the family doing? (**Possible responses:** *Another photograph might show the family playing games or eating cake. More people might come to the party.*) *(Creative)*

5. Can you think of other family members who might be part of the birthday celebration? (**Possible responses:** *I think the boy's aunt and uncle might come. Maybe the boy's cousins would come.*) *(Creative)*

6. How does "Birthday Fun" tell about growing and changing? (**Possible response:** *The boy is a year older. He is growing bigger and smarter.*) *(Critical)*

During the discussion, children will need to

- **recognize** the main character in the wordless story.
- **interpret** the main character's feelings.
- **explain** how each family member makes the birthday fun.
- **predict** other activities that might occur at the party.
- **evaluate** why the story belongs in the thematic unit.

You may wish to model responses to the questions. Use the possible responses given.

Tips for Evaluating the Oral Response

- Children should speak clearly and at the appropriate volume.
- Children should respond in complete thoughts.
- Children should ask relevant questions.

Additional Discussion Questions

Notes for Evaluating the Oral Response

Think and Write

Cooperative Learning

Cooperative learning suggestions for *Think and Write* appear at the beginning of the *Teacher's Edition.*

Making the Assignment

Review that all the family members worked together to make the birthday party fun for the little boy. Have children think about the many different things their own family members do for them each day. Tell them that now they are going to write a note thanking one family member for something he or she has done. They will give or send the thank-you note to that person.

Using the Writing Process

Prewriting   Ask children to name family members and the things they do for them. List their responses on the chalkboard or on chart paper. Point to and read each response after you write it, and ask children to read it.

People in My Family	Things They Do for Me
Mother	cooks dinner for me
Father	takes me to school
Brother	plays with me
Sister	teaches me to read
Aunt	takes me to the park
Uncle	takes me fishing
Grandfather	plays football with me
Grandmother	sings songs with me

Notes for Cooperative Learning

Notes for Making the Assignment

Drafting Have children write a thank-you note to a family member of their choosing. Have children dictate words to you to complete the following letter.

Dear _____.

    Thank you for _____.

               Love,

             _____

Begin by modeling a response on the chalkboard or on chart paper. An example follows.

Dear Aunt Mary,

    Thank you for taking me to the park.

               Love,
               Melissa

    Write each child's dictated thank-you note on a piece of paper. Then follow this procedure.

- Read the thank-you note to the child.
- Read the thank-you note with the child.
- Have the child read the thank-you note.
- Have the child illustrate the thank-you note, if he or she wishes.

Responding/Revising/Editing After each child has dictated a thank-you note and illustrated it, read aloud the letters the children dictated. Draw attention to conventions of letter writing such as the greeting, the message, the closing, and the signature.

Postwriting (Sharing) Have each child "address" an envelope for the letter by dictating the name of the person to whom the letter is written. (**Possible responses:** *Aunt Mary, Mommy*) Children may take home the letters to hand deliver or a parent or older family member can address the envelope properly so that it can be mailed.

Notes for Using the Writing Process

Notes for Evaluating the Written Response

Develop Skills

Strategies for developing concepts and skills related to "Birthday Fun" are included in this section. Select appropriate activities to teach to the whole class, small groups, or individual children.

Developing Concepts and Skills

Language: Words That Name Family Members

Composition: Story

Auditory Discrimination: Names of Family Members

Visual Discrimination: Big and Small; Young and Old

Sound-Letter Correspondences: Initial Correspondence /f/f

Focusing on Language

Using Words that Name Family Members Tell children that some words name the members of a family. Remind them they have just read a wordless story about a family making a birthday fun for a little boy. Have them look once again at the photographs and think about who the members of the family are.

Use *Activity Book* pages 4 and 5 with children. Have them identify the pictures of the family members at the top of the pages. As each is identified, have them find the word, run their fingers under it, and say it aloud. Have each child draw pictures of family members and dictate to you words that name the people he or she drew. Write the names on the writing rule for the child. You may wish to have some children copy the words.

Focusing on the Writer's Use of Language

Ask children how the writer of "Birthday Fun" told a story. (**Possible response:** *The writer told a story by using photographs.*) Ask them why they think the writer chose to use photographs to tell a story. (**Possible responses:** *The writer wanted to make the story look as if it were happening right now. The photographs help us to think about real parties we have had with our own families.*)

 Cooperative Learning

Focusing on Visual Discrimination can be used for cooperative learning. Divide children into groups of four members. Ask each group member to draw a picture of one of the following: young family members, old family members, small family members, big family members. Have group members share their ideas with each other. All group members must agree on each other's work before they share it with the class.

Focusing on Composition

Note: Through observing and evaluating children's writing in a variety of situations and at different times, you can gather data which can help you understand children's writing development. Use the *Checklist for Observing and Evaluating Writing* in the **Evaluation Resources** section of the *Teacher's Edition* to gather data.

Writing About a Special Activity   Ask children to think about special activities they have done with their families such as having a birthday party, going on a vacation, or having a picnic. Have them write a story about the fun they had with their families during an activity.

Accept their writing regardless of its stage of development. Many children will draw pictures, while others scribble, write letters, or use invented spelling. Have children share their writing by reading it to family members.

Focusing on Auditory Discrimination

Listening for Names of People in a Family   Ask children to look at the story "Birthday Fun" and tell the story to each other. The children listening to the storyteller should point to the pictures of the family members in the story as the names are read aloud.

Focusing on Visual Discrimination

Noticing the Difference Between Big/Small and Young/Old   Review with children that there were seven different family members at the birthday party. Point out that the family members are not the same age or the same size. Have children examine the photographs in the story and identify which family members are young, old, big and small.

Focusing on Sound-Letter Correspondences

Recognizing Initial /f/f   Ask children to listen as you read the title of the information story "Birthday Fun." Then repeat the words *family* and *fun* and write them on the chalkboard. Ask children to repeat the word. Circle the first letter in each word and explain that each word begins with the letter *f*.

Use **Activity Book** page 6 with children. Have them repeat the words *family* and *fun* as they finger-trace the uppercase *F* and the lowercase *f*.

Have children identify the pictures at the top of the page. As each is identified, have them find the word, run their fingers under it, and say it aloud. Explain that each picture begins with the same sound they hear at the beginning of the words *family* and *fun*.

Ask children to identify the letter each word begins with. Tell them that the letter *f* usually stands for the same sound they hear at the beginning of *family* and *fun*. Then have children listen for the /f/ sound as you say the word *father*.

Have children name other words that begin with the same sound they hear at the beginning of *family* and *father*. Then ask each child to draw a picture of something whose name begins with the same sound and dictate to you a word that names the picture. Write the word on the writing rule for the child. You may wish to have some children copy the word.

Activity Book: Language

Naming Words

father   sister   grandfather

IMAGINATION, *Hello Friends!,* "Birthday Fun."   4

Activity Book: Language

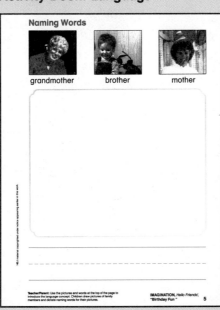

Naming Words

grandmother   brother   mother

IMAGINATION, *Hello Friends!,* "Birthday Fun."   5

Activity Book: Sound/Letter

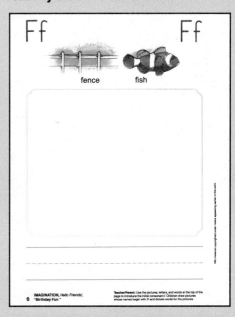

Ff   Ff

fence   fish

IMAGINATION, *Hello Friends!,* "Birthday Fun."   6

Think and Extend

Cooperative Learning

Cooperative learning suggestions for *Think and Extend* appear at the beginning of the **Teacher's Edition.**

For the Classroom

Art—Designing a Greeting Card Talk about the many different kinds of greeting cards you can buy in the stores to send to family members or friends for various occasions. Show examples of these cards to children.

Then distribute sheets of drawing paper for children to use to design their own greeting cards. Encourage them to draw colorful pictures or designs on the front of the cards and have them dictate a message for the inside. They may have a particular person and a special occasion in mind when they create their greeting cards.

When finished, suggest that the children give the cards to the persons for whom they were made. They may deliver the cards or send them by mail.

Social Studies—Learning About the Mail Process
Discuss what happens to a letter once it is mailed. *(The Post Office Book* by Gail Gibbons [Harper & Row, 1982] illustrates the mail process for children.) You may wish to do the following experiment with children.

1. With the class, write a reminder note about an upcoming activity or event children are involved in.
2. Self-address an envelope.
3. Write the return address.
4. Place a stamp on the envelope.
5. Mail the letter. (If possible, take children to a local post office or a mail box.) Record the time and date it is mailed.

Once the letter is mailed, discuss what happens to the letter.

- The letter is taken by a postal employee and then the letter is taken to the Post Office and sorted with the other mail.
- The letter is picked up by a postal employee and then taken to the Post Office and sorted with the other mail.
- It is taken to the Post Office in that city where it is again sorted.
- A mail carrier delivers the letter to the address on the envelope.

When the letter arrives, write the day and time it arrived. Ask children to help you determine how long it took to be delivered.

Notes for Cooperative Learning

Additional Classroom Activities

For the Home

The homework assignment that follows also appears on **Homework Notebook copying master 2.** You may wish to distribute the copying masters to the children.

Writing Have children find a family photograph at home to write about. Have a family member help the child attach the photograph to a sheet of paper. Then have the child dictate sentences telling about the occasion for which the photograph was taken. Encourage family members to follow this procedure after taking the child's dictation.

- Read the sentences to the child.
- Read the sentences with the child.
- Have the child illustrate the sentences.
- Children may wish to illustrate their sentences.

Reading Suggest that each child read the story "Birthday Fun" to parents or older family members. Encourage them to discuss times when the family gathers for special celebrations such as birthdays. Have them talk about things the grown-ups do together, things the children do together, and things everyone does together. Ask children to share these stories and family traditions with the class the following day.

For Extended and Recreational Reading

You may wish to recommend the following books about family activities and relationships for children to share with family members. Encourage family members to visit the public library with children to select the books to be read.

Books About Families

Umbrella by Taro Yashima. Viking, 1958.

Friday Night is Papa Night by Ruth Sonneborn. Penguin, 1987.

Ask Mister Bear by Marjorie Flack. Macmillan, 1986.

Blueberries for Sal by Robert McCloskey. Puffin, 1976.

More Books About Families:

Happy Birthday, Sam by Pat Hutchins. Greenwillow Books, 1978.

A Birthday Wish by Ed Emberley. Little, Brown, 1977.

My Old Grandad by Wolf Harranth. Oxford, 1984.

Paul's Christmas Birthday by Carol Carrick. Greenwillow, 1978.

Additional Home Activities

Additional Books for Extended and Recreational Reading

Notes

Ideas for Cooperative Learning

Ideas for Meeting the Needs of Individual Students

Questioning Strategies

Focusing on "Story Time at School"

While **listening** to and **reading** the selection, children will focus on things we do in school. Children will also use **writing, listening,** and **speaking** skills as they respond to the selection. They will use higher-level **thinking** skills throughout the lesson.

OBJECTIVES

WRITING/THINKING

- To dictate a response to literature using the writing process.
- To write in the practical/informative domain.
- To use action words.
- To write about a favorite activity.

READING/THINKING

- To compare characters to identify similarities.
- To evaluate the author's choice of a story title.
- To place oneself in the story setting.
- To recognize the effectiveness of a wordless story.
- To listen to the class's oral reading of a selection.
- To recognize initial correspondences. (/s/s)

SPEAKING/THINKING

- To discuss personal experiences before reading a selection.
- To participate in shared reading.
- To participate in group discussions.
- To dictate a response to literature.
- To pantomime actions suggested by a wordless story.

LISTENING/THINKING

- To listen to the class' oral reading of a selection.
- To listen to and analyze response to opinions about a selection.
- To listen for and identify sounds in a classroom.
- To listen for initial sounds. (/s/)

LEARNING STRATEGIES

- Brainstorming ideas related to children's own experiences.
- Previewing the selection and making predictions about the content.
- Completing a drawing to help comprehension.
- Completing a chart to help organize writing.
- Analyzing the writer's use of language.

Summary

Children are actively participating in the classroom during storytime in this wordless story. The picture shows what the children are doing and encourages the readers to think about things they do at school.

INDIVIDUAL NEEDS

Suggestions for teaching children with special needs are provided on *Teacher's Edition* page 1.

- The blue objectives may require direct instruction.

PLANNING CALENDAR

		STUDENT'S EDITIONS	TEACHER'S EDITION	ACTIVITY BOOK
DAY 1 INTO THE SELECTION	**THINK AND READ**			
	Preparing to Read	● *pages 16–17* ■ *pages 16–17*	*page 37*	
	Planning a Reading Strategy	● *pages 16–17* ■ *pages 16–17*	*page 38*	
DAYS 2-4 THROUGH THE SELECTION	**THINK AND DISCUSS**			
	Remembering the Selection	● *pages 16–17* ■ *pages 16–17*	*page 40*	
	Discussing the Selection	● *pages 16–17* ■ *pages 16–17*	*page 41*	
	THINK AND WRITE			
	Making the Assignment		*page 42*	
	Using the Writing Process		*page 43*	
	Develop Skills			
	Focusing on Language		*page 44*	*pages 7–8*
	Focusing on Composition		*pages 44, 45*	
	Focusing on Auditory Discrimination		*page 45*	
	Focusing on Visual Discrimination		*page 45*	
	Focusing on Sound-Letter Correspondences		*page 45*	*page 9*
	Focusing on the Writer's Use of Language		*page 44*	
DAY 5 BEYOND THE SELECTION	**THINK AND EXTEND**			
	For the Classroom		*pages 46–47*	
	For the Home		*page 47*	
			▲ Homework Notebook copying master 3	

● ***Happy Times! Story Land 1***
■ ***Hello Friends!*** Storybook

▲ ***Learning Resources File***

Note: Through observing and evaluating children's reading in a variety of situations and at different times, you can gather data which can help you understand and support individual children's reading development. Use the *Checklist for Observing and Evaluating Reading* in the **Evaluation Resources** section of the *Teacher's Edition.*

Cooperative Learning

Cooperative learning suggestions for *Think and Read* appear at the beginning of the *Teacher's Edition.*

Preparing to Read

▶**Relating to Children's Experiences** Ask how many children enjoy listening to stories. Have them name their favorite stories. Display the storybooks named, if available. Then have children discuss ways they share these stories with friends at school or with family members at home.

After the discussion, teach children the following fingerplay about reading and sharing books.

My Favorite Book

I looked in a book
  [*pantomime opening a book*]
And what did I see?
  [*point to eyes*]
A group of friendly faces
  [*make a big smile*]
Smiling at me.
  [*point to self*]
I listened to a story
  [*cup hand by one ear*]
And what did I hear?
  [*point to both ears*]
A very funny tale
  [*pantomime laughing*]

Notes for Cooperative Learning

Notes for Preparing to Read

That made me laugh and cheer.
   [*raise arms to cheer*]
I took my favorite book
   [*pantomime opening a book*]
And shared it with a friend.
   [*sit with a friend*]
We read the story together
   [*pretend to read*]
From beginning to end.

▶Previewing and Predicting Explain to children that they will be looking at a picture that will tell them a story. Write the title of the wordless story, "Story Time at School," on the chalkboard and read it to the children. Ask them to name things they do when the class reads stories together in the classroom. You may wish to model a response.

We sit together on the rug and look at picture books. Sometimes we stand up and pretend we are part of the story.

▶Setting a Purpose Tell children that they will be making up their own story about the picture they see. As they look at the wordless story, they should be thinking about what the children and teacher are doing.

Planning a Reading Strategy

Sharing Reading Ask children to take turns telling the story in their own words. Suggest that they point to the various details in the illustration as their stories are being told.

   Encourage children to react spontaneously with comments and questions, following each child's interpretation of the wordless story.

Reading Silently Give children a period of time to examine the picture carefully. Have them think about who is in the wordless story and what they are doing and saying.

Reading Orally Ask children to select a person pictured in the wordless story and pantomime what that person is doing. As each pantomime is finished, ask children in the class to identify the activity by responding with a sentence telling about it.

Story Time at School

16

17

Think and Discuss

Note: Through observing and evaluating children's oral language (listening and speaking) in a variety of situations and at different times, you can gather data that will help you understand and support individual children's oral development. Use the *Checklist for Evaluating Oral Language* in the **Evaluation Resources** section of the *Teacher's Edition.*

Cooperative Learning

Cooperative learning suggestions for *Think and Discuss* appear at the beginning of the **Teacher's Edition.**

Remembering the Selection

Ask children to re-examine the picture that tells the wordless story and identify what the children in the story are doing during story time. As children examine the illustration and express their ideas, you may wish to record their responses in a cluster.

Story Time at School

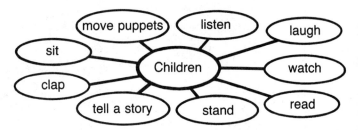

Discussing the Selection

The following questions focus on things children do in school. As children respond to the questions, ask them to support their answers with examples from the wordless story. Encourage children to agree or disagree with their classmates' responses and to substantiate their opinions.

Remind children to speak clearly and loudly enough so they can be heard and understood.

Notes for Cooperative Learning

Notes for Remembering the Selection

1. What is alike about all the children in the story? (**Possible responses:** *All the children are in school. All the children are in the same class. All the children are having story time.*) *(Literal)*

2. What do you think the children did to get ready for the puppet show? (**Possible response:** *They read the story; they made the puppets, stage, and scenery; they decided who would work each puppet; they practiced telling the story and moving the puppets.*) *(Interpretive)*

3. Why did the writer call this wordless story "Story Time at School"? (**Possible response:** *The picture shows the actions that children would do during story time at school.*) *(Critical)*

4. Would you like to be a student in this classroom? Why or why not? (**Possible response:** *I would like to be in this classroom because the children look like they are having fun. I would also like to be in a puppet show.*) *(Critical)*

5. What other things could the writer have shown children doing in school? (**Possible response:** *The writer could have shown children writing, painting, singing, counting, or playing a game.*) *(Critical)*

During the discussion, children will need to

- **compare** the children in the story and their actions and tell how they are alike.

- **determine** what the children did to prepare for a classroom activity.
- **evaluate** why the writer entitled the wordless story "Story Time at School."
- **consider** whether they would like to be in the class depicted in the story.
- **recognize** other classroom activities the writer could have pictured in a wordless story.

You may wish to model responses to the questions. Use the possible responses given.

Tips for Evaluating the Oral Response

- Children should speak clearly and at the appropriate volume.
- Children should respond in complete thoughts.
- Children should ask relevant questions.

Additional Discussion Questions   Notes for Evaluating the Oral Response

Think and Write

Cooperative Learning

Cooperative learning suggestions for *Think and Write* appear at the beginning of the *Teacher's Edition.*

Making the Assignment

Review that the wordless story showed what children do in school during story time. Remind children that they do many different things in school and having story time is just one of them. Tell children that they are now going to write about the different things they do in school. They will make a class book of their writing.

Notes for Cooperative Learning

Notes for Making the Assignment

Using the Writing Process

Prewriting Ask children to think about the various things they do in school throughout the week. Write the following on the chalkboard. Point to each word as you read it.

We _____ in school.

Have children think of words that can finish the sentence. The words will name the things they do in school. List their responses on chart paper. Point to and read each response after you write it. A sample chart follows.

> We _____ in school.
>
> sing songs
> read books
> count
> write letters
> play games
> color pictures

Drafting   Have children dictate sentences to you that tell what they do in school. Begin by modeling a response and writing on the chalkboard or on chart paper. An example follows.

We sing songs in school.

Write each child's dictated sentence at the bottom of a piece of paper. Then follow this procedure.

- Read the sentence to the child.
- Read the sentence with the child.
- Have the child read the sentence.
- Have the child illustrate the sentence.

Responding/Revising/Editing   After each child has dictated a sentence and illustrated it, reread the sentence you wrote. Draw attention to conventions of writing such as beginning sentences with a capital letter, leaving spaces between words, ending sentences with a period, and following left-to-right progression.

Postwriting (Sharing)   Compile children's papers in a class book entitled "Things We Do at School." Display the book in the reading corner for children to read independently or with each other.

Notes for Using the Writing Process

Notes for Evaluating the Written Response

Develop Skills

Strategies for developing concepts and skills related to "Story Time at School" are included in this section. Select appropriate activities to teach to the whole class, small groups, or individual children.

Developing Concepts and Skills

Language:	Action Words
Composition:	Story
Auditory Discrimination:	Sounds in the Classroom
Visual Discrimination:	Things We Use in the Classroom
Sound-Letter Correspondences:	Initial Correspondence /s/s

Focusing on Language

Using Action Words   Tell children that some words are special because they name actions. Have children look once again at the wordless story "Story Time at School." Have them suggest words that name actions that tell what the children are doing. As each action word is suggested, write it on the chalkboard and read it aloud.

Continue by using **Activity Book** pages 7 and 8 with children. Have them identify what the children are in each picture are doing. As each picture is identified, have them find the word that names the action, run their fingers under it, and say the word aloud. Have each child draw a picture of an action they do in school and dicate to you the action illustrated. Write the action word(s) on the writing rule for the child. You may wish to have some children copy the word(s).

Focusing on the Writer's Use of Language

Explain to children that there are different ways for a writer to tell a story. A writer can tell a story through words, through pictures, or through both pictures and words. Ask the children if the writer's pictures make it easy to understand that the story is happening at school.
(**Possible responses:** *Yes, because the writer shows desks, a flag, books, a teacher and children, school supplies, a chalkboard, and a bulletin board. These are things found in a classroom at school.*)

 Cooperative Learning

The *Focusing on Visual Discrimination* activity can be used for cooperative learning. Have children work in pairs. Ask one child to name one thing in the classroom used for work and the second child to name one thing used for play. Have the partners share their ideas with each other. Both partners must agree on each other's ideas before they both draw pictures of the objects and one child shares the pictures with the class.

Focusing on Composition

Note: Through observing and evaluating children's writing in a variety of situations and at different times, you can gather data which can help you understand children's writing development. Use the *Checklist for Observing and Evaluating Writing* in the **Evaluation Resources** section of the **Teacher's Edition.**

Writing About School Activities   Ask children to think about the different things they do at school. Have them think about their favorite thing they like to do and write about it. Encourage children to tell what their favorite thing to do is and why they like to do it.

Accept their writing regardless of its stage of development. Many children will draw pictures while others scribble, write letters, and use invented spelling. Have children share their writing about their favorite things to do at school by reading it aloud to you, a group of classmates, or family members.

Focusing on Auditory Discrimination

Identifying Sounds in the Classroom   Ask children to look at the wordless story and name the sounds they might hear if they were in that classroom. (**Possible responses:** *children talking; clapping; the sound of a musical instrument; feet shuffling; the sound of turning pages; walking; paper rustling*)

Then ask children to close their eyes and listen to the sounds around them. Ask them to name the sounds they hear.

Focusing on Visual Discrimination

Classifying Things in the Classroom According to Use   Remind children that the picture in the wordless story shows a classroom and many things that can be found there. Ask children if some of the same things are found in their own classroom.

Discuss that the many things in a classroom are used for different reasons. Ask children to walk around the room and identify things that are used for work or play at school.

Focusing on Sound-Letter Correspondences

sentences that tells about things they do in school. Read the sentence *We sing songs in school.* Then write the words *sing* and *songs* on the chalkboard. Have children repeat the words. Trace over the initial *s* in each word and explain that each word begins with the letter *s*.

Use **Activity Book** page 9 with children. Have them name the letter *s* and repeat the sound /s/ as they finger-trace the uppercase *S* and the lowercase *s*. Then ask them to repeat the words *sing* and *songs*.

Have children identify the pictures at the top of the page. As each is identified, have them find the word, run their fingers under it, and say it aloud. Explain that each picture begins with the same sound they hear at the beginning of the words *sing* and *songs*.

Have children name other words that begin with the same sound they hear at the beginning of *sun* and *seal*. Then ask each child to draw a picture of something whose name begins with the same sound and dictate to you a word that names the picture. Write the word on the writing rule for the child. You may wish to have some chlidren copy the word.

Activity Book: Language

Activity Book: Language

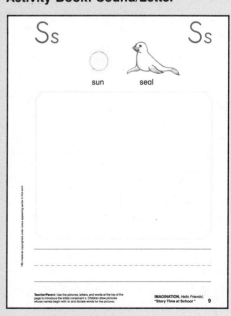

Activity Book: Sound/Letter

Think and Extend

Cooperative Learning

Cooperative learning suggestions for *Think and Extend* appear at the beginning of the **Teacher's Edition.**

For the Classroom

Science—Examining Sense of Hearing   Remind children that they hear many sounds around them each day. Among the special sounds they hear are the voices of others. Take time to privately record each child's voice. Encourage each child to say a short message, recite a rhyme, or even sing a song. Once all the children's voices have been taped, play the recording of each voice and ask children to guess who is speaking. Ask children to raise their hands when they are ready to guess rather than shout out, since some children may wish to hear the recording more than once.

Art—Making Action Puppets   Give children five cut-out body parts such as those shown. Help children attach the body parts using brads.

Once the bodies are attached, children can color in facial features, hair, and clothing. When the puppets are ready, allow students to play with their puppet, moving its arms and legs to demonstrate various actions.

Allow each child to introduce his or her puppet to the class. As each puppet is introduced have the class ask, "What can your puppet do?" At that signal, the child responds with, "My puppet can ____," using action words and moving the puppet to demonstrate.

Notes for Cooperative Learning

Additional Classroom Activities

For the Home

The homework assignment that follows also appears on **Homework Notebook copying master 3.** You may wish to distribute the copying masters to the children.

Writing   Have children dictate sentences to an older family member, telling about "Work Time at Home." The children will dictate sentences that tell what they do to help out at home. Encourage family members to follow this procedure after taking the child's dictation.

- Read the sentences to the child.
- Read the sentences with the child.
- Have the child read the sentences.
- Have the child illustrate the sentences.

Suggest that children share their sentences with classmates the following day.

Reading   Have family members listen as children read a wordless story to them. Family members may even want to take turns telling their own version of the story.

For Extended and Recreational Reading

You may wish to recommend the following wordless stories for children to read to family members. Encourage family members to select a wordless book from home or visit the public library.

Recommended Wordless Stories

The Snowman by Raymond Briggs. Random House, 1978.

Deep in the Forest by Brinton Turkle. Dutton, 1976.

Ah-Choo! by Mercer Mayer. Dial, 1976.

Noah's Ark by Peter Spier. Doubleday, 1977.

A Boy, a Dog and a Frog by Mercer Mayer. Dial, 1967.

More Stories for Children to Share

Here Comes Alex Pumpernickel by Fernando Krahn. Little, Brown, 1981.

The Knight and The Dragon by Tomie De Paola. G. P. Putnam's Sons, 1980.

Snow by Isao Sasaki. Viking Press, 1980.

The Story of a Little Mouse Trapped in a Book by Monique Felix. Green Tiger Press, 1980.

The Hunter and the Animals by Tomie De Paola. Holiday House, 1981.

Additional Home Activities

Additional Books for Extended and Recreational Reading

Notes

Ideas for Cooperative Learning

Ideas for Meeting the Needs of Individual Students

Questioning Strategies

Focusing on "Silly Goose"

While **listening** to and **reading** the selection, children will focus on actions that imitate animals. Children will also use **writing, listening,** and **speaking** skills as they respond to the selection. They will use higher-level **thinking** throughout the lesson.

OBJECTIVES

WRITING/THINKING

- To dictate a response to literature using the writing process.
- To write in the imaginative/narrative domain.
- To use words that name actions.
- To write an imaginative story.

READING/THINKING

- To interpret a character's actions.
- To analyze the writer's purpose.
- To recognize the use of action words in a selection.
- To discriminate colors.
- To recognize initial correspondences. (/l/)

SPEAKING/THINKING

- To discuss personal experiences before reading a selection.
- To participate in shared reading.
- To participate in group discussions.
- To dictate a response to literature.
- To use creative dramatics to interpret a story.

LISTENING/THINKING

- To listen to the oral reading of a selection.
- To listen to and analyze responses to and opinions about a selection.
- To identify different animal sounds.
- To listen for initial sounds. (/l/)

LEARNING STRATEGIES

- Brainstorming ideas related to children's own experiences.
- Previewing the selection and making predictions about the content.
- Completing a chart to help comprehension.
- Completing a chart to help organize writing.
- Analyzing the writer's use of language.

Summary

A little girl delights in imitating the actions of various animals and wins the name "silly goose" from her mother.

INDIVIDUAL NEEDS

Suggestions for teaching children with special needs are provided on **Teacher's Edition** page 1.

- The blue objectives may require direct instruction.

PLANNING CALENDAR

		STUDENT'S EDITIONS	TEACHER'S EDITION	ACTIVITY BOOK
DAY 1 **INTO THE SELECTION**	**THINK AND READ** Preparing to Read Planning a Reading Strategy	● *pages 18–33* ■ *pages 18–33* ● *pages 18–33* ■ *pages 18–33*	*page 51* *page 52*	
DAYS 2-4 **THROUGH THE SELECTION**	**THINK AND DISCUSS** Remembering the Selection Discussing the Selection	● *pages 18–33* ■ *pages 18–33* ● *pages 18–33* ■ *pages 18–33*	*page 58* *pages 58–59*	
	THINK AND WRITE Making the Assignment Using the Writing Process **Develop Skills** Focusing on Language Focusing on Composition Focusing on Auditory Discrimination Focusing on Visual Discrimination Focusing on Sound-Letter Correspondences Focusing on the Writer's Use of Language		 *page 60* *page 61* *page 62* *page 63* *page 63* *page 63* *page 63* *page 62*	 *pages 10–11* *page 12*
DAY 5 **BEYOND THE SELECTION**	**THINK AND EXTEND** For the Classroom For the Home		*page 64* *page 65* ▲ Homework Notebook copying master 4	

● *Happy Times! Story Land 1*
■ *Hello Friends!* Storybook

▲ *Learning Resources File*

Cooperative Learning

Cooperative learning suggestions for *Think and Read* appear at the beginning of the *Teacher's Edition.*

Preparing to Read

▶**Relating to Children's Experiences** Ask children to recall times when someone may have called them silly. Have children explain what they were doing to be called silly. Discuss different ways to be silly and allow children to demonstrate actions or noises that seem silly. Ask children to tell how they feel when they act silly and how they make others feel.

After the discussion, have children listen as you read the poem "That's Silly." Teach them to reply, "No, that's silly!" after every verse except for the final verse which ends with "Yes!"

That's Silly

Did you ever make a sandwich?
And wear it in your hair?
No, that's silly!

Did you ever open your lunchbox
And find a bear in there?
No, that's silly!

Did you ever take a mop
And ride on it to school?
No, that's silly!

Notes for Cooperative Learning

Notes for Preparing to Read

Did you ever pour bubble bath
Into a swimming pool?
No, that's silly!

Did you ever put potatoes
On top of apple pie?
No, that's silly!

Do you like to act silly?
Did you ever even try?
Yes!

▶**Previewing and Predicting**   Point to the story title and read it to the children. Then ask them to look at each of the eight sets of pictures and ask if they notice anything the same about the little girl and each animal. You may wish to model a response.

I see the little girl swinging in the air like the monkey. I think she is trying to act like a monkey.

▶**Setting a Purpose**   Tell children that as they listen to "Silly Goose" they should think about the kinds of things both the little girl and the animals do.

Planning a Reading Strategy

Sharing Reading   Read aloud the story, sharing the illustrations by pointing to the girl each time the word I is read and to the animal each time its name is read. Emphasize the action words as you read.

Encourage children to react spontaneously with comments and questions after you have read the story. Encourage creative dramatics by allowing children to move about the classroom imitating the movements of each animal as you read.

Reading Orally   Read aloud the story once again and ask children to say each animal name. Pause each time after reading the words, "I swing like a . . . .," allowing children the opportunity to say the animal name.

Reading Silently   Give children the opportunity to read the story independently. Explain that the pictures will help them remember what is happening in the story.

Silly Goose

A story by Jan Ormerod

I swing like a monkey.

18   19

55

Look at me!
My Mom says . . .

sometimes I'm just
as silly as a goose.

32

33

56

Notes

Ideas for Cooperative Learning

Ideas for Meeting the Needs of Individual Students

Questioning Strategies

Think and Discuss

Cooperative Learning

Cooperative learning suggestions for *Think and Discuss* appear at the beginning of the **Teacher's Edition.**

Remembering the Selection

Ask children to recall the story and identify

- each action the little girl does.
- each animal the little girl imitates.

Suggest that children look at each illustration to recall the information. You may wish to use the following incomplete sentence for children to slot appropriate action words and animal names and then record them on a class chart. Explain to children that you will use red chalk to write the name of the action and blue chalk to write the name of the animal.

I _____ like a _____.

Discussing the Selection

The following questions focus on actions that imitate the things animals do. As children respond to the questions, ask them to support their answers with examples from the story. Encourage children to agree or disagree with their classmates' responses and to substantiate their opinions.

Remind children to speak clearly and loudly enough so they can be heard and understood.

1. What does the little girl in the story like to do? (**Possible response:** *She likes to be silly and act like different animals.*) *(Literal)*
2. Do you think the girl is a silly goose? (**Possible response:** *Yes, because a goose moves about in funny ways just as the girl does when she acts like the animals.*) *(Interpretive)*
3. How does a goose move? *(Have children demonstrate their ideas.) (Creative)*
4. Can you think of another animal the writer could have used to show the action word swing?

Notes for Cooperative Learning

Notes for Remembering the Selection

(**Possible responses:** *The writer could have used an ape or an opossum.*)

. . . to show the action word hop?

(**Possible responses:** *The writer could have used a bird or rabbit.*)

. . . to show the action word jump?

(**Possible responses:** *The writer could have used a frog or grasshopper.*)

. . . to show the action word paddle?

(**Possible responses:** *The writer could have used a swan or turtle.*)

. . . to show the action word hide?

(**Possible responses:** *The writer could have used a turtle, crab, or snake.*) *(Creative)*

5. What does the story have to do with friendship?

(**Possible response:** *The story is about the little girl and her friends, the animals.*) *(Critical)*

During the discussion, children will need to

- **recall** what the girl in the story does.
- **interpret** how the girl in the story acts.
- **demonstrate** how a certain animal moves.
- **classify** animals by their actions.
- **evaluate** why the story belongs in the thematic unit.

You may wish to model responses to the questions. Use the possible responses given.

 Cooperative Learning

The fourth question Discussing the Selection can be used for cooperative learning. Have children work in pairs. Assign one action word to each pair of children. Have them draw animals that the writer could have used in place of the one in the story. Have partners share their pictures with each other. Both partners must agree on each other's work before one child shares the pictures with the class.

Tips for Evaluating the Oral Response

- Children should speak clearly and at the appropriate volume.
- Children should respond in complete thoughts.
- Children should ask relevant questions.

Additional Discussion Questions

Notes for Evaluating the Oral Response

Think and Write

Cooperative Learning

Cooperative learning suggestions for *Think and Write* appear at the beginning of the **Teacher's Edition.**

Making the Assignment

Tell children that they are going to add more to the story "Silly Goose" by thinking of new animals and the actions they do. They will make a big book of their writing.

Notes for Cooperative Learning

Notes for Making the Assignment

Using the Writing Process

Prewriting Ask children to name animals and words that tell about the actions the animals do. List their responses on the chalkboard or on chart paper. Point to and read each word after you write it. A sample chart follows.

Animal		Action
tiger		run
fish		swim
snake		crawl
dog		dig

Drafting Have children dictate sentences to you that tell ways they can act like an animal. Begin by modeling a response and writing it on the chalkboard or on chart paper. An example follows.

I run like a tiger.

Write each child's dictated sentence at the bottom of a large sheet of paper (select a paper size suitable for a big book.) Then follow this procedure.

- Read the sentence to the child.
- Read the sentence with the child.
- Have the child read the sentence.
- Have the child illustrate the sentence.

Responding/Revising/Editing After each child has dictated a sentence and illustrated it, reread the sentence you wrote. Draw attention to conventions of writing such as beginning sentences with a capital letter, leaving spaces between words, ending sentences with a period, and following left-to-right progression.

Postwriting (Sharing) Compile children's papers in a class big book entitled "Silly Goose." Read the big book with children and then display it in the reading corner for children to read independently or with each other.

Notes for Using the Writing Process

Notes for Evaluating the Written Response

Develop Skills

Strategies for developing concepts and skills related to "Silly Goose" are included in this section. Select appropriate activities to teach to the whole class, small groups, or individual children.

Developing Concepts and Skills

Language:	Words That Name Actions
Composition:	Imaginative Story
Auditory Discrimination:	Animal Sounds
Visual Discrimination:	Colors
Sound-Letter Correspondences:	initial correspondence /l/

Focusing on Language

Using Words that Name Actions of Animals Review that action words tell how people and animals move. Ask children to listen for words that tell how the girl in the story moves as you reread "Silly Goose."

After reading the story, ask children to name the action words. Write each word on a card and place it on the chalkledge or in a pocket chart. Then play a game of "Follow the Leader" with children. Ask volunteers to take turns being the leader by selecting one action word and holding it for the class to see. Say the word, have children repeat the word and then have the leader demonstrate the action while the others follow the leader.

Use *Activity Book* pages 10–11 with children. Have them identify the pictures (of people and animals in action) at the top of each page. As each is identified, have them find the action word, run their fingers under it, and say it aloud. Have each child draw a picture of an animal (page 10) or themselves (page 11) doing something or moving a particular way and dictate to you a word that names the action shown.
Write the action word on the writing rule for the child. You may wish to have some children copy the word.

Focusing on the Writer's Use of Language

Help children locate the name of the writer of the story (Jan Ormerod.) Discuss what this writer wanted to tell us by showing that we move in the same ways that animals move. Discuss how we know that people and animals move in many different ways. (**Possible responses:** *The writer uses many different action words to tell us what these different ways are. The pictures in the story help us to see the different actions we and animals can do.*)

Focusing on Composition

Note: Through observing and evaluating children's writing in a variety of situations and at different times, you can gather data which can help you understand and support individual children's writing development. Use the *Checklist for Observing and Evaluating Writing* in the **Evaluation Resources** section of the **Teacher's Edition** to gather data.

Writing An Imaginative Story   Have children think about their favorite animal. Ask children to write a story about their favorite animal telling what they would like to say to the animal and what they would like to do.

Accept their writing regardless of its stage of development. Many children will draw pictures while others scribble, write letters, and use invented spelling. Have children share their writing by reading it aloud to you, a group of classmates, or family members.

Focusing on Auditory Discrimination

Identifying Animal Sounds   Have children look again at the animals featured in "Silly Goose." Discuss the sounds these animals make. Imitate the more familiar sounds such as the monkey, duck, bat, and goose and ask children to repeat them. Then ask children to name other familiar animals and imitate their animal sounds (dog, cat, horse, cow, pig, chicken, bird, turkey, snake, frog, lion, bear, elephant).

Review all animal sounds by playing a guessing game. Ask volunteers to make different animal sounds while classmates guess the animal names.

Another variation of the guessing game would be to show children a picture of an animal, make two different animal sounds, and have them identify the animal and the correct sound it makes.

Focusing on Visual Discrimination

Identify the Colors of Animals   Ask children to examine the pictures of the animals in "Silly Goose" and name ways the animals are different. Then focus on the different colors of animals. Name each animal in the story and help children describe its colors. Point out and identify the colors noted and compare them to similarly colored objects in the room.

Focusing on Sound-Letter Correspondences

Recognizing Initial /l/   Ask children to listen for the word *like* as you read aloud the class big book. After reading, write on the chalkboard the word *like*. Have children say the word. Then circle the first letter of *like* and explain that the word begins with the letter *l*.

Use **Activity Book** page 12 with children. Have them repeat the word *like* and name the letter *l* as they finger-trace the uppercase *L* and the lowercase *l*.

Have children identify the pictures at the top of the page. As each is identified, have them find the word, run their fingers under it, and say it aloud. Explain that each picture begins with the same sound they hear at the beginning of the word *like*.

Ask children to identify the letter each word begins with. Tell them that the letter *l* usually stands for the same sound they hear at the beginning of *like*. Then have children listen for the /l/ sound as you say the words *lamb* and *lizard*.

Have children name other words that begin with the same sound they hear at the beginning of *lamb* and *lizard*. Then ask each child to draw a picture of something whose name begins with the same sound and dictate to you a word that names the picture. Write the word on the writing rule for the child. You may wish to have some children copy the word.

Activity Book: Language

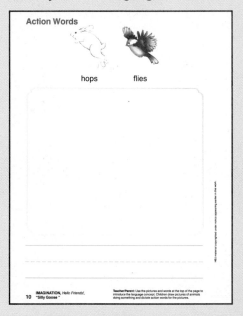

Action Words

hops   flies

IMAGINATION, *Hello Friends!*, 10 "Silly Goose"

Activity Book: Language

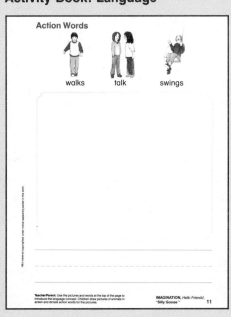

Action Words

walks   talk   swings

IMAGINATION, *Hello Friends!*, "Silly Goose" 11

Activity Book: Sound/Letter

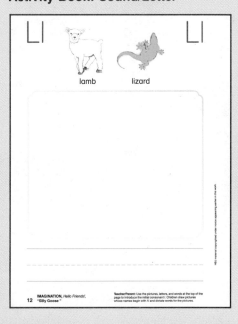

Ll   Ll

lamb   lizard

12 IMAGINATION, *Hello Friends!*, "Silly Goose"

Think and Extend

Cooperative Learning

Cooperative learning suggestions for *Think and Extend* appear at the beginning of the *Teacher's Edition.*

For the Classroom

Health/Physical Education—Learning New Exercises

Discuss how exercising makes our bodies strong and healthy. Then play some lively music for children to move to. As the music begins, and periodically throughout the workout, call out, "Move like a . . .," adding various animal names. This will be a signal for children to imitate the movements of that particular animal.

Prior to this activity you may wish to share with children the story *Petunia Takes a Trip* by Roger Duvoisin (Knopf, 1953). The story tells how Petunia, the silly goose, does calisthenics to lose weight so that she can fly. Children can follow the art in the book and do the same calisthenics as Petunia.

Music—Learning a Song

You may wish to teach children the song "Sammy" by Hap Palmer. The music and lyrics are found in the **Teacher's Resource** section of the *Teacher's Edition.*

Notes for Cooperative Learning

Additional Classroom Activities

64

For the Home

The homework assignment that follows also appears on **Homework Notebook copying master 4.** You may wish to distribute the copying masters to the children.

Writing   Have children ask family members to help them watch an animal near their homes as it moves. This animal could be a pet or a wild animal such as a squirrel, chipmunk, bird, toad, or insect. Then have children dictate sentences about the animal. Encourage family members to follow this procedure after taking the child's dictation.

- Read the sentences to the child.
- Read the sentences with the child.
- Have the child read the sentences.
- Have the child illustrate the sentences.

Suggest that children share their sentences with classmates the following day.

Reading   Suggest that children read a story or poem about silly animals with a parent or older family member. Encourage them to discuss silly things they have seen animals do.

For Extended and Recreational Reading

You may wish to recommend the following books about silly animals. Encourage family members to visit the public library with children to select the books to be read.

Books About Silly Animals

Bedtime for Frances by Russell Hoban. Harper & Row, 1960.

The Tale of Peter Rabbit by Beatrix Potter in *The Complete Adventures of Peter Rabbit.* Puffin, 1984.

Amos and Boris by William Steig. Farrar, Straus & Giroux, 1971.

A Bear Called Paddington by Michael Bond. Dell, 1968.

Frog and Toad Are Friends by Arnold Lobel. Harper & Row, 1979.

The Adventures of Paddy Pork by John Goodall. Harcourt, 1968.

More Books About Silly Animals

Paddy's New Hat by John Goodall. Atheneum, 1980.

Frederick by Leo Lionni. Pantheon, 1966.

Additional Home Activities

Additional Books for Extended and Recreational Reading

Notes

Ideas for Cooperative Learning

Ideas for Meeting the Needs of Individual Students

Questioning Strategies

Focusing on "Very Tall Mouse and Very Short Mouse"

While **listening** to and **reading** the selection, children will focus on friendship. Children will also use **writing, listening,** and **speaking** skills as they respond to the selection. They will use higher-level **thinking** skills throughout the lesson.

OBJECTIVES

WRITING/THINKING

- To dictate a response to literature using the writing process.
- To write in the practical/informative domain.
- To use describing words that are opposites.
- To write a description.

READING/THINKING

- To recall the actions of characters.
- To draw conclusions about the characters.
- To recognize the writer's use of words that are opposite in meaning.
- To discriminate between short and tall.
- To recognize initial correspondences. (/v/v) and (/r/r)

SPEAKING/THINKING

- To discuss personal experiences before reading a selection.
- To participate in shared reading.
- To participate in group discussions.
- To dictate a response to literature.
- To orally reread parts of a story.

LISTENING/THINKING

- To listen to the oral reading of the selection.
- To listen to and analyze responses to opinions about a selection.
- To distinguish story characters by their voices.
- To listen for initial sounds. (/v/) and (/r/)

LEARNING STRATEGIES

- Brainstorming ideas related to children's own experiences.
- Previewing the selection and making predictions about the content.
- Completing a chart to help comprehension.
- Completing a chart to help organize writing.
- Analyzing the writer's use of language.

Summary

- Very Tall Mouse and Very Short Mouse see and greet different things as they walk together. Very Tall Mouse sees things that are high up. Very Short Mouse sees things that are low. A storm forces the two mice indoors, where they enjoy seeing the same thing—a rainbow.

INDIVIDUAL NEEDS

Suggestions for teaching children with special needs are provided on *Teacher's Edition* page 1.

- The blue objectives may require direct instruction.

PLANNING CALENDAR

		STUDENT'S EDITIONS	TEACHER'S EDITION	ACTIVITY BOOK
DAY 1 **INTO THE SELECTION**	**THINK AND READ**			
	Preparing to Read	● *pages 34–41* ■ *pages 34–41*	*page 69*	
	Planning a Reading Strategy	● *pages 34–41* ■ *pages 34–41*	*page 70*	
DAYS 2-4 **THROUGH THE SELECTION**	**THINK AND DISCUSS**			
	Remembering the Selection	● *pages 34–41* ■ *pages 34–41*	*page 72*	
	Discussing the Selection	● *pages 34–41* ■ *pages 34–41*	*page 72*	
	THINK AND WRITE			
	Making the Assignment		*page 76*	
	Using the Writing Process		*page 77*	
	Focusing on Language		*page 78*	*pages 13–14*
	Focusing on Composition		*pages 78–79*	
	Focusing on Auditory Discrimination		*page 79*	
	Focusing on Visual Discrimination		*page 79*	
	Focusing on Sound-Letter Correspondences		*page 79*	*pages 15–16*
	Focusing on the Writer's Use of Language		*page 78*	
DAY 5 **BEYOND THE SELECTION**	**THINK AND EXTEND**			
	For the Classroom		*page 80*	
	For the Home		*page 81*	
			▲ Homework Notebook copying master 5	

● *Happy Times!* **Story Land 1**
■ *Hello Friends!* **Storybook**

▲ *Learning Resources File*

Think and Read

Note: Through observing and evaluating children's reading in a variety of situations and at different times, you can gather data which can help you understand and support individual children's reading development. Use the *Checklist for Observing and Evaluating Reading* in the **Evaluation Resources** section of the *Teacher's Edition.*

Cooperative Learning

Cooperative learning suggestions for *Think and Read* appear at the beginning of the *Teacher's Edition.*

Preparing to Read

▶**Relating to Children's Experiences**   Take children on a walk around the schoolyard. Upon returning, record what was seen by writing children's responses on chart paper. A sample follows.

Things We Saw on Our Walk	
children playing softball	⚾
birds eating worms	🐦🐦
cars passing on the street	🚗
men fixing a fence	▦

▶**Previewing and Predicting**   Point to the title of the story and read it to children. Ask children to tell what they think the story might be about. You may wish to model a response.

I think the story will be about a mouse who is very tall and a mouse who is very short because I see two mice and they are different sizes.

Notes for Cooperative Learning

Notes for Preparing to Read

Then have children look at the pictures of the two mice walking together and looking at things. Ask children what they think the two mice will see as they walk. You may wish to model a response.

I think Very Tall Mouse will see birds flying high in the sky. I think Very Short Mouse will see bugs crawling on the ground.

▶**Setting a Purpose**   Tell children that as they listen to "Very Tall Mouse and Very Short Mouse" they should think about why each mouse sees different things as they walk.

Planning a Reading Strategy

Sharing Reading   Read aloud the story, sharing the illustrations. Use a deep voice when reading the lines of Very Tall Mouse and a lighter voice when reading the lines of Very Short Mouse.

Read the story a second time, having children wave high in the air or low toward the floor each time Very Tall Mouse or Very Short Mouse speaks.

Encourage children to react spontaneously with comments and questions after you read the story.

Reading Orally   Read aloud the story. Encourage children to join in and repeat with you each time Very Tall Mouse or Very Short Mouse says hello. Point to the picture and have children say, "Hello, _____," using the appropriate voices.

Reading Silently   Give children the opportunity to "read" the story independently. Explain that the illustrations will help them remember what Very Tall Mouse and Very Short Mouse see on their walk and to what they say hello.

VERY TALL MOUSE
and
VERY SHORT MOUSE

Story and pictures by Arnold Lobel

Once there was a very tall mouse
and a very short mouse
who were good friends.

When they met
Very Tall Mouse would say,
"Hello, Very Short Mouse."
And Very Short Mouse would say,
"Hello, Very Tall Mouse."

34

The two friends would often
take walks together.
As they walked along
Very Tall Mouse would say,
"Hello, birds."
And Very Short Mouse would say,
"Hello, bugs."

35

70

When they
passed by a garden,
Very Tall Mouse would say,
"Hello, flowers."
And Very Short Mouse
would say,
"Hello, roots."

When they passed by a house,
Very Tall Mouse would say,
"Hello, roof."
And Very Short Mouse
would say,
"Hello, cellar."

One day the two mice
were caught in a storm.
Very Tall Mouse said,
"Hello, raindrops."
And Very Short Mouse said,
"Hello, puddles."

They ran indoors to get dry.
"Hello, ceiling,"
said Very Tall Mouse.
"Hello, floor,"
said Very Short Mouse.

Soon the storm was over.
The two friends
ran to the window.

Very Tall Mouse held
Very Short Mouse up to see.

"Hello, rainbow!"
they both said together.

40

When he was seven years old, Arnold Lobel began telling stories. First he made up stories for his friends at school. Then he made up stories for his own children when they were small. Arnold Lobel was an author and illustrator of books. Many children enjoy his stories and drawings.

Arnold Lobel said, "When I write my stories, I always sit in the same chair. I do my writing in the late afternoon. That is a good time to think about frogs and toads and mice and crickets."

More Books by Arnold Lobel

Mouse Tales   (Harper & Row, 1972)
Frog and Toad Together   (Harper & Row, 1972)
Days with Frog and Toad   (Harper & Row, 1979)
Owl at Home   (Harper & Row, 1975)
Fables   (Harper & Row, 1980)

41

Notes

Ideas for Cooperative Learning

Ideas for Meeting the Needs of Individual Students

Questioning Strategies

Think and Discuss

Cooperative Learning

Cooperative learning suggestions for *Think and Discuss* appear at the beginning of the **Teacher's Edition.**

Remembering the Selection

Ask children to recall the story and identify the things Very Tall Mouse and Very Short Mouse say hello to.

Encourage children to look at the story's illustrations to help themselves recall the information. You may wish to create a class chart to record children's responses.

A sample chart follows.

VERY TALL

birds   flowers
roof   raindrops
ceiling   rainbow

VERY SHORT

bugs   roots
cellar   puddles
floor   rainbow

Notes for Cooperative Learning

Notes for Remembering the Selection

Discussing the Selection

The following questions focus on friendship. As children respond to the questions, ask them to support their answers with examples from the story. Encourage children to agree or disagree with their classmates' responses and to substantiate their opinions.

Remind children to speak clearly and loudly enough so they can be heard and understood.

1. What did the mice like to do together? (**Possible responses:** *The mice liked to take walks together; talk; look at rainbows.*) *(Literal)*
2. Why did Very Tall Mouse and Very Short Mouse see things differently on their walk? (**Possible response:** *The two mice were different heights. Very Tall Mouse saw only things that were high up. Very Short Mouse saw only things that were low.*) *(Interpretive)*
3. How do we know the two mice are friends? (**Possible response:** *The story told us they were friends. They liked to do things together.*) *(Interpretive)*
4. How would the story be different if both mice had been the same size? (**Possible response:** *The two mice would have seen the same things.*) *(Critical)*
5. Name ways you and your friends are the same. Name ways you and your friends are different.

(**Possible responses:** *My friends and I like to play baseball and tag, and ride bikes. My friends and I do not look the same or talk the same.*) *(Creative)*

During the discussion, children will need to

- **recall** what the mice liked to do together.
- **explain** why the mice saw things differently.
- **conclude** why the two mice are friends.
- **analyze** how the story would be different if the mice had been the same size.
- **recognize** how they and their friends are the same and different.

You may wish to model responses to the questions. Use the possible responses given.

Tips for Evaluating the Oral Response

- Children should speak clearly and at the appropriate volume.
- Children should respond in complete thoughts.
- Children should ask relevant questions.

Additional Discussion Questions

Notes for Evaluating the Oral Response

Think and Discuss

Talking About Stories and Poems

The children have read the stories and poems in "Hello Friends!" Have children compare and contrast the selections. Use the discussion questions and the possible responses provided.

1. How do you and your family act like the family members in the stories "Birthday Fun" and "Silly Goose"? (**Possible responses:** *My family has a party for everyone's birthday. We have cake and give presents and have fun. I show my mother and father things I have learned to do. Sometimes they laugh and call me silly.*)
2. Do you think the little girl in "Goodbye, Hello" and the little girl in "Silly Goose" could be friends? Tell why you think as you do. (**Possible response:** *I think they could be good friends because they like to play.*)
3. If Very Tall Mouse and Very Short Mouse came to visit the class, what game would you ask them to play with you? (**Possible responses:** *I would ask them to play hide-and-seek. We could play a game of tag.*)
4. Which character from one poem or story would you like to be your friend? Tell why. (*Encourage children to share their thoughts.*)

During the discussion children will talk about

- how they are very much like some of the characters they read about.
- how characters from the different stories could be friends.
- how the selections relate to the theme of the unit.

Bookshelf

Introduce children to these and other selections that relate to the theme of the unit.

Nicolas, Where Have You Been? by Leo Lionni. Alfred A. Knopf, 1987. Nicolas and his mice friends dislike all birds until a bird family befriends Nicolas and keeps him safe from danger.

Faye and Dolores by Barbara Samuels. Bradbury Press, 1985. Join sisters Faye and Dolores during daily activities, including playtime, snacktime, and bedtime.

Danny's Birthday by Edith Kunhardt. Greenwillow, 1986. Danny's father videotapes Danny's fifth birthday so he can relive the festivities again and again.

Best Friends by Steven Kellogg. Dial Books, 1986. Kathy and Louise are best friends, but when Louise goes away for the summer, Kathy misses her terribly and begins to feel some resentment.

Lizzie and Harold by Elizabeth Winthrop. Lothrop, Lee & Shepard, 1986. Six-year-old Lizzie wants a best girlfriend until Harold, who lives next door, proves to be a wonderful friend.

Notes

Ideas for Cooperative Learning

Ideas for Meeting the Needs of Individual Students

Questioning Strategies

Think and Write

Making the Assignment

Review that friends like to do many different things together. Tell them that they are going to write about things they do with their friends. They will draw pictures of the things they do and will post them on the bulletin board.

Notes for Cooperative Learning

Notes for Making the Assignment

Using the Writing Process

Prewriting   Ask children to name the different things they enjoy doing with friends. List their responses on the chalkboard or on chart paper. Point to and read the words after writing them. A sample chart follows.

Friends

ride bikes

play ball

play games

swing

Drafting   Have children dictate sentences to you that tell what they do with a friend. Begin by modeling a response and writing it on the chalkboard or on chart paper. An example follows.

My friend and I walk to school.

Write each child's dictated sentence at the bottom of a piece of paper. Then follow this procedure.

- Read the sentence to the child.
- Read the sentence with the child.
- Have the child read the sentence.
- Have the child illustrate the sentence.

Responding/Revising/Editing   After each child has dictated a sentence and illustrated it, reread the sentence you wrote. Draw attention to conventions of writing such as beginning sentences with a capital letter, leaving spaces between words, ending sentences with a period, and following left-to-right progression.

Postwriting (Sharing)   Display children's sentences and pictures on the bulletin board. Ask children for suggestions for a title for the display, such as "What Friends Do Together" or "Friends Are Fun to Be With." Write the title, pin it to the bulletin board, and read it to children.

Notes for Using the Writing Process

Notes for Evaluating the Written Response

Develop Skills

Strategies for developing concepts and skills related to "Very Tall Mouse and Very Short Mouse" are included in this section. Select appropriate activities to teach to the whole class, small groups, or individual children.

Developing Concepts and Skills

Language:	Words That Name Short and Tall Things
Composition:	Story
Auditory Discrimination:	Distinguishing the Voices of Story Characters
Visual Discrimination:	Short and Tall
Sound-Letter Correspondences:	Initial correspondences /v/v and /r/r

Focusing on Language

Using Words That Name Short and Tall Things
Recall from the story that Very Tall Mouse was able to see things that were very high in the air because he was tall. Demonstrate this by showing children things you are able to see that they are not because they are high above their heads.

Use **Activity Book** pages 13 and 14 with children. Have them identify the pictures at the top of the pages. As each is identified, have them find the word, run their fingers under it, and say it aloud. Have each child draw a picture of something that is very tall on the first page and dictate to you a word that names the thing he or she drew. Write the naming word on the writing rule for the child. You may wish to have some children copy the word. Follow the same procedure for page 14 and ask children to draw pictures of short objects.

Focusing on Composition

Note: Through observing and evaluating children's writing in a variety of situations and at different times,

Focusing on the Writer's Use of Language

If you haven't done so, read aloud the information about the writer Arnold Lobel on page 41 of **Story Land 1** to children.

Ask children to recall Very Tall Mouse and Very Short Mouse saying hello to different things as they walked, until the very end of the story when they both said hello to the rainbow. Discuss why the writer may have decided to have the two mice looking at different things rather than the same things. (**Possible responses:** *The writer wanted to show us that two friends can be very different but still get along and share.*)

Activity Book: Language

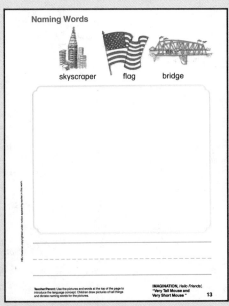

you can gather data which can help you understand children's writing development. Use the *Checklist for Observing and Evaluating Writing* in the **Evaluation Resources** section of the *Teacher's Edition.*

Writing About a Best Friend   Ask each child to think about his or her very best friend and then to write about this friend telling what he or she is like. Accept their writing regardless of its stage of development. Encourage children to write in a way that is most comfortable for them and share the writing with their best friend.

Focusing on Auditory Discrimination

Distinguishing the Voices of Very Tall Mouse and Very Short Mouse   Read aloud the first page of the story. Use a deep voice when Very Tall Mouse speaks and a lighter voice when Very Short Mouse speaks. Ask children if they can tell the difference between voices.

Stick puppets of Very Tall Mouse and Very Short Mouse can be made by having children draw pictures of each mouse and by taping the pictures to sticks or pencils or by duplicating pictures of the mice to distribute to children to use.

After rereading the story, ask volunteers to vary their voices and use their puppets to say hello to other tall and short things.

Focusing on Visual Discrimination

Identifying Tall and Short Objects   Review with children that in "Very Tall Mouse and Very Short Mouse" the two friends said hello to different things because of their sizes.

Divide the class in half. Give one half of the children pictures of Very Tall Mouse. Have them move about the classroom and tape the pictures to objects that are tall or high. Children may need assistance to reach high places. Then give the remaining children pictures of Very Short Mouse to tape to objects that are short or near the floor.

Focusing on Sound-Letter Correspondences

Recognizing Initial /v/v   Ask children to listen for the word *very* as you read aloud the first page of the story. After reading, write on the chalkboard the word *very*. Have children say the word. Then circle the first letter of *very* and explain that the word begins with the letter *v*.

Use *Activity Book* page 15 with children. Have them repeat the word *very* as they finger-trace the uppercase *V* and the lower case *v*. Have children name other words that begin with the same sound they hear at the beginning of *violin* and *vegetable*. Then ask each child to draw a picture of something whose name begins with the same sound and dictate to you a word that names the picture. Write the word on the writing rule for the child. You may wish to have some children copy the word.

Recognizing Initial /r/r   Review with children the things Very Tall Mouse and Very Short Mouse saw. When words with initial sound *r* are mentioned, write the words on the chalkboard. Have children repeat the words beginning with the letter *r*. Using *Activity Book* page 16, follow the same procedure from the previous page.

Activity Book: Language

Activity Book: Sound/Letter

Activity Book: Sound/Letter

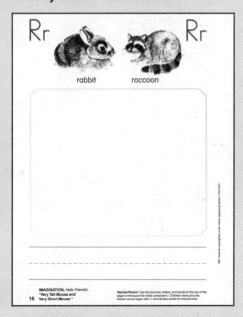

Think and Extend

Cooperative Learning

Cooperative learning suggestions for *Think and Extend* appear at the beginning of the **Teacher's Edition.**

For the Classroom

Science—Learning About Mice Ask how many students have seen a real mouse. Have them describe what it looked like. For children who have not seen a real mouse, display pictures for them to look at while you read aloud the following poem.

Mice
by Rose Fyleman

I think mice
Are rather nice.
  Their tails are long,
  Their faces small,
  They haven't any
  Chins at all.
  Their ears are pink,
  Their teeth are white,
  They run about
  The house at night.

They nibble things
They shouldn't touch
And no one seems
To like them much.
But I think mice
Are nice.

Ask children what they learned about mice from listening to the poem. Discuss the homes, food, and habits of mice. Then have each child draw a picture of a real mouse in a proper setting. Display the finished pictures and discuss what each picture tells about mice.

Art—Painting Mice
Materials: sponges cut into small pieces
            bowls with different colors of tempera paint
            drawing paper
            stencils of mice
Demonstrate sponge painting by dipping a sponge into paint and dabbing it on paper. Then place a stencil of a mouse in the center of the child's paper. Show him or her how to hold the stencil in place while sponge painting around it.

Notes for Cooperative Learning

Additional Classroom Activities

For the Home

The homework assignment that follows also appears on **Homework Notebook copying master 5.** You may wish to distribute the copying master to the children.

Writing   Have children dictate a note to a friend or special relative to say hello. Encourage family members to follow this procedure after taking the child's dictation.

- Read the sentences to the child.
- Read the sentences with the child.
- Have the child read the sentences.
- Have the child illustrate the sentences if he or she wishes.

Suggest that parents address and mail the notes for children. Encourage children to tell classmates to whom they wrote friendly notes.

Reading   Have family members read and discuss with children stories about friends, realistic or animal, or some of Arnold Lobel's other stories.

For Extended and Recreational Reading

You may wish to recommend the following books about friends for children to share with family members. Encourage family members to visit the public library with children to select the books to be read.

Books About Friends

May I Bring a Friend? by Beatrice Schenk de Regniers. Atheneum, 1964.

Corduroy by Don Freeman. Viking Press, 1968.

George and Martha by James Marshall. Houghton Mifflin, 1972.

The Snowman by Raymond Briggs. Random House, 1978.

Will I Have a Friend? by Miriam Cohen. Macmillan, 1967.

Mouse Tales by Arnold Lobel. Harper & Row, 1972.

Additional Books About Friends

Best Friends by Miriam Cohen. Macmillan, 1971.

A New Home, A New Friend by Hans Wilhelm. Random House, 1985.

Friend Dog by Arnold Doff. J.B. Lippincott, 1980.

We Are Best Friends by Aliki. Greenwillow Books, 1982.

Additional Home Activities

Additional Books for Extended and Recreational Reading

Unit 2

Places I Know

Theme: Discovering the world around us

Reading Selections	Writing Assignments
• A House Is a House for Me	• Dictate Sentences About Different Kinds of Houses
• The Chick and the Duckling	• Dictate Dialogue for Story Characters
• Connections: Count the Friends	• Dictate Sentences About Counting
• Uno, Dos, Tres, Cho— One, Two, Three, Four, Five	• Dictate Sentences About Children Counting
• Higher Than a House Star Light, Star Bright	• Sentences About Wishes

Unit Resources

As you work through the Integrated Instructional Plans in this unit, you may want to use the following resources included in the **Student/Teacher Resources** and **Evaluation Resources** sections of the **Teacher's Edition.**

Student/Teacher Resources

- Home Letters 3A and 3B
- Extended and Recreational Reading Ideas

Evaluation Resources

- Observation and Evaluation Guides

Students With Individual Needs

	Limited-English-Proficient Students	Less-Prepared Students	Gifted Students	Special Education Students
Think and Read	• Assist students with previewing strategies. Focus on gaining meaning from illustrations. • Use pictures and filmstrips to provide additional background information. • Use audiovisual aids to help students understand difficult concepts.	• Frequently model and review strategies for recalling and applying prior knowledge. • Use shared reading strategies. Discuss vocabulary and content after each selection is read. • Encourage students to talk about previous experiences related to the selections. Remind them to use *I* and *me* in their statements.	• After modeling effective prereading strategies, have students lead the discussions that focus on previewing and predicting. • After modeling effective thinking strategies, have students lead the discussions that focus on summarizing.	• Review individualized education programs (IEPs) with special education staff and discuss necessary modification of curriculum. • For visually-impaired students, provide specialized resources, such as large-print books, books in braille, or recordings.
Think and Discuss	• Model by reading aloud questions and possible responses. Have students repeat each question and add additional responses. • Have students work in cooperative learning groups. (See the suggestions at the front of this *Teacher's Edition.*)	• Help students identify details from the selections to support answers to interpretive and critical questions. Model the thinking process for students. • Have students brainstorm ideas to aid them in answering creative questions.	• After modeling effective questioning strategies, have students lead the discussions that focus on the selection and its theme. • Have students work in cooperative learning groups. (See the suggestions at the front of this *Teacher's Edition.*)	• During discussion, have notetakers record and transmit hearing-impaired students' responses. • For hearing-impaired students, use visual aids, such as slides and overhead projectors, to reinforce learning.
Think and Write	• Have students work in cooperative learning groups. (See the suggestions at the front of this *Teacher's Edition.*) • Provide pictures to stimulate prewriting. Then help students brainstorm and list descriptive words.	• During the writing process, have students work in cooperative learning groups. (See the suggestions at the front of this *Teacher's Edition.*) • Review with students the purpose and the intended audience of each writing assignment. Remind them to consider their purpose and audience during the entire writing process.	• Encourage students to consider different ways to publish their writing for assignments in *Think and Write*. • After modeling responses for *Thinking Back*, have students lead the discussions.	• Review lesson plans with special education staff to discuss any necessary modification of curriculum. • For visually-impaired students, record the directions for the stages of the writing process. Have students record their compositions.
Think and Extend	• Encourage students to participate in *Think and Extend* activities that require speaking. • For social studies activities, have students share related information about their cultural experiences.	• Provide manipulatives for students to use while completing mathematics activities. • Have students work in cooperative learning groups. (See the suggestions for cooperative learning activities at the front of the *Teacher's Edition.*)	• Have students work in cooperative learning groups. (See the suggestions at the front of this *Teacher's Edition.*) • Ask students to think of additional *Think and Extend* activities. When appropriate, assign the student-generated activities instead of the activities in the *Writer's Corner.*	• Review lesson plans with special education staff to discuss any necessary modification of curriculum. • For visually-impaired students, record the directions for the activities.

Unit 2

FIRE HOUSE

LIBRARY

42

Introducing the Unit

Talking About the Theme   To introduce children to the unit, point to and read aloud the title "Places I Know." Ask children to look at the picture that illustrates the opening of the unit. Begin a discussion about every person, animal, and thing having its own special place by having children answer the following questions about the picture.

1. Name the special places you see in the picture. (**Possible responses:** *There are stores in the picture. There is a fire engine in the picture.*)
2. Who or what is in each special place? (**Possible responses:** *The fire engine is in the firehouse. The boy and girl are standing on the sidewalk.*)
3. Name other people, animals, or things that might make their homes in the places you see in the picture. (**Possible responses:** *There might be a squirrel or a bird in the tree. People work in the stores.*)

4. Why do you think it is important for everyone and everything to have its own special place? (*Encourage children's responses.*)
5. What kinds of special places do you think you might read about in the stories and poems in this unit? (**Possible response:** *I think the stories might be about special places for things.*)

2 Places I Know

43

Extending Reading   The following books extend the theme of the unit. You may want to share these books as children listen to and "read" the selections in Unit 2. Have children discuss the special places for people, animals, and things.

The Little House by Virginia Lee Burton. Houghton Mifflin, 1978. The little house starts out life far in the country, but slowly the city grows up around it.

The Biggest House in the World by Leo Lionni. Alfred A. Knopf, 1968. A wise father snail convinces his son that a small, easy-to-carry shell is better than the biggest house in the world.

Anno's Counting House by Mitsumasa Anno. Philomel, 1982. Through the cutouts in the pages, the reader can watch young children move from house to house.

Ten, Nine, Eight by Molly Bang. Greenwillow, 1983. A father counts backward to help his daughter sleep.

Bulletin Board Suggestion

Make a class bulletin board showing *Places I Know.* Have children draw or cut pictures that show special places for people and animals. The pictures they choose can be places people live, work or play and places animals live. Ask children to name the special places. Label each special place. Point to each name and have children repeat it. Talk about what makes each place special and ask how many children have seen such a place.

Unit 2

Unit Activities

The following optional unit activities relate to the theme of the unit. The activities may be completed during or after unit instruction. Instructions for setting up learning centers appear at the front of the *Teacher's Edition.*

LISTENING Corner

Objective: To listen to directions.
Procedure: Play a simple game of "Simon Says" using the idea of "a place for everything" to tie in the actions. For example, have children pantomime the actions for the following directions:

"Put your hands in your pockets."
"Put a ring on your finger."
"Put shoes on your feet."
"Put a watch on your wrist."
"Put a hat on your head."

You may wish to have children play the leader and give directions to other children.

SPEAKING Corner

Objective: To introduce children to the concept of visiting a home.
Materials: blocks and classroom furniture
Procedure: Have children set up a house in a corner of the room using blocks and classroom furniture. Tell them to take turns pretending to live in the house and inviting friends over to visit. Have other children visit the house. As they pretend, ask them to think about how they should act when they visit someone. Encourage them to share with each other and then switch roles.

READING Corner

Objective: To read books about special places for people, animals, and things.
Materials: books about special places that may include titles from page 85 in the *Teacher's Edition.*
Procedure: Ask children to select a book. You may wish to read it aloud to a group of children. After you have read aloud the story, encourage children to draw a picture of the character in the story and share it with other classmates.

WRITING Corner

Objective: To keep a log of special places visited during the week.
Materials: booklets made by stapling together four or five sheets of paper.
Procedure: Ask children to think about special places they visit during the week. Have them draw a picture of one place on the first page of the booklet. You may wish to continue the project on the following day and have children draw a picture of another place they visited. Continue until the booklet is filled.

Have children dictate to you naming words that tell about the places they visited. Write the naming words in the booklet. Finally, have children share their logs with the class or with a small group.

Note: Some children will prefer to dictate their sentences as you write. Others will want to write on their own. Accept their writing regardless of its stage of development. Allow them to draw, scribble, or write using their own spelling.

Focusing on "A House Is a House for Me"

While **listening** to and **reading** the selection, children will focus on the idea that everything has a home. Children will also use **writing, listening,** and **speaking** skills as they respond to the selection. They will use higher-level **thinking** skills throughout the lesson.

OBJECTIVES

WRITING/THINKING

- To dictate a response to literature using the writing process.
- To write in the imaginative/narrative domain.
- To use naming words.
- To write about a personal experience.

READING/THINKING

- To draw conclusions about the information in the poem.
- To evaluate the placement of the poem in a thematic unit.
- To interpret the writer's purpose.
- To make comparisons.
- To locate details in the selection.
- To recognize initial correspondences. (/h/h)

SPEAKING/THINKING

- To discuss personal experiences before reading a selection.
- To participate in shared reading.
- To participate in group discussions.
- To dictate a response to literature.
- To read aloud parts of the poem.

LISTENING/THINKING

- To listen to the oral reading of a selection.
- To listen to and analyze responses to opinions about a selection.
- To listen for rhyming words.
- To listen for initial sounds. (/h/)

LEARNING STRATEGIES

- Brainstorming ideas related to children's own experiences.
- Previewing the selection and making predictions about the content.
- Completing a chart to help comprehension.
- Completing a list to help organize writing.
- Analyzing the writer's use of language.

Summary

Every thing, animal, and person has a special place of its own called a house. The poem names many kinds of houses, ending with the earth which houses us all.

INDIVIDUAL NEEDS

Suggestions for teaching children with special needs are provided on *Teacher's Edition* page 82.

- The blue objectives may require direct instruction.

PLANNING CALENDAR

		STUDENT'S EDITIONS	TEACHER'S EDITION	ACTIVITY BOOK
DAY 1 **INTO THE SELECTION**	**THINK AND READ**			
	Preparing to Read	● *pages 44–53* ■ *pages 2–11*	*page 89*	
	Planning a Reading Strategy	● *pages 44–53* ■ *pages 2–11*	*page 90*	
DAYS 2-4 **THROUGH THE SELECTION**	**THINK AND DISCUSS**			
	Remembering the Selection	● *pages 44–53* ■ *pages 2–11*	*page 94*	
	Discussing the Selection	● *pages 44–53* ■ *pages 2–11*	*page 95*	
	THINK AND WRITE			
	Making the Assignment		*page 96*	
	Using the Writing Process		*pages 96–97*	
	Develop Skills			
	Focusing on Language		*page 98*	*pages 17–18*
	Focusing on Composition		*page 99*	
	Focusing on Auditory Discrimination		*page 99*	
	Focusing on Visual Discrimination		*page 99*	
	Focusing on Sound-Letter Correspondences		*page 99*	*page 19*
	Focusing on the Writer's Use of Language		*page 98*	
DAY 5 **BEYOND THE SELECTION**	**THINK AND EXTEND**			
	For the Classroom		*page 100*	
	For the Home		*page 101*	
			▲ Homework Notebook copying master 6	

● *Happy Times!* **Story Land 1**
■ *Places I Know* **Storybook**

▲ *Learning* **Resources File**

Note: Through observing and evaluating children's reading in a variety of situations and at different times, you can gather data which can help you understand and support individual children's reading development. Use the *Checklist for Observing and Evaluating Reading* in the **Evaluation Resources** section of the *Teacher's Edition.*

Cooperative Learning

Cooperative learning suggestions for *Think and Read* appear at the beginning of the *Teacher's Edition.*

Preparing to Read

▶**Relating to Children's Experiences** Ask children to discuss what they think about when they hear the word house. After the discussion, have children listen as you read the poem for the fingerplay "A Good House." Ask children to think about whether their houses look like the one being described in the poem. Then reread the poem and teach children the actions.

A Good House

This is the roof on the house so good.
  [*make roof with hands*]
These are the walls that are made of wood.
  [*hands straight, palms parallel*]
These are the windows that let in the light.
  [*thumbs and forefingers for windows*]
This is the door that shuts so tight.
  [*hands straight side by side*]
This is the chimney so straight and tall.
  [*arms straight up*]
Oh! What a good house for one and all.
  [*arms at angle for roof*]

▶**Previewing and Predicting** Point to the title of the selection and read it to children. Then ask them to tell what they think the poem will be about. You may wish to model a response.

Notes for Cooperative Learning

Notes for Preparing to Read

People live in different kinds of houses. I think the poem will tell about these houses.

▶**Setting a Purpose**   Tell children that as they listen to "A House Is a House for Me" they should think about the different kinds of things that are houses.

Planning a Reading Strategy

Sharing Reading   Read aloud the poem several times, sharing the illustrations and pointing to the text. Stress the words that name various houses and emphasize the line that is repeated.

Encourage children to react spontaneously with comments and questions after you read the poem.

Reading Orally   Read aloud the poem. Encourage children to join in by repeating the line, "And a house is a house for me." Read aloud the poem a second time having children insert the names of the houses pictured on each page. As you read, point to the picture of the house and pause long enough for children to respond. For example: *A [point to the picture of the hill] is a house for an ant, an ant.*

Reading Silently   Give children the opportunity to "read" the poem independently. Explain that the illustrations will help them remember the house named.

A House Is a House for Me

From a poem by Mary Ann Hoberman

Pictures by Janet La Salle

A hill is a house for an ant, an ant.
A hive is a house for a bee.

A hole is a house for a mole or
   a mouse
And a house is a house for me!

2

3

A web is a house for a spider.
A bird builds its nest in a tree.

There is nothing so snug as a bug
in a rug
And a house is a house for me!

A glove is a house for a hand, a hand.
A stocking's a house for a knee.

A shoe or a boot is a house for a foot
And a house is a house for me!

A book is a house for a story.
A rose is a house for a smell.

My head is a house for a secret,
A secret I never will tell.

A flower's at home in a garden.
A donkey's at home in a stall.

Each creature that's known has a
house of its own
And the earth is a house for us all.

Notes

Ideas for Cooperative Learning

Ideas for Meeting the Needs of Individual Students

Questioning Strategies

Think and Discuss

Note: Through observing and evaluating children's oral language (listening and spoeaking) in a variety of situations and at different times, you can gather data which can help you understand and support individual children's oral development. Use the *Checklist for Observing and Evaluating Writing* in the **Evaluation Resources** section of the *Teacher's Edition.*

Cooperative Learning

Cooperative learning suggestions for *Think and Discuss* appear at the beginning of the **Teacher's Edition.**

Remembering the Selection

Ask children to recall the poem and identify

- the name of each house mentioned in the poem.
- the name of the person, animal, or thing living in each house.

Encourage children to look at the poem's illustrations to help recall the information. You may wish to pantomime or use noises to help children make associations and remember the animals and their houses. For example: *A hill (make a hill with hands and arms) is a house for an ant. A hive is a house for a bee (buzz like a bee). A web is a house for a spider (hand motion like a spider).*

Notes for Cooperative Learning

Notes for Remembering the Selection

Discussing the Selection

The following questions focus on homes and houses. As children respond to the questions, ask them to support their answers with examples from the poem. Encourage children to agree or disagree with their classmates' responses and to substantiate their opinions.

Remind children to speak clearly and loudly enough so they can be heard and understood.

1. Are all houses exactly alike? Why or why not? (**Possible responses:** *No because some houses are small and some are large. Houses can be different things or places where people, animals, or things live.*) (*Interpretive*)
2. What is the writer trying to tell us in this poem? (**Possible responses:** *Everything has its own house; we all share the earth as a house.*) (*Critical*)
3. What does the writer mean when she writes "and a house is a house for me?" (**Possible responses:** *A house is where children live.*) (*Critical*)
4. Think of another animal not mentioned in the story. Where does that animal live? (*Invite children to respond.*) (*Creative*)
5. Why do you think it's important to have a home? (**Possible responses:** *It is important to have a home because everyone needs a place to live. It's important to have a home so that you feel safe.*) (*Critical*)

During the discussion, children will need to

- **conclude** whether or not all houses are alike.
- **interpret** the writer's message.
- **explain** the meaning of "a house is a house for me."
- **identify** another animal and its home.
- **evaluate** the story in the thematic unit.

You may wish to model responses to the questions. Use the possible responses given.

Tips for Evaluating the Oral Response

- Children should speak clearly and at the appropriate volume.
- Children should respond in complete thoughts.
- Children should ask relevant questions.

Additional Discussion Questions

Notes for Evaluating the Oral Response

Think and Write

Making the Assignment

Review that people, animals, and things have houses
that are special places for them to feel at home. Tell
children that they will write about animals and their
houses. Then they will make a class poem of their
writing.

Notes for Cooperative Learning

Notes for Making the Assignment

Using the Writing Process

Prewriting   Ask children to suggest the names of various animals and the names of the places where they live. List their responses on the chalkboard or on chart paper. Point to and read each word after you write it. A sample chart follows.

Animals and Their Homes	
bird	nest
squirrel	tree
skunk	woods
frog	pond
rabbit	hole

Drafting   Have children dictate sentences by using words from the chart to fill in the blanks.
A ____ is a house for a ____.
Begin by modeling a response and writing on the chalkboard. An example follows.
   A nest is a house for a bird.
   Write each child's dictated sentence at the bottom of a piece of paper. Then follow this procedure.

- Read the sentence to the child.
- Read the sentence with the child.
- Have the child read the sentence.
- Have the child illustrate the sentence.

Responding/Revising/Editing   After each child has dictated a sentence and illustrated it, reread the sentence you wrote. Draw attention to conventions of writing such as beginning sentences with a capital letter, leaving spaces between words, ending sentences with a period, and following left-to-right progression.

Postwriting (Sharing)   Use children's sentences to write a class poem. Have each child dictate his or her sentence as you write it on chart paper. End the poem with the sentence, "And a house is a house for me." Also have children decide on a title for their class poem. Write it at the top of the chart paper. Display the poem on a bulletin board in the school library for other classes to read and enjoy.

Notes for Using the Writing Process

Notes for Evaluating the Written Response

Develop Skills

Strategies for developing concepts and skills related to "A House Is a House for Me" are included in this section. Select appropriate activities to teach to the whole class, small groups, or individual children.

Developing Concepts and Skills

Language:	Naming Words
Composition:	Story
Auditory Discrimination:	Rhyming Words
Visual Discrimination:	Details
Sound-Letter Correspondences:	Initial correspondence /h/h

Focusing on Language

Using Naming Words Recall that some words in the poem named animals and the houses they lived in. Ask children to listen carefully as you reread the poem "A House Is a House for Me."

Use *Activity Book* pages 17 and 18 with children. Have them identify the pictures. As each is identified, have them find the word, run their fingers under it, and say it aloud. Have each child draw a picture of an animal and dictate to you a word that names the animal on page 17. Write the naming word on the writing rule for the child. You may wish to have some children copy the words. Follow the same procedure for page 18. Ask children to think of a house they would like to live in. Have children draw pictures of themselves in their own "house."

Focusing on Composition

Note: Through observing and evaluating children's writing in a variety of situations and at different times, you can gather data which can help you understand children's writing development. Use the *Checklist for*

Focusing on the Writer's Use of Language

If you haven't done so, point out the writer's name (Mary Ann Hoberman) and the illustrator's name (Janet LaSalle) printed at the beginning of the selection.

With children recall words the writer used to name different kinds of houses. *(hill, hive, hole, house, web, nest, rug, glove, stocking, shoe, boot, book, rose, head, garden, stall, earth)* Ask why the writer decided to name so many different kinds of houses. (**Possible responses:** *The writer wanted us to understand that everyone and everything in the world has a special place. A house can be anything that makes a person, animal, or thing feel safe and comfortable.*)

Observing and Evaluating Writing in the **Evaluation Resources** section of the *Teacher's Edition.*

Writing About a Personal Experience   Ask children to think about a time when they went to someone's house for a special visit. Encourage children to think about a special activity they did, like play with new friends or eat a new food. Have them write about the experience.

Accept their writing regardless of its stage of development. Many children will draw pictures while others scribble, write letters, or use invented spelling. Have children share their writing by reading it aloud to a group of classmates.

Focusing on Auditory Discrimination

Listening for Rhyming Words   Read aloud the first two pages of the poem. Then repeat the words *bee* and *me.* Ask children to tell how the words sound the same. (**Possible response:** *They both have the same ending sound.*)

Then ask children to name other words that have the same ending sounds they hear in *bee* and *me.* Tell children that words that end with the same ending sound are called **rhyming words.**

Reread "A House Is a House for Me," pausing after every two pages. Ask children to name the rhyming words they hear. Ask children why they think the writer used rhyming words in the poem.

Focusing on Visual Discrimination

Noticing the Differences Between Houses   Review with children that in the poem "A House Is a House for Me" every person, animal, and thing had its own special place called a house. Have children look at the pictures

illustrated and identify the houses for the ants and the bees. Ask children how the houses are different. Encourage them to compare the sizes, shapes, and colors of the two houses. Then have children compare other houses in the remaining illustrations.

Focusing on Sound-Letter Correspondences

Recognizing Initial /h/h   Ask children to listen for the word *house* as you read aloud the class poem they wrote for *Think and Write.* After reading the class poem, write on the chalkboard the word *house.* Have children say the word.

Use *Activity Book* page 19 with children. Have them repeat the word *house* as they finger-trace the uppercase H and the lowercase h.

Have children identify the pictures at the top of the page. As each is identified, have them find the word, run their fingers under it, and say it aloud. Explain that each picture begins with the same sound they hear at the beginning of *house.*

Ask children to identify the letter each word begins with. Tell them that the letter *h* usually stands for the same sound they hear at the beginning of *house.*

Then have children listen for the /h/ sound as you say the words *hill, hive,* and *hole.*

Have children name other words that begin with the same sound they hear at the beginning of *hill, hive,* and *hole.* Then ask each child to draw a picture of something whose name begins with the same sound and dictate to you a word that names the picture. Write the word on the writing rule for the child. You may wish to have some children copy the word.

Activity Book: Language

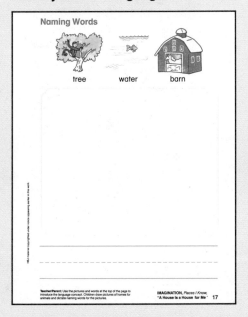

Naming Words

tree   water   barn

Teacher/Parent: Use the pictures and words at the top of the page to introduce the language concept. Children draw pictures of homes for animals and dictate naming words for the pictures.

IMAGINATION, *Places I Know,* "A House Is a House for Me"   17

Activity Book: Language

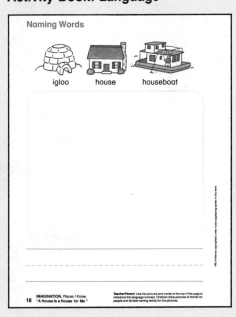

Naming Words

igloo   house   houseboat

18   "A House Is a House for Me"

Teacher/Parent: Use the pictures and words at the top of the page to introduce the language concept. Children draw pictures of homes for people and dictate naming words for the pictures.

IMAGINATION, *Places I Know,* "A House Is a House for Me"

Activity Book: Sound/Letter

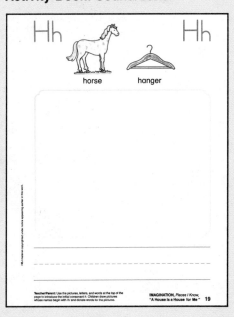

Hh   Hh

horse   hanger

Teacher/Parent: Use the pictures, letters, and words at the top of the page to introduce the initial consonant h. Children draw pictures whose names begin with /h/ and dictate words for the pictures.

IMAGINATION, *Places I Know,* "A House Is a House for Me"   19

Think and Extend

Cooperative Learning

Cooperative learning suggestions for *Think and Extend* appear at the beginning of the *Teacher's Edition.*

For the Classroom

Social Studies—Identifying Things That Belong in a Home   Discuss various things we need and we use in our homes. Have children cut pictures from magazines and catalogues that show people, furniture, appliances, and so on. After the collages are finished, ask children to share their collages of things that belong in a home.

Science—Identifying Animals That Have the Same Homes   Discuss how some animals live in the same kinds of houses. Mount on large sheets of drawing paper a picture of a forest, an ocean, a tree, and a cave. (Include additional animal homes if you wish.) Display these pictures of animal homes. Ask children to identify each and name different animals that make each place their home. Place each animal home in a different area of the classroom and invite children to walk about the room and draw a picture of an appropriate animal on the sheet picturing its home.
Example:

Notes for Cooperative Learning

Additional Classroom Activities

For the Home

The homework assignment that follows also appears on **Homework Notebook copying master 6.** You may wish to distribute the copying masters to the children.

Writing Have children dictate sentences to family members describing some special qualities about their house. Include the writing of the child's home address. You may want to suggest that the child begin by dictating "I live at _____." Encourage family members to follow this procedure after taking the child's dictation.

- Read the sentences to the child.
- Read the sentences with the child.
- Have the child read the sentences.
- Have the child illustrate the sentences by drawing a picture of the family home.

Reading Have parents or older family members show children a family phone directory. Have children read names and phone numbers of family and friends with them. Children may wish to have their special phone numbers written on a separate page.

For Extended and Recreational Reading

You may wish to recommend the following books about homes and houses for children to share with family members. Encourage family members to visit the public library with children to select the books to be read.

Books About Houses and Homes

The Little House by Virginia Lee Burton. Houghton Mifflin, 1978.

Listen, Children, Listen: An Anthology of Poems for the Very Young by Myra Cohn Livingston. Harcourt Brace Jovanovich, 1972.

The Biggest House in the World by Leo Lionni. Alfred A. Knopf, 1968.

More Books About Houses and Homes

Animals Live Here by Muriel Batherman. Greenwillow Books, 1979.

Tony's Hard Work Day by Alan Arkin. Harper & Row, 1972.

Benedict Finds a Home by Chris L. Demarest. Lothrop, Lee & Shepard, 1982.

Animal Houses by Aileen Fisher. Bowmar-Noble, 1978.

Additional Home Activities

Additional Books for Extended and Recreational Reading

Notes

Ideas for Cooperative Learning

Ideas for Meeting the Needs of Individual Students

Questioning Strategies

Focusing on "The Chick and the Duckling"

While **listening** to and **reading** the selection, children will focus on knowing yourself. Children will also use **writing, listening,** and **speaking** skills as they respond to the selection. They will use higher-level **thinking** skills throughout the lesson.

OBJECTIVES

WRITING/THINKING

- To dictate a response to literature using the writing process.
- To write in the imaginative/narrative domain.
- To use action words.
- To write about personal accomplishments.

READING/THINKING

- To analyze a character's motives.
- To make predictions about a character.
- To compare two characters.
- To compare similarities and differences of animals.
- To recognize initial correspondences. (/d/d)

SPEAKING/THINKING

- To discuss personal experiences before reading a selection.
- To participate in shared reading.
- To participate in group discussions.
- To dictate a response to literature.
- To participate in the oral rereading of the story.

LISTENING/THINKING

- To listen to the oral reading of a selection.
- To listen to and analyze responses to opinions about a selection.
- To listen for details.
- To listen for initial sounds. (/d/)

LEARNING STRATEGIES

- Brainstorming ideas related to children's own experiences.
- Previewing the selection and making predictions about the content.
- Completing a drawing to help comprehension.
- Completing a chart to help organize writing.
- Analyzing the writer's use of language.

Summary

A newly hatched chick imitates a duckling until a troublesome swim teaches the chick to think for himself.

INDIVIDUAL NEEDS

Suggestions for teaching children with special needs are provided on *Teacher's Edition* page 82.

- The blue objectives may require direct instruction.

PLANNING CALENDAR

		STUDENT'S EDITIONS	TEACHER'S EDITION	ACTIVITY BOOK
DAY 1 **INTO THE SELECTION**	**THINK AND READ** Preparing to Read Planning a Reading Strategy	● *pages 54–72* ■ *pages 12–30* ● *pages 54–72* ■ *pages 12–30*	*page 105* *page 106*	
DAYS 2-4 **THROUGH THE SELECTION**	**THINK AND DISCUSS** Remembering the Selection Discussing the Selection	● *pages 54–72* ■ *pages 12–30* ● *pages 54–72* ■ *pages 12–30*	*page 112* *page 113*	
	THINK AND WRITE Making the Assignment Using the Writing Process **Develop Skills** Focusing on Language Focusing on Composition Focusing on Auditory Discrimination Focusing on Visual Discrimination Focusing on Sound-Letter Correspondences Focusing on the Writer's Use of Language		*page 114* *pages 114–115* *page 116* *page 117* *page 117* *page 117* *page 117* *page 116*	*pages 20–21* *page 22*
DAY 5 **BEYOND THE SELECTION**	**THINK AND EXTEND** For the Classroom For the Home		*page 118* *page 119* ▲ Homework Notebook copying master 7	

● *Happy Times! Story Land 1*   ▲ *Learning*
■ *Places I Know* Storybook   *Resources File*

Note: Through observing and evaluating children's reading in a variety of situations and at different times, you can gather data which can help you understand and support individual children's reading development. Use the *Checklist for Observing and Evaluating Reading* in the **Evaluation Resources** section of the *Teacher's Edition.*

Cooperative Learning

Cooperative learning suggestions for *Think and Read* appear at the beginning of the *Teacher's Edition.*

Preparing to Read

▶**Relating to Children's Experiences**   Ask children if they ever learned to do something by watching someone else. Discuss the idea of learning from other people.

After the discussion, have children listen as you read aloud the poem "Watch Me." Ask children to listen for the names of things you can learn to do by watching another person. Then read the poem a second time and have children pantomime each action mentioned.

Watch Me

I can make a mud pie.
I can turn a key.
I can catch a butterfly.
I can climb a tree.
You can do it too.
Just watch me.

I can roller skate.
I can ride a bike.
I can plant some flowers.
I can take a hike.
You can do it too.
Watch me, if you like.

Notes for Cooperative Learning

Notes for Preparing to Read

I can tie my shoelaces.
I can milk a cow.
I can paint a picture.
I will start right now.
You can learn to do it.
I will show you how.

▶**Previewing and Predicting** Point to the title of the story and read it to the children. Then ask them to look at the second set of pictures and identify the chick and the duckling.

Ask children what they think the story might tell about the chick and the duckling. You may wish to model a response.

I think the story will tell about the things a chick and a duckling can do because the chick and the duckling are hatching out of eggs.

▶**Setting a Purpose** Tell children that "That Chick and the Duckling" is a story with few words. The story has just enough words to tell us what the chick and the duckling say to each other. Tell children as they listen to the story, they should think about which animal is speaking and what it says it can do.

Planning a Reading Strategy

Sharing Reading Divide the class into two groups. As you read the story once again, have one group pantomime the role of the chick and the other group pantomime the role of the duckling.

Encourage children to react spontaneously with comments and questions after you have read the story.

Reading Orally Read aloud the story. Encourage children to join in by pretending they are the chick. Each time the duckling tells what she is doing, have the children respond with "Me too."

Reading Silently Give children the opportunity to read the story independently. Explain that the illustrations will help them remember what is happening in the story.

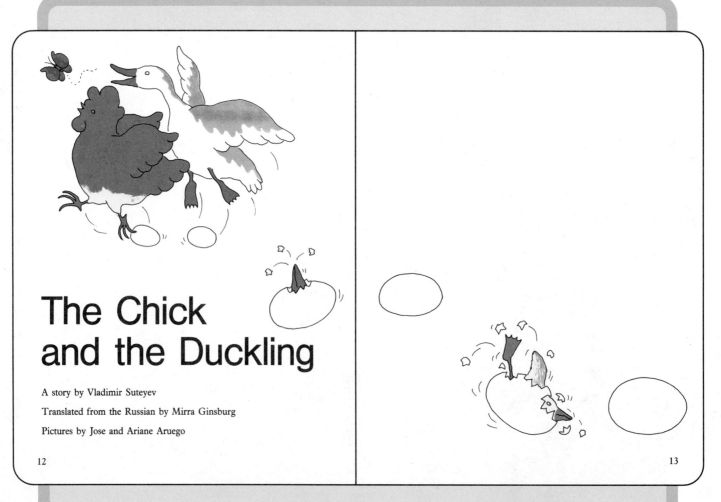

The Chick
and the Duckling

A story by Vladimir Suteyev

Translated from the Russian by Mirra Ginsburg

Pictures by Jose and Ariane Aruego

12

13

A Duckling came out
of the shell.
''I am out!'' the Duckling said.

''Me too,'' said the Chick.

''I am taking a walk,''
said the Duckling.

''Me too,''
said the Chick.

"I am digging a hole,"
said the Duckling.

"Me too,"
said the Chick.

18

19

"I have found a worm,"
said the Duckling.

"Me too,"
said the Chick.

20

21

"I am swimming,"
said the Duckling.

"Me too!"
said the Chick.

22

23

24

25

The Duckling pulled
the Chick out.

"I am going for another swim,"
said the Duckling.

"Not me,"
said the Chick.

30

Think and Discuss

Note: Through observing and evaluating children's oral language (listening and speaking) in a variety of situations and at different times, you can gather data which can help you understand and support individual children's oral development. Use the *Checklist for Observing and Evaluating Oral Language* in the **Evaluation Resources** section of the *Teacher's Edition*

Cooperative Learning

Cooperative learning suggestions for *Think and Discuss* appear at the beginning of the **Teacher's Edition.**

Remembering the Selection

Ask children to recall the story and identify

- each thing the chick does to copy the duckling.
- the order in which each thing happens.

Ask children to look at the story with you and help you count the number of things the chick does to copy the duckling *(hatches; takes a walk; digs; finds a worm; swims)*. Then make a drawing to show what happened in order. Use pictures to represent the actions. A sample drawing follows.

Things Chick Does			
1. hatches	2. walks	3. digs	4. swims

Ask children to retell the story by looking at the pictures. Then have children explain how the story ends.

Notes for Cooperative Learning   **Notes for Remembering the Selection**

Discussing the Selection

The following questions focus on self-concept. As children respond to the questions, ask them to support their answers with examples from the story. Encourage children to agree or disagree with their classmates' responses and to substantiate their opinions.

Remind children to speak clearly and loudly enough so they can be heard and understood.

1. How are the chick and the duckling the same? (**Possible responses:** *They are both yellow. The chick and the duckling have wings and beaks. They hatched from eggs and eat worms.*) *(Interpretive)*

2. How are the chick and the duckling different? (**Possible responses:** *They have different beaks and feet. The duckling is larger. They have different parents.*) *(Interpretive)*

3. Why do you think the chick thought it could swim like the duckling? (**Possible response:** *He thought he could do everything else the duckling did.*) *(Critical)*

4. What might be something the chick can show the duckling to do? (**Possible response:** *The chick might show the duckling how to catch a butterfly or scratch in the dirt.*) *(Creative)*

5. Why did the chick have to learn how to do things by himself? (**Possible responses:** *The chick had to learn to do some things by himself because he*

couldn't swim like the duckling. The chick realizes he did not have to be with the duckling all the time.) *(Interpretive)*

During the discussion, children will need to

- **interpret** why the chick went off on his own.
- **compare** the characteristics and actions of the two animals.
- **analyze** the chick's motives for copying the duckling.
- **predict** something new the chick might do.

You may wish to model responses to the questions. Use the possible responses given.

Tips for Evaluating the Oral Response

- Children should speak clearly and at the appropriate volume.
- Children should respond in complete thoughts.
- Children should ask relevant questions.

Additional Discussion Questions

Notes for Evaluating the Oral Response

Think and Write

Cooperative Learning

Cooperative learning suggestions for *Think and Write* appear at the beginning of the *Teacher's Edition.*

Making the Assignment

Have children recall that the story told about things the chick and duckling can do. Tell children that now they are going to write about more things the chick and duckling do. They will write what the duckling says. They will write what the chick says. Then they will make a class book of their writing.

Notes for Cooperative Learning

Notes for Making the Assignment

Using the Writing Process

Prewriting   Ask children to name things a chick can do and name things a duckling can do. List their responses on the chalkboard or on chart paper. Point to and read each response after you write it. You may wish to include picture clues with the responses. A sample chart follows.

Chick can	Duckling can
walk	walk
peep	quack
dig	dig
find a worm	swim
run	catch a fish

Drafting   Have children dictate sentences to you that tell what the duckling says he can do followed by what the chick says he can do. Begin by modeling sentences and writing on the chalkboard or on chart paper. An example follows.

"I quack," said the Duckling.
"I peep," said the Chick.

Write each child's dictated sentences at the bottom of a piece of paper. Then follow this procedure.

- Read the sentences to the child.
- Read the sentences with the child.
- Have the child read the sentences.
- Have the child illustrate the sentences.

Responding/Revising/Editing   After each child has dictated sentences and illustrated them, reread the sentences you wrote. Draw attention to conventions of writing such as beginning sentences with a capital letter, leaving spaces between words, ending sentences with a period, and following left-to-right progression.

Postwriting (Sharing)   Compile children's pages in a class book entitled "The Chick and the Duckling." Display the book in the reading corner for children to read independently or with each other.

Notes for Using the Writing Process

Notes for Evaluating the Written Response

Develop Skills

Strategies for developing concepts and skills related to "The Chick and the Duckling" are included in this section. Select appropriate activities to teach to the whole class, small groups, or individual children.

Developing Concepts and Skills

Language:	Action Words
Composition:	Story
Auditory Discrimination:	Dialogue
Visual Discrimination:	Animals
Sound-Letter Correspondences:	Initial Correspondence /d/d

Focusing on Language

Using Action Words Tell children that some words tell what a person, animal, or thing is doing. Ask children to listen for words that tell what the duckling and chick are doing as you reread the story "The Chick and the Duckling."

Use **Activity Book** page 20 with children. Have them identify the actions of the duckling and the chick in the pictures at the top of the page. As each action is identified, have them find the action word, run their fingers under it, and say it aloud. Have each child draw a picture of an animal of their choice doing something and dictate to you a word that names the action of the animal he or she drew. Write the action word on the writing rule for the child. You may wish to have some children copy the word.

Discuss with children some of the actions they can do. Have children identify the actions of the chick and the duckling in the picture at the top of **Activity Book** page 21, find the action word under it and say it aloud. Have each child draw a picture of an action they can do. Follow the same procedure used for the previous **Activity Book** page.

Focusing on the Writer's Use of Language

Point out the author's name (Vladimir Suteyev) on the first page of the selection and examine the pictures in "The Chick and the Duckling" with children. Ask them how the pictures help them know which animal is always first to do and say something. (**Possible response:** *The duckling did things first and he is always first in the pictures.*)

Focusing on Composition

Note: Through observing and evaluating children's writing in a variety of situations and at different times, you can gather data which can help you understand children's writing development. Use the *Checklist for Observing and Evaluating Writing* in the **Evaluation Resources** section of the **Teacher's Edition.**

Writing About an Accomplishment Discuss with children some of the things they can do. Explain that there are some things children can do better than animals like chick and duckling. Work with children to name some of these actions.

Accept their writing regardless of its stage of development. Many children will draw pictures, while others scribble, write letters, or use invented spelling. Have children share their writing with classmates.

Focusing on Auditory Discrimination

Matching the Speakers to the Story Dialogue
Divide the class in half. Ask one half to be the chick and the other half to be the duckling. Then explain that you are going to read the lines from the story that tell what the animals are saying. They will have to listen carefully to decide if the duckling or the chick is speaking. They may look at the pictures in the story as you read. When the first group hears the words duckling says, they should raise their hands. When the second group hears words the chick is saying they should raise their hands.

Begin the activity with the picture showing the duckling hatching on the first page. Read only the dialogue and wait for children's response.

Focusing on Visual Discrimination

Noticing the Differences Between Animals
Review with children that in "The Chick and the Duckling" the two animals did many things that were the same and yet the chick discovered he was different in some ways. Ask children to think of ways animals are the same. You may wish to give them two animals to compare such as a dog and a cat. Then ask children to name ways they are different. Have children look at the pictures of the duckling and the chick and name things that are the same and things that are different. Then continue by comparing the other animals pictured in the story including the hen, goose, worm, fish, and butterfly.

Focusing on Sound-Letter Correspondences

Recognizing Initial /d/d Ask children to listen for the word *duckling* as you read aloud the class book they wrote for *Think and Write.* After you read the class book, write on the chalkboard the word *duckling.* Have children say the word. Then circle the first letter of *duckling* and explain that the word begins with the letter d.

Use **Activity book** page 22 with children. Have them repeat the word *duckling* as they finger-trace the uppercase *D* and the lowercase *d.* Have children identify the pictures at the top of the page.

Have children name other words that begin with the same sound they hear at the beginning of *dinosaur* and *dog.* Then ask each child to draw a picture of something whose name begins with the same sound and dictate to you a word that names the picture. Write the word on the writing rule for the child. You may wish to have some children copy the word.

Activity Book: Language

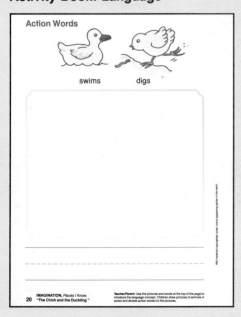

Activity Book: Language

Activity Book: Sound/Letter

Think and Extend

Cooperative Learning

Cooperative learning suggestions for *Think and Extend* appear at the beginning of the **Teacher's Edition.**

For the Classroom

Science—Discovering Things That Sink or Float

Discuss the reasons why the chick sinks. Show children how some nonliving things might sink or float if placed in water.

Fill a glass bowl with water. Gather items such as a sheet of paper, a toy boat, a rock, a pencil, a plastic lid, a coin, a cork, a spoon, a sponge and so on. Have children name each item and predict whether it will sink or float. Ask a volunteer to drop the item in the water. Record all the results on chart paper by listing the names of the items that sink or float.

Mathematics—Counting Chicks

Use the following poem to review counting from one to ten. In preparation, draw ten chicks on a sheet, leaving space between each.

Duplicate the picture and give one copy to each child. Help children cut apart the ten chicks and place them in a row on their desks. Have children count the chicks with you from one to ten. Then read the following poem, giving directions as you read.

Ten Little Chicks

Two little chicks looking for some more.
  [Children place two chicks in the center of the desk. Count one, two.]
Along came another two, and they made four.
  [Place two more chicks in the center. Count from one to four.]
Four little chicks hopping over sticks. Along came another two, and they made six.
  [Place two more chicks in the center. Count from one to six.]
Six little chicks perching on a gate. Along came another two, and they made eight.
  [Place two more chicks in the center. Count from one to eight.]
Eight little chicks ran to the pen. Along came another two, and they made ten.
  [Place the last chicks in the center. Count from one to ten.]

Notes for Cooperative Learning

Additional Classroom Activities

For the Home

The homework assignment that follows also appears on **Homework Notebook copying master 7.** You may wish to distribute the copying masters to the children.

Writing Have children dictate to a parent or other family member the names of objects with which the child plays. Ask the family member to write the naming word on a small piece of paper or index card. Encourage family members to follow this procedure after taking the child's dictation.

- Read the words to the child.
- Read the words with the child.
- Have the child read the words.
- Have the child attach the card to the object.

Reading Suggest that each child read a story with parents or other family members. Encourage them to discuss things the child can do well. Have them discuss times when the child acted independently or responsibly. acted independently or responsibly.

Additional Home Activities

Additional Books for Extended and Recreational Reading

Notes

Ideas for Cooperative Learning

Ideas for Meeting the Needs of Individual Students

Questioning Strategies

Focusing on
"Count the Friends"

While **listening** to and **reading** the selection, children will focus on individual and group activities. Children will also use **writing, listening,** and **speaking** skills as they respond to the selection. They will use higher-level **thinking** skills throughout the lesson.

OBJECTIVES

WRITING/THINKING

- To dictate a response to literature using the writing process.
- To write in the analytical/expository domain.
- To use counting words to describe how many.
- To write about a personal experience.

READING/THINKING

- To use story details to draw conclusions.
- To evaluate the importance of a story message.
- To identify activities children do alone and with others.
- To recognize the use of illustrations to tell a story.
- To recognize different numbers shown by illustrations.
- To recognize initial correspondences. (/k/c)

SPEAKING/THINKING

- To discuss personal experiences before reading a selection.
- To participate in shared reading.
- To participate in group discussions.
- To dictate a response to literature.
- To pantomime story actions.

LISTENING/THINKING

- To listen to the oral interpretation of a wordless story.
- To listen to and analyze responses to opinions about a selection.
- To listen for counting words that tell how many.
- To listen for initial sounds. (/k/)

LEARNING STRATEGIES

- Brainstorming ideas related to children's own experiences.
- Previewing the selection and making predictions about the content.
- Completing a chart to help comprehension.
- Completing a chart to help organize writing.
- Analyzing the writer's use of language.

Summary

A child playing alone is eventually joined by two, then three, then four, then five friends.

INDIVIDUAL NEEDS

Suggestions for teaching children with special needs are provided on *Teacher's Edition* page 82.

- The blue objectives may require direct instruction.

PLANNING CALENDAR

		STUDENT'S EDITIONS	TEACHER'S EDITION	ACTIVITY BOOK
DAY 1 **INTO THE SELECTION**	**THINK AND READ**			
	Preparing to Read	● pages 73–77 ■ pages 31–35	page 123	
	Planning a Reading Strategy	● pages 73–77 ■ pages 31–35	page 124	
DAYS 2-4 **THROUGH THE SELECTION**	**THINK AND DISCUSS**			
	Remembering the Selection	● pages 73–77 ■ pages 31–35	page 126	
	Discussing the Selection	● pages 73–77 ■ pages 31–35	page 127	
	THINK AND WRITE			
	Making the Assignment		page 128	
	Using the Writing Process		pages 128–129	
	Develop Skills			
	Focusing on Language		page 130	pages 23–24
	Focusing on Composition		page 131	
	Focusing on Auditory Discrimination		page 131	
	Focusing on Visual Discrimination		page 131	
	Focusing on Sound-Letter Correspondences		page 131	page 25
	Focusing on the Writer's Use of Language		page 130	
DAY 5 **BEYOND THE SELECTION**	**THINK AND EXTEND**			
	For the Classroom		page 132	
	For the Home		page 133	
			▲ Homework Notebook copying master 8	

● *Happy Times! Story Land 1*
■ *Places I Know* Storybook

▲ *Learning Resources File*

Think and Read

Note: Through observing and evaluating children's reading in a variety of situations and at different times, you can gather data which can help you understand and support individual children's reading development. Use the *Checklist for Observing and Evaluating Reading* in the **Evaluation Resources** section of the *Teacher's Edition*.

Cooperative Learning

Cooperative learning suggestions for *Think and Read* appear at the beginning of the **Teacher's Edition.**

Preparing to Read

▶**Relating to Children's Experiences** Ask children to name the games they like to play with friends. These things may include sharing toys, taking turns, being polite, inviting everyone to play.

▶**Previewing and Predicting** Point to the title of the wordless story and read it to the children. Ask them to tell what they think the selection might be about. You may wish to model a response.

I think the story might be about friends because it looks like the girl is waiting for her friends.

▶**Setting a Purpose** Tell children that as they look at the pictures in the wordless story "Count the Friends," they should think about how many friends are together and what they are doing.

Notes for Cooperative Learning

Notes for Preparing to Read

Planning a Reading Strategy

Sharing Reading   Ask volunteers to pantomime the actions of the children in each illustration. Begin with one child and gradually add four others. Ask other children to narrate as the children pantomime the five activities.

Reading Silently   Have children spend time examining the illustrations in the selection. Have them think about who is in each picture and what they are doing and saying. Have children think about the story the pictures tell.

Reading Orally   Invite children to take turns telling the story in their own words. Suggest that children point to the illustrations as they tell their stories. Also suggest that they use number words to tell how many friends are doing things together in each illustration.

Encourage children to react spontaneously with comments and questions after children have given their versions of the story.

Connections

Count the Friends

31

32

33

34

35

Think and Discuss

Cooperative Learning

Cooperative learning suggestions for *Think and Discuss* appear at the beginning of the **Teacher's Edition.**

Remembering the Selection

Ask children to recall the story and identify

- the number of children in each illustration.
- the various activities the children are doing.

Encourage children to look at the story's illustrations to help themselves recall the information. You may wish to create a class chart to record the children's responses. A sample chart follows.

"Count the Friends"		
😊 one		swings
😊😊 two		walk
😊😊😊 three		eat lunch
😊😊😊😊 four		play soccer
😊😊😊😊😊 five		ride bikes

Notes for Cooperative Learning

Notes for Remembering the Selection

Discussing the Selection

The following questions focus on individual and group activities. As children respond to the questions, ask them to support their answers with examples from the story. Encourage children to agree or disagree with their classmates' responses and to substantiate their opinions.

Remind children to speak clearly and loudly enough so they can be heard and understood.

1. Do you need a friend to ride on a swing with you? to dance? Why or why not? *(Interpretive)* (**Possible responses:** *You can swing by yourself. You can listen to music and dance by yourself too, but it is always more fun to do these things with a friend.*)

2. Four friends are playing soccer. If more children came along, could they play too? Why or why not? *(Interpretive)* (**Possible responses:** *Yes, more than four friends can play soccer. You need two teams to play and each team can have eleven players.*)

3. What things do you like to play by yourself? What things do you play with friends? *(Critical)* (**Possible responses:** *I like to play with my dolls. My friends and I go to the playground to play.*)

4. If there could be one more picture in the story, what might it show six friends doing? *(Creative)* (**Possible responses:** *Six friends might play tag; play a game of dodgeball; or have running races.*)

5. Why do you think the children in the pictures are friends? *(Interpretive)* (**Possible responses:** *The children are friends because they like to do things together. The children are friends because they like each other.*)

During the discussion, children will need to

- **analyze** why some activities can be done alone or with a friend.
- **explain** why several children could participate in a certain game.
- **identify** activities they do alone and with others.
- **predict** additional games children might play.
- **appraise** the value of friendship

You may wish to model responses to the questions. Use the possible responses given.

Tips for Evaluating the Oral Response

- Children should speak clearly and at the appropriate volume.
- Children should respond in complete thoughts.
- Children should ask relevant questions.

Additional Discussion Questions

Notes for Evaluating the Oral Response

Think and Write

Making the Assignment

Review the various activities different numbers of children did in the story. Tell children that now they are going to write about friends and things they do together. They will make a class book of their writing.

Notes for Cooperative Learning

Notes for Making the Assignment

128

Using the Writing Process

Prewriting   Ask children to name things they play alone and things they play with friends. List their responses on the chalkboard or on chart paper. Point to and read each response after you write it. A sample chart follows.

Games to Play Alone	Games to Play with Friends
jump rope	tag
blocks	hopscotch
painting	dodge ball
Tinkertoys	checkers
drawing	hide-and-seek
jacks	kickball
bike riding	jumprope

Drafting   Have children dictate sentences to you that tell the number of friends playing and the name of the game that is being played. Begin by modeling a response and writing on the chalkboard or on chart paper.

Two friends play checkers.

Write each child's dictated sentence at the bottom of a piece of paper. Then follow this procedure:

- Read the sentence to the child.
- Read the sentence with the child.
- Have the child read the sentence.
- Have the child illustrate the sentence.

Responding/Revising/Editing   After each child has dictated a sentence and illustrated it, reread the sentence you wrote. Draw attention to conventions of writing such as beginning sentences with a capital letter, leaving spaces between words, ending sentences with a period, and following left-to-right progression.

Postwriting (Sharing)   Arrange children's pages according to the number of friends they wrote about. The first pages will feature activities done by one friend and the remaining pages will follow in order from two friends to several. Compile the pages into a class book entitled "Count the Friends." Display the book in the reading corner for children to read independently or with a friend.

Notes for Using the Writing Process

Notes for Evaluating the Written Response

Develop Skills

Strategies for developing concepts and skills related to "Count the Friends" are included in this section. Select appropriate activities to teach to the whole class, small groups, or individual children.

Developing Concepts and Skills

Language:	Number Words
Composition:	Story
Auditory Discrimination:	Number Words
Visual Discrimination:	Numbers of People and Things in Illustrations
Sound-Letter Correspondences:	Initial Correspondence /k/c

Focusing on Language

Using Number Words Tell children that there are some words that tell how many. These are number words. Ask children to follow the story pictures and tell about the number of children in each picture.

Use **Activity Book** page 23 with children. Have them identify the objects and count the numbers in the pictures at the top of the page. As each is identified, have them find the word, run their fingers under it, and say it aloud. Have each child draw a picture of one or more objects and dictate to you a counting word. Write the word on the writing rule for the child. You may wish to have some children copy the word.

Activity Book page 24 also focuses on counting. Follow the same procedure used for the previous page.

Focusing on Composition

Note: Through observing and evaluating children's writing in a variety of situations and at different times, you can gather data which can help you understand children's writing development. Use the *Checklist for*

Focusing on the Writer's Use of Language

Review the pictures with children and explain that each picture changes in the story. Ask children why they think the writer decided to show a different number of children in each group. (**Possible response:** *The different numbers of children tell a story of how one friend is joined by another and another until finally there are five friends riding bikes together.*)

Writing About an Activity Ask children to think about a favorite activity they do with friends and to write about their experiences. Accept their writing regardless of its stage of development. Encourage children to draw or make attempts to write and spell. Have children share their writing by reading it aloud to a group of classmates.

Focusing on Auditory Discrimination

Telling How Many Have children listen carefully as you clap your hands three times. Ask children to tell how many times you clapped. Then clap three times again and have them count aloud one, two, three. Repeat the activity, varying the number of times you clap. Then invite children to take turns clapping as their classmates listen and identify the number.

Focusing on Visual Discrimination

Determining Numbers of People or Things in Illustrations Review with children that in "Count the Friends" different numbers of children are doing different things. Have children look at the first picture in the story and identify how many children swing *(one).* Then have them look at the second picture and tell how many children walk the dog. *(two)* Ask which picture shows more children playing together. *(the second picture)* Ask which picture shows fewer children. *(the first picture)* Then continue by comparing the numbers of children in the remaining pictures.

Focusing on Sound-Letter Correspondences

Recognizing Initial /k/c Ask the children to count from one to ten with you. After counting, write on the chalkboard the word *count.* Have children say the word. Then circle the first letter of count and explain that the word begins with the letter *c.*

Use *Activity Book* page 25 with children. Have them repeat the word count as they finger-trace the uppercase *C* and the lowercase *c.*

Have children identify the pictures at the top of the page. As each is identified, have them find the word, run their fingers under it, and say it aloud. Explain that each picture begins with the same sound they hear at the beginning of count.

Ask children to identify the letter each word begins with. Tell them that the letter c sometimes stands for the same sound they hear at the beginning of count. Then have children listen for the /k/ sound as you say the words *cup* and *car.*

Have children name other words that begin with the same sound they hear at the beginning of *cup* and *car.* Some children may name words that begin with the letter *k.* Explain that both letters sometimes make the same sound. Help them select words using the letter c spelling. Then ask each child to draw a picture of something whose name begins with the /k/ sound spelled with a c and dictate to you a word that names the picture. Write the word on the writing rule for the child. You may wish to have some children copy the word.

Activity Book: Language

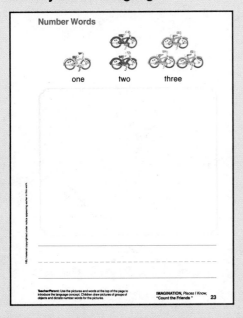

Activity Book: Language

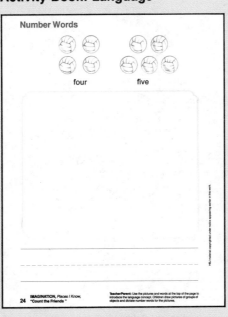

Activity Book: Sound/Letter

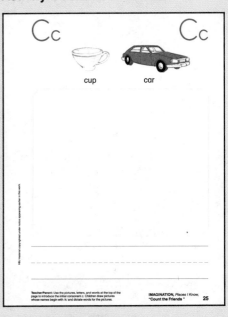

Think and Extend

Cooperative Learning

Cooperative learning suggestions for *Think and Extend* appear at the beginning of the *Teacher's Edition.*

For the Classroom

Mathematics—Using Counting Words On a very large sheet of butcher paper or newsprint draw ten large circles. Inside each circle draw a different number of objects (like squares, circles, hearts and triangles) ranging from one to ten. To play, give one child a beanbag to toss onto the sheet. Then have the child look at the circle of objects on which the beanbag has landed and count the number of objects inside. Have the child respond by completing the sentence "I see (number) (name of objects) inside the circle."

Health—Learning About Safe and Cooperative Play
Talk with children about some of the things they do to play safely and fairly. You may wish to invite a safety or fair play "expert" from the school such as the school nurse or physical education instructor. Ask children to talk about some of the things they have learned about safety and fair play by themselves. If possible, have children demonstrate or pantomime safety or fair play practices.

Notes for Cooperative Learning

Additional Classroom Activities

132

For the Home

The homework assignment that follows also appears on **Homework Notebook copying master 8.** You may wish to distribute the copying masters to the children.

Writing Have children draw a picture of their family and count the number of people. Have children dictate the number to a parent or other family member.

Encourage family members to follow this procedure after taking the child's dictation.

- Read the word to the child.
- Read the word with the child.
- Have the child read the word.

Suggest that children share their family portraits with classmates the following day.

Reading Suggest that family members find a new game to play together. Have parents or other family members read the rules for the new game so that everyone can play together cooperatively. Encourage children to tell classmates about the new family game the following day.

Additional Home Activities

For Extended and Recreational Reading

Family members may wish to read and discuss with children other books that deal with counting. You may wish to recommend the following books.

Books About Counting

1, 2, 3, to the Zoo by Eric Carle. World, 1968.

The Very Hungry Caterpillar by Eric Carle. Puffin, 1984.

Anno's Counting Book by Mitsumasa Anno. Thomas Y. Crowell, 1975.

Ten, Nine, Eight by Molly Bang. Greenwillow, 1983.

Moja Means One: Swahili Counting Book by Muriel Feelings. Dial, 1971.

Numbers by John J. Reiss. Bradbury Press, 1971.

More Books About Counting

Don't Count Your Chicks by Ingri D'Aulaire and Edgar P. D'Aulaire. Doubleday, 1973.

The Berenstain Bear's Counting Book by Stan and Jan Berenstain. Random House, 1976.

Count and See by Tana Hoban. Macmillan, 1973.

One, Two, Three: An Animal Counting Book by Marc Brown. Little, Brown, 1976.

Additional Books for Extended and Recreational Reading

Notes

Ideas for Cooperative Learning

Ideas for Meeting the Needs of Individual Students

Questioning Strategies

Focusing on "Uno, Dos, Tres, Cho-" and "One, Two, Three, Four, Five"

While **listening** to and **reading** the selection, children will focus on counting. Children will also use **writing, listening,** and **speaking** skills as they respond to the selection. They will use higher-level **thinking** skills throughout the lesson.

OBJECTIVES

WRITING/THINKING

- To dictate a response to literature using the writing process.
- To write in the practical/informative domain.
- To use describing words.
- To write about an imaginary experience.

READING/THINKING

- To analyze the writers' purposes.
- To demonstrate the actions suggested by a rhyme.
- To recognize the use of number words in rhymes.
- To identify numbers with their corresponding numerals and objects.
- To recognize initial correspondences. (/b/b)

SPEAKING/THINKING

- To discuss personal experiences before reading a selection.
- To participate in shared reading.
- To participate in group discussions.
- To dictate a response to literature.
- To interpret a rhyme through choral speaking.

LISTENING/THINKING

- To listen to the oral reading of a selection.
- To listen for number words in Spanish and English.
- To listen to and analyze responses to and opinions about a selection.
- To listen for rhyming words.
- To listen for initial sound. (/b/)

LEARNING STRATEGIES

- Brainstorming ideas related to children's own experiences.
- Previewing the selection and making predictions about the content.
- Completing a chart to help comprehension.
- Completing a list to help organize writing.
- Analyzing the writer's use of language.

Summary

"Uno, Dos, Tres, Cho-" and "One, Two, Three, Four, Five" illustrate the use of number words to create rhyme in both Spanish and English.

INDIVIDUAL NEEDS

Suggestions for teaching children with special needs are provided on *Teacher's Edition* page 82.

- The blue objectives may require direct instruction.

PLANNING CALENDAR

		STUDENT'S EDITIONS	TEACHER'S EDITION	ACTIVITY BOOK
DAY 1 **INTO THE SELECTION**	**THINK AND READ**			
	Preparing to Read	● *pages 78–83* ■ *pages 36–41*	*page 137*	
	Planning a Reading Strategy	● *pages 78–83* ■ *pages 36–41*	*page 138*	
DAYS 2-4 **THROUGH THE SELECTION**	**THINK AND DISCUSS**			
	Remembering the Selection	● *pages 78–83* ■ *pages 36–41*	*page 140*	
	Discussing the Selection	● *pages 78–83* ■ *pages 36–41*	*page 141*	
	THINK AND WRITE			
	Making the Assignment		*page 142*	
	Using the Writing Process		*pages 142–143*	
	Develop Skills			
	Focusing on Language		*page 144*	*pages 26–27*
	Focusing on Composition		*page 145*	
	Focusing on Auditory Discrimination		*page 145*	
	Focusing on Visual Discrimination		*page 145*	
	Focusing on Sound-Letter Correspondences		*page 145*	*page 28*
	Focusing on the Writer's Use of Language		*page 144*	
DAY 5 **BEYOND THE SELECTION**	**THINK AND EXTEND**			
	For the Classroom		*page 146*	
	For the Home		*page 147*	
			▲ Homework Notebook copying master 9	

● *Happy Times!* **Story Land 1**
■ *Places I Know* **Storybook**

▲ **Learning Resources File**

136

Note: Through observing and evaluating children's reading in a variety of situations and at different times, you can gather data which can help you understand and support individual children's reading development. Use the *Checklist for Observing and Evaluating Reading* in the **Evaluation Resources** section of the ***Teacher's Edition.***

Cooperative Learning

Cooperative learning suggestions for *Think and Read* appear at the beginning of the ***Teacher's Edition.***

Preparing to Read

▶**Relating to Children's Experiences** Ask children to name any songs or rhymes they know that have helped them learn to count. Sing or chant those that are commonly known. *("One, Two, Buckle My Shoe," "One Potato, Two Potato, " "This Old Man.")* Encourage children to demonstrate any actions they use while chanting or singing these rhymes and songs.

▶**Previewing and Predicting** Point to the title of the first rhyme and read it to the children. Explain that the words *uno, dos, tres* are Spanish meaning *one, two, three.* Have them examine the picture for a moment. Then point to the title of the second rhyme and read it to the children. Have them examine the pictures that accompany this rhyme. Then ask children why they think both are called counting rhymes. You may wish to model a response.

I know the words one, two, three, four, and five. *I use these words to count. The names of the rhymes use number words so the rhymes must teach you to count.*

▶**Setting a Purpose** Tell children that as you read each rhyme, they should listen for the number words that are used and think about the actions in each rhyme.

Notes for Cooperative Learning

Notes for Preparing to Read

Planning a Reading Strategy

Sharing Reading Read aloud each rhyme several times, sharing the illustrations and pointing to the text. Draw attention to the number words that are used, both Spanish and English and ask children to count with you as you read the rhymes.

Encourage children to react spontaneously with comments and questions after you have read the rhymes. You may wish to have children move their bodies to accompany the rhythm of the two rhymes.

Reading Orally Read aloud the rhymes. Encourage children to join in by reciting the number words in each rhyme. After hearing each several times, children may be able to recite them with you.

Reading Silently Give children the opportunity to read the rhymes independently. Explain that the illustrations may help them remember the lines of the rhymes.

Uno, Dos, Tres, Cho-

A Mexican counting rhyme

Uno, dos, tres, cho-
ōō′·nō, dōs, tres, chō-

Uno, dos, tres, co-
ōō′·nō, dōs, tres, kō-

Uno, dos, tres, la-
ōō′·nō, dōs, tres, lä-

Uno, dos, tres, te.
ōō′·nō, dōs, tres, tā.

Chocolate, chocolate,
chō′·kō·lä·tā, chō′·kō·lä·tā

¡bate, bate, el chocolate!
bä′·tā, bä′·tā, el chō′·kō·lä·tā

36

Picture by Sharon Harker

37

138

One, Two, Three, Four, Five

An old counting rhyme

One, two, three, four, five,

I caught a fish alive,

Pictures by Dennis Ziemienski

38

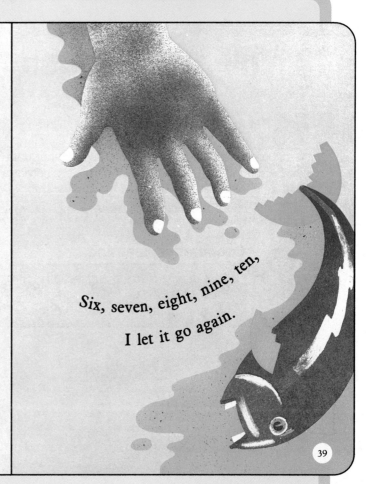

Six, seven, eight, nine, ten,

I let it go again.

39

Why did you let it go?
Because it bit my finger so.

40

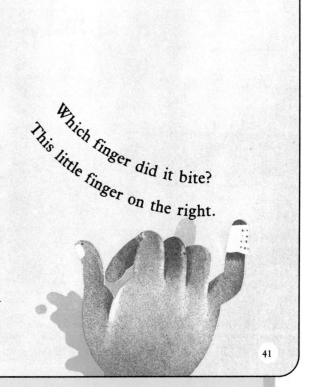

Which finger did it bite?
This little finger on the right.

41

Think and Discuss

Note: Through observing and evaluating children's oral language (listening and speaking) in a variety of situations and at different times, you can gather data which can help you understand and support individual children's oral development. Use the *Checklist for Observing and Evaluating Oral Language* in the **Evaluation Resources** section of the *Teacher's Edition.*

Cooperative Learning

Cooperative learning suggestions for *Think and Discuss* appear at the beginning of the **Teacher's Edition.**

Remembering the Selection

Ask children to recall the rhymes and identify

- number words in English.
- number words in Spanish.

Encourage children to look at the rhymes and the accompanying illustrations to recall the number words. You may wish to create a class chart to show the number words with the corresponding numerals as well as pictures to serve as a visual aid. A sample chart follows.

Numbers		
1 one	1 uno	
2 two	2 dos	
3 three	3 tres	
4 four		
5 five		
6 six		
7 seven		
8 eight		
9 nine		
10 ten		

Notes for Cooperative Learning

Notes for Remembering the Selection

140

Discussing the Selection

The following questions focus on counting rhymes. As children respond to the questions, ask them to support their answers with examples from the rhymes. Encourage children to agree or disagree with their classmates' responses and to substantiate their opinions.

Remind children to speak clearly and loudly enough so they can be heard and understood.

1. What do you think the writers want you to learn from both rhymes? (**Possible response:** *The writers want me to learn how to count and speak in two languages.*) *(Critical)*

2. Show what someone might be doing while saying the rhyme "Uno, Dos, Tres, Cho-." (**Possible response:** *Child may demonstrate mixing a chocolate drink.*) *(Interpretive)*

3. Name different times when you use counting to do something. (**Possible responses:** *I count when I play Hide and Seek. I count when I jump rope. I count when I want to know how many pennies I have.*) *(Creative)*

4. How high can you count? (*Encourage children to count aloud.*) *(Literal)*

5. Why do you think it is important to know how to count? (**Possible responses:** *You have to know how to count if you want to buy something. If you want to do well in school, you have to count.*) *(Critical)*

During the discussion, children will need to

- **analyze** the writer's purpose.
- **demonstrate** the actions suggested by the rhyme "Uno, Dos, Tres, Cho-."
- **relate** the act of counting to their everyday experiences.
- **measure** their counting skills.
- **appraise** the value of learning how to count.

You may wish to model responses to the questions. Use the possible responses given.

Tips for Evaluating the Oral Response

- Children should speak clearly and at the appropriate volume.
- Children should respond in complete thoughts.
- Children should ask relevant questions.

Additional Discussion Questions

Notes for Evaluating the Oral Response

Think and Write

Cooperative Learning

Cooperative learning suggestions for *Think and Write* appear at the beginning of the *Teacher's Edition.*

Making the Assignment

Review with children that the two rhymes used number words to help them learn to count. Tell them now they will use number words to write about things in their classroom. They will make a class counting book of their writing.

Notes for Cooperative Learning

Notes for Making the Assignment

Using the Writing Process

Prewriting   Ask children to look about the classroom and to name different things they see. Have them count the number of different things. List their responses on the chalkboard or on chart paper. Point to and read each word after you write it. A sample chart follows.

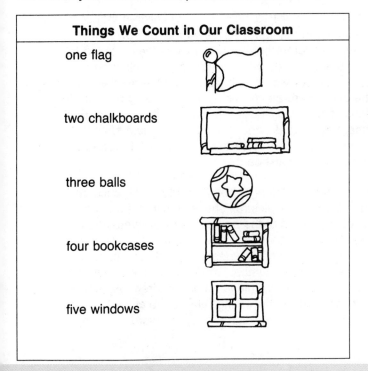

Things We Count in Our Classroom	
one flag	
two chalkboards	
three balls	
four bookcases	
five windows	

Drafting   Have children dictate sentences to you that tell about the number of things they have in the classroom. Begin by modeling a response and writing on the chalkboard or on chart paper. An example follows.

We have one flag in our classroom.

Write each child's dicated sentence at the bottom of a piece of paper. Then follow this procedure.

- Read the sentence to the child.
- Read the sentence with the child.
- Have the children read the sentence.
- Have the child illustrate the sentence showing the number of objects.

Responding/Revising/Editing   After each child has dictated a sentence and illustrated it, read the sentences they wrote. Draw attention to conventions of writing such as beginning sentences with a capital letter, leaving spaces between words, ending sentences with a period, and following left-to-right progression.

Postwriting (Sharing)   Arrange children's sentences in numerical order. Compile the papers into a class counting book entitled "We Can Count." Display the book in the reading corner along with other counting books for children to read independently or with each other.

Notes for Using the Writing Process

Notes for Evaluating the Written Response

Develop Skills

Strategies for developing concepts and skills related to "Uno, Dos, Tres, Cho-" and "One, Two, Three, Four, Five" are included in this section. Select appropriate activities to teach to the whole class, small groups, or individual children.

Developing Concepts and Skills

Language:	Describing Words
Composition:	Recipe
Auditory Discrimination:	Rhyming Words
Visual Discrimination:	Counting
Sound-Letter Correspondences:	Initial correspondence /b/b

Focusing on Language

Using Describing Words   Tell children that some words name numbers. These words tell how many. Remind children that the two rhymes they listened to used the number words one through ten. Ask children to say these number words with you. Write the number words on the chalkboard as children say them. Sing or chant the song "One, Two Buckle My Shoe" with children. Each time they hear a number word they should raise their hands. When they raise their hands, point to the number word on the chalkboard.

Use **Activity Book** pages 26 and 27 with children. Have them identify the pictures showing different numbers of things at the top of the pages. As each number word is identified, have them find the word, run their fingers under it, and say it aloud. Have each child draw a picture representing one number word and dictate to you the word that tells how many things he or she drew. Write the number word on the writing rule for the child. You may wish to have some children copy the word.

Focusing on the Writer's Use of Language

Ask children to identify the number words the writers used in their rhymes. Discuss why the writers used number words in their rhymes. (**Possible responses:** *The number words make the rhymes sound fun to read. Using number words in rhymes is a good way to teach children how to count. Some of the number words rhyme with other words.*)

Focusing on Composition

Note: Through observing and evaluating children's writing in a variety of situations and at different times, you can gather data which can help you understand children's writing development. Use the *Checklist for Observing and Evaluating Writing* in the **Evaluation Resources** section of the *Teacher's Edition.*

Writing a Recipe   Ask children to make up their own recipe for their favorite meal.

Accept their writing regardless of its stage of development. Many children will draw pictures, numbers or make attempts to spell. Have children share their writing by reading it aloud to you, a group of classmates, or family members.

Focusing on Auditory Discrimination

Rhyming Words   Read aloud the rhyme "One, Two, Three, Four, Five." Then repeat the words *five* and *alive*. Ask children to tell how the words sound the same. (**Possible response:** *They both have the same ending sounds.*) Then ask children to name other words that have the same ending sound they hear in *five* and *alive. (dive, hive)* Tell children that the words that end with the same ending sounds are called **rhyming words.**

Focusing on Visual Discrimination

Matching Numerals and Objects   Make the following puzzle activity for children to use independently to review numerals. You will need construction paper and markers to make the puzzle pieces.

- On one half of each puzzle piece write a numeral from one to ten and the corresponding number word. On the second half of the puzzle piece draw the corresponding number of objects. Example:

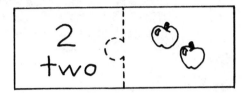

- Make a puzzle piece for each of the numerals from one to ten. Cut the pieces apart and scramble them. Have children match the pieces.

Focusing on Sound-Letter Correspondences

Recognizing Initial /b/b   Use *Activity Book* page 28 with children. Have them repeat the word *bite* as they finger-trace the uppercase *B* and the lowercase *b.*

Have children identify the pictures at the top of the page. As each is identified, have them find the word, run their fingers under it, and say it aloud. Explain that each picture begins with the same sound they hear at the beginning of *bite.*

Then ask each child to draw a picture of something whose name begins with the same sound and dicate to you a word that names the picture. Write the word on the writing rule for the child. You may wish to have some children copy the word.

Activity Book: Language

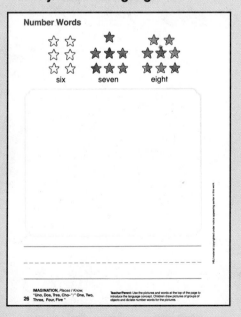

Activity Book: Language

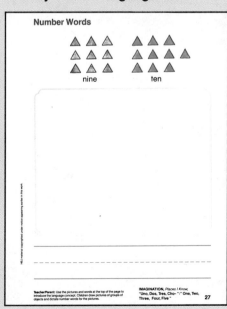

Activity Book: Sound/Letter

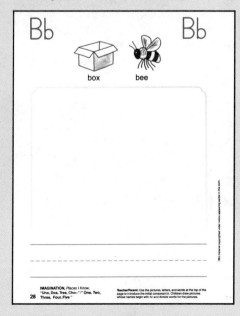

Think and Extend

Cooperative Learning

Cooperative learning suggestions for *Think and Extend* appear at the beginning of the *Teacher's Edition.*

For the Classroom

Mathematics—Fishing for Numbers Make a fishing game for children to play to review numbers.

- Draw ten doubled fish shapes from construction paper. Fold each fish along the dotted line. On the outside of each fish draw dots to represent a number from one to ten.

- On the inside of the fish write the corresponding number and number word from one to ten to represent the number of dots.

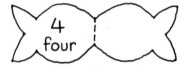

- Use a large paper clip to keep each fish closed so the numeral and number word cannot be seen.
- Place the ten fish dot-side up on the floor.
- Allow the children to fish using a pole made from a magnet tied to a length of string that has been attached to the end of a ruler.
- When a child "catches" a fish, he or she must count the dots, and say the number. Some children may be able to write the numeral on a separate sheet. The answer can be checked by looking inside the fish. If the answer is correct, the player may keep the fish. The player with the most fish at the end of the game is the winner.

Social Studies—Counting in Other Languages
Review counting from one to three in English and Spanish. Then teach children to count from one to three in one of the following languages.

French		Japanese	
un	/än/	ichi	/ē′•chē/
deux	/du/	ni	/nē/
trois	/twä/	san	/sän/

Swahili	
moja	/mo′•jä/
mbili	/mə•bē•lē/
tatu	/tä′•too/

Notes for Cooperative Learning   **Additional Classroom Activities**

For the Home

The homework assignment that follows also appears on **Homework Notebook copying master 9.** You may wish to distribute the copying masters to the children.

Writing Have children ask parents to help them take an inventory of things at home such as the number of rooms in the house, number of chairs, number of windows, number of tables, and so on. Have children dictate sentences, naming these items and using number words. Encourage family members to follow this procedure after taking the child's dictation.

- Read the sentences to the child.
- Read the sentences with the child.
- Have the child read the sentences.
- Have the child illustrate the sentences showing how many of each.

Suggest that children share their inventories with classmates the following day.

Reading Have family members read and discuss with children the importance of things around the house that have numerals on them. Suggest that parents read the numerals on the telephone as well as write and read the family's home phone number, the numerals on the house or mailbox, the numerals on a clock, and the numerals (and letters) on car license plates.

For Extended and Recreational Reading

You may wish to recommend the following books about counting for children to share with family members. Encourage family members to visit the public library with children to select books to be read.

Books About Counting

Ten, Nine, Eight by Molly Bang. Greenwillow Books, 1983.

Anno's Counting House by Mitsumasa Anno. Philomel/Putnam, 1982.

Numbers by John J. Reiss. Bradbury, 1971.

Inch by Inch by Leo Lionni. Astor-Honor, 1962.

Moja Means One: Swahili Counting Book by Muriel Feelings. Dial, 1971.

More Books About Counting

One Wide River to Cross by Barbara Emberley. Prentice-Hall, 1966.

Over in the Meadow by John Langstaff. Harcourt Brace Jovanovich, 1957.

Cat Count by Betsy Lewin. Dodd, Mead, 1981.

Harriet Goes to the Circus by Betsy Maestro and Guilo Maestro. Crown, 1977.

Additional Home Activities

Additional Books for Extended and Recreational Reading

Notes

Ideas for Cooperative Learning

Ideas for Meeting the Needs of Individual Students

Questioning Strategies

Focusing on "Higher Than a House" and "Star Light, Star Bright"

While **listening** to and **reading** the selection, children will focus on wishes. Children will also use **writing, listening,** and **speaking** skills as they respond to the selection. They will use higher-level **thinking** skills throughout the lesson.

OBJECTIVES

WRITING/THINKING

- To dictate a response to literature using the writing process.
- To write in the imaginative/narrative domain.
- To use naming words.
- To write about an imaginary experience.

READING/THINKING

- To identify possible answers to a riddle.
- To relate personal experiences to the theme of a rhyme.
- To recognize the use of an asking sentence in a riddle.
- To distinguish between high and low.
- To recognize initial correspondences. (/w/w, /h/h)

SPEAKING/THINKING

- To discuss personal experiences before reading a selection.
- To participate in shared reading.
- To participate in group discussions.
- To dictate a response to literature.
- To read aloud a riddle.
- To participate in a choral reading of a rhyme.

LISTENING/THINKING

- To listen to the oral reading of a selection.
- To listen to and analyze responses to and opinions about a selection.
- To listen for rhyming words.
- To listen for initial sounds. (/w/, /h/)

LEARNING STRATEGIES

- Brainstorming ideas related to children's own experiences.
- Previewing the selection and making predictions about the content.
- Completing a chart to help comprehension.
- Completing a chart to help organize writing.
- Analyzing the writer's use of language.

Summary

You must imagine yourself gazing into the sky above rooftops and treetops to suggest an answer to the old riddle "Higher Than a House." The popular rhyme "Star Light, Star Bright" is said by many people when they see the first star of the evening.

INDIVIDUAL NEEDS

Suggestions for teaching children with special needs are provided on *Teacher's Edition* page 82.

- The blue objectives may require direct instruction.

PLANNING CALENDAR

		STUDENT'S EDITIONS	TEACHER'S EDITION	ACTIVITY BOOK
DAY 1 INTO THE SELECTION	**THINK AND READ**			
	Preparing to Read	● *pages 84–85* ■ *pages 42–43*	*page 151*	
	Planning a Reading Strategy	● *pages 84–85* ■ *pages 42–43*	*page 152*	
DAYS 2-4 THROUGH THE SELECTION	**THINK AND DISCUSS**			
	Remembering the Selection	● *pages 84–85* ■ *pages 42–43*	*page 154*	
	Discussing the Selection	● *pages 84–85* ■ *pages 42–43*	*page 155*	
	THINK AND WRITE			
	Making the Assignment		*page 158*	
	Using the Writing Process		*page 159*	
	Develop Skills			
	Focusing on Language		*page 160*	*pages 29–30*
	Focusing on Composition		*page 161*	
	Focusing on Auditory Discrimination		*page 161*	
	Focusing on Visual Discrimination		*page 161*	
	Focusing on Sound-Letter Correspondences		*page 161*	*pages 31–32*
	Focusing on the Writer's Use of Language		*page 160*	
DAY 5 BEYOND THE SELECTION	**THINK AND EXTEND**			
	For the Classroom		*page 162*	
	For the Home		*page 163*	
			▲ Homework Notebook copying master 10	

● ***Happy Times! Story Land 1***
■ ***Places I Know* Storybook**

▲ *Learning Resources File*

150

Note: Through observing and evaluating children's reading in a variety of situations and at different times, you can gather data which can help you understand and support individual children's reading development. Use the *Checklist for Observing and Evaluating Reading* in the **Evaluation Resources** section of the *Teacher's Edition.*

Cooperative Learning

Cooperative learning suggestions for *Think and Read* appear at the beginning of the **Teacher's Edition.**

Preparing to Read

►**Relating to Children's Experiences**   Have children look outside through classroom windows or a doorway. Call on volunteers to name the things they see in the sky. Then have children imagine the nighttime sky. Have them tell you what they see.

   After the discussion, have children listen as you read aloud the poem "Day Sky, Night Sky." Ask children to name the things mentioned in the poem that are seen in the day sky and in the night sky.

Day Sky, Night Sky

The day sky is full of wonderful sights.
Butterflies and birds
That sing a pretty song.
The brightly shining sun
Smiling all day long.
Colorful rainbows,
Kites flying high,
Jet planes soaring
Across blue sky.

The night sky is full of wonderful sights.
Twinkling stars
That fill the black sky,
With a cloud or two
Slowly passing by.

(poem continues on next page)

Notes for Cooperative Learning

Notes for Preparing to Read

A tiny firefly
Shines a bright light,
While the moon overhead
Wishes us a good night.

▶**Previewing and Predicting**   Point to the title of the riddle and then to the title of the rhyme. Ask the children to look at the pictures that go with the two selections and tell what they think the riddle and rhyme will be about. You may wish to model a response.

I think the riddle and rhyme might be about the sky at night because the sky looks dark and I see some stars in the sky.

▶**Setting a Purpose**   Tell children that as they listen to "Higher Than a House" and "Star Light, Star Bright" they should think about ways that the riddle and the rhyme are alike.

Planning a Reading Strategy

Sharing Reading   Read aloud the riddle several times, sharing the illustration with children. As you read ask the children to look in the picture for clues to the answer. Place special emphasis on the question that ends the riddle by pausing slightly after reading the first two lines. At this time you may wish to ask children for possible answers to the riddle. Point out that the riddle can have more than one answer.

Then read aloud the rhyme "Star Light, Star Bright," sharing the illustrations and pointing to the text. Encourage children to react spontaneously with comments and questions, after you have read the rhyme.

Reading Orally   Read aloud the riddle "Higher Than a House." Ask children to join in by reading the question with you. Then have the children read the entire riddle with you. Read aloud the rhyme "Star Light, Star Bright" and ask children to recite the rhyme with you.

Reading Silently   Give children the opportunity to "read" the riddle and the rhyme independently. Children may want to read in pairs and then ask each other to answer the riddle or share wishes they would make on a star.

Picture by Jane Teiko Oka

Higher Than a House

An old riddle

Higher than a house,
Higher than a tree,
Oh, whatever can that be?

(Many answers,
such as a star,
the moon, a spaceship.)

42

Star Light, Star Bright

An old rhyme

Star light, star bright,
First star I see tonight,
I wish I may, I wish I might,
Have the wish I wish tonight.

43

152

Notes

Ideas for Cooperative Learning

Ideas for Meeting the Needs of Individual Students

Questioning Strategies

Think and Discuss

Cooperative Learning

Cooperative learning suggestions for *Think and Discuss* appear at the beginning of the **Teacher's Edition.**

Remembering the Selection

Ask children to recall the riddle and the rhyme and identify

- the answer to the riddle "Higher Than a House."
- what in the sky they need to wish on when they recite the rhyme "Star Light, Star Bright."

Encourage children to look at the illustration shown with the riddle and the rhyme for ideas. Discuss how the riddle and rhyme both tell about things in the sky. Have children recall the names of these things. Begin by reading the upside-down answers to the riddle with children. You may wish to create a class chart to record children's responses. Point to and read each word after writing.

Things in the Night Sky	
moon	🌙
stars	⭐
airplane	✈
skyscrapers	🏙

Notes for Cooperative Learning

Notes for Remembering the Selection

Discussing the Selection

The following questions focus on wishes. As children respond to the questions, ask them to support their answers with examples from the riddle and rhyme. Encourage children to agree or disagree with their classmates' responses and to substantiate their opinions. Remind children to speak clearly and loudly.

1. What does the rhyme say you should do when you see the first star in the sky? (**Possible response:** *The rhyme says you should make a wish on the first star you see.*) *(Literal)*

2. Why do you think people look for the first star and make a wish? (**Possible responses:** *They want something very special. They want their wish to come true.*) *(Critical)*

3. Name different times when you can make wishes. (**Possible responses:** *I can make a wish when I blow out the candles on a birthday cake or when I break off the larger piece of a wishbone or when I throw a coin in a wishing well.*) *(Creative)*

4. Have you ever had a wish come true? What was your wish? *(Encourage children to share their wishes.) (Creative)*

5. Do wishes always come true? (**Possible responses:** *No, they do not always come true. Even when you wish very hard, they may not happen.*) *(Critical)*

During the discussion, children will need to

- **identify** what people do when they see the first star in the sky.
- **analyze** why people look for the first bright star in the evening sky.
- **recall** situations in which they have made wishes and times when they have come true.
- **evaluate** the theme of the poem "Star Light, Star Bright."

You may wish to model responses to the questions. Use the possible responses given.

Tips for Evaluating the Oral Response

- Children should speak clearly and at the appropriate volume.
- Children should respond in complete thoughts.
- Children should ask relevant questions.

Additional Discussion Questions

Notes for Evaluating the Oral Response

Think and Discuss

Talking About Stories and Poems

The children have read the stories and poems in "Places I Know." Have children compare and contrast the selections. Use the discussion questions and the possible responses provided.

1. Do you think the chick would want to follow you to city places? Why or why not? (**Possible responses:** *The city would be too dangerous for the chick. There are too many people walking and too many cars, buses, and trucks in the streets. The chick might get hurt.*)
2. How might the house for a chick, a duck, a cow, a horse, and a donkey be alike? (**Possible responses:** *All these animals could live in the country. They all might have a home on a farm.*)
3. If the duckling could fly higher than a house, do you think the chick would follow? Why or why not? (**Possible responses:** *Chicks cannot fly that high. If the chick tried to fly that high, she might get hurt, or she might land on a roof and not be able to get down.*)
4. Which special place mentioned in the poems and stories in this unit would you like to be in? *(Encourage children to share their ideas.)*

During the discussion children will talk about

- how some places are suitable for certain people, animals, and things while other places are not.
- how the selections relate to the theme of the unit.

Bookshelf

Suggest the following books for children to read. Introduce children to these and other selections that relate to the theme of the unit.

A New Home, a New Friend by Hans Wilhelm. Random House, 1985. The new house Michael just moved into seems big and gloomy until he finds Waldo, a shaggy dog, to help him explore.

Oscar Mouse Finds a House by Moira Miller. Dial Books, 1985. Oscar Mouse hunts and hunts until he finds just the right place for his new house.

This Is the Place for Me by Joanna Cole. Scholastic, 1986. Clumsy Morty Bear makes a mess at home and searches for a better place to live, but none is quite right.

Demi's Count the Animals 1, 2, 3 by Demi. Grosset, 1986. Read the rhymes and carefully count all the animals in the pictures.

Goodbye, House by Frank Asch. Prentice-Hall, 1986. Bear experiences a painful feeling when he is faced with moving from his home.

Notes

Ideas for Cooperative Learning

Ideas for Meeting the Needs of Individual Students

Questioning Strategies

Think and Write

Making the Assignment

Review that the old rhyme "Star Light, Star Bright" is often said when making a wish on the first star seen in the nighttime sky. Tell children that they are now going to write about wishes they have. They will make a bulletin board display of their writing.

Notes for Cooperative Learning

Notes for Making the Assignment

Using the Writing Process

Prewriting Ask children to name things they wish they could have. List their responses on the chalkboard or on chart paper. Point to and read each word after you write it. A sample chart follows.

Things We Wish For
puppy
kitten
swings
bike

Drafting Have children dictate sentences to you that tell what they wish for. Begin by modeling a response and writing it on the chalkboard or on chart paper. An example follows.

I wish for a puppy.

Write each child's dictated sentence at the bottom of a piece of paper. Then follow this procedure.

- Read the sentence to the child.
- Read the sentence with the child.
- Have the child read the sentence.
- Have the child illustrate the sentence.

Responding/Revising/Editing After each child has dictated a sentence and illustrated it, reread the sentence you wrote. Draw attention to conventions of writing such as beginning sentences with a capital letter, leaving spaces between words, ending sentences with a period, and following left-to-right progression.

Postwriting (Sharing) Attach each child's paper to the center of a large construction paper star. Pin all the stars on the bulletin board with a caption such as "Wishing on a Star." Invite children to visit the bulletin board and read the wishes of their classmates.

Notes for Using the Writing Process

Notes for Evaluating the Written Response

Develop Skills

Strategies for developing concepts and skills related to "Higher Than a House" and "Star Light, Star Bright" are included in this section. Select appropriate activities to teach to the whole class, small groups, or individual children.

Developing Concepts and Skills

Language:	Naming Words
Composition:	Story
Auditory Discrimination:	Rhyming Words
Visual Discrimination:	High and Low
Sound-Letter Correspondences:	Initial Correspondence /w/w and /h/h

Focusing on Language

Using Naming Words   Reread the riddle "Higher Than a House." Have children recall the names of the things in the sky that were answers to the riddle "Higher Than a House." Then reread the rhyme "Star Light, Star Bright" and ask children to name the thing in the sky that you can wish on. Write the words that name things in the sky on the chalkboard as children dictate. Point to each word and read it after writing.

Use **Activity Book** page 29 with children. Have them identify the pictures of things in the sky at the top of the page. As each is identified, have them find the word, run their fingers under it, and say it aloud. Have each child draw a picture of something found in the sky and dictate to you a word that names the thing. Write the naming word on the writing rule for the child. You may wish to have some children copy the word.

Activity Book page 30 focuses on things that fly in the sky. Follow the same procedure used for the previous page. This time, ask children to think of an imaginary vehicle they would wish for so they could fly in the sky.

Focusing on the Writer's Use of Language

Help children identify the words the writer used in the riddle "Higher Than a House" to ask a question. *(Oh, whatever can that be?)* Ask why the writer may have decided to end the riddle with a sentence that asks a question. (**Possible responses:** *Many riddles end with asking sentences. The writer is asking the reader to answer the riddle.*)

Activity Book: Language

Focusing on Composition

Note: Through observing and evaluating children's writing in a variety of situations and at different times, you can gather data which can help you understand children's writing development. Use the *Checklist for Observing and Evaluating Writing* in the **Evaluation Resources** section of the *Teacher's Edition.*

Writing About A Star Have children pretend they each have their very own star in the sky. Have them think about what the star looks like, how big and bright it is, what they would do with such a star, and what they would name it. Have children then write about their stars.

Accept their writing regardless of its stage of development. Many children will draw pictures while others scribble, write letters, or use invented spelling. Have children share their writing by reading it aloud to you, a group of classmates, or family members.

Focusing on Auditory Discrimination

Listening for Rhyming Words Read aloud the rhyme "Star Light, Star Bright." Then repeat the words light and bright. Ask children to tell how the words sound the same. *(They both have the same ending sounds.)* Then ask children to find other words in the rhyme that have the same ending sounds as *light* and *bright. (might, tonight)* Review that words that end with the same ending sounds are called **rhyming words.**

Focusing on Visual Discrimination

Discriminating Objects That Are High and Low
Review with children that in the riddle and rhyme they read about and talked about things that were higher than a house and a tree. Have children look at the illustrations for both "Higher Than a House" and "Star Light, Star Bright." Have them compare the heights of things.

Focusing on Sound-Letter Correspondences

Recognizing Initial /w/w Use **Activity Book** page 31 with children. Have them repeat the word *wish* as they finger-trace the uppercase *W* and the lowercase *w*. Have children identify the pictures at the top of the page. As each is identified, have them find the word, run their fingers under it. and say it aloud. Explain that each word begins with the same sound they hear at the beginning of *wish:*

Have children name other words that begin with the same sound they hear at the beginning of *watch* and *window.* Then ask each child to draw a picture of something whose name begins with the same sound and dictate to you a word that names the picture. Write the word on the writing rule for the child. You may wish to have some children copy the word.

Recognizing Initial /h/h Ask children to listen for the word *higher* as you reread aloud the riddle "Higher Than a House." After rereading the selection, write on the chalkboard the word *higher.* Have children say the word. Explain that the word begins with the letter *h*.

Use **Activity Book** page 32 with children, Have them repeat the word *higher* as they finger-trace the uppercase *H* and the lowercase *h*. Follow the same procedure used for the previous sound-letter correspondence and have children draw pictures of something whose name begins with the sound /h/.

Activity Book: Language

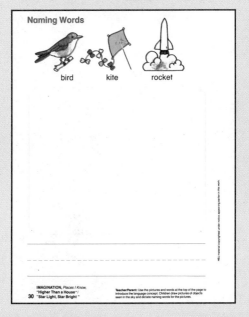

Activity Book: Sound/Letter

Activity Book: Sound/Letter

Think and Extend

For the Classroom

Science—Observing Things in the Sky   Conduct an outdoor activity with children that enables them to experience things going up in the air toward the sky.
Option 1: Bring helium filled balloons to school. Have children help you compose a friendly note to attach to each balloon including your name and school address. Someone finding the balloon may want to respond with a note. Have children take the balloons outside and let them go. Allow children to watch until they are out of sight. Upon returning to the classroom, have children recall what happened to the balloons and where they went. Record their responses on an experience chart.
Option 2:   Have children help you assemble a kite from a kit and take it outdoors to fly on a windy day. You may wish to have children take turns flying the kite.

Music—Learning a Song   Teach children the music and words to the song "Twinkle, Twinkle, Little Star." Then have children make twinkling stars to use while singing the song.

- Give each child two identical star shapes cut from construction paper.
- Have them apply glue to one side of each star and sprinkle glitter on the glue.
- Once the glue has dried, take each child's two stars and place them back to back with an unsharpened pencil in between. The glitter will be on the outside. Staple the two stars together. Tape the bottom of the stars to the pencil. See the illustration.

- Have children take the pencil, hold it between their two palms, and move it back and forth so that the glittering star twirls and sparkles.
- As children sing the song, have them make their stars twinkle by turning them.

Notes for Cooperative Learning

Additional Classroom Activities

For the Home

The homework assignment that follows also appears on **Homework Notebook copying master 10.** You may wish to distribute the copying masters to the children.

Writing   Suggest that children go outside on a clear night with a parent or family member to do some star gazing. Then have them dictate sentences telling what they see in the sky. Encourage family members to follow this procedure after taking the child's dictation.

- Read the sentences to the child.
- Read the sentences with the child.
- Have the child read the sentences.
- Have the child illustrate the sentences.

Suggest that children share their sentences with classmates the following day.

Reading   Have family members read, make up, and discuss riddles and jokes and their possible answers.

For Extended and Recreational Reading

You may wish to recommend the following books of riddles and rhymes for children to share with family members.

Encourage family members to visit the public library with children to select riddle books.

Books of Riddles

The Riddle of the Drum, A Tale from Tizapan, Mexico retold by Verna Aardema. Four Winds Press, 1979.

Sylvester and the Magic Pebble by William Steig. Windmill Books, 1969.

Why the Sun and the Moon Live in the Sky by Elphinstone Dayrell. Houghton Mifflin, 1977.

London Bridge Is Falling Down by Peter Spier. Doubleday, 1985.

Father Fox's Pennyrhymes by Clyde Watson. Harper & Row, 1971.

The Cloud Book by Tomie De Paola. Holiday, 1975.

More Books of Riddles and Rhymes

The Carsick Zebra and Other Animal Riddles by David Adler. Holiday, 1983.

The Hodgepodge Book by Duncan Emrich. Four Winds Press, 1972.

Additional Home Activities

Additional Books for Extended and Recreational Reading

Unit 3

Imagine That!

Theme: The strange and wondrous possibilities of make-believe

Reading Selections	Writing Assignments
• The Three Bears	• Dictate Sentences About the Three Bears
• Changes, Changes	• Dictate Sentences About the Story
• Connections: Dress for the Weather	• Dictate a Weather Report
• The Mitten	• Dictate a Conversation
• Five Little Pumpkins	• Dictate a Scary Poem

Unit Resources

As you work through the Integrated Instructional Plans in this unit, you may want to use the following resources included in the **Student/Teacher Resources** and **Evaluation Resources** sections of the *Teacher's Edition.*

Student/Teacher Resources

- Home Letters 4A and 4B
- Extended and Recreational Reading Ideas

Evaluation Resources

- Observation and Evaluation Guides

Students With Individual Needs

	Limited-English-Proficient Students	Less-Prepared Students	Gifted Students	Special Education Students
Think and Read	• Explain the meanings of idiomatic expressions found in the selections. • Have students work in cooperative learning groups to complete the *Think and Read* chart. (See the suggestions at the front of this *Teacher's Edition*.)	• Provide additional background information when personal experiences are limited. Use pictures, magazines, and filmstrips. • Emphasize strategies included in *Setting a Purpose*. Model strategies for students.	• After modeling effective prereading strategies, have students lead the discussions that focus on previewing and predicting. • After modeling effective thinking strategies, have students lead the discussions that focus on summarizing the reading process.	• Review individualized education programs (IEPs) with special education staff and discuss necessary modification of curriculum. • For visually-impaired students, provide specialized resources such as large print books, books in braille, or recordings.
Think and Discuss	• Provide students opportunities to listen to and repeat native-English speakers' language. • Pair students with native-English speakers to answer questions.	• During discussions, model strategies for asking additional questions. (See the strategies for generating questions at the front of this *Teacher's Edition*.) • Model by reading aloud questions and possible responses. Have students add original responses.	• Model strategies for listening tolerantly and thoughtfully to classmates' opinions. • During the discussions, help students focus their abstract thoughts. Model effective strategies. • Encourage students to explain complex thoughts and ideas their classmates do not understand. Model strategies for students.	• Review lesson plans with special education staff to discuss any necessary modification of curriculum. • Develop a specialized listening program for visually-impaired students.
Think and Write	• Have students sketch story events and arrange the pictures in order, before they dictate stories. • During prewriting, ask students to act out words and phrases. Help students verbalize their thoughts.	• Model the use of prewriting strategies to organize ideas. • During revising, encourage students to expand one or two sentences. Model the process for students.	• During responding, revising, and editing, help students expand complex thoughts. Model effective strategies. • Have students work in cooperative learning groups. (See the suggestions at the front of this *Teacher's Edition*.)	• Review lesson plans with special education staff to discuss any necessary modification of curriculum. • For visually-impaired students, record the directions for the stages of the writing process. Have students record their compositions.
Think and Extend	• Explain vocabulary necessary to complete the activities. Integrate appropriate lessons from science and social studies textbooks. • Have students work in cooperative learning groups. (See the suggestions at the front of this *Teacher's Edition*.)	• Have students work in cooperative learning groups. (See the suggestions for cooperative learning activities at the front of the *Teacher's Edition*.) • Provide manipulatives for students to use while completing mathematics activities.	• Ask students to think of additional *Think and Extend* activities. When appropriate, assign the student-generated activities instead of the activities in the **Writer's Corner**. • Have students work in cooperative learning groups. (See the suggestions at the front of this *Teacher's Edition*.)	• For hearing-impaired students, use visual aids, such as slides and overhead projectors, to reinforce learning. • For visually-impaired students, record the directions for the activities.

Unit 3

86

Introducing the Unit

Talking About the Theme   To introduce children to the unit, point to and read aloud the title "Imagine That!" Ask children to look at the picture that illustrates the opening of the unit. Begin a discussion about imaginary happenings in a make-believe world by having children answer the following questions about the picture.

1. What is happening in the picture? (**Possible responses:** *There is a woman flying a plane. She has a dog in the plane with her.*)
2. Are the characters you see real or make-believe? (**Possible responses:** *The dog looks make-believe. Dogs don't really fly in a plane like that.*)
3. Would you like to travel to a make-believe place? Tell why or why not. (**Possible responses:** *I would like to fly a plane to a make-believe place because I could meet new friends there.*)
4. Which character would you like to have for a friend?

Tell why. (**Possible responses:** *I would like to be friends with the dog. He seems very friendly.*)
5. What do you think the stories and poems in this unit might be about? (**Possible response:** *The stories might be about traveling to make-believe places.*)

3 Imagine That!

87

Extending Reading The following books extend the theme of the unit. You may wish to share these books as children listen to and "read" the selections in Unit 3. Have children discuss the make-believe things in the stories.

The Turnip illustrated by Janina Domansa. Macmillan, 1969. When all the people and animals could not pull the turnip out of the ground, the magpie landed on the last one in line and that did it.

One Fine Day by Nonny Hogrogian. Macmillan, 1971. The fox's greed leads him to a lost tail in this cumulative story.

Corduroy by Don Freeman. Viking, 1968. A teddy bear search through a department store for his lost button ends when a little girl buys him.

The Little Red Hen by Paul Galdone. Scholastic, 1973. A hen tries unsuccessfully to enlist the help of animal friends as she turns a grain of wheat into a loaf of bread.

Bulletin Board Suggestion

Write the caption "Imagine That!" for a bulletin board. Then cut from paper a long winding road and pin it to the board. You may wish to include a few trees along the road and clouds with a sun above. (Children could help make these details.) Then ask children to think of make-believe animals and things they might see if they went to a make-believe land named "Imagine That!" Have them draw, color, and cut out their pictures and place them on the bulletin board to complete the scene.

Unit 3

Unit Activities

The following optional unit activities relate to the theme of the unit. The activities may be completed during or after unit instruction. Instructions for setting up learning centers appear at the front of the *Teacher's Edition.*

LISTENING Corner

Objective: To listen to a make-believe story and predict an ending.

Materials: books such as the titles found on page 167 in the *Teacher's Edition,* paper and crayons

Procedure: Read aloud a story with a make-believe theme. Choose a stopping place in the story where children can predict the outcome by drawing a picture. Ask children to think about the next thing that will happen in the story and draw a picture.

After children finish their drawings, read aloud the rest of the story and have children discuss their drawings.

SPEAKING Corner

Objective: To create a make-believe story.

Procedure: Work with a small group or the entire class. Have children sit in a circle. Begin a story with a familiar introduction such as, "Once upon a time there was a . . ." Have children take turns adding sentences to the story. You may wish to have children act out the story as it is created.

Reading Corner

Objective: To read about imaginary happenings in a make-believe world.

Materials: books about make-believe that may include titles from page 167 in the *Teacher's Edition.*

Procedure: Ask children to select a book. You may wish to read aloud to children. Encourage them to share the book with each other and retell the story.

WRITING Corner

Objective: To draw a make-believe object and dictate sentences about it.

Materials: box with toys such as stuffed animals, dolls, wooden soldiers, trucks, and cars; paper and crayons

Procedure: Gather toys and place them in a box labeled "Story Box." Ask children to choose a toy from the box. Encourage them to pretend that it is magical and that it comes to life.

Have children draw a picture of their magical toy and dictate a name for the toy and sentences telling what the magical toy can do.

Note: Some children will prefer to dictate their sentences as you write. Others will want to write on their own. Accept their writing regardless of its stage of development. Allow them to draw, scribble, or write using their own spelling.

Focusing on "The Three Bears"

While **listening** to and **reading** the selection, children will focus on understanding feelings. Children will also use **writing, listening,** and **speaking** skills as they respond to the selection. They will use higher-level **thinking** throughout the lesson.

OBJECTIVES

WRITING/THINKING

- To dictate a response to literature using the writing process.
- To write in the sensory/descriptive domain.
- To use words that name opposites.
- To write a story extension.

READING/THINKING

- To identify sequence in a story.
- To interpret how characters feel.
- To evaluate the placement of a story in a thematic unit.
- To discriminate sizes.
- To recognize initial correspondences. (/j/j/)

SPEAKING/THINKING

- To discuss personal experiences before reading a selection.
- To participate in shared reading.
- To use the **Story Theater** technique.
- To participate in group discussions.
- To dictate a response to literature.

LISTENING/THINKING

- To listen to the oral reading of a selection.
- To listen to and analyze responses to opinions about a selection.
- To listen for changes in volume of voice.
- To listen for initial sounds. (/j/)

LEARNING STRATEGIES

- Brainstorming ideas related to children's own experiences.
- Previewing the selection and making predictions about the content.
- Completing a chart to help comprehension.
- Completing a chart to help organize writing.
- Analyzing the writer's use of language.

Summary

A family of three bears goes for a walk while their porridge cools. While they are gone, a girl enters their empty house. She samples their porridge and compares the comforts of their three chairs and three beds. When the bears return, they find Baby Bear's bowl empty, his chair broken, and the little girl asleep in his bed. When she awakens, she runs away as the surprised bears look on in wonder.

INDIVIDUAL NEEDS

Suggestions for teaching children with special needs are provided on *Teacher's Edition* page 164.

- The blue objectives may require direct instruction.

PLANNING CALENDAR

		STUDENT'S EDITIONS	TEACHER'S EDITION	ACTIVITY BOOK
DAY 1 **INTO THE SELECTION**	**THINK AND READ** Preparing to Read Planning a Reading Strategy	● *pages 88–101* ■ *pages 2–15* ● *pages 88–101* ■ *pages 2–15*	*page 171* *page 172*	
DAYS 2-4 **THROUGH THE SELECTION**	**THINK AND DISCUSS** Remembering the Selection Discussing the Selection	● *pages 88–101* ■ *pages 2–15* ● *pages 88–101* ■ *pages 2–15*	*page 176* *page 177*	
	THINK AND WRITE Making the Assignment Using the Writing Process **Develop Skills** Focusing on Language Focusing on Composition Focusing on Auditory Discrimination Focusing on Visual Discrimination Focusing on Sound-Letter Correspondences Focusing on the Writer's Use of Language		 *page 178* *page 179* *page 180* *page 181* *page 181* *page 181* *page 181* *page 180*	 *pages 33–34* *page 35*
DAY 5 **BEYOND THE SELECTION**	**THINK AND EXTEND** For the Classroom For the Home		*page 182* *page 183* ▲ Homework Notebook copying master 11	

● ***Happy Times! Story Land 1***   ▲ *Learning*
■ ***Imagine That!*** Storybook   *Resources File*

Note: Through observing and evaluating children's reading in a variety of situations and at different times, you can gather data that will help you understand and support individual children's reading development. Use the *Checklist for Observing and Evaluating Reading* in the **Evaluation Resources** section of the *Teacher's Edition*.

Cooperative Learning

Cooperative learning suggestions for *Think and Read* appear at the beginning of the **Teacher's Edition.**

Preparing to Read

▶**Relating to Children's Experiences**   Ask children if they have ever seen real bears. Encourage them to discuss where they saw the bears, how the bears looked and behaved, and whether they were frightened when they saw the bears.

▶**Previewing and Predicting**   Point to the title of the story and read it to the children. Then have them look at the pictures and identify the characters and what they are doing. Ask children if there are similarities to a story that they may have already read about three bears. You may wish to model a response.

I see three bears eating cereal. This might be the story of "Goldilocks and the Three Bears."

▶**Setting a Purpose**   Tell children that as you read "The Three Bears" they should listen to find out what happens to the three bears and to think about how the bears feel.

Notes for Cooperative Learning

Notes for Preparing to Read

Planning a Reading Strategy

Sharing Reading   Read aloud the story, paying particular attention to the tone of voice in order to convey the emotions of surprise, anger, fear, and happiness of the characters. Draw attention to the "speech balloons," explaining that they point out the character who is talking. As you share the illustrations, remind children to note each character's expressions. You may wish to have children use facial expressions to show how they think each character feels as you read the story. Encourage children to react spontaneously with comments and questions after you have read the story.

Reading Orally   Invite children to join in as you read aloud the story. Encourage them to use their voices expressively to indicate the emotions of the characters.

You may wish to divide children into small groups to "read" the parts of the three bears and the girl. As children become more comfortable and familiar with the dialogue, begin to assign parts to individual children. Refer to the techniques described in Story Theater at the beginning of this *Teacher's Edition* and have the children perform "The Three Bears."

Reading Silently   Give children the opportunity to "read" the story independently. Explain that the illustrations will help them to remember what is happening in the story and how each character feels.

4

5

6

7

Think and Discuss

Cooperative Learning

Cooperative learning suggestions for *Think and Discuss* appear at the beginning of the **Teacher's Edition.**

Remembering the Selection

Ask children to recall the story and identify the characters and what they do. Encourage children to look at the story illustrations, paying particular attention to characters' actions and expressions to help themselves recall the information. You may wish to create a class chart to record children's responses.

What the Little Girl Does
She goes into the bears'
She eats the bears'
She sits on the bears'
She runs away from the bears.

Notes for Cooperative Learning

Notes for Remembering the Selection

Discussing the Selection

The following questions focus on feelings. As children respond to the questions, ask them to support their answers with examples from the story. Encourage children to agree or disagree with their classmates' responses and to substantiate their opinions.

Remind children to speak clearly and loudly enough so they can be heard and understood.

1. Why do you think the little girl goes into the three bears' house? (**Possible responses:** *She is looking for someone to play with. She thinks she is at her friend's house.*) *(Critical)*

2. How does the little girl feel when she sees the three bears looking at her? Why? (**Possible response:** *The little girl is surprised when she sees the bears. She doesn't expect to see anyone.*) *(Interpretive)*

3. How do you think the three bears feel when they return home? Why? (**Possible responses:** *The bears are surprised when they return home. They find the little girl in their house and she is using their things.*) *(Interpretive)*

4. What do you think the three bears do after the little girl runs away? (**Possible response:** *The bears probably clean up the mess and cook another pot of porridge.*) *(Creative)*

5. What happens in the story that tells you this is make-believe? *(Critical)* (**Possible response:** *I know it is make-believe because the bears live in a house and talk.*)

During the discussion, children will need to

- **recall** the sequence of events of the story.
- **interpret** the feelings of the characters.
- **predict** the actions of the characters.
- **relate** what they might do if they were the little girl.
- **evaluate** why the story belongs in the thematic unit.

You may wish to model responses to the questions. Use the possible responses given.

Tips for Evaluating the Oral Response

- Children should speak clearly and at the appropriate volume.
- Children should respond in complete thoughts.
- Children should ask relevant questions.

Additional Discussion Questions

Notes for Evaluating the Oral Response

Think and Write

Cooperative Learning

Cooperative learning suggestions for *Think and Write* appear at the beginning of the **Teacher's Edition.**

Making the Assignment

Review the "The Three Bears" with children. Ask them to think about how the bears look and feel. Then tell children that they will write a description of one of the bears and make a bulletin board display.

Notes for Cooperative Learning

Notes for Making the Assignment

178

Using the Writing Process

Prewriting Draw the following figures on the chalkboard or on chart paper. Ask children to think of words to describe each of the bears. List their responses in the appropriate figures. Point to and read each word after you write it. Sample responses are included.

Papa Bear   Mama Bear   Baby Bear

Drafting Have children dictate sentences to you that describe one of the bears. Refer to the words listed in the drawings. Begin by modeling a response and writing it on the chalkboard or on chart paper. Examples follow.

Papa Bear is very big.
Baby Bear is sad because his chair is broken.
Mama Bear is unhappy because the house is messy.

Write each child's dictated sentence at the bottom of a piece of paper. Then follow this procedure.

- Read the sentence to the child.
- Read the sentence with the child.
- Have the child read the sentence.
- Have the child illustrate the sentence.

Responding/Revising/Editing After each child has dictated sentences and illustrated them, reread the sentences you wrote. Draw attention to conventions of writing such as beginning sentences with a capital letter, leaving spaces between words, ending sentences with a period, and following left-to-right progression.

Postwriting (Sharing) Have the children take turns reading aloud their writing to classmates and then add their illustrations and sentences to a bulletin board display entitled "The Three Bears."

Notes for Using the Writing Process

Notes for Evaluating the Written Response

Develop Skills

Strategies for developing concepts and skills related to "The Three Bears" are included in this section. Select appropriate activities to teach the whole class, small groups, or individual children.

Developing Concepts and Skills

Language:	Words That Name Opposites
Composition:	Story Extension
Auditory Discrimination:	Volume of Voice
Visual Discrimination:	Sizes
Sound-Letter Correspondences:	Initial Correspondence /j/j

Focusing on Language

Using Opposites   Tell children that there are many different kinds of words and that some words describe how things look and feel. Some pairs of describing words have opposite meanings. Ask children to name pairs of describing words whose meanings are opposite Write each pair of opposites on the chalkboard and read them aloud.

Use *Activity Book* page 33 with children. Have them identify the objects in each picture and find the describing word under it and say it aloud. Discuss the relative sizes of each object. Have children draw a picture of a pair of opposites from the story. Have the children dictate the names of the objects drawn and write the names on the writing rule for the children.

Follow a similar procedure with *Activity Book* page 34. Identify the pictures of Goldilocks at the top of the page. In the space provided, have them draw a pair of opposites.

Focusing on the Writer's Use of Language

Show children the writer's name (Kinuko Craft) printed on the first page.

Ask children to recall the words the little girl used to describe Papa Bear's and Mama Bear's chairs and beds. (*hard/soft*) Remind children that these words are opposites. Ask children how the opposites big and small helped them understand the things that happened to Goldilocks. (**Possible responses:** *When Goldilocks sat on the small chair, I knew it belonged to baby bear. Goldilocks was small, like baby bear.*)

Focusing on Composition

Note: Through observing and evaluating children's writing in a variety of situations and at different times, you can gather data that will help you understand and support individual children's writing development. Use the *Checklist for Observing and Evaluating Writing* in the **Evaluation Resources** section of the *Teacher's Edition* to gather data.

Writing a Story Extension   Recall with children that the little girl ran out of the house after waking up and seeing the three bears. Have children look at the very last picture in the story and ask them to write about her. Children may wish to tell how she felt, where she ran to, or what she did after leaving the house of the three bears.

Accept their writing regardless of its stage of development. Many children will draw pictures while others will scribble, write letters, and use invented spelling. Have children share their writing by reading it aloud to each other.

Focusing on Auditory Discrimination

Identifying Characters According to Volume of Voice   Have children look at the speech balloons in the story. Ask children how and why the words look different in each of the balloons. (**Possible responses:** *Words spoken by Papa Bear are darkest and largest. Words spoken by Baby Bear are lightest and smallest. Words indicate who is speaking and the volume of the speaker's voice.*)

Then have children close their books. Read the words adjusting the volume and pitch of your voice to indicate the characters. Have children identify the speaker and then tell how they decided.

Focusing on Visual Discrimination

Identifying Sizes   Discuss the fact that the Papa Bear's bowl is big and that Baby Bear's bowl is small. Review the opposites big and small. Continue by explaining that Papa Bear's bowl is the biggest of the three and that Baby Bear's bowl is the smallest. Then ask children to identify the biggest and the smallest things in the remaining illustrations.

Focusing on Sound-Letter Correspondences

Recognizing Initial /j/j   Use *Activity Book* page 35 with children. Have them repeat the word *just* as they finger-trace the uppercase *J* and the lowercase *j*.

Use *Activity Book* page 35 with children. Have them repeat the word *just* as they finger-trace the uppercase *J* and the lowercase *j*.

Have children identify the pictures at the top of the page. As each is identified, have them find the word, run their fingers under it, and say it aloud. Explain that each picture begins with the same sound they hear at the beginning of *just*.

Ask children to identify the letter each word begins with. Tell them that the letter *j* usually stands for the same sound they hear at the beginning of *just*. Then have children listen for the /j/ sound as you say the words *jar* and *jacket*.

Have children name other words that begin with the same sound they hear at the beginning of *just*. Then ask each child to draw a picture of something whose name begins with the same sound and dictate to you a word that names the picture. Write the word on the writing rule for the child. You may wish to have some children copy the word.

Activity Book: Language

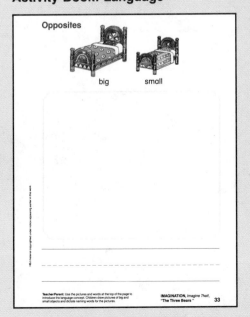

Activity Book: Language

Activity Book: Sound/Letter

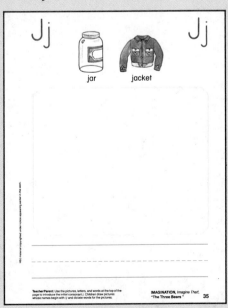

Think and Extend

Cooperative Learning

Cooperative learning suggestions for *Think and Extend* appear at the beginning of the **Teacher's Edition.**

For the Classroom

Health—Talking About Breakfast Ask children to recall what the three bears were going to eat for breakfast *(porridge).* Explain that porridge is a hot cereal like oatmeal and is made by boiling cereal in water or milk until thick.

Discuss the importance of eating a nutritious breakfast. Point out that a good breakfast will give them the energy they need to run, play, and think, and stay well. Continue discussing things that are good to eat for breakfast. Then provide children with paper plates, old magazines, and glue. Have children cut out pictures of foods that make up a good breakfast and glue them to the paper plates. Provide children with the opportunity to share their breakfast plates by naming the foods.

Mathematics—Learning About Telling Time Ask children to recall the time of day that the three bears went for a walk. *(morning)* Then have children turn to the first page of the story and locate the clock in the picture. Ask if anyone can tell the time. *(seven o'clock)*

Using a model clock, point out the hands and the numbers 1–12, and demonstrate how to tell the time on the hour. As you change the hour, have children take turns telling the new time. You may wish to have children make their own clocks using paper plates for the clock face, tag board strips for the hands, and paper fasteners to attach the hands. Children can then practice showing and reading the time.

Notes for Cooperative Learning

Additional Classroom Activities

182

For the Home

The homework assignment that follows also appears on **Homework Notebook copying master 11.** You may wish to distribute the copying masters to the children.

Writing Have children dictate sentences to an older family member telling who the biggest and the smallest (tallest/shortest) family members are. Encourage family members to follow this procedure after taking the child's dictation.

- Read the sentences to the child.
- Read the sentences with the child.
- Have the child read the sentences.
- Have the child illustrate the sentences.

Suggest that children share their sentences and pictures with classmates the following day.

Reading Ask children and family members to discuss opposites that are found in the home. Have the child dictate the names of opposites and a parent or older family member write the opposites on small pieces of paper or index cards so that children can tape the card to the object and read the words with the family member.

For Extended and Recreational Reading

You may wish to recommend the following traditional folktales like "The Three Bears" for children to share with family members. Encourage family members to visit the public library with children to select the books to be read.

Folk Tales

Little Red Riding Hood by Jacob and Wilhelm Grimm. Troll, 1981.

The Little Red Hen by Paul Galdone. Houghton Mifflin, 1973.

Snow White and the Seven Dwarfs by Jacob and Wilhelm Grimm. Translated by Randal Jarrell. Farrar, Straus & Giroux, 1972.

Marguerite De Angeli's Book of Nursery and Mother Goose Rhymes by Marguerite De Angeli. Doubleday, 1979.

The Gift of the Sacred Dog by Paul Goble. Bradbury, 1984.

More Folk Tales

Two Greedy Bears: Adapted from a Hungarian Folk Tale by Mirra Ginsburg. Macmillan, 1976.

The Valentine Bears by Eve Bunting, illustrated by Jan Brett. Clarion Books, 1982.

Additional Home Activities

Additional Books for Extended and Recreational Reading

Notes

Ideas for Cooperative Learning

Ideas for Meeting the Needs of Individual Students

Questioning Strategies

Focusing on "Changes, Changes"

While **listening** to and **reading** the selection, children will focus on problem solving. Children will also use **writing, listening,** and **speaking** skills as they respond to the selection. They will use higher-level **thinking** skills throughout the lesson.

OBJECTIVES

WRITING/THINKING

- To dictate a response to literature using the writing process.
- To write in the analytical/expository domain.
- To use action words.
- To write a story ending.

READING/THINKING

- To identify characters' actions.
- To recognize sequence.
- To infer the emotions of characters.
- To evaluate the placement of a story in a thematic unit.
- To identify shapes of objects.
- To recognize initial correspondences. (/f/f)

SPEAKING/THINKING

- To discuss personal experiences before reading the selection.
- To participate in shared reading.
- To participate in group discussions.
- To participate in Creative Dramatics/Improvisation.
- To dictate a response to literature.

LISTENING/THINKING

- To listen to the oral reading of the selection.
- To listen to and analyze responses to opinions about a selection.
- To distinguish sounds that objects make.
- To listen for initial sounds. (/f/)

LEARNING STRATEGIES

- Brainstorming ideas related to children's own experiences.
- Previewing the selection and making predictions about the content.
- Completing a chart to help comprehension.
- Completing a chart to help organize writing.
- Analyzing the writer's use of language.

Summary

This wordless story is about two toy people who solve problems by making changes. They rearrange building blocks to make a house where they can live, a firetruck to put out a fire, and a boat to survive a flood.

INDIVIDUAL NEEDS

Suggestions for teaching children with special needs are provided on *Teacher's Edition* page 164.

- The blue objectives may require direct instruction.

PLANNING CALENDAR

		STUDENT'S EDITIONS	TEACHER'S EDITION	ACTIVITY BOOK
DAY 1 **INTO THE SELECTION**	**THINK AND READ**			
	Preparing to Read	● pages 102–114 ■ pages 16–28	page 187	
	Planning a Reading Strategy	● pages 102–114 ■ pages 16–28	page 188	
DAYS 2-4 **THROUGH THE SELECTION**	**THINK AND DISCUSS**			
	Remembering the Selection	● pages 102–114 ■ pages 16–28	page 192	
	Discussing the Selection	● pages 102–114 ■ pages 16–28	page 193	
	THINK AND WRITE			
	Making the Assignment		page 194	
	Using the Writing Process		page 195	
	Develop Skills			
	Focusing on Language		page 196	pages 36–37
	Focusing on Composition		page 197	
	Focusing on Auditory Discrimination		page 197	
	Focusing on Visual Discrimination		page 197	
	Focusing on Sound-Letter Correspondences		page 197	page 38
	Focusing on the Writer's Use of Language		page 196	
DAY 5 **BEYOND THE SELECTION**	**THINK AND EXTEND**			
	For the Classroom		page 198	
	For the Home		page 199	
			▲ Homework Notebook copying master 12	

● *Happy Times!* Story Land 1
■ *Imagine That!* Storybook
▲ *Learning Resources File*

Note: Through observing and evaluating children's reading in a variety of situations and at different times, you can gather data that will help you understand and support individual children's reading development. Use the *Checklist for Observing and Evaluating Reading* in the **Evaluation Resources** section of the *Teacher's Edition.*

Cooperative Learning

Cooperative learning suggestions for *Think and Read* appear at the beginning of the *Teacher's Edition.*

Preparing to Read

▶**Relating to Children's Experiences** Ask children to identify some of the shapes found in the room. You may want to draw a circle, a square, and a triangle on the chart or chalkboard.

After the discussion have children listen as you read aloud the poem "Draw a Circle." Ask children to listen for the shapes mentioned in the poem and to think about how they look.

Draw a Circle

Draw a circle, draw a circle,
Round as can be;
  [Draw a circle in the air with pointer finger.]
Draw a circle, draw a circle,
Just for me.
  [Point to self.]

Draw a square, draw a square,
Shaped like a door;
  [Draw a square in the air.]
Draw a square, draw a square,
With corners four.

Draw a triangle, draw a triangle,
With corners three;
  [Draw a triangle in the air.]

(poem continued on the next page)

Notes for Cooperative Learning

Notes for Preparing to Read

Draw a triangle, draw a triangle,
Just for me.
[Point to self.]

▶**Previewing and Predicting** Point to the title of the story and read it to the children. Then have them observe the first illustration. Ask children to think about the changes that might happen in the story. You may wish to model a response.

I think the man and woman want to build something with the blocks.

▶**Setting a Purpose** Before reading the selection, encourage children to observe the changes that occur in the story.

Planning a Reading Strategy

Sharing Reading Explain to children that although there are no words, the illustrations in "Changes, Changes" tell the story. Share the illustrations. Draw children's attention to the details in each illustration to determine what each problem is and how the characters solve it. Encourage children to react spontaneously with their comments and questions.

Reading Orally Have children take turns telling the story. Have children give the man and woman names. You may want to start by saying:

Fred and his wife, Freida, collect blocks of wood. One day they decide to build a house. Fred and Freida work very hard building it.

Have children continue building and embellishing it with details from the illustrations. Encourage them to use dialogue that shows what the characters said to themselves or to each other at various points in the story.

You may then wish to have children work in pairs to take the parts of the man and the woman. Encourage children to show in their voices and expressions how they think the man and woman feel as they face and solve their problems. Refer to the Creative Dramatics/Improvisation techniques described in the beginning of this *Teacher's Edition* for suggestions.

Reading Silently Give children the opportunity to read the story independently. Explain that the illustrations will help them remember what is happening in the story.

Changes, Changes

A story in pictures by Pat Hutchins

16

17

18

19

20

21

22

23

24

25

26

27

28

Think and Discuss

Cooperative Learning

Cooperative learning suggestions for *Think and Discuss* appear at the beginning of the **Teacher's Edition.**

Remembering the Selection

Ask children to recall the story and identify

- the problems that the man and woman faced.
- the changes the man and woman made to solve the problems.

Encourage children to look at the story illustrations to help themselves recall the information. You may wish to create a class chart to record children's responses.

Changes the Man and Woman Make

They build a

They build a

They build a

Notes for Cooperative Learning

Notes for Remembering the Selection

192

Discussing the Selection

The following questions focus on problem solving. As children respond to the questions, ask them to support their answers with examples from the story. Encourage children to agree or disagree with their classmates' responses and to substantiate their opinions.

Remind children to speak clearly and loudly enough so they can be heard and understood.

1. Why do the man and woman build a fire truck? (**Possible response:** *The man and woman build a fire truck so they can put out the fire.*) *(Literal)*
2. What problem do they solve by building a boat? (**Possible response:** *The man and woman are able to save themselves from the flood.*) *(Literal)*
3. How do you think they feel when they realize that their house is burning? Why? (**Possible response:** *The man and woman are surprised. They have their hands in the air and their faces look surprised.*) *(Interpretive)*
4. What would you do if you saw a house on fire? (**Possible response:** *I would probably be very scared, but I would try to get help right away.*) *(Creative)*

5. In the story why do the man and the woman make changes? (**Possible response:** *The man and the woman make changes because they need a place to live.*) *(Critical)*

During the discussion, children will need to

- **analyze** why the man and woman built a fire truck.
- **identify** the problem the man and woman solved by building a boat.
- **interpret** how the man and woman felt during the fire.
- **relate** how they might feel in a similar situation.
- **evaluate** why the story belongs in the thematic unit.

You may wish to model responses to the questions. Use the possible responses given.

Tips for Evaluating the Oral Response

- Children should speak clearly and at the appropriate volume.
- Children should respond in complete thoughts.
- Children should ask relevant questions.

Additional Discussion Questions

Notes for Evaluating the Oral Response

Think and Write

Making the Assignment

Review with children that the man and woman in "Changes, Changes" had a series of problems to solve. Children will write sentences to tell what happens in the story.

Notes for Cooperative Learning

Notes for Making the Assignment

Using the Writing Process

Prewriting Ask children to name what the man and woman do in the order in which it happens. List their responses on the chalkboard or on chart paper. A sample chart follows.

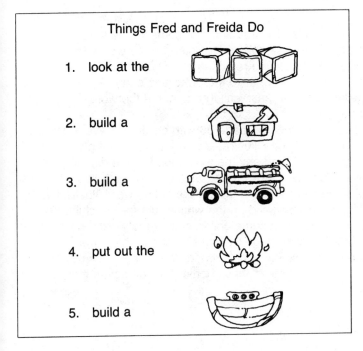

Things Fred and Freida Do

1. look at the
2. build a
3. build a
4. put out the
5. build a

Drafting Have children decide which part of the story they want to write about and then dictate a sentence to tell what the man and woman do. Begin by modeling responses and writing them on the chalkboard or on chart paper. Examples follow.

Fred and Freida build a house.
They build a fire truck.

Write each child's dictated sentence at the bottom of a piece of paper. Then follow this procedure.

- Read the sentence to the child.
- Read the sentence with the child.
- Have the child read the sentence.
- Have the child illustrate the sentence.

Responding/Revising/Editing After each child has dictated sentences and illustrated them, reread the sentence you wrote. Draw attention to conventions of writing such as beginning sentences with a capital letter, leaving spaces between words, ending sentences with a period, and following left-to-right progression.

Postwriting (Sharing) Have children take turns reading aloud their writing to classmates and then add their illustrations and sentences to a bulletin board display entitled "Changes, Changes." Arrange the illustrations according to the order in which they happened in the story.

Notes for Using the Writing Process   Notes for Evaluating the Written Response

Develop Skills

Strategies for developing concepts and skills related to "Changes, Changes" are included in this section. Select appropriate activities to teach the whole class, small groups, or individual children.

Developing Concepts and Skills

Language: Action Words

Composition: Story

Auditory Discrimination: Sounds

Visual Discrimination: Shapes

Sound-Letter Correspondences: Initial Correspondence /f/f

Focusing on Language

Using Action Words Tell children that there are many different kinds of words and that some words name actions. Then ask children to listen for the words that name actions as you retell the story "Changes, Changes." You may wish to refer to the prewriting chart. After retelling the story, ask children to name the words that name actions.

Use *Activity Book* page 36 with children. Have them identify the actions illustrated and the word that names the action under it and say the word aloud. Then direct children to draw a picture of another action the two toys do in the selection and dictate the action word illustrated. Write the action word on the writing rule for the child. You may wish to have some children copy the word.

Activity Book page 37 can be used in the same manner. In this case, children identify things they do. In their own illustration, they should draw an action they do in the classroom.

Focusing on the Writer's Use of Language

If you haven't done so, point out the writer's name (Pat Hutchins) on the first page of the selection.

Remind children that "Changes, Changes" is a wordless story. Discuss with children how the writer used illustrations to show actions in a story. Ask them why the writer did this. (**Possible responses:** *I could understand the story by looking at the pictures. The pictures told what the man and woman were doing.*)

Focusing on Composition

Note: Through observing and evaluating children's writing in a variety of situations and at different times, you can gather data that will help you understand and support individual children's writing development. Use the *Checklist for Observing and Evaluating Writing* in the **Evaluation Resources** section of the *Teacher's Edition.*

Writing a Story Extension Recall with children how the man and woman solved their problems. Have children make up their own endings to the story "Changes, Changes." Tell them to continue the story to include one more problem and the change the people had to make before they were safe and sound.

Accept their writing regardless of its stage of development. Many children will draw pictures while others scribble, write letters, and use invented spellings. Have children share their story with the rest of the class.

Focusing on Auditory Discrimination

Identifying Sounds Explain that things can be identified by the sounds they make. You may wish to demonstrate by having the children close their eyes and listen as you close a door, knock on a door, move a chair, whistle, play a musical instrument, or write on the chalkboard. Have children identify the sounds and explain how they decided what made the sounds.

Focusing on Visual Discrimination

Identifying the Shapes of Objects Using construction paper or blocks, review the characteristics of the square, triangle, circle and rectangle. Have children then find these shapes in the selection.

Focusing on Sound-Letter Correspondences

Recognizing Initial /f/f Locate examples of children's writing completed for *Think and Write* that contain words beginning with /f/ spelled *f*. Possible words may include *fire, first, finish, fun.* After reading their sentences, write the words beginning with *f* on the chalkboard. Have children say the words. Then circle the first letter of each word and explain that they begin with the letter *f*.

Use *Activity Book* page 38 with children. Have them repeat the word *fire* as they finger-trace the uppercase *F* and the lowercase *f*.

Have children identify the pictures at the top of the page. As each is identified, have them find the word, run their fingers under it, and say it aloud. Explain that each word begins with the same sound they hear at the beginning of *fire*.

Have children name other words that begin with the same sound they hear at the beginning of *fire*. Then ask each child to draw a picture of something whose name begins with the same sound and dictate to you a word that names the picture. Write the word on the writing rule for the child. You may wish to have some children copy the word.

Activity Book: Language

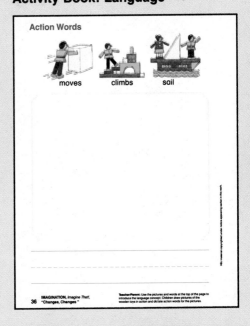

Activity Book: Language

Activity Book: Sound/Letter

Think and Extend

For the Classroom

Art/Mathematics—Working with Shapes Provide children and yourself with the same number of triangles, circles, rectangles, and squares cut from colored construction paper.

Identify the shapes with children. Then begin by arranging several of the shapes into simple patterns. Examples follow.

Have children repeat the patterns using their own shapes. Next, begin a pattern for children to complete by telling which shape should come next.

Finally, encourage children to experiment on their own by arranging shapes into designs, patterns, or figures. When children are satisfied with their creations, help them glue the shapes onto a sheet of construction paper. Then have children dictate or write their own sentence about their work. Stage an art exhibit so that children can compare the variety of designs, patterns, and figures that were created even though everyone used the same shapes.

Art—Identifying Color Changes
Materials Needed: Glasses or clear plastic containers
Water
Food coloring
Celery stalks
Coffee stirrers

Into one glass of water, drop yellow food coloring and show it to children. Ask them to identify the color. In another glass, drop blue food coloring and have children identify the color. Mix the two colors in another glass. Ask children to identify the color. (*green*) Using the same procedure, mix red and blue to make purple, yellow and red to make orange. Have children identify colors each time.

Take celery stalks and place them in glasses of bright-colored water (red, orange, and purple work well). Leave the glasses overnight and have children observe the changes the next morning.

Notes for Cooperative Learning

Additional Classroom Activities

198

For the Home

The homework assignment that follows also appears on **Homework Notebook copying master 12.** You may wish to distribute the copying masters to the children.

Writing   Suggest that children compare their appearance in a baby photo with the way they look now. Have children dictate sentences about how they have changed. Encourage family members to follow this procedure after taking the child's dictation.

- Read the sentences to the child.
- Read the sentences with the child.
- Have the child read the sentences.
- Have the child illustrate how he or she looks now.

Suggest that children share their illustrations and sentences with classmates the following day.

Reading   Have children and a parent or older family member look through a newspaper. Encourage them to talk about the newspaper as a source of information and entertainment. Children may be interested in photographs, cartoons, or advertisements. Read the name of the newspaper, the date at the top of the page, and the weather report.

For Extended and Recreational Reading

You may wish to recommend the following books related to problem-solving and changes. Encourage family members to visit the public library with children to select the books to be read.

Books About Changes

Pig Pig Grows Up by David McPhail. Dutton, 1980.

There's a Nightmare in My Closet by Mercer Mayer. Dial, 1968.

Noah's Ark by Peter Spier. Doubleday, 1977.

The Little House by Virginia L. Burton. Houghton Mifflin, 1978.

More Books About Changes

Building a House by Byron Barton. Greenwillow Books, 1981.

Who Needs a Bear by Barbara Dillon. William Morrow, 1981.

The Cozy Book by Mary Ann Hoberman. Viking Press, 1982.

Don't Forget the Bacon! by Pat Hutchins. Greenwillow Books, 1985.

The House That Sailed Away by Pat Hutchins. Greenwillow Books, 1975.

Additional Home Activities

Additional Books for Extended and Recreational Reading

Notes

Ideas for Cooperative Learning

Ideas for Meeting the Needs of Individual Students

Questioning Strategies

Focusing on "Dress for the Weather"

While **listening** to and **reading** the selection, children will focus on the weather. Children will also use **writing, listening,** and **speaking** skills as they respond to the selection. They will use higher-level **thinking** skills throughout the lesson.

OBJECTIVES

WRITING/THINKING

- To dictate a response to literature using the writing process.
- To write in the sensory/descriptive domain.
- To use describing words.
- To write about a personal experience.

READING/THINKING

- To recognize how illustrations provide information.
- To recognize cause-and-effect relationships.
- To evaluate the placement of a story in a thematic unit.
- To identify the weather from illustrations.
- To recognize initial correspondences. (/w/w)

SPEAKING/THINKING

- To discuss personal experiences before reading a selection.
- To participate in shared reading.
- To participate in group discussions.
- To dictate a response to literature.

LISTENING/THINKING

- To listen to the oral reading of a selection.
- To listen to and analyze responses to opinions about a selection.
- To identify simple sentences and asking sentences.
- To listen for initial sounds. (/w/)

LEARNING STRATEGIES

- Brainstorming ideas related to children's own experiences.
- Previewing the selection and making predictions about the content.
- Completing a chart to help comprehension.
- Completing a chart to help organize writing.
- Analyzing the writer's use of language.

Summary

The selection illustrates different kinds of weather and clothing two children wear in the snow, rain, sun, and wind.

INDIVIDUAL NEEDS

Suggestions for teaching children with special needs are provided on *Teacher's Edition* page 164.

- The blue objectives may require direct instruction.

PLANNING CALENDAR

		STUDENT'S EDITIONS	TEACHER'S EDITION	ACTIVITY BOOK
DAY 1 INTO THE SELECTION	**THINK AND READ**			
	Preparing to Read	● *pages 115–121* ■ *pages 29–35*	*pages 203–204*	
	Planning a Reading Strategy	● *pages 115–121* ■ *pages 29–35*	*page 204*	
DAYS 2-4 THROUGH THE SELECTION	**THINK AND DISCUSS**			
	Remembering the Selection	● *pages 115–121* ■ *pages 29–35*	*page 208*	
	Discussing the Selection	● *pages 115–121* ■ *pages 29–35*	*page 209*	
	THINK AND WRITE			
	Making the Assignment		*page 210*	
	Using the Writing Process		*page 211*	
	Develop Skills			
	Focusing on Language		*page 212*	*pages 39–40*
	Focusing on Composition		*page 213*	
	Focusing on Auditory Discrimination		*page 213*	
	Focusing on Visual Discrimination		*page 213*	
	Focusing on Sound-Letter Correspondences		*page 213*	*page 41*
	Focusing on the Writer's Use of Language		*page 212*	
DAY 5 BEYOND THE SELECTION	**THINK AND EXTEND**			
	For the Classroom		*page 214*	
	For the Home		*page 215*	
			▲ Homework Notebook copying master 13	

● ***Happy Times!* Story Land 1**
■ ***Imagine That!* Storybook**

▲ *Learning Resources File*

Note: Through observing and evaluating children's reading in a variety of situations and at different times, you can gather data that will help you understand and support individual children's reading development. Use the *Checklist for Observing and Evaluating Reading* in the **Evaluation Resources** section of the *Teacher's Edition* to gather data.

Cooperative Learning

> Cooperative learning suggestions for *Think and Read* appear at the beginning of the **Teacher's Edition.**

Preparing to Read

▶**Relating to Children's Experiences** Ask children to describe today's weather and the clothing they are wearing. Discuss with children why they are dressed the way they are and how they knew what to wear today.

After the discussion, have children listen as you read aloud the poem "Winter Clothes." Ask children to recall what the child is wearing and to think about what the weather might be like.

Winter Clothes
by Karla Kuskin

Under my hood I have a hat
And under that
My hair is flat.
Under my coat
My sweater's blue.
My sweater's red.
I'm wearing two.
My muffler muffles to my chin
Around my neck
And then tucks in.
My gloves were knitted
By my aunts.
I've mittens too
And pants

(poem continued on the next page)

Notes for Cooperative Learning

Notes for Preparing to Read

And pants
And boots
And shoes
With socks inside.
The boots are rubber, red and wide.
And when I walk
I must not fall
Because I can't get up at all.

▶**Previewing and Predicting**   Point to the title of the story and read it to the children. Have children look at the title and the pictures to decide what the story might be about. You may wish to model a response.

It looks like it is fall because I see two children raking leaves and they are dressed in warm clothes.

▶**Setting a Purpose**   Tell children that as you read "Dress for the Weather" they should think about changes and what happens in the pictures.

Planning a Reading Strategy

Sharing Reading   Read aloud the story several times, sharing the illustrations and pointing to the text. Draw attention to the changes in the weather and how the children are dressed.

Ask children to pantomime putting on the clothes illustrated in the selection. Have children do things such as put on boots, mittens, hat, and sunglasses and open an umbrella.

Reading Orally   Read aloud the story. Invite children to join in by saying the line that repeats

We dress for the weather.

Then have children work in pairs. Encourage one child to "read" about the weather and the other child to "read" about how the children are dressed for the weather.

Reading Silently   Give children the opportunity to "read" the story independently. Explain that the illustrations will help them to remember what is happening in the story.

Connections

Dress for the Weather

What is today's weather?
What are you wearing?

29

204

Today is snowy.
Today is cold.

30

We dress for the weather.

31

Today is rainy.
Today is warm.

32

We dress for the weather.

33

Today is sunny.
Today is hot.

We dress for the weather.

34

35

Notes

Ideas for Cooperative Learning

Ideas for Meeting the Needs of Individual Students

Questioning Strategies

Think and Discuss

Cooperative Learning

Cooperative learning suggestions for *Think and Discuss* appear at the beginning of the **Teacher's Edition.**

Remembering the Selection

Ask children to recall the story and identify

- each type of weather.
- what the children wear.

Encourage children to look at the story illustrations to help themselves recall the information. You may wish to record the class responses in the following manner:

Notes for Cooperative Learning

Notes for Remembering the Selection

208

Discussing the Selection

The following questions focus on the weather. As children respond to the questions, ask them to support their answers with examples from the story. Encourage children to agree or disagree with their classmates' responses and to substantiate their opinions.

Remind children to speak clearly and loudly enough so they can be heard and understood.

1. What kinds of weather are illustrated in the story? (**Possible response:** *The story shows a cold and snowy day, a rainy and warm day, a sunny and hot day, and a windy and cool day.*) *(Literal)*
2. Which is your favorite kind of weather? Why? (**Possible response:** *I like hot and sunny days because I can go swimming.*) *(Critical)*
3. What time of year do we have snow? *(Encourage children to answer questions appropriately, depending on your geographic area.) (Interpretive)*
4. In the story, the children rake leaves on a windy day. What else might children do outdoors on a windy day? (**Possible responses:** *Children can fly kites on a windy day. Children can sail boats on a windy day.*) *Extend questioning to include what else children might do on a hot and sunny day, a cold and snowy day, and a warm and rainy day. (Creative)*

5. How does the appearance of the children change in each picture? (**Possible responses:** *The children wear different clothes in each picture. They are doing different things in each picture.*) *(Interpretive/ Critical)*

During the discussion, children will need to

- **identify** the kinds of weather.
- **relate** which kind of weather they like best and tell why.
- **differentiate** seasons of the year.
- **relate** other things that children might do outdoors during different kinds of weather.
- **evaluate** why the story belongs in the thematic unit.

You may wish to model responses to the questions. Use the possible responses given.

Tips for Evaluating the Oral Response

- Children should speak clearly and at the appropriate volume.
- Children should respond in complete thoughts.
- Children should ask relevant questions.

Additional Discussion Questions

Notes for Evaluating the Oral Response

Think and Write

Cooperative Learning

Cooperative learning suggestions for *Think and Write* appear at the beginning of the **Teacher's Edition.**

Making the Assignment

Review that the children in the story dressed for different weather conditions throughout the year. Tell children that now they are going to write a weather report. They will pretend to be TV weather forecasters and give their reports to their viewers on the morning news.

Notes for Cooperative Learning

Notes for Making the Assignment

Using the Writing Process

Prewriting   Ask children to name different weather conditions. Then have them recommend what kind of clothing people should wear. List their responses on the chalkboard or on chart paper. Point to and read each word after you write it. A sample chart follows.

cold	cool and rainy	hot and sunny
gloves scarf hat coat boots	raincoat rain hat boots umbrella	shorts shirt bathing suit sandals

Drafting   Have children dictate an imaginary weather report for the morning news. Sentences should describe the weather for the day. Begin by modeling a response.

Today is Wednesday.
It is sunny and very hot.
You should wear shorts and a T-shirt.

Write each child's dictated sentence at the bottom of a piece of paper. Then follow this procedure.

- Read the sentences to the child.
- Read the sentences with the child.
- Have the child read the sentences.
- Have the child illustrate the sentences.

Responding/Revising/Editing   After each child has dictated sentences and illustrated them, reread the sentences you wrote. Draw attention to conventions of writing such as beginning sentences with a capital letter, ending a sentence with a period, leaving spaces between words, and following left-to-right progression.

Postwriting (Sharing)   Have children pretend to be TV weather forecasters and read aloud their weather reports. Children's reports can be added to a bulletin board display entitled "The Weather."

Notes for Using the Writing Process

Notes for Evaluating the Written Response

211

Develop Skills

Strategies for developing concepts and skills related to "Dress for the Weather" are included in this section. Select appropriate activities to teach the whole class, small groups, or individual children.

Developing Concepts and Skills

Language:	Weather Words
Composition:	Story
Auditory Discrimination:	Simple Sentences
Visual Discrimination:	Details in Illustrations
Sound-Letter Correspondences:	Initial Correspondence /w/w

Focusing on Language

Using Describing Words for Weather   Tell children that there are many different kinds of words and that some words describe the weather. Then ask children to listen for the words that describe the weather in "Dress for the Weather."

Use **Activity Book** pages 39 and 40 with children. Have children identify the pictures at the top of the pages. As each is identified, have them find the word, run their fingers under it and say it aloud. Have children draw pictures of weather scenes and dictate to you words that describe the pictures. Write the words on the writing rules for the children. You may wish to have other children copy the words.

Focusing on Composition

Note: Through observing and evaluating children's writing in a variety of situations and at different times, you can gather data that will help you understand and support individual children's writing development. Use the *Checklist for Observing and Evaluating Writing* in the **Evaluation Resources** section of the **Teacher's Edition.**

Focusing on the Writer's Use of Language

Review with children the use of the sentence "We dress for the weather" throughout the selection. Ask children why the writer chose to repeat the sentence. (**Possible responses:** *It is repeated because the children are properly dressed. The children are dressed for the different kinds of weather.*)

Writing About a Favorite Season   Have children think about their favorite kind of weather and the things they like to do in that weather, such as swimming, sledding, bicycling and boating. Have them write about something special they have seen or done.

Accept their writing regardless of its stage of development. Many children will draw pictures while others scribble, write letters, and use invented spelling. Have children share their writing by reading it aloud to you, a group of classmates, or family members.

Focusing on Auditory Discrimination

Identifying Simple Sentences   Read aloud the sentences in "Dress for the Weather." Remind children that these are examples of sentences. Point out that one kind of sentence tells about something. Another kind of sentence asks a question. Reread "Dress for the Weather" two pages at a time. Have children identify the telling and asking sentences. Discuss why the writer used these sentences in the story.

Focusing on Visual Discrimination

Identifying the Weather From Illustrations   Turn to the first page of "Dress for the Weather" and have children identify the season and the weather (fall day, windy, cool). Discuss the fact that the leaves are falling from the trees and the wind is blowing them around. Point out that it must be cool because children are wearing sweaters and long pants. Ask children to discuss the weather in the rest of the illustrations. Encourage them to explain how the illustrations help them to know the weather.

Focusing on Sound-Letter Correspondences

Recognizing Initial /w/w   Ask children to listen for the word *weather* as you reread "Dress for the Weather."

After rereading the story, write on the chalkboard the word *weather*. Have children say the word. Then circle the first letter of *weather* and explain that the word begins with the letter *w*.

Use *Activity Book* page 41 with children. Have them repeat the word *weather* as they finger-trace the uppercase *W* and the lowercase *w*.

Have children identify the pictures at the top of the page. As each is identified, have them find the word, run their fingers under it, and say it aloud. Explain that each word begins with the same sound they hear at the beginning of *weather*.

Ask children to identify the letter each word begins with. Tell them that the letter *w* usually stands for the same sound they hear at the beginning of *weather*. Then have children listen for the /w/ sound as you say the words *wagon* and *worm*.

Have children name other words that begin with the same sound they hear at the beginning of *wagon* and *worm*. Then ask each child to draw a picture of something whose name begins with the same sound and dictate to you a word that names the picture. Write the word on the writing rule for the child. You may wish to have some children copy the word.

Activity Book: Language

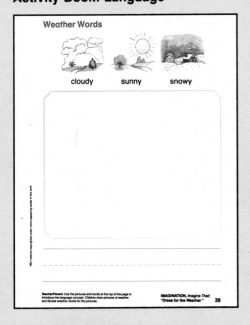

Weather Words

cloudy   sunny   snowy

Activity Book: Language

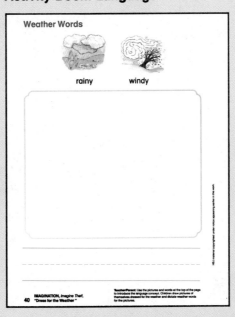

Weather Words

rainy   windy

Activity Book: Sound/Letter

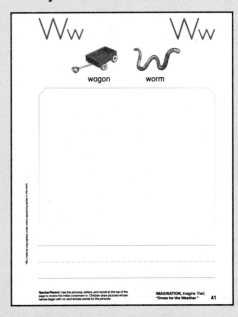

Ww   Ww

wagon   worm

Think and Extend

Cooperative Learning

Cooperative learning suggestions for *Think and Extend* appear at the beginning of the **Teacher's Edition.**

For the Classroom

Science—Watching and Recording the Weather
Review the symbols that show the different kinds of weather. Using the symbols, keep a chart of the weather. Have children discuss the weather conditions, and record their class response.

You may wish to keep a second chart to record the TV or radio weather predictions. Children can listen to weather reports and report the forecast to the class. At the end of the week, compare the two charts, noting the changes in the weather and the accuracy of the weather reports.

Art—Making a Rainy Day Book   Have children make a rainy day book. Ask children to think about all the things they like to do or make when they cannot go out to play on a rainy day. Have them draw a picture to show each activity. Help children compile their papers into a book entitled "My Rainy Day Book."

Notes for Cooperative Learning

Additional Classroom Activities

For the Home

The homework assignment that follows also appears on **Homework Notebook copying master 13.** You may wish to distribute the copying masters to the children.

Writing Have each child and family member talk about some of the birthdays in the family and the seasons in which they fall. On a calendar, point out the child's birthday and discuss the season it falls in. Have the child write a sentence about their birthday and how they usually celebrate it. Encourage family members to follow this procedure after taking the child's dictation.

- Read the sentence to the child.
- Read the sentence with the child.
- Have the child read the sentence.
- Have the child illustrate the sentence.

Reading Suggest that children and family members read a story or poem about weather. Encourage them to talk about the stories and some of their own personal experiences with the weather.

Additional Home Activities

For Extended and Recreational Reading

You may wish to recommend the following books about weather and the seasons. Encourage family members to visit the public library with children to select the books to be read.

Books About Weather and Seasons

The Cloud Book by Tomie dePaola. Holiday, 1975.

A Tree is Nice by Janice Udry. Harper and Row, 1956.

Peter Spier's Rain by Peter Spier. Doubleday, 1982.

Katy and the Big Snow by Virginia L. Burton. Houghton Mifflin, 1943.

First Snow by Helen Coutant. Knopf, 1974.

More Books About Weather and Seasons

On the Town: A Book of Clothing Words by Betsy Maestro et al. Crown, 1983.

All Wet! All Wet! by James Skofield. Harper & Row, 1984.

A January Fog Will Freeze a Hog and Other Weather Folklore by Hubert Davis. Crown, 1977.

On Sunday the Wind Came by Alan Elliott. William Morrow, 1980.

Additional Books for Extended and Recreational Reading

Notes

Ideas for Cooperative Learning

Ideas for Meeting the Needs of Individual Students

Questioning Strategies

Focusing on "The Mitten"

While **listening** to and **reading** the selection, children will focus on sharing. Children will also use **writing, listening,** and **speaking** skills as they respond to the selection. They will use higher-level **thinking** skills throughout the lesson.

OBJECTIVES

WRITING/THINKING

- To dictate a response to literature using the writing process.
- To write in the imaginative/narrative domain.
- To use naming words.
- To write a story extension.

READING/THINKING

- To distinguish between fact and fantasy.
- To understand the sequence in a cumulative story.
- To interpret how characters feel.
- To evaluate the placement of a story in a thematic unit.
- To classify likenesses and differences of animals/objects.
- To recognize initial correspondences. (/m/m)

SPEAKING/THINKING

- To discuss personal experiences before reading a selection.
- To participate in shared reading.
- To participate in group discussions.
- To dictate a response to literature.

LISTENING/THINKING

- To listen to an oral reading of the selection.
- To listen to and analyze responses to opinions about a selection.
- To listen for details from a class oral reading.
- To listen for initial sounds. (/m/)

LEARNING STRATEGIES

- Brainstorming ideas related to children's own experiences.
- Previewing the selection and making predictions about the content.
- Completing a chart to help comprehension.
- Completing a chart to help organize writing.
- Analyzing the writer's use of language.

Summary

In this Ukrainian folktale, a boy drops his mitten on a winter day. It becomes home for a mouse, a squirrel, a rabbit, a fox and her cub. When an insect moves in, the mitten bursts.

INDIVIDUAL NEEDS

Suggestions for teaching children with special needs are provided on *Teacher's Edition* page 164.

- The blue objectives may require direct instruction.

PLANNING CALENDAR

		STUDENT'S EDITIONS	TEACHER'S EDITION	ACTIVITY BOOK
DAY 1 **INTO THE SELECTION**	**THINK AND READ** Preparing to Read Planning a Reading Strategy	● *pages 122–131* ■ *pages 36–45* ● *pages 122–131* ■ *pages 36–45*	*page 219* *page 220*	
DAYS 2-4 **THROUGH THE SELECTION**	**THINK AND DISCUSS** Remembering the Selection Discussing the Selection	● *pages 122–131* ■ *pages 36–45* ● *pages 122–131* ■ *pages 36–45*	*page 224* *page 225*	
	THINK AND WRITE Making the Assignment Using the Writing Process Focusing on Language Focusing on Composition Focusing on Auditory Discrimination Focusing on Visual Discrimination Focusing on Sound-Letter Correspondences Focusing on the Writer's Use of Language		*page 226* *page 227* *page 228* *page 229* *page 229* *page 229* *page 229* *page 228*	 *pages 42–43* *page 44*
DAY 5 **BEYOND THE SELECTION**	**THINK AND EXTEND** For the Classroom For the Home		*page 230* *page 231* ▲ Homework Notebook copying master 14	

● *Happy Times! Story Land 1*
■ *Imagine That! Storybook*

▲ *Learning Resources File*

Note: Through observing and evaluating children's reading in a variety of situations and at different times, you can gather data that will help you understand and support individual children's reading development. Use the *Checklist for Observing and Evaluating Reading* in the **Evaluation Resources** section of the *Teacher's Edition.*

Cooperative Learning

Cooperative learning suggestions for *Think and Read* appear at the beginning of the *Teacher's Edition.*

Preparing to Read

▶**Relating to Children's Experiences** Ask children to discuss and name the different types of clothing worn when it is cold or when it is snowing.

After the discussion have children listen as you read the poem "Mitten Weather." Ask children to show how their fingers look when wearing mittens and tell how mittens help "when the cold winds moan."

Mitten Weather
by Audrey Olson Leighton

Thumb in the thumb place,
Fingers all together.

This is the rhyme we say,
In mitten weather.
   [*hold fingers together and thumb apart*]
Fingers in the wide part,
Thumb stands all alone.
Mittens keep fingers warm,
When the cold winds moan.
   [*blow through hands; makes "Ooooo" sound*]

▶**Previewing and Predicting** Point to the title of the story and read it to the children. Have them observe and discuss the irst illustration. Ask them to determine the time of year and give reasons why they know this. Ask where the mitten came from and what the mouse might be thinking. You may wish to model a response.

It looks like a cold, winter day because there is snow on the ground. A boy may have dropped his mitten. The mouse sees it and wants to get warm.

▶**Setting a Purpose** Ask children to think about how the mitten changes in each picture of the story.

Notes for Cooperative Learning

Notes for Preparing to Read

Planning a Reading Strategy

Sharing Reading   Explain to children that although there are no words, the illustrations in "The Mitten" tell the story. Share the illustrations. Draw children's attention to the details as each animal makes the mitten its home. Point out the changes of seasons in the illustrations, if children do not notice. Encourage children to react spontaneously with their comments and questions.

You may wish to have children pantomime the actions of the characters as they join the mouse in the mitten.

Reading Orally   Have the children take turns telling the story themselves. They may use the selection to help them remember all the details. Have the children first decide upon a name for the boy and the animals.

Once upon a time on a cold winter's day in the Ukraine there lived a boy named _____. He put on his warmest coat, hat, and scarf. The boy buckled his boots and pulled on his very warmest pair of mittens. He took his sled and went deep into the forest. There, he gathered wood to keep his family's house warm. As he was pulling a sled full of wood, . . .

Have the children continue building and embellishing it with details from the illustrations.

You may then wish to have children take the parts of the animals in "The Mitten" and have them develop or improvise their own dialogue. Refer to the *Creative Dramatic/Improvisation* techniques described at the beginning of this **Teacher's Edition.**

Reading Silently   Give children the opportunity to read the story independently. Explain that the illustrations will help them remember what is happening in the story.

The Mitten

A Ukrainian folk tale retold in pictures by Willi Baum

36

37

38

39

40

41

42

43

44

45

Notes

Ideas for Cooperative Learning

Ideas for Meeting the Needs of Individual Students

Questioning Strategies

Think and Discuss

Cooperative Learning

Cooperative learning suggestions for *Think and Discuss* appear at the beginning of the **Teacher's Edition.**

Remembering the Selection

Ask children to recall the story and identify each character who comes to share the mitten.

Encourage children to look at the story illustrations to help themselves recall the information. You may wish to use the following simple illustration to record responses.

Notes for Cooperative Learning

Notes for Remembering the Selection

224

Discussing the Selection

The following questions focus on the mouse that shared the mitten with the other animals. As children respond to the questions, ask them to support their answers with examples from the story. Encourage children to agree or disagree with their classmates' responses and to substantiate their opinions.

Remind children to speak clearly and loudly enough so they can be heard and understood.

1. Which animal finds the mitten? (**Possible response:** *The mouse finds the mitten.*) *(Literal)*
2. Name the animals with which the mouse shares the mitten. (**Possible responses:** *The mouse shared the mitten with the squirrel, the rabbit, the fox and its cub and the bug.*) *(Literal)*
3. Why do you think the mouse shares the mitten with the other animals? (**Possible responses:** *The mouse is lonely. The mouse feels sorry for the other animals.*) *(Critical)*
4. What would you do if you were the mouse? (**Possible response:** *I would share too, because it's fun to be with friends.*) *(Creative)*
5. Why is the story of the mitten make-believe? (**Possible response:** *Most of the animals can't really fit in a mitten. A rabbit wouldn't live with a fox because the fox would eat it.*) *(Critical)*

During the discussion, children will need to

- **identify** the animals who shared the mitten.
- **analyze** why the mouse shared the mitten.
- **justify** what they would do if they had been the mouse.
- **interpret** why the young fox was crying.
- **evaluate** why the story belongs in the thematic unit.

You may wish to model responses to the questions. Use the possible responses given.

Tips for Evaluating the Oral Response

- Children should speak clearly and at the appropriate volume.
- Children should respond in complete thoughts.
- Children should ask relevant questions.

Additional Discussion Questions

Notes for Evaluating the Oral Response

Think and Write

Cooperative Learning

Cooperative learning suggestions for *Think and Write* appear at the beginning of the *Teacher's Edition.*

Making the Assignment

Review with children the fact that each illustration tells part of the story and that by looking at the illustrations, they know what is happening. Tell them that now they are going to write what they think the animals say to each other.

Notes for Cooperative Learning

Notes for Making the Assignment

Using the Writing Process

Prewriting Ask children to name all the animals that share the mitten in the story. Then have children tell what the animals might say to each other in the story. Cluster their responses on the chalkboard or on chart paper. Point to and read each word after you write it.

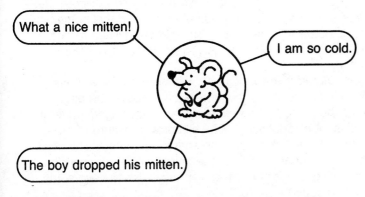

Drafting Have children dictate sentences to you that tell what each animal might say in the story. Begin by modeling a response and writing on the chalkboard or on the chart next to the animal's name.

Write each child's dictated sentence at the top of a piece of paper with balloon around it. Then follow this procedure.

- Read the sentence to the child.
- Read the sentence with the child.
- Have the child read the sentence.
- Have the child illustrate the sentence.

Responding/Revising/Editing After children have dictated sentences and illustrated them, reread the sentence you wrote. Draw attention to conventions of writing such as beginning sentences with a capital letter, leaving spaces between words, ending sentences with a period, and following left-to-right progression.

Postwriting (Sharing) Have the children take turns reading aloud their writing to classmates and then add their illustrations and sentences to a bulletin board display entitled "The Mitten."

Notes for Using the Writing Process

Notes for Evaluating the Written Response

Develop Skills

Strategies for developing concepts and skills related to "The Mitten" are included in this section. Select appropriate activities to teach the whole class, small groups, or individual children.

Developing Concepts and Skills

Language:	Words That Name Animals
	Words That Name Things
Composition:	Story
Auditory Discrimination:	Details
Visual Discrimination:	Likenesses and Differences
Sound-Letter Correspondences:	Initial Correspondence /m/m

Focusing on Language

Using Words That Name Animals Tell children that there are many different kinds of words and that some words name animals. Then ask children to listen for the words that name animals as you retell the story "The Mitten."

Use **Activity Book** page 42 with children. Have them identify the picture of the mouse at the top of the page. Have them find the printed word, run their fingers under it and say it aloud. Have each child draw a picture of an animal with whom the mouse shared the mitten. The child should dictate the name of the animal. Write the word on the writing rule for the child. You may wish to have some children copy the word.

Using Words That Name Things Explain that some words name things. At the top of **Activity Book** page 43, things found in the selection are pictured. Follow the same procedure from previous page for these pictures. Each child should draw a picture of any object or thing from the story. The child should dictate the name of the object drawn.

Focusing on the Writer's Use of Language

Turn to the first page of the story and read aloud the writer's name (Willi Baum).

Remind children that "The Mitten" is a story without words. Ask the children why the writer told the story using pictures only. Discuss how they were able to understand the story without words. (**Possible responses:** *The pictures told the story. We didn't need to know the words to the story. The pictures helped me see what happened to the mouse and the mitten.*)

Focusing on Composition

Note: Through observing and evaluating children's writing in a variety of situations and at different times, you can gather data that will help you understand and support individual children's writing development. Use the *Checklist for Observing and Evaluating Writing* in the **Evaluation Resources** section of the *Teacher's Edition.*

Writing a Story Extension Recall with children that the boy in "The Mitten" dropped his hat as he was picking up his lost mitten. Have children look at the very last picture in the story and ask them to write about what might happen next.

Accept their writing regardless of its stage of development. Many children will draw pictures while others scribble, write letters, and use invented spellings. Have children share their writing by reading it aloud to you, a group of classmates, or family members.

Focusing on Auditory Discrimination

Listening for Details Recall with children that "The Mitten" is a wordless story. Ask children to listen as you give a description of each animal and to give the animal's name. You may wish to use the following samples.

I am small. I have two wings and two antennae. Who am I? *(bug)*
I am small. I have a bushy tail and I can climb trees. Who am I? *(squirrel)*
I have two big ears and I can hop. Who am I? *(rabbit)*

Focusing on Visual Discrimination

Identifying Likenesses and Differences Have the children locate the mouse, squirrel, rabbit, and foxes from "The Mitten." You may wish to write the name of each animal on the chalkboard. Next, have the children identify those characteristics shared by the animals (head, legs, paws, tail). Then have the children identify how the animals differ from one another (color, size, length of tail, and size of ears).

Focusing on Sound-Letter Correspondences

Recognizing Initial /m/m Locate examples of children's writing completed for *Think and Write* that contain the words *mouse* or *mitten*. Ask children to listen for the words *mouse* or *mitten* as you read aloud the writing. Then write the words *mouse* and *mitten* on the chalkboard. Have children say the words. Then circle the first letter of *mouse* and *mitten* and explain that the words begin with the letter *m.*

Use **Activity Book** page 44 with children. Have them repeat the word *mitten* as they finger-trace the uppercase *M* and the lowercase *m.*

Have children identify the pictures at the top of the page. As each is identified, have them find the word, run their fingers under it, and say it aloud. Explain that each picture begins with the same sound they hear at the beginning of *mitten.*

Have children name other words that begin with the same sound they hear at the beginning of *mitten.* Then ask each child to draw a picture of something whose name begins with the same sound and dictate to you a word that names the picture. Write the word on the writing rule for the child. You may wish to have some children copy the word.

Activity Book: Language

Naming Words

mouse

Teacher/Parent: Use the pictures and words at the top of the page to introduce the language concept. Children draw pictures of other animals that share the mitten with the mouse and dictate naming words for the pictures.

Activity Book: Language

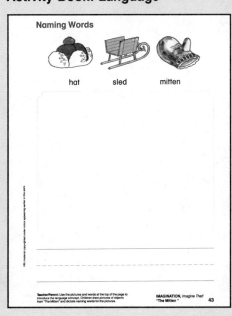

Naming Words

hat   sled   mitten

Teacher/Parent: Use the pictures and words at the top of the page to introduce the language concept. Children draw pictures of objects from "The Mitten" and dictate naming words for the pictures.

Activity Book: Sound/Letter

Mm   Mm

mountain   monkey

Teacher/Parent: Use the pictures, letters, and words at the top of the page to introduce the initial consonant m. Children draw pictures whose names begin with /m/ and dictate words for the pictures.

Think and Extend

Cooperative Learning

Cooperative learning suggestions for *Think and Extend* appear at the beginning of the *Teacher's Edition.*

For the Classroom

Science—Investigating Animal Homes Discuss with children the need for safe and warm places to live. Ask them why people live in houses or apartments. Explain that animals also need places to live and that some animals need extra protection from the cold and snow and from their enemies.

Bring in pictures of some animals in their homes and ask children to name some of them. For example, bird/nest, rabbit/burrow, squirrel/tree, fish/pond, crab/shell. You may wish to have children draw pictures of animals in their homes and display them on a bulletin board titled, "Animal Homes."

Health—Talking About Safety Discuss with children the idea of things being lost and found. Ask children what they would do if they were ever lost.

You may wish to ask children what they would do if they were lost in a store or mall, on a camping trip, or in a busy and crowded area like a football/baseball game. Record children's answers on the chalkboard or on chart paper and title them "Things To do if I am Lost."

Notes for Cooperative Learning

Additional Classroom Activities

For the Home

The homework assignment that follows also appears on **Homework Notebook copying master 14.** You may wish to distribute the copying masters to the children.

Writing Have the child dictate naming words to an older family member. Have the child name five things in the kitchen. Have the older family member write the names down on small cards. Encourage family member to follow this procedure.

- Read the words to the child.
- Read the words with the child.
- Have the child read the words.
- Have the child tape the card to the object.

Suggest that the child "read" the cards each day for a week and make up five new naming cards for objects in the home.

Reading Have family members review with children the numbers on the telephone, and post on or near the telephone the numbers for police/fire departments and numbers needed for neighbors or relatives in case of emergency. Encourage them to read aloud the names and numbers to children.

For Extended and Recreational Reading

You may wish to recommend the following books about animals and their adventures. Encourage family members to visit the public library with children to select the books to be read.

Books About Animals

The Turnip illustrated by Janina Domanska. Macmillan, 1969.

One Fine Day by Nonny Hogrogian. Macmillan, 1971.

Corduroy by Don Freeman. Viking Press, 1968.

The Tale of Peter Rabbit by Beatrix Potter. Troll, 1979.

Pinkerton, Behave! by Steven Kellogg. Dial, 1979.

More Books About Animals and Their Adventures

The Little Girl and the Big Bear by Paul Galdone. Clarion Books, 1980.

Henny Penny by Paul Galdone. Seabury Press, 1968.

Silly Goose by Jack Kent. Prentice-Hall, 1983.

Additional Home Activities

Additional Books for Extended and Recreational Reading

Notes

Ideas for Cooperative Learning

Ideas for Meeting the Needs of Individual Students

Questioning Strategies

Focusing on "Five Little Pumpkins"

While **listening** to and **reading** the selection, children will focus on scary things. Children will also use **writing, listening,** and **speaking** skills as they respond to the selection. They will use higher-level **thinking** skills throughout the lesson.

OBJECTIVES

WRITING/THINKING

- To dictate a response to literature using the writing process.
- To write in the sensory/descriptive domain.
- To use number words.
- To write about a personal experience.

READING/THINKING

- To identify characters' point of view.
- To identify mood in a poem.
- To evaluate the placement of a poem in a thematic unit.
- To identify colors and shapes.
- To recognize initial correspondences. (/s/s)

SPEAKING/THINKING

- To discuss personal experiences before reading a selection.
- To participate in shared reading.
- To participate in oral reading using creative dramatics/improvisation.
- To participate in group discussions.
- To dictate a response to literature.

LISTENING/THINKING

- To listen to the oral reading of a selection.
- To listen to and analyze responses to opinions about a selection.
- To listen for rhyming words.
- To listen for initial sounds. (/s/)

LEARNING STRATEGIES

- Brainstorming ideas related to children's own experiences.
- Previewing the selection and making predictions about the content.
- Completing a chart to help comprehension.
- Completing a chart to help organize writing.
- Analyzing the writer's use of language.

Summary

Five jack-o'-lanterns sit on a fence and discuss the emotions and events of Halloween night.

INDIVIDUAL NEEDS

Suggestions for teaching children with special needs are provided on *Teacher's Edition* page 164.

> • The blue objectives may require direct instruction.

PLANNING CALENDAR

		STUDENT'S EDITIONS	TEACHER'S EDITION	ACTIVITY BOOK
DAY 1 **INTO THE SELECTION**	**THINK AND READ** Preparing to Read Planning a Reading Strategy	● *pages 132–137* ■ *pages 46–51* ● *pages 132–137* ■ *pages 46–51*	*page 235* *page 236*	
DAYS 2-4 **THROUGH THE SELECTION**	**THINK AND DISCUSS** Remembering the Selection Discussing the Selection	● *pages 132–137* ■ *pages 46–51* ● *pages 132–137* ■ *pages 46–51*	*page 238* *page 239*	
	THINK AND WRITE Making the Assignment Using the Writing Process **Develop Skills** Focusing on Language Focusing on Composition Focusing on Auditory Discrimination Focusing on Visual Discrimination Focusing on Sound-Letter Correspondences Focusing on the Writer's Use of Language		 *page 242* *pages 242–243* *page 244* *page 245* *page 245* *page 245* *page 245* *page 244*	 *pages 45–46* *page 47*
DAY 5 **BEYOND THE SELECTION**	**THINK AND EXTEND** For the Classroom For the Home		*page 246* *page 247* ▲ Homework Notebook copying master 15	

● *Happy Times!* **Story Land 1**　　▲ *Learning*
■ *Imagine That!* **Storybook**　　　**Resources File**

Note: Through observing and evaluating children's reading in a variety of situations and at different times, you can gather data that will help you understand and support individual children's reading development. Use the *Checklist for Observing and Evaluating Reading* in the **Evaluation Resources** section of the *Teacher's Edition.*

Cooperative Learning

Cooperative learning suggestions for *Think and Read* appear at the beginning of the **Teacher's Edition.**

Preparing to Read

▶**Relating to Children's Experiences**   Ask children if they have ever seen or made jack-o'-lanterns. Encourage children to describe jack-o'-lanterns and how they are made. Point out that jack-o'-lanterns are often associated with Halloween when apples, corn, and pumpkins are harvested and when the leaves on the trees change color.

▶**Previewing and Predicting**   Point to the title of the poem and read it aloud to the children. Then ask them to look at the title pictures and tell what they think the poem might be about. You may wish to model a response.

I think the poem is about Halloween because there are five jack-o'-lanterns sitting on a gate. The leaves on the trees are beginning to turn color.

▶**Setting a Purpose**   Tell children that as they listen to the poem, they should think about what happens to the five little pumpkins that might be a little bit scary.

Notes for Cooperative Learning

Notes for Preparing to Read

Planning a Reading Strategy

Sharing Reading Read aloud "Five Little Pumpkins" several times, sharing the illustrations and pointing to the text. You may wish to draw their attention to the quotation marks. Explain that these indicate the exact words of each pumpkin.

Encourage children to react spontaneously with comments and questions after you have read the poem. You may wish to have the children perform the poem as a finger play. Have them wiggle successive fingers on one hand as each pumpkin's line is recited, then blow on their hands as the wind says, "Oo—oo!" and finally hide their hands behind their backs to show the pumpkins rolling out of sight.

Reading Orally Read aloud the poem. Encourage children to join in repeating the lines that each pumpkin said.

You may wish to choose five children to be pumpkins. Have them sit in chairs at the front of the classroom. Assign each child to be a different pumpkin. The five children can recite their lines of dialogue with you. Have the rest of the class recite the narration with you. Have the pumpkins roll away by running to the back of the class. Continue the activity with five different children.

Refer to *Creative Dramatics/Improvisation* at the beginning of the **Teacher's Edition** for additional suggestions.

Reading Silently Give children the opportunity to "read" the poem independently. Ask children to notice how the pictures become progressively darker as they read the poem. Explain that the illustrations will help them remember what is happening in the poem and how the pumpkins feel.

Five Little Pumpkins

A rhyme

Five little pumpkins
Sitting on a gate,
The first one said,
"Oh, my, it's getting late."

46

Pictures by Christa Kieffer

47

The second one said,
"There are witches in the air."
The third one said,
"But we don't care."

48

The fourth one said,
"Let's run and run and run."
The fifth one said,
"I'm ready for some fun."

49

"Oo-oo!" went the wind
And out went the light,
And the five little pumpkins
Rolled out of sight.

50

51

Think and Discuss

Note: Through observing and evaluating children's oral language (listening and speaking) in a variety of situations and at different times, you can gather data that will help you understand and support individual children's oral language development. Use the *Checklist for Observing and Evaluating Oral Language* in the **Evaluation Resources** section of the *Teacher's Edition.*

Cooperative Learning

Cooperative learning suggestions for *Think and Discuss* appear at the beginning of the **Teacher's Edition.**

Remembering the Selection

Ask children to recall the poem and identify who the speakers are and what the speakers say. Encourage children to look at the illustrations to recall the information.

Five Little Pumpkins

The first said, "_____ ."

The second said, "_____ ."

The third said, "_____ ."

The fourth said, "_____ ."

The fifth said, "_____ ."

Notes for Cooperative Learning

Notes for Remembering the Selection

Discussing the Selection

The following questions focus on what scares the five pumpkins. As children respond to the questions, ask them to support their answers with examples from the poem. Encourage children to agree or disagree with their classmates' responses and to substantiate their opinions.

Remind children to speak clearly and loudly enough so they can be heard and understood.

1. How do you think the first pumpkin feels? Why? (**Possible response:** *The first pumpkin feels worried because it is getting late.*) *(Interpretive)*
2. What does the second pumpkin see? (**Possible response:** *The second pumpkin sees witches in the air.*) *(Literal)*
3. What things happen that make all five pumpkins roll out of sight? (**Possible responses:** *The wind goes "Oo—oo!" The light in the lantern blows out. The lights in the house go out. The sky grows darker.*) *(Interpretive)*
4. If you were in this poem, which pumpkin would you like to be? Why? (**Possible response:** *I would be the third pumpkin because he isn't afraid.*) *(Critical)*

5. Why is the story of the "Five Little Pumpkins" make-believe? (**Possible response:** *"Five Little Pumpkins" is a make-believe poem because pumpkins can't talk, feel afraid, or roll away by themselves.*) *(Critical)*

During the discussion, children will need to

- **interpret** what each pumpkin felt.
- **identify** what the pumpkins did and saw.
- **decide** which pumpkin they would choose to be in the poem.
- **evaluate** why the poem belongs in the thematic unit.

You may wish to model responses to the questions. Use the possible responses given.

Tips for Evaluating the Oral Response

- Children should speak clearly and at the appropriate volume.
- Children should respond in complete thoughts.
- Children should ask relevant questions.

Additional Discussion Questions

Notes for Evaluating the Oral Response

Think and Discuss

Talking About Stories and Poems

The children have read the stories and poems in "Imagine That!" Have children compare and contrast the selections. Use the discussion questions and the possible responses provided.

1. What do you think the three bears would do if the five little pumpkins rolled into their house? (**Possible response:** *The three bears would be very mad because the pumpkins would mess up the house.*)
2. Would the mouse have invited Goldilocks to come into the mitten? Why or why not? (**Possible response:** *If the mouse had enough room in the mitten, he would let Goldilocks come in, too.*)
3. What could the two people build with their wooden blocks if suddenly the weather changed and it began to snow? (**Possible responses:** *They could build an igloo. They could build a furnace to keep them warm.*)
4. How can you tell that all the stories you read are make-believe? (**Possible responses:** *The stories tell about characters or things that are not real: Bears can't talk and live in houses. Toy people can't build things from blocks. Animals can't live in a mitten. Jack-o'-lanterns do not talk.*)

During the discussion children will talk about

- how characters from different stories would respond to each other.
- how story characters would act in a new situation.
- how the selections relate to the theme of the unit.

Bookshelf

Introduce children to these and other selections that relate to the theme of the unit.

The Magic Fish by Freya Littledale. Scholastic, 1986. A simple version of Grimm's tale about a fisherman, his greedy wife, and a fish who grants wishes.

Pig Pig and the Magic Photo Album by David McPhail. E.P. Dutton, 1986. Pig Pig discovers a magic photo album that takes him on exciting adventures to faraway places.

Have You Even Seen? . . . An ABC Book by Beau Gardner. Dodd, Mead, 1986. Comical combinations, such as an "Egg with Ears" and a "Jellybean Jump-Rope" are found in this lively ABC book.

Teeny Tiny by Jill Bennett. Putnam, 1986. After finding a bone in a churchyard, the teeny tiny woman plans to use it for supper until a ghost begins to haunt her.

Tomie dePaola's Favorite Nursery Tales by Tomie de Paola. G.P. Putnam, 1986. A collection of favorite poems, fables, and traditional tales.

Notes

Ideas for Cooperative Learning

Ideas for Meeting the Needs of Individual Students

Questioning Strategies

Think and Write

Making the Assignment

Reread "Five Little Pumpkins" and review with children why all the little pumpkins were scared by the end of the poem. Tell them that now they will write a class poem about pumpkins. They will dramatize and pantomime their own class poem.

Using the Writing Process

Prewriting Ask children to look at the pictures of the five little pumpkins and tell how each one feels. List their responses on the chalkboard or on chart paper. Point to and read their responses after writing each one. A sample chart follows.

> The Five Little Pumpkins
>
> 1 tired
> 2 surprised
> 3 happy
> 4 scared
> 5 excited

Notes for Cooperative Learning

Notes for Making the Assignment

Drafting Explain to children that they will pretend they are pumpkins sitting on the fence on the scary night. Have each child then decide which pumpkin he or she would want to be. For example:

The first pumpkin said, "Let's get out of here."

Have children dictate a sentence of dialogue for the pumpkin. Write the sentence on the chalkboard or chart paper. Then follow this procedure after each child's sentence.

- Read the sentence to the child.
- Read the sentence with the child.
- Have the child read the sentence.

Copy all the sentences onto a large piece of paper and call the poem "More About the Five Little Pumpkins." Display the poem on a bulletin board or wall.

Responding/Revising/Editing You may wish to have children make small construction paper jack-o'-lanterns to glue onto the poem.

After children have completed their artwork, reread what you wrote. Draw attention to conventions of writing such as beginning sentences with a capital letter, leaving spaces between words, ending sentences with a period, adding quotation marks around the exact words each pumpkin says, and following left-to-right progression.

Postwriting (Sharing) As you read the class poem pause after each line. Ask each child to repeat their line of dialogue with you and pantomime the actions if possible.

You may wish to have children recite and perform their "Little Pumpkins" poem.

Notes for Using the Writing Process

Notes for Evaluating the Written Response

Develop Skills

Strategies for developing concepts and skills related to "Five Little Pumpkins" are included in this section. Select appropriate activities to teach the whole class, small groups, or individual children.

Developing Concepts and Skills

Language:	Ordinal Numbers
Composition:	Scary Story
Auditory Discrimination:	Rhyming Words
Visual Discrimination:	Colors and Shapes
Sound-Letter Correspondences:	Initial Correspondence /s/s

Focusing on Language

Using Ordinal Numbers Tell children that there are words that name which one (ordinal numbers). Then ask them to listen for the words that name which pumpkin spoke as you reread "Five Little Pumpkins." (You may wish to replace the word *one* with the word *pumpkin* as you read the lines.)

After rereading the poem, ask children to identify the words that name which pumpkin spoke. Write the words *first, second, third, fourth,* and *fifth* on the chalkboard and read each one aloud.

Use *Activity Book* page 45 with children. Have children count the scarecrows at the top of the page *(three)*. Ask children to draw a picture of one of the pumpkins from the poem and dictate its ordinal number in the poem.

Use *Activity Book* page 46. Have children identify the objects pictured and find the number word under each and say it aloud with you. Have them draw a picture of the people in their family, including themselves. Count with them so they can determine their ordinal number in the family portrait.

Focusing on the Writer's Use of Language

Ask children to recall the words the writer used to name which pumpkin was speaking in "Five Little Pumpkins." Remind them that the writer didn't give the pumpkins names. He called them in the order they were sitting on the fence. Discuss with children how these words helped them to understand the poem. (**Possible responses:** *When I looked at the pictures, I could see which one was first.*)

Focusing on Composition

Note: Through observing and evaluating children's writing in a variety of situations and at different times, you can gather data that will help you understand and support individual children's writing development. Use the *Checklist for Observing and Evaluating Writing* in the **Evaluation Resources** section of the *Teacher's Edition.*

Writing a Scary Story Recall with children that the pumpkins were frightened by the sound of the wind and the darkness. Ask children to make up a scary story to tell a family member at home.

Accept their writing regardless of its stage of development. Many children will draw pictures while others scribble, write letters, and use invented spelling. Have children share their writing by reading it aloud to you, a group of classmates, or family members.

Focusing on Auditory Discrimination

Listening for Rhyming Words Read aloud the first four lines of "Five Little Pumpkins." Then repeat the words *gate* and *late*. Ask children to tell how the words are the same. *(They both have the same ending sounds.)* Then ask children to name other words that have the same ending sound they hear in *gate* and *late*. Tell children that words that have the same ending sound are called **rhyming words.**

Reread "Five Little Pumpkins" a page at a time. Ask children to name the rhyming words they hear.

Focusing on Visual Discrimination

Identifying Colors and Shapes Draw a yellow circle and an orange triangle on a chart or chalkboard. Identify the shapes. Then have children look at the pictures that accompany "Five Little Pumpkins" and locate triangles and circles. Discuss the fact that these shapes can be seen in things that we use and see every day. Work with children to discover triangles and circles and their colors in the classroom.

Focusing on Sound-Letter Correspondences

Recognizing Initial /s/s Ask children to listen for the word *said* as you read aloud the writing they did for *Think and Write.* After reading the poem, write on the chalkboard the word *said.* Have children say the word. Then circle the first letter and explain that the word begins with the letter *s.*

Use *Activity Book* page 47 with children. Have them repeat the word *said* as they finger-trace the uppercase *S* and the lowercase *s.*

Have children identify the pictures at the top of the page. As each is identified, have them find the word, run their fingers under it, and say it aloud. Explain that each picture begins with the same sound they hear at the beginning of *said.*

Ask children to identify the letter each word begins with. Then have children listen for the /s/ sound as you say the words *soap* and *saw.*

Have children name other words that begin with the same sound they hear at the beginning of *said.* Then ask each child to draw a picture of something whose name begins with the same sound and dictate to you a word that names the picture. Write the word on the writing rule for the child. You may wish to have some children copy the word.

Activity Book: Language

Activity Book: Language

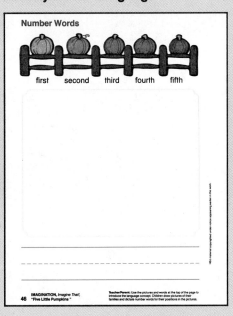

Activity Book: Sound/Letter

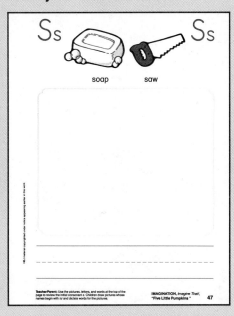

Think and Extend

Cooperative Learning

Cooperative learning suggestions for *Think and Extend* appear at the beginning of the *Teacher's Edition.*

For the Classroom

Science—Investigating Pumpkins Buy a pumpkin. Encourage the children to describe its size, weight, texture, and color. Have children design a face for the pumpkin by drawing on it with crayon or marking pen. Cut the top from the pumpkin and have children explore and describe the inside. Clean out the inside of the pumpkin and carve out the face.

When the face is complete, wash the seeds to prepare them for planting. Children can plant seeds in a planter, paper cup, or egg carton. After the seeds germinate, they can be transplanted into larger containers containers.

Mathematics—Talking About Order Remind children that in the poem five pumpkins sat in a row. Ask them to think of times when people or animals sit or stand in a row (in a race, waiting for a bus, in line at the grocery store, in a dog show, in a pet store). Provide each child with a large sheet of paper and drawing materials. Have children then look through magazines and cut out five pictures of animals or people. Next have children glue the pictures in a row. Then have children draw things around the people or animals to show where they are. Children should then practice naming the person or animal who is first, second, third, fourth, and fifth.

Notes for Cooperative Learning

Additional Classroom Activities

For the Home

The homework assignment that follows also appears on **Homework Notebook copying master 15.** You may wish to distribute the copying masters to the children.

Writing Have children and older family members discuss the things they do in the morning before they leave for school. Have children draw a picture of themselves waking up in the morning and dictate sentences tell what they do first, second, and third. Encourage family members to follow this procedure after taking the child's dictation.

- Read the sentences to the child.
- Read the sentences with the child.
- Have the child read the sentences.

Suggest that children share their sentences with classmates the following day.

Reading Have older family members read and discuss with children rhymes or stories about Halloween. Suggest that they talk about their own Halloween stories.

For Extended and Recreational Reading

You may wish to recommend the following books about imaginary things and Halloween for children to share with family members. Encourage family members to visit the public library with children to select the books to be read.

Books About Imaginary Things

Strega Nona by Tomie dePaola. Prentice Hall, 1975.

Harry and the Terrible Whatzit by Dick Gackenbach. Houghton Mifflin, 1978.

The Cat in the Hat by Dr. Seuss. Beginner, 1957.

Where the Wild Things Are by Maurice Sendak. Harper and Row, 1963.

More Books About Halloween

Riddles That Rhyme for Halloween Time by Leonard Kessler. Garrard, 1978.

Georgie's Halloween by Robert Bright. Doubleday, 1971.

Hey-How for Halloween! by Lee Bennett Hopkins. Harcourt Brace Jovanovich, 1974.

Halloween Hecatee and Other Rhymes To Skip To by Cynthia Mitchell. Harper & Row, 1979.

Additional Home Activities

Additional Books for Extended and Recreational Reading

Unit 4

Oh, What Fun!

Theme: The excitement of learning new things

Reading Selections	Writing Assignments
• Quack! Quack! Quack!	• Dictate Sentences About Animal Sounds
• Mix a Pancake Singing-Time	• Dictate a Recipe
• Quick As a Cricket	• Dictate Sentences Describing Yourself
• Connections: How Do They Feel?	• Dictate Sentences About the Story
• Over, Under, and Through	• Dictate Sentences Naming Positions

Unit Resources

As you work through the Integrated Instructional Plans in this unit, you may want to use the following resources included in the **Student/Teacher Resources** and **Evaluation Resources** sections of the *Teacher's Edition.*

Student/Teacher Resources

• Home Letters 5A and 5B
• Extended and Recreational Reading Ideas

Evaluation Resources

• Observation and Evaluation Guides
• **Listening** Comprehension Evaluation

Students With Individual Needs

	Limited-English-Proficient Students	Less-Prepared Students	Gifted Students	Special Education Students
Think and Read	• Encourage students to participate in prereading activities by discussing relevant facts about their native countries. • Explain unfamiliar vocabulary. Make words concrete by using objects, pictures, and demonstrations. • Use recordings to help students "hear" fluent language.	• Frequently model and review strategies for recalling and applying prior knowledge. • Use shared reading strategies. Discuss vocabulary and content after each selection is read. • Encourage students to talk about previous experiences related to the selections. Remind them to use *I* and *me* in their statements.	• After modeling effective prereading strategies, have students lead the discussions that focus on previewing and predicting. • After modeling effective thinking strategies, have students lead the discussions that focus on summarizing the reading process.	• Review individualized education programs (IEPs) with special education staff and discuss necessary modification of curriculum. • For visually-impaired students, provide specialized resources such as large print books, books in braille, or recordings.
Think and Discuss	• Model by reading aloud questions and possible responses. Have students repeat each question and add additional responses. • Have students work in cooperative learning groups. (See the suggestions at the front of this *Teacher's Edition*.)	• Have students work in cooperative learning groups to answer questions. (See the suggestions at the front of this *Teacher's Edition*.) • Help students identify details from the selections to support answers to interpretive and critical questions. Model the thinking process for students.	• After modeling effective questioning strategies, have students lead the discussions that focus on the selection and its theme. • Have students work in cooperative learning groups. (See the suggestions at the front of this *Teacher's Edition*.) • Model strategies for listening tolerantly and thoughtfully to classmates' opinions.	• For hearing-impaired students, use visual aids, such as slides and overhead projectors, to reinforce learning. • During discussion, have notetakers record and transmit hearing-impaired students' responses.
Think and Write	• Have students dictate as you record their drafts. Read aloud their drafts before students read aloud what they have composed. • Have students work in cooperative learning groups. (See the suggestions at the front of this *Teacher's Edition*.)	• During the writing process, have students work in cooperative learning groups. (See the suggestions at the front of this *Teacher's Edition*.) • Review with students the purpose and the intended audience of each writing assignment. Remind them to consider their purpose and audience during the entire writing process.	• Encourage students to consider different ways to publish their writing for assignments in *Think and Write*. • After modeling responses for *Thinking Back*, have students lead the discussions.	• Review lesson plans with special education staff to discuss any necessary modification of curriculum. • For visually-impaired students, record the directions for the stages of the writing process. Have students record their compositions.
Think and Extend	• Encourage students to participate in *Think and Extend* activities that require speaking. • For social studies activities, have students share related information about their cultural experiences.	• Encourage students to participate in *Think and Extend* activities that require speaking. • Provide manipulatives for students to use while completing mathematics activities.	• Have students work in cooperative learning groups. (See the suggestions at the front of this *Teacher's Edition*.) • Ask students to think of additional *Think and Extend* activities. When appropriate, assign the student-generated activities instead of the activities in the **Writer's Corner**.	• Review lesson plans with special education staff to discuss any necessary modification of curriculum. • For hearing-impaired students, use visual aids, such as slides and overhead projectors, to reinforce learning.

Introducing the Unit

Talking About the Theme To introduce children to the unit, point to and read aloud the title "Oh, What Fun!" Ask children to look at the picture that illustrates the opening of the unit. Begin a discussion about different ways people have fun by having children answer the following questions about the picture.

1. What do you see in the picture? (**Possible responses:** *I see two children flying on a big bird. They are waving hello.*)
2. How do you think the children in the picture feel? (**Possible response:** *The children look very happy.*)
3. What are the children doing to have fun? (**Possible response:** *The children are traveling to a new place.*)
4. What would you be doing to have fun if you were in this picture? (*Accept children's responses.*)
5. The stories and poems in this unit all go together. What do you think the stories and poems will be about? (**Possible responses:** *The stories might be about doing things that are fun.*)

Extending Reading The following books extend the theme of the unit. You may want to share these books as children listen to and "read" the selections in Unit 4. Have children discuss what the characters in the stories do to have fun.

The Popcorn Book by Tomie dePaola. Harper & Row, 1978. Tony likes to cook and Tim likes to read, but both twins like to eat . . . POPCORN!

Danny and the Dinosaur by Syd Hoff. Harper & Row, 1958. A dinosaur from a museum follows Danny around town and has a great time playing with children.

4 Oh, What Fun!

Petunia by Roger Duvoisin. Alfred A. Knopf, 1977. Funny, muddled Petunia always manages to solve life's problems in her own hilarious ways.

Curious George by H. A. Rey. Houghton Mifflin, 1973. George is a funny little monkey whose curiosity always gets the best of him.

Bulletin Board Suggestion

Have children paint a large mural showing themselves doing various playtime activities. Entitle the mural "Oh, What Fun!" and display it on a bulletin board or tape it to the wall. Once the mural is finished, allow children to point out their pictures and explain what they are doing to have fun.

Unit 4

Unit Activities

The following optional unit activities relate to the theme of the unit. The activities may be completed during or after unit instruction. Instructions for setting up learning centers appear at the front of the **Teacher's Edition.**

LISTENING Corner

Objective: To listen to and repeat a silly rhyme or song.
Materials: a book of silly rhymes or songs such as *The Random House Book of Mother Goose: A Timeless Treasury of 306 Nursery Rhymes* selected and illustrated by Arnold Lobel (Random House, 1986.)
Procedure: Read aloud or sing a silly rhyme or song. Silly rhymes such as "Pease Porridge Hot," "It's Raining, It's Pouring," and "Yankee Doodle," can be found in any collection of rhymes.

Work with children to help them learn the rhyme or song. Have children work in small groups and practice saying or singing what they learned.

SPEAKING Corner

Objective: To develop and expand use of naming words, action words, and position words.
Materials: small toys such as small stuffed animals, dolls, airplanes, trucks, blocks, and wooden shapes
Procedure: Place a number of small toys in a box. Explain to children that they will play the "Talking Game" with a partner. Have children choose a toy and put it in different places.

You may wish to give an example by placing a toy under a chair. Have children ask their partner, "Where is the toy?" The partner should respond with the correct answer.

READING Corner

Objective: To read about making each day fun and exciting.
Materials: humorous books about having fun that may include titles from page 251 in the **Teacher's Edition.**
Procedure: Ask children to select a book. Read aloud the story to the class. Ask children questions about the story and have them pantomime the actions of the characters in the story.

WRITING Corner

Objective: To have children write about enjoyable experiences.
Materials: paper and crayons
Procedure: Have children think about something they have done that was enjoyable because it was fun to do. Have children draw a picture of this activity. Ask children to dictate sentences describing the activity. Then have them share their sentences and drawings with the class.

Note: Some children will prefer to dictate their sentences as you write. Others will want to write on their own. Accept their writing regardless of its stage of development. Allow them to draw, scribble, or write using their own spelling.

Focusing on "Quack! Quack! Quack!"

While **listening** to and **reading** the selection, children will focus on sounds. Children will also use **writing, listening,** and **speaking** skills as they respond to the selection. They will use higher-level **thinking** skills throughout the lesson.

OBJECTIVES

WRITING/THINKING

- To dictate a response to literature using the writing process.
- To write in the sensory/descriptive domain.
- To use action words.
- To write about an imaginary situation.

READING/THINKING

- To interpret actions of one character.
- To evaluate the placement of a poem in a thematic unit.
- To recognize patterns in a selection.
- To recognize colors.
- To recognize initial correspondences. (/d/d)

SPEAKING/THINKING

- To discuss personal experiences before reading a selection.
- To participate in shared reading.
- To participate in group discussions.
- To dictate a response to literature.
- To recite a poem in unison.

LISTENING/THINKING

- To listen to the oral reading of a selection.
- To listen to and analyze responses to opinions about a selection.
- To listen for rhyming words.
- To listen for initial sounds. (/d/)

LEARNING STRATEGIES

- Brainstorming ideas related to children's own experiences.
- Previewing the selection and making predictions about the content.
- Completing a chart to help comprehension.
- Completing a chart to help organize writing.
- Analyzing the writer's use of language.

Summary

In this old rhyme, five ducks waddle down to the river for a swim. All is well except for the one little duck with a feather on his back who can do nothing but, "Quack! Quack! Quack!"

INDIVIDUAL NEEDS

Suggestions for teaching children with special needs are provided on *Teacher's Edition* page 248.

- The blue objectives may require direct instruction.

PLANNING CALENDAR

		STUDENT'S EDITIONS	TEACHER'S EDITION	ACTIVITY BOOK
DAY 1 **INTO THE SELECTION**	**THINK AND READ**			
	Preparing to Read	● *pages 2–3* ■ *pages 2–3*	*page 255*	
	Planning a Reading Strategy	● *pages 2–3* ■ *pages 2–3*	*page 256*	
DAYS 2-4 **THROUGH THE SELECTION**	**THINK AND DISCUSS**			
	Remembering the Selection	● *pages 2–3* ■ *pages 2–3*	*page 258*	
	Discussing the Selection	● *pages 2–3* ■ *pages 2–3*	*page 259*	
	THINK AND WRITE			
	Making the Assignment		*page 260*	
	Using the Writing Process		*pages 260–261*	
	Develop Skills			
	Focusing on Language		*page 262*	*pages 48–49*
	Focusing on Composition		*page 263*	
	Focusing on Auditory Discrimination		*page 263*	
	Focusing on Visual Discrimination		*page 263*	
	Focusing on Sound-Letter Correspondences		*page 263*	*page 50*
	Focusing on the Writer's Use of Language		*page 262*	
DAY 5 **BEYOND THE SELECTION**	**THINK AND EXTEND**			
	For the Classroom		*page 264*	
	For the Home		*page 265*	
			▲ Homework Notebook copying master 16	

● *Happy Times!* **Story Land 2**
■ *Oh, What Fun!* Storybook

▲ *Learning Resources File*

Think and Read

Preparing to Read

▶Relating to Children's Experiences   Ask how many children have ever seen a real duck and where they might see one. Have them tell what a duck looks like, how it moves, and the sounds it makes. For children who have never seen a real duck, have pictures available for them to look at.

Then have them listen as you read aloud the poem "Four Little Ducks." Following the reading, discuss what they learned about ducks from the poem.

Four Little Ducks

The little yellow duck
with the long, orange beak
Said, "I hatched from an egg
Just last week!"

The little black duck
With a funny little quack
Said, "I wish I had
More feathers on my back."

The little white duck
With big webbed feet
Said, "I'm looking for
A fish to eat!"

(poem continued on the next page)

Note: Through observing and evaluating children's reading in a variety of situations and at different times, you can gather data which can help you understand and support individual children's reading development. Use the *Checklist for Observing and Evaluating Reading* in the **Evaluation Resources** section of the *Teacher's Edition.*

Cooperative Learning

Cooperative learning suggestions for *Think and Read* appear at the beginning of the *Teacher's Edition.*

Notes for Cooperative Learning

Notes for Preparing to Read

The little brown duck
Who was coming up last
Said, "Watch me in the pond
While I swim real fast."

▶Previewing and Predicting   Point to the title of the selection and read it to children. Then ask them to look at the two pages of the selection and identify what animal the poem may be about. You may wish to model a response.

I see ducks in the picture. I know that ducks say, "Quack," so I think the poem is about ducks.

You may also want to draw attention to the small pictures found next to certain lines of the poem and ask children what these pictures might show.

▶Setting a Purpose   Tell children that as they listen to "Quack! Quack! Quack!" they should think about the thing that happens again and again.

Planning a Reading Strategy

Sharing Reading   Read aloud the poem several times, sharing illustrations and pointing to the text. Draw attention to the lines that are repeated three times.

Encourage children to react spontaneously with comments and questions, after you have read the poem. Then teach children the actions that accompany each line and read the poem again as they do the fingerplay.

Reading Orally   Read aloud the rhyme while children perform the fingerplay. Encourage children to join in by saying the lines that are repeated:

But the one little duck with the
Feather on his back,
All he could do was, "Quack! Quack!
Quack!"
All he could do was, "Quack! Quack!
Quack!"

Children will eventually join in by reciting the entire poem.

Reading Silently   Give children the opportunity to "read" the poem independently. Explain that the fingerplay illustrations and the lines that are repeated will help them remember what is happening in the poem.

Quack! Quack! Quack!
A hand rhyme by Marc Brown

Five little ducks that I once knew,

Big ones, little ones, skinny ones, too.

But the one little duck with the

Feather on his back,

All he could do was, "Quack! Quack! Quack!"

All he could do was, "Quack! Quack! Quack!"

Down to the river they would go,

Waddling, waddling, to and fro.

But the one little duck with the

Feather on his back,

All he could do was, "Quack! Quack! Quack!"

All he could do was, "Quack! Quack! Quack!"

Up from the river they would come.

Ho, ho, ho, ho, hum, hum, hum.

But the one little duck with the

Feather on his back,

All he could do was, "Quack! Quack! Quack!"

All he could do was, "Quack! Quack! Quack!"

2

3

Notes

Ideas for Cooperative Learning

Ideas for Meeting the Needs of Individual Students

Questioning Strategies

Think and Discuss

Note: Through observing and evaluating children's oral language (listening and speaking) in a variety of situations and at different times, you can gather data which can help you understand and support individual children's oral development. Use the *Checklist for Observing and Evaluating Oral Language* in the **Evaluation Resources** section of the *Teacher's Edition*.

Cooperative Learning

Cooperative learning suggestions for *Think and Discuss* appear at the beginning of the **Teacher's Edition**.

Remembering the Selection

Ask children to recall the poem and identify

- what the ducks do that is the same.
- what one duck does to be different.

Encourage children to look at the poem's illustration and to think about the words of the poem to help themselves recall the information. You may wish to illustrate their responses. A sample chart follows.

All the Ducks	One Duck
waddle swim	quacks

Notes for Cooperative Learning

Notes for Remembering the Selection

Discussing the Selection

The following questions focus on sounds and animal habits. As children respond to the questions, ask them to support their answers with examples from the poem. Encourage children to agree or disagree with their classmates' responses and to substantiate their opinions.

Remind children to speak clearly and loudly enough so they can be heard and understood.

1. How many ducks does the poem tell about? (**Possible response:** *The poem tells about five ducks.*) *(Literal)*
2. Which duck is quacking? (**Possible response:** *The little duck with the feather on his back is quacking.*) *(Literal)*
3. Why do you think the one little duck is always quacking? (**Possible responses:** *The little duck thinks it is fun to make a lot of noise. He wants the other ducks to notice him.*) *(Interpretive)*
4. When do you make a lot of noise like the little duck does? (**Possible responses:** *I make a lot of noise when I'm playing outside. I make a lot of noise when I'm excited.*) *(Creative)*
5. What kind of noises do you make when you are happy? When you are sad? (**Possible responses:** *When I'm happy, I say "Yeah!" I cry when I am sad.*) *(Interpretive)*

6. Why do ducks say "quack, quack"? (**Possible responses:** *Ducks cannot talk, so they say "quack, quack". When a duck wants to say something, it must say "quack, quack".*) *(Critical)*

During the discussion, children will need to

- **recall** details about the ducks in the poem.
- **identify** when they make a lot of noise and what kind of noise they make.
- **interpret** the actions of one duck.
- **evaluate** why the poem belongs in a thematic unit.

You may wish to model responses to the questions. Use the possible responses given.

Tips for Evaluating the Oral Response

- Children should speak clearly and at the appropriate volume
- Children should respond in complete thoughts.
- Children should ask relevant questions.

Additional Discussion Questions   Notes for Evaluating the Oral Response

Think and Write

Cooperative Learning

Cooperative learning suggestions for *Think and Write* appear at the beginning of the **Teacher's Edition.**

Making the Assignment

Review that the one little duck was always making noise. Ask children to make the sounds of the one little duck. Tell them that now they are going to write about different animals and the sounds they make. They will make a class book of their writing.

Notes for Cooperative Learning

Notes for Making the Assignment

Using the Writing Process

Prewriting Ask children to name animals and the sounds they make. List their responses on the chalkboard or on chart paper. Point to and read each word after you write it. A sample chart follows.

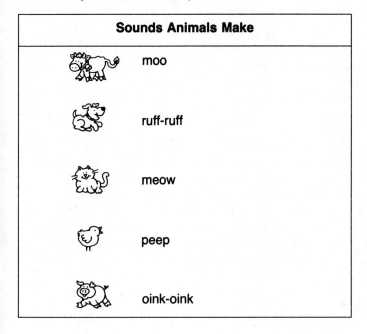

Sounds Animals Make	
	moo
	ruff-ruff
	meow
	peep
	oink-oink

Drafting Have children dictate sentences to you that tell what one animal says. Begin by modeling a response and writing on the chalkboard or on chart paper. An example follows.

A cow says moo.

Write each child's dictated sentence at the bottom of a piece of paper.
Then follow this procedure.

- Read the sentence to the child.
- Read the sentence with the child.
- Have the child read the sentence.
- Have the child illustrate the sentence.

Responding/Revising/Editing After each child has dictated a sentence and illustrated it, reread the sentence you wrote. Draw attention to conventions of writing such as beginning sentences with a capital letter, leaving spaces between words, ending sentences with a period, and following left-to-right progression.

Postwriting (Sharing) Compile children's papers in a class book entitled "Animal Talk." Display the book in the reading corner for children to read independently or with each other.

Notes for Using the Writing Process

Notes for Evaluating the Written Response

Develop Skills

Strategies for developing concepts and skills related to "Quack! Quack! Quack!" are included in this section. Select appropriate activities to teach to the whole class, small groups, or individual children.

Developing Concepts and Skills

Language:	Action Words
Composition:	Dialogue
Auditory Discrimination:	Rhyming Words
Visual Discrimination:	Colors
Sound-Letter Correspondences:	Initial Correspondence /d/d

Focusing on Language

Using Action Words   Review with children that some words name actions. Ask them to listen for words that name the actions of the ducks as you reread the poem "Quack! Quack! Quack!" Doing the fingerplay as you read may help them recognize certain actions. *(go, waddle, quack)* (You may wish to teach children the song "Six Little Ducks" in the **Resource Section** of the *Teacher's Edition.*)

After reading the poem, ask children to identify the words that name actions for animals like the ducks. Write each action word on the chalkboard and read it aloud.

Use *Activity Book* page 48 with children. Have them identify the animal action pictured at the top of the page. As each is identified, have them find the word, run their fingers under it, and say it aloud. Have each child draw a picture of an animal doing an action and dictate to you a word that names the action he or she drew. Write the action word on the writing rule for the child. You may wish to have some children copy the word.

Activity Book page 49 focuses on action words for people. Follow the same procedure used for the previous *Activity Book* page. Ask children to draw a picture of themselves doing an action.

Focusing on the Writer's Use of Language

Review with children the words the writer used over and over again in the poem. *(But the one little duck with the feather on his back, all he could do was, "Quack! Quack! Quack!" All he could do was, "Quack! Quack! Quack!")* Ask why the writer may have decided to repeat these words many times. (**Possible responses:** *The words used over and over make the poem sound funny when it is read aloud. The words tell that the one little duck keeps doing the same thing over and over again and this makes the poem funny.*)

Focusing on Composition

Note: Through observing and evaluating children's writing in a variety of situations and at different times, you can gather data which can help you understand children's writing development. Use the *Checklist for Observing and Evaluating Writing* in the **Evaluation Resources** section of the *Teacher's Edition.*

Writing an Imaginary Dialogue   Ask children to think about an imaginary situation in which they are able to talk with and understand an animal. Have them decide which animal they would like to be able to talk with and what they would say. Have them write about their imaginary experience.

Accept their writing regardless of its stage of development. Many children will draw pictures, while others scribble, write letters, or use invented spelling. Have children share their writing by reading it aloud to you, a group of classmates, or family members.

Focusing on Auditory Discrimination

Listening for Rhyming Words   Read aloud the first five lines of the selection. Then repeat the words *back* and *quack.* Ask children to tell how the words sound the same. (They both have the same ending sounds.) Then ask children to name other words that have the same ending sounds they hear in *back* and *quack.* (**Possible responses:** *jack, pack, sack, tack, shack, black, crack, track, stack, snack*) Review with children that words that end with the same ending sounds are called rhyming words.

Reread the poem, five lines at a time. Ask children to name the **rhyming words** they hear.

Focusing on Visual Discrimination

Recognizing Colors   Show children the illustration for "Quack! Quack! Quack!" Ask children to identify the colors of the ducks. *(yellow)* Ask children to name other things that are yellow. (**Possible responses:** *a school bus, a banana, a lemon*)

Follow the same procedure for the color of the water. *(blue)* You may wish to have children draw and color their responses.

Focusing on Sound-Letter Correspondences

Recognizing Initial /d/d   Ask children to listen for the words *duck* and *do* as you reread the first five lines of the poem. After reading, write on the chalkboard the words *duck* and *do.* Have children say the words. Then circle the first letter in each word and explain that each word begins with the letter *d.*

Use *Activity Book* page 50 with children. Have them repeat the words duck and do as they finger-trace the uppercase *D* and the lowercase *d.*

Have children identify the pictures at the top of the page. As each is identified, have them find the word, run their fingers under it, and say it aloud. Explain that each picture begins with the same sound they hear at the beginning of *duck* and *do.*

Have children name other words that begin with the same sound they hear at the beginning of *doll* and *doctor.* Then ask each child to draw a picture of something whose name begins with the same sound and dictate to you a word that names the picture. Write the word on the writing rule for the child. You may wish to have some children copy the word.

Activity Book: Language

Activity Book: Language

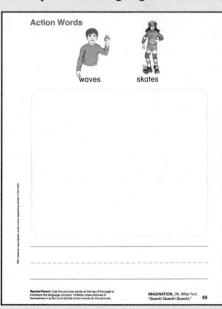

Activity Book: Sound/Letter

Think and Extend

For the Classroom

▶Science—Learning How Animals Move   Discuss the different ways that ducks can move. List words on the board. A sample list follows.

Ways Ducks Move

walk   waddle

run   swim

fly

Then have children think of the names of other animals that move in the same ways. Ask children to suggest animal names. (**Possible responses:** *Cats, dogs, hens, and turtles walk. Fish, turtles, and frogs swim.*

Mathematics—Identifying Numerals   Make the following matching activity for children to use to practice identifying numerals.

- Cut five duck shapes from construction paper.
- Cut a slit in the back of each duck.
- Write a numeral from 1 to 5 on each duck.
- Cut fifteen small feathers from construction paper.

Have children work independently, with a partner or in a small group. Children must correctly insert in the back of each duck the number of feathers that corresponds with the numeral on the duck. After practicing with numerals 1 to 5, you may wish to use additonal ducks for practice with numerals 6 through 10.

Notes for Cooperative Learning

Additional Classroom Activities

For the Home

The homework assignment that follows also appears on **Homework Notebook copying master 16.** You may wish to distribute the copying master to the children.

Writing Have children think about the special sounds they hear around the house and what these sounds mean, such as the doorbell or telephone ringing, friends calling their names, the ringing of the alarm clock, or the whistling of the teakettle. Have them dictate sentences telling about some of these sounds around the house. Encourage family members to follow this procedure after taking the child's dictation.

- Read the sentences to the child.
- Read the sentences with the child.
- Have the child read the sentences.
- Have the child illustrate the sentences.

Suggest that children share their sentences and drawings with classmates the following day.

Reading Have family members read with children rhymes, poems, or stories. Children may already know some such as "Eensy, Weensy Spider" and "This Little Pig." Ask children to share these rhymes and fingerplays with the class the following day.

For Extended and Recreational Reading

You may wish to recommend the following books of poems, rhymes and stories that use many sound words. Encourage family members to visit the public library with children to select books to be read.

Rhymes, Poems and Fingerplays

Father Fox's Pennyrhymes by Clyde Watson. Harper & Row, 1971.

Petunia by Roger Duvoisin. Knopf, 1950.

More Songs, Rhymes and Fingerplays

Eye Winker, Tom Tinker, Chin Chopper: 50 Musical Fingerplays by Tom Glazer. Doubleday, 1978.

Do Your Ears Hang Low?: 50 More Musical Fingerplays by Tom Glazer. Doubleday, 1980.

Out Loud by Eve Merriman. Atheneum, 1973.

Animal, Animal, Where Do You Live? by Jane Moncure. Children's Press, 1975.

The Farmer in the Dell illustrated by Diane Zuromskis. Little, Brown, 1978.

Old Macdonald Had a Farm illustrated by Robert Quackenbush. Harper & Row, 1972.

Additional Home Activities

Additional Books for Extended and Recreational Reading

Notes

Ideas for Cooperative Learning

Ideas for Meeting the Needs of Individual Students

Questioning Strategies

While **listening** to and **reading** the selections, children will focus on morning activities. Children will also use **writing, listening,** and **speaking** skills as they respond to the selection. They will use higher-level **thinking** skills throughout the lesson.

OBJECTIVES

WRITING/THINKING

- To dictate a response to literature using the writing process.
- To write in the practical/informative domain.
- To use action words.
- To write about a personal experience.

READING/THINKING

- To analyze the importance of sequential order.
- To relate a poem's theme to personal experiences.
- To recognize the use of action words in poetry.
- To place events in sequential order.
- To recognize initial correspondences. (/p/p)

SPEAKING/THINKING

- To discuss personal experiences before reading the selections.
- To participate in shared reading.
- To participate in group discussions.
- To dictate a response to literature.
- To recite a poem in unison.

LISTENING/THINKING

- To listen to the oral reading of the selections.
- To listen to and analyze responses to opinions about the selections.
- To listen for rhyming words.
- To listen for initial sounds. (/p/)

LEARNING STRATEGIES

- Brainstorming ideas related to children's own experiences.
- Previewing the selection and making predictions about the content.
- Completing a chart to help comprehension.
- Completing a drawing to help organize writing.
- Analyzing the writer's use of language.

Summary

The speaker in the poem "Singing-Time" wakes up early and greets the morning with song. "Mix a Pancake" describes in verse the actions involved in making pancakes.

INDIVIDUAL NEEDS

Suggestions for teaching children with special needs are provided on **Teacher's Edition** page 248.

- The blue objectives may require direct instruction.

PLANNING CALENDAR

		STUDENT'S EDITIONS	TEACHER'S EDITION	ACTIVITY BOOK
DAY 1 **INTO THE SELECTION**	**THINK AND READ** Preparing to Read	● *pages 4–7* ■ *pages 4–7*	*page 269*	
	Planning a Reading Strategy	● *pages 4–7* ■ *pages 4–7*	*page 270*	
DAYS 2-4 **THROUGH THE SELECTION**	**THINK AND DISCUSS** Remembering the Selection	● *pages 4–7* ■ *pages 4–7*	*page 272*	
	Discussing the Selection	● *pages 4–7* ■ *pages 4–7*	*page 273*	
	THINK AND WRITE Making the Assignment		*page 274*	
	Using the Writing Process		*page 275*	
	Develop Skills Focusing on Language		*page 276*	*pages 51–52*
	Focusing on Composition		*pages 276–277*	
	Focusing on Auditory Discrimination		*page 277*	
	Focusing on Visual Discrimination		*page 277*	
	Focusing on Sound-Letter Correspondences		*page 277*	*page 53*
	Focusing on the Writer's Use of Language		*page 276*	
DAY 5 **BEYOND THE SELECTION**	**THINK AND EXTEND** For the Classroom		*page 278*	
	For the Home		*page 279*	
			▲ Homework Notebook copying master 17	

● *Happy Times! Story Land 2*   ▲ *Learning Resources File*
■ *Oh, What Fun!* Storybook

Note: Through observing and evaluating children's reading in a variety of situations and at different times, you can gather data which can help you understand and support individual children's reading development. Use the *Checklist for Observing and Evaluating Reading* in the **Evaluation Resources** section of the *Teacher's Edition*.

Cooperative Learning

Cooperative learning suggestions for *Think and Read* appear at the beginning of the *Teacher's Edition*.

Preparing to Read

▶**Relating to Children's Experiences** Ask children to think about the different things they do when they get up each morning. Ask volunteers to pantomime actions showing what they do while classmates guess.

You may wish to teach children the song "This Is The Way We Get Up in the Morning" by Hap Palmer. The music and lyrics are in the **Teacher's Resource** section of the *Teacher's Edition*.

▶**Previewing and Predicting** Point to the title of each poem and read it to the children. Ask them to look at the pictures for each poem and tell what they think is happening. You may wish to model a response.

I see children making something in one picture. I think they are making pancakes because it looks like there is a pancake in the pan.

▶**Setting a Purpose** Tell children that as they listen to "Mix a Pancake" and "Singing-Time," they should think about what happens step-by-step.

Notes for Cooperative Learning

Notes for Preparing to Read

Planning a Reading Strategy

Sharing Reading   Read aloud the poems several times, sharing the illustrations and pointing to the text. Draw attention to each word that expresses an action.

Encourage children to react spontaneously with comments and questions after you have read the poems. You may wish to have children pantomime each action as it is mentioned in the poems.

Reading Orally   Divide the class into two groups. Have one half of the class recite the poem "Mix a Pancake" with you while the second half of the class pantomimes the actions. Then have the two groups switch roles. Follow the same procedure for reciting the lines and pantomiming the actions for "Singing-Time."

Reading Silently   Give children the opportunity to "read" the poems independently. Explain that the action pictures will help them remember what is happening in the poems.

Mix a Pancake

A poem by Christina Rossetti

Mix a pancake,
Stir a pancake,
   Pop it in the pan;
Fry the pancake,
Toss the pancake,—
   Catch it if you can.

4

Pictures by Marie-Louise Gay

5

270

Singing-Time

A poem by Rose Fyleman

I wake in the morning early
And always, the very first thing,
I poke out my head and I sit up in bed
And I sing and I sing and I sing.

6

7

Think and Discuss

Cooperative Learning

Cooperative learning suggestions for *Think and Discuss* appear at the beginning of the **Teacher's Edition.**

Remembering the Selection

Ask children to recall each poem and identify

- the six steps involved in making pancakes.
- what one child does each morning upon awakening.

Encourage children to look at the poems' illustrations to help themselves recall the order of things that happened. You may wish to create a class chart to record children's responses. A sample chart follows.

"Mix a Pancake"	"Singing-Time"
1. mix	1. wake up
2. stir	2. sit up
3. pop	3. sing
4. fry	
5. toss	
6. catch	

Notes for Cooperative Learning

Notes for Remembering the Selection

Discussing the Selection

The following questions focus on wake-up time. As children respond to the questions, ask them to support their answers with examples from the poems. Encourage children to agree or disagree with their classmates' responses and to substantiate their opinions.

Remind children to speak clearly and loudly enough so they can be heard and understood.

1. What time of the day does each poem tell about? (**Possible responses:** *The poems tell about the morning. This is the time when you wake up. It is also the time when we usually eat pancakes.*) *(Interpretive)*

2. How does the child in "Singing-Time" feel about the morning? (**Possible response:** *I think the child is happy about the morning because he is singing.*) *(Interpretive)*

3. For what meal might the children be making pancakes? (**Possible response:** *The children might be making pancakes for breakfast.*) *(Interpretive)*

4. What kinds of breakfast foods do you like to eat or make? (**Possible responses:** *I like to make toast and cereal. I like my mom to make scrambled eggs and oatmeal for me.*) *(Creative)*

5. What can you do in the morning to make the day begin in a happy way? (**Possible responses:** *I can say good morning with a smile. I can help my mom and dad make breakfast. I can get ready for school by myself.*) *(Creative)*

During the discussion, children will need to

- **recognize** the time of day suggested by the poems.
- **interpret** the feelings of the child in "Singing-Time."
- **identify** breakfast foods.
- **propose** ways in which they make morning a happy time at home.

You may wish to model responses to the questions. Use the possible responses given.

Tips for Evaluating the Oral Response

- Children should speak clearly and at the appropriate volume.
- Children should respond in complete thoughts.
- Children should ask relevant questions.

Additional Discussion Questions

Notes for Evaluating the Oral Response

Think and Write

Cooperative Learning

Cooperative learning suggestions for *Think and Write* appear at the beginning of the *Teacher's Edition.*

Making the Assignment

Review that the poem "Mix a Pancake" tells the steps for making pancakes. Tell children that now they are going to write the steps for making another kind of food that they like to eat. They will make a class recipe book of their writing.

Notes for Cooperative Learning

Notes for Making the Assignment

274

Using the Writing Process

Prewriting Ask children to name foods they enjoy eating and would like to help prepare at home. Cluster their responses on the chalkboard or on chart paper. A sample drawing follows.

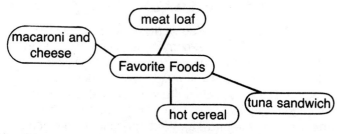

Drafting Have children dictate sentences to you that tell how to prepare a favorite dish. Have them dictate what they would do first, next, then, and last. Begin by modeling a response and writing it on the chalkboard or on chart paper. An example follows.

Peanut Butter and Jelly Sandwich

1. Scoop peanut butter from the jar.
2. Spread it on one slice of bread.
3. Spread jelly on top of the peanut butter.
4. Put another slice of bread on top.

Write each child's dictated sentences at the bottom of a piece of paper. Then follow this procedure.

- Read the sentences to the child.
- Read the sentences with the child.
- Have the child read the sentences.
- Have the child illustrate the sentences.

Responding/Revising/Editing After each child has dictated sentences for a recipe and illustrated the sentences, reread the recipe you wrote. Draw attention to conventions of writing, such as beginning sentences with a capital letter, leaving spaces between words, ending sentences with a period, and following left-to-right progression.

Postwriting (Sharing) Compile children's papers in a class recipe book. Have children suggest a title for the book, such as "Class Cookbook." Display the book in the reading corner for children to read independently or with each other. You may also want to consider duplicating the book and sending a copy home with each child. Families will enjoy reading the original recipes.

Notes for Using the Writing Process

Notes for Evaluating the Written Response

Develop Skills

Strategies for developing concepts and skills related to "Mix a Pancake" and "Singing-Time" are included in this section. Select appropriate activities to teach to the whole class, small groups, or individual children.

Developing Concepts and Skills

Language:	Action Words
Composition:	Story
Auditory Discrimination:	Rhyming Words
Visual Discrimination:	Sequential Order
Sound-Letter Correspondences:	Initial Correspondence /p/p

Focusing on Language

Using Action Words   Use *Activity Book* pages 51 and 52 with children. Have them identify the actions in the pictures at the top of the pages. As each is identified, have them find the word, run their fingers under it, and say it aloud. Have each child draw pictures of actions he or she can do and dictate to you words that name the actions shown in the drawing. Write the action words on the writing rules for the child. You may wish to have some children copy the words.

Focusing on Composition

Note: Through observing and evaluating children's writing in a variety of situations and at different times, you can gather data which can help you understand and support individual children's writing development. Use the *Checklist for Observing and Evaluating Writing* in the **Evaluation Resources** section of the *Teacher's Edition.*

Focusing on the Writer's Use of Language

Show children the writers' names on the first pages of the poems (Christina Rosetti and Rose Fyleman). Review with children the action words these writers used in the poems. *(mix, stir, pop, fry, toss, catch; wake, poke, sit, sing)* Ask why the writers of the poems used action words. **(Possible responses:** *The writer of "Mix a Pancake" used action words to tell us how to do something. The writer of "Singing-Time" used action words to tell us what one child does at wake-up time.)*

Writing About Morning Activities   Ask children to think about what they do in the morning and then to write about these activities. Have them think about the family members or friends they see every morning before they come to school.

Accept their writing regardless of its stage of development. Many children will draw pictures, while others scribble, write letters, or use invented spelling. Have children share their writing by reading it aloud to you, a group of classmates, or family members.

Focusing on Auditory Discrimination

Listening for Rhyming Words   Read aloud the poem "Singing-Time." Then repeat the words *thing* and *sing*. Ask children to tell how the words sound the same. *(They both have the same ending sound.)* Then ask children to name other words that have the same ending sound they hear in *thing* and *sing*. (**Possible responses:** *ring, king, bring, spring, swing, string*) Remind children that words that end with the same sound are called **rhyming words.**

Reread "Mix a Pancake" and ask children to name the rhyming words they hear.

Focusing on Visual Discrimination

Noticing Sequence in Illustrations   Review with children that the poem "Mix a Pancake" tells how to make pancakes. Have children look at the illustrations for the poem. Have them point to each illustration as they recite each step of the poem with you. Ask them to tell how they know which picture to point to for each step. Elicit that the pictures are numbered in order from 1 to 6 and that each picture shows an action.

Focusing on Sound-Letter Correspondences

Recognizing Initial /p/p   Ask children to listen for the word *pancake* as you read aloud the poem "Mix a Pancake." After you read the poem, write on the chalkboard the word *pancake.* Have children say the word. Then circle the first letter of *pancake* and explain that the word begins with the letter *p.*

Use *Activity Book* page 53 with children. Have them repeat the word *pancake* as they finger-trace the uppercase *P* and the lowercase *p.*

Have children identify the pictures at the top of the page. As each is identified, have them find the word, run their fingers under it, and say it aloud. Explain that each word begins with the same sound they hear at the beginning of *pancake.*

Ask children to identify the letter each word begins with. Tell them that the letter *p* usually stands for the same sound they hear at the beginning of *pancake.* Then have children listen for the /p/ sound as you say the words *pig* and *panda.*

Have children name other words that begin with the same sound they hear at the beginning of *pig* and *panda.* Then ask each child to draw a picture of something whose name begins with the same sound and dictate to you a word that names the picture. Write the word on the writing rule for the child. You may wish to have some children copy the word.

Activity Book: Language

Activity Book: Language

Activity Book: Sound/Letter

Think and Extend

Cooperative Learning

Cooperative learning suggestions for *Think and Extend* appear at the beginning of the **Teacher's Edition.**

For the Classroom

Health—Planning a Healthful Breakfast   Discuss the importance of eating a good breakfast and suggest foods that are nutritious to eat. Then make available magazines for children to look through and cut pictures from. They will need pictures of healthful foods that they can paste on paper plates. Display the paper plate collages on a bulletin board with the caption "Start Your Day with a Smile and a Good Breakfast."

Social Studies—Learning About Where Food Comes From   List the names of some of the children's favorite foods for breakfast as well as other meals. Talk about where the food comes from.

Notes for Cooperative Learning

Additional Classroom Activities

For the Home

The homework assignment that follows also appears on **Homework Notebook copying master 17.** You may wish to distribute the copying masters to the children.

Writing Have children think about what they like to do in the afternoon after school. Then have them dictate sentences to family members. Encourage family members to follow this procedure after taking the child's dictation.

- Read the sentences to the child.
- Read the sentences with the child.
- Have the child read the sentences.
- Have the child illustrate the sentences.

Suggest that children share their sentences with classmates the following day.

Reading Have a parent or older family member read and discuss the steps of a favorite recipe and then allow the child to help prepare the dish. Children can help by gathering ingredients and cooking utensils, by telling the order of the steps, and by completing simple tasks. Ask children to share their cooking activity with the class the following day.

For Extended and Recreational Reading

You may wish to recommend the following books about food and cooking for children to share with family members. Encourage family members to visit the public library with children to select the books to be read.

Books About Food

The Very Hungry Caterpillar by Eric Carle. Puffin, 1984.

Bread and Jam for Frances by Russell Hoban. Harper and Row, 1964.

The Popcorn Book by Tomie dePaola. Holiday House, 1978.

The Pancake by Anita Lobel. Greenwillow, 1978.

More Books About Cooking and Food

Eats: Poems by Arnold Adoff. Lothrop, Lee & Shepard, 1979.

Cloudy with a Chance of Meatballs by Judith Barrett. Atheneum, 1978.

Pancakes for Breakfast by Tomie de Paola. Harcourt Brace Jovanovich, 1978.

Avocado Bay by John Burningham. Harper & Row, 1982.

Additional Home Activities

Additional Books for Extended and Recreational Reading

Notes

Ideas for Cooperative Learning

Ideas for Meeting the Needs of Individual Students

Questioning Strategies

Focusing on "Quick as a Cricket"

While **listening** to and **reading** the selection, children will focus on positive self-image. Children will also use **writing, listening,** and **speaking** skills as they respond to the selection. They will use higher-level **thinking** skills throughout the lesson.

OBJECTIVES

WRITING/THINKING

- To dictate a response to literature using the writing process.
- To write in the sensory/descriptive domain.
- To use describing words.
- To write about a personal accomplishment.

READING/THINKING

- To identify the speaker in a story.
- To evaluate the placement of a story in a thematic unit.
- To recognize patterns in a selection.
- To identify opposites.
- To recognize initial correspondences. (/t/t)

SPEAKING/THINKING

- To discuss personal experiences before reading a selection.
- To participate in shared reading.
- To participate in group discussions.
- To dictate a response to literature.
- To read aloud parts of a story.

LISTENING/THINKING

- To listen to the oral reading of a selection.
- To listen to and analyze responses to opinions about a selection.
- To listen for alliteration.
- To listen for initial sounds. (/t/)

LEARNING STRATEGIES

- Brainstorming ideas related to children's own experiences.
- Previewing the selection and making predictions about the content.
- Completing a chart to help comprehension.
- Completing drawings to help organize writing.
- Analyzing the writer's use of language.

Summary

"Quick as a cricket" is just one of the ways a young boy describes himself in this story which is joyful celebration of a child's self-awareness.

INDIVIDUAL NEEDS

Suggestions for teaching children with special needs are provided on *Teacher's Edition* page 248.

- The blue objectives may require direct instruction.

PLANNING CALENDAR

		STUDENT'S EDITIONS	TEACHER'S EDITION	ACTIVITY BOOK
DAY 1 INTO THE SELECTION	**THINK AND READ**			
	Preparing to Read	● *pages 8–21* ■ *pages 8–21*	*page 283*	
	Planning a Reading Strategy	● *pages 8–21* ■ *pages 8–21*	*page 284*	
DAYS 2-4 THROUGH THE SELECTION	**THINK AND DISCUSS**			
	Remembering the Selection	● *pages 8–21* ■ *pages 8–21*	*page 288*	
	Discussing the Selection	● *pages 8–21* ■ *pages 8–21*	*page 289*	
	THINK AND WRITE			
	Making the Assignment		*page 290*	
	Using the Writing Process		*pages 290–291*	
	Develop Skills			
	Focusing on Language		*page 292*	*pages 54–55*
	Focusing on Composition		*page 293*	
	Focusing on Auditory Discrimination		*page 293*	
	Focusing on Visual Discrimination		*page 293*	
	Focusing on Sound-Letter Correspondences		*page 293*	*page 56*
	Focusing on the Writer's Use of Language		*page 292*	
DAY 5 BEYOND THE SELECTION	**THINK AND EXTEND**			
	For the Classroom		*page 294*	
	For the Home		*pages 294–295*	
			▲ Homework Notebook copying master 18	

● ***Happy Times! Story Land 2***
■ ***Oh, What Fun!* Storybook**

▲ **Learning Resources File**

Note: Through observing and evaluating children's reading in a variety of situations and at different times, you can gather data which can help you understand and support individual children's reading development. Use the *Checklist for Observing and Evaluating Reading* in the **Evaluation Resources** section of the *Teacher's Edition.*

Cooperative Learning

Cooperative learning suggestions for *Think and Read* appear at the beginning of the *Teacher's Edition.*

Preparing to Read

▶**Relating to Children's Experiences** Ask children to think about their experiences with animals. Discuss how animals are different sizes, act differently, and certainly look different from one another.

After the discussion, have children listen as you read the following poem about animals. Ask children to name the words that tell what the different animals are like.

One-by-One

It's fun to look at animals one-by-one.
I see a little bird high up in a tree.
I see a pretty butterfly chasing after me.
I see a wiggly worm crawling on the ground.
I see a silly pig that is fat and round.
I see a friendly cow saying, "Moo, moo!"
I see a tall giraffe living in a zoo.
Big or small, short or tall,
I love the animals, one and all.
I always have such fun,
Looking at animals one-by-one.

▶**Previewing and Predicting** Point to the title of the story and read it to the children. Then ask them to look at the pictures and tell what they think the story might be about. You may wish to model a response.

Notes for Cooperative Learning

Notes for Preparing to Read

I see a boy with some crickets.
The boy is jumping like a cricket.
I think the boy feels he can jump
just as fast as a cricket jumps.

▶**Setting a Purpose** Tell children that as they listen to "Quick as a Cricket" they should think about the different things the boy feels he can do and how he feels about himself.

Planning a Reading Strategy

Sharing Reading Read aloud the story several times, sharing the illustrations and pointing to the text. Draw attention to the pattern the writer uses. (I am as _____ as a _____.)

Encourage children to react spontaneously with comments and questions, after you read the story. You may wish to have children pretend they are the boy and pantomime the actions of the animals described in the story as you read it to them.

Reading Orally Make name tags with the name of each animal mentioned in the story. Ask for ten volunteers to be the animals. Pin one tag on each volunteer. Read the name of the animal on each tag and have the child repeat the name. Then invite all children to "help" you read the story by finishing each sentence as you read the first part, such as "I'm as quick as a _____. The volunteers will pantomime the actions of each animal as it is mentioned.

Reading Silently Give children the opportunity to "read" the story independently. Explain that the illustrations will help them remember what is happening in the story.

Quick as a Cricket

From a story by Audrey Wood

I'm as quick as a cricket.

8

9

I'm as slow as a snail.

10

I'm as large as a whale.

12

I'm as small as an ant.

11

13

I'm as sad as a basset.

14

I'm as happy as a lark.

15

I'm as cold as a toad.

16

I'm as hot as a fox.

17

I'm as loud as a lion.

I'm as quiet as a clam.

Put it all together,
And you've got me!

Think and Discuss

Note: Through observing and evaluating children's oral language (listening and speaking) in a variety of situations and at different times, you can gather data which can help you understand and support individual children's oral language development. Use the *Checklist for Observing and Evaluating Oral Language* in the **Evaluation Resources** section of the *Teacher's Edition*.

Cooperative Learning

Cooperative learning suggestions for *Think and Discuss* appear at the beginning of the **Teacher's Edition.**

Remembering the Selection

Ask children to recall the story and identify

- each word used to describe the boy.
- each animal associated with the describing word.

Encourage children to look at the story's illustrations to help themselves recall the information. You may wish to create a class chart to record children's responses.

Boy	Animal
quick	cricket
slow	snail
small	ant
large	whale
sad	basset

Discussing the Selection

The following questions focus on positive self-image. As children respond to the questions, ask them to support their answers with examples from the story. Encourage children to agree or disagree with their classmates' responses and to substantiate their opinions.

Remind children to speak clearly and loudly enough so they can be heard and understood.

1. Who is telling the story in "Quick as a Cricket"? (**Possible response:** *The boy is telling the story.*) (*Interpretive*)

2. How do you think the boy feels about himself? (**Possible response:** *I think the boy feels good about himself because he is able to do different kinds of things.*) (*Interpretive*)

3. In the picture on page 11 of the Big Book the boy is small as an ant. Why might a child feel very small? (**Possible responses:** *A child might feel small because grownups and older children are much taller. A child might feel small when he cannot do the things older people can do.*) (*Critical*)

4. If you could be one of the animals in the story for a day, which would be the most exciting? (*Encourage children to express their ideas.*) (*Creative*)

5. Do you think the boy is having fun? Tell why or why not. (**Possible responses:** *The boy is having fun because he is playing with the animals. The boy can talk to the animals.*) (*Critical*)

During the discussion, children will need to

- **identify** the speaker in the story.
- **interpret** the character's feelings from his words and actions.
- **analyze** why the character might feel a certain way.
- **specify** which animals they might like to be for a day.
- **evaluate** the story in the thematic unit.

You may wish to model responses to the questions. Use the possible responses given.

Tips for Evaluating the Oral Response

- Children should speak clearly and at the appropriate volume.
- Children should respond in complete thoughts.
- Children should ask relevant questions.

Additional Discussion Questions

Notes for Evaluating the Oral Response

Think and Write

Cooperative Learning

Cooperative learning suggestions for *Think and Write* appear at the beginning of the *Teacher's Edition.*

Making the Assignment

Review that the boy in the story told how he is like the different animals. Tell children that now they are going to write about themselves, using words that tell what they are like. They will make booklets about themselves with their writing.

Using the Writing Process

Prewriting   Ask children to name words that describe animals. List their responses on the chalkboard or on chart paper. Draw a circle around each describing word. Then have them name various animals that can be described by each word. Write these animal names in a cluster around each describing word.

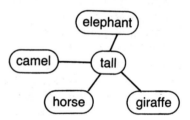

Notes for Cooperative Learning

Notes for Making the Assignment

290

Drafting   Have children dictate sentences to you that tell what animal they are like. Begin by modeling a response and writing on the chalkboard or on chart paper. An example follows.

I am as silly as a monkey.

Encourage the children to write as many sentences as they wish. Write each dictated sentence for the child at the bottom of a separate piece of paper. Then follow this procedure.

- Read each sentence to the child.
- Read each sentence with the child.
- Have the child read each sentence.
- Have the child illustrate each sentence.

Responding/Revising/Editing   After each child has dictated sentences and illustrated them, reread the sentence you wrote. Draw attention to the conventions of writing such as beginning sentences with a capital letter, leaving spaces between words, ending sentences with a period, and following left-to-right progression.

Postwriting (Sharing)   Compile each child's papers into a booklet. Have each child write his or her name on the cover for the title of the booklet. Display the booklets in the reading corner for children to read independently or to share with each other.

Notes for Using the Writing Process

Notes for Evaluating the Written Response

Develop Skills

Strategies for developing concepts and skills related to "Quick as a Cricket" are included in this section. Select appropriate activities to teach to the whole class, small groups, or individual children.

Developing Concepts and Skills

Language:	Describing Words
Composition:	Story
Auditory Discrimination:	Alliteration
Visual Discrimination:	Opposites
Sound-Letter Correspondences:	Initial Correspondences /t/t

Focusing on Language

Using Describing Words   Tell children that there are certain words that tell what people and animals are like. Ask them to listen as you reread the first line in the story "Quick as a Cricket." Have them name the word that tells what the boy is like and what the cricket is like *(quick)*. Write the word *quick* on the chalkboard. Point to and read the word aloud. Then follow the same procedure as you read the remaining pages in the story.

Use *Activity Book* page 54 with children. Have them identify the pictures at the top of the page. As each is identified, have them find the word, run their fingers under it, and say it aloud. Have each child draw a picture of an animal and dictate to you a word that describes the animal. Write the describing word on the writing rule for the child. You may wish to have some children copy the word.

Activity Book page 55 also focuses on describing words. This time ask children to use a word that describes themselves. Have children draw a picture and dictate the describing word to you. Follow the same procedure used for the previous *Activity Book* page.

Focusing on the Writer's Use of Language

Review with children how most of the lines in the story are the same. *(All story lines except for the final page use the same pattern: I'm as _____ as a _____.)* Ask why the writer may have decided to repeat these words. (**Possible responses:** *The words make the story easy to read. The words help you know that the boy is going to name how he is like another animal. The sentences are fun to read.*)

Focusing on Composition

Note: Through observing and evaluating children's writing in a variety of situations and at different times, you can gather data which can help you understand children's writing development. Use the *Checklist for Observing and Evaluating Writing* in the **Evaluation Resources** section of the *Teacher's Edition.*

Writing About a Special Talent   Ask children to think about something they can do well and then to write about this special ability they have. Accept their writing regardless of its stage of development. Many children will draw pictures, while others scribble, write letters, or use invented spelling. Have children share their writing by reading it aloud to you, a group of classmates, or family members.

Focusing on Auditory Discrimination

Listening for Alliteration   Read aloud the last pages of the selection. Repeat the words *loud* and *lion.* Ask children to tell how the words are the same. *(They both begin with the same sound.)* Then ask children to think of and name other words that begin like *loud* and *lion.*

Reread "Quick as a Cricket" one page at a time. Ask children to listen for other words that begin with the same sounds.

Focusing on Visual Discrimination

Identifying Opposites   Have children look at pairs of pages in "Quick as a Cricket" to identify words that are opposite in meaning. Then write the words *quick* and *slow* on the chalkboard. Read the words. Then ask children to identify the difference between how a cricket moves and how a snail moves. Ask if they move in the same way or in different ways. Have them demonstrate the movements to show the differences.

Continue in the same manner with the remaining pairs of opposites: small-large, sad-happy, cold-hot, loud-quiet. Have the children use objects, body movements, or facial expressions to show the differences in meanings.

Focusing on Sound-Letter Correspondences

Recognizing Initial /t/t   Ask children to listen for the word *toad* as you read page 16. Have them raise their hands when they hear the word. Then ask children to listen for the word *together* as you read the last page. Have them raise their hands when they hear the word. Write the words *toad* and *together* on the chalkboard. Have children say the words. Then circle the first letter in each word and explain that both words begin with the letter *t.*

Use **Activity Book** page 56 with children. Have them repeat the words *toad* and *together* as they finger-trace the uppercase *T* and the lowercase *t.*

Have children identify the pictures at the top of the page. As each is identified, have them find the word, run their fingers under it, and say it aloud. Explain that each word begins with the same sound they hear at the beginning of *toad* and *together.*

Have children name other words that begin with the same sound they hear at the beginning of *tiger* and *turtle.* Then ask each child to draw a picture of something whose name begins with the same sound and dictate to you a word that names the picture. Write the word on the writing rule for the child. You may wish to have some children copy the word.

Activity Book: Language

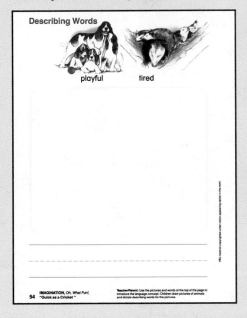

Activity Book: Language

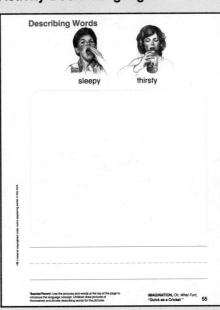

Activity Book: Sound/Letter

Think and Extend

For the Classroom

Mathematics—Constructing a Pictograph Have each child draw a picture of an animal on an index card. Label each picture with the child's name (Karin's Dog; Michael's Moose). Construct a graph that lists the describing words used in the story. Discuss the characteristics of the animals drawn by the children and have children decide which word best describes each of their animals. Pin the pictures next to the appropriate describing words to form a pictograph. Analyze the information on the graph. Have children count the number of animals in each category. Have them tell you which category has the most and which has the least.

Science/Art—Constructing Special Zoos Teach children how to make a zoo animal using paper. You will need drawing paper. Have each child select a zoo animal to draw and color on the drawing paper. Then have children decide what kind of zoo their animal should live in. The types of zoos include: Big Zoo, Small Zoo, Loud Zoo, and Quiet Zoo.

Then have children decide what kind of zoo their animal should live in. The types of zoos include: Big Zoo, Small Zoo, Loud Zoo, and Quiet Zoo.

Label four different areas in the classroom or on a bulletin board with the zoo names. Have children categorize their animals by placing them in zoos that appropriately describe them. If more than one zoo is appropriate, have children choose one.

Notes for Cooperative Learning

Additional Classroom Activities

For the Home

The homework assignment that follows also appears on **Homework Notebook copying master 18.** You may wish to distribute the copying masters to the children.

Writing Have children think of something special about each member of their families and dictate sentences that tell about them. For example: *Mom is the best cook in the world. Dad is the best ballplayer I know. Grandpa knows everything about wild animals.* Suggest that parents follow this procedure after taking the child's dictation.

- Read the sentences to the child.
- Read the sentences with the child.
- Have the child read the sentences.
- Have the child illustrate the sentences with a family portrait.

Suggest that children share their sentences with classmates the following day.

Reading Suggest that children and older family members look at refrigerated food and their containers. Encourage them to read the food containers and point out words that desribe the food products. Have an older family member copy the words onto a piece of paper and read the words with the child.

For Extended and Recreational Reading

You may wish to recommend the following books about developing a positive self-image. Encourage family members to visit the public library with children to select the books to be read.

Books About Developing a Positive Self-Image

William's Doll by Charlotte Zolotow. Harper & Row, 1985.

Look What I Can Do by Jose Aruego. Scribner, 1971.

The Carrot Seed by Ruth Krauss. Harper & Row, 1945.

Story of Ferdinand by Munro Leaf. Penguin, 1977.

Nobody Listens to Andrew by Elizabeth Guilfoile. Modern Curriculum, 1957.

More Books About Developing a Positive Self-Image

By Myself compiled by Lee Bennett Hopkins. Harper & Row, 1980.

Humphrey the Dancing Pig by Arthur Getz. Dial Press, 1980.

Herbert Hated Being Small by Karla Kuskin. Houghton Mifflin, 1979.

Additional Home Activities

Additional Books for Extended and Recreational Reading

Notes

Ideas for Cooperative Learning

Ideas for Meeting the Needs of Individual Students

Questioning Strategies

Focusing on "How Do They Feel?"

While **listening** to and **reading** the selection, children will focus on understanding others' feelings. Children will also use **writing, listening,** and **speaking** skills as they respond to the selection. They will use higher-level **thinking** skills throughout the lesson.

OBJECTIVES

WRITING/THINKING

- To dictate a response to literature using the writing process.
- To write in the analytical/expository domain.
- To use describing words.
- To write about a personal experience.

READING/THINKING

- To interpret the feelings of characters.
- To make predictions about characters.
- To evaluate the placement of a story in a thematic unit.
- To recognize the use of photographs to tell a story.
- To identify feelings shown by facial expressions.
- To recognize initial correspondences. (/f/f)

SPEAKING/THINKING

- To discuss personal experiences before reading a selection.
- To participate in shared reading.
- To participate in group discussions.
- To dictate a response to literature.
- To tell a story about a set of illustrations.

LISTENING/THINKING

- To listen to the oral reading of a selection.
- To listen to and analyze responses to opinions about a selection.
- To listen for telling sentences and asking sentences.
- To listen for initial sounds. (/f/)

LEARNING STRATEGIES

- Brainstorming ideas related to children's own experiences.
- Previewing the selection and making predictions about the content.
- Completing a drawing to help comprehension.
- Completing a chart to help organize writing.
- Analyzing the writer's use of language.

Summary

Various situations cause children to express different feelings. A boy is happy because his dog wins a ribbon. A girl is upset when she falls off her bicycle. Two children laugh as they read a funny book. A boy is sad when he cannot play baseball because of rain.

INDIVIDUAL NEEDS

Suggestions for teaching children with special needs are provided on *Teacher's Edition* page 248.

- The blue objectives may require direct instruction.

PLANNING CALENDAR

		STUDENT'S EDITIONS	TEACHER'S EDITION	ACTIVITY BOOK
DAY 1 INTO THE SELECTION	**THINK AND READ**			
	Preparing to Read	● *pages 22–25* ■ *pages 22–25*	*pages 299–300*	
	Planning a Reading Strategy	● *pages 22–25* ■ *pages 22–25*	*page 300*	
DAYS 2-4 THROUGH THE SELECTION	**THINK AND DISCUSS**			
	Remembering the Selection	● *pages 22–25* ■ *pages 22–25*	*page 302*	
	Discussing the Selection	● *pages 22–25* ■ *pages 22–25*	*pages 302–303*	
	THINK AND WRITE			
	Making the Assignment		*page 304*	
	Using the Writing Process		*page 305*	
	Develop Skills			
	Focusing on Language		*page 306*	*pages 57–58*
	Focusing on Composition		*page 307*	
	Focusing on Auditory Discrimination		*page 307*	
	Focusing on Visual Discrimination		*page 307*	
	Focusing on Sound-Letter Correspondences		*page 307*	*page 59*
	Focusing on the Writer's Use of Language		*page 306*	
DAY 5 BEYOND THE SELECTION	**THINK AND EXTEND**			
	For the Classroom		*pages 308–309*	
	For the Home		*page 309*	
			▲ Homework Notebook copying master 19	

● ***Happy Times! Story Land 2***
■ ***Oh, What Fun!*** Storybook

▲ ***Learning Resources File***

298

Note: Through observing and evaluating children's reading in a variety of situations and at different times, you can gather data that can help you understand and support individual children's reading development. Use the *Checklist for Observing and Evaluating Reading* in the **Evaluation Resources** section of the *Teacher's Edition* to gather data.

Cooperative Learning

Cooperative learning suggestions for *Think and Read* appear at the beginning of the *Teacher's Edition.*

Preparing to Read

▶**Relating to Children's Experiences**   Ask children to recall how they felt when they got up this morning. As they respond, write the words that name their feelings on the chalkboard. Their list may include *tired, sleepy, happy, excited, grumpy, good.* Discuss why they did not all feel the same way. Stress that it is all right to have different feelings.

After the discussion, have children listen as you read the fingerplay "When I Am . . ." and name the different feelings a person can have. Then teach children the actions for the fingerplay.

When I Am . . .

When I am sad, I want to cry.
  [rub eyes]
When I am proud, I want to fly.
  [extend arms outwards, veer]
When I am curious, I want to know.
  [scratch head, puzzled, wave hand as if to teacher]
When I am impatient, I want to go.
  [cross arms, tap foot]
When I am bored, I want to play.
  [yawn, look around]
When I am happy, I smile all day.
  [grin]

(poem continued on the next page)

Notes for Cooperative Learning

Notes for Preparing to Read

When I am shy, I want to hide.
  [peer over shoulder with back to audience]
When I am depressed, I stay inside.
  [rest jaws on fists]
When I am puzzled, I want to shrug.
  [shrug]
When I am loving, I kiss and hug.
  [hold arms out and draw in, as if embracing someone]

▶**Previewing and Predicting** Point to the title of the story and read it to the children. Have them glance at the illustrations and tell what they think the story might be about. You may wish to model a response.

I see children in the pictures. They are doing different things. I think the story tells how these children feel.

▶**Setting a Purpose** Tell children that as they look at the illustrations in the story, they should think about how each boy and girl feels and why.

Planning a Reading Strategy

Sharing Reading Allow children to take turns telling about one page of the story. Encourage them to point to details in the illustrations as they tell what is happening. Make certain they answer the question, "How do they feel?" as their narration is given.

Encourage children to react spontaneously with comments and questions after they have shared the story.

Reading Orally Ask volunteers to perform the roles of the children in the story by pantomiming the actions suggested by each illustration. Ask other children to narrate as others pantomime.

Reading Silently Have children carefully examine the illustrations in the wordless story. Tell them to think about who is in each illustration and what the child is doing and saying. Have them also think about how each child must feel.

Connections
How Do They Feel?

22

23

24

25

Think and Discuss

Note: Through observing and evaluating children's oral language (listening and speaking) in a variety of situations and at different times, you can gather data that can help you understand and support individual children's oral development. Use the *Checklist for Evaluating Oral Language* in the **Evaluation Resources** section of the *Teacher's Edition.*

Cooperative Learning

Cooperative learning suggestions for *Think and Discuss* appear at the beginning of the **Teacher's Edition.**

Remembering the Selection

Ask children to recall the story and identify the feelings of the children shown in the illustrations. List their responses on the chalkboard or on chart paper. Point to and read each response after writing it. A sample chart follows.

How do they feel?
His dog won a ribbon.
She fell off her bike.
They read a funny book.
He cannot play baseball.

Discussing the Selection

The following questions focus on understanding others' feelings. As children respond to the questions, ask them to support their answers with examples from the story. Encourage children to agree or disagree with their classmates' responses and to substantiate their opinions.

Remind children to speak clearly and loudly enough so they can be heard and understood.

Notes for Cooperative Learning

Notes for Remembering the Selection

302

1. What causes the children in the story to have different feelings? (**Possible response:** *The things that happen to the children make them have different kinds of feelings.*) *(Interpretive)*
2. Which children in the story look happy? (**Possible response:** *The boy with the dog looks happy. The girl and the boy are laughing at the book.*) *(Literal)*
3. How do you know the children are happy? (**Possible responses:** *The boy is smiling. The two children are laughing.*) *(Interpretive)*
4. Which children look unhappy? (**Possible responses:** *The girl who fell off the bike is crying. The boy is frowning because he cannot go outside.*) *(Literal)*
5. If you knew the children who are unhappy, what would you say or do to make them happy again? (**Possible responses:** *I would invite the boy over to my house to play. I would tell the girl that I fell off my bike once . . .*) *(Creative)*
6. Think about the boy in the story "Quick as a Cricket." If he were in this story, how would he feel? (**Possible responses:** *I think he would feel happy because he has fun acting like the different animals. I think he would feel proud because he can do many things.*) *(Critical)*

During the discussion, children will need to
- **relate** what they would do if they were friends with these children.
- **recognize** the feelings of characters by their facial expressions and actions.
- **evaluate** the story in the thematic unit.

You may wish to model responses to the questions. Use the possible responses given.

Tips for Evaluating the Oral Response

- Children should speak clearly and at the appropriate volume.
- Children should respond in complete thoughts.
- Children should ask relevant questions.

Additional Discussion Questions

Notes for Evaluating the Oral Response

Think and Write

Making the Assignment

Review that the children in the story had different feelings because of things that happened to them. Tell children that they are now going to add a page to the story. They will write a sentence about a feeling and illustrate it. They will make a class book about feelings.

Notes for Cooperative Learning

Notes for Making the Assignment

Using the Writing Process

Prewriting   Ask children to recall the feelings of each person in the story and what happened to make each person have those feelings. Encourage children to look at each illustration and suggest words that name feelings. Ask children to think of some other feelings that were not in the story. The following questions may help ellicit responses.

How did you feel on the first day of school?
How do you feel when your friends can't play with you?
How do you feel when you are sick?
How do you feel when you fall down?
How do you feel when you wake up in the morning?

You may wish to create a class cluster to record children's responses.

Drafting   Explain to children that now they must think of a make-believe character to add to the story. It can be a boy or a girl or both. Have children dictate sentences to you that tell about the feelings of these make-believe people. Begin by modeling a response and writing on the chalkboard or on chart paper. An example follows.

The boy feels excited because he is going on a vacation.

Write each child's sentences on a piece of paper. Then follow this procedure.

- Read the sentences to the child.
- Read the sentences with the child.
- Have the child read the sentences.
- Have the child illustrate the sentences.

Responding/Revising/Editing   After each child has dictated sentences, reread the sentence you wrote. Draw attention to conventions of writing such as beginning sentences with a capital letter, leaving spaces between words, ending sentences with a period, and following left-to-right progression.

Postwriting (Sharing)   Invite children to read their sentences about the story. Then collect the drawings and sentences and compile them in a book called "Everyone Has Feelings." Display the book in the reading corner for children to read independently or with each other.

Notes for Using the Writing Process

Notes for Evaluating the Written Response

Develop Skills

Strategies for developing concepts and skills related to "How Do They Feel?" are included in this section. Select appropriate activities to teach the whole class, small groups, or individual children.

Developing Concepts and Skills

Language:	Describing Words
Composition:	Story
Auditory Discrimination:	Telling and Asking Sentences
Visual Discrimination:	Facial Expressions
Sound-Letter Correspondences:	Initial Correspondence /f/f

Focusing on Language

Using Words That Describe Feelings   Tell children that there are certain words that tell how a person feels. Ask them to listen for words that tell how the children feel as you read examples from the sentences children wrote for *Think and Write.*

After you read their sentences, ask children to name words that tell how people feel. Write each word on the chalkboard and read it aloud. Ask children to think of other feeling words they would like to add to the list.

Use *Activity Book* page 57 with children. Have them identify the pictures of children at the top of the page. As each is identified, have them find the word, run their fingers under it, and say it aloud. Have each child draw a picture of a child and dictate to you a word that describes how the child feels. Write the describing word on the writing rule for the child. You may wish to have some children copy the word.

Activity Book page 58 also focuses on feelings. Follow the same procedure used for the previous page. Have children draw a picture of themselves doing something that makes them happy.

Focusing on the Writer's Use of Language

Discuss with children how the writer tells the story. *(The writer uses pictures to tell the story.)* Ask why the writer may have decided to use only pictures. (**Possible responses:** *The writer uses pictures to show the faces of real children like ourselves so we can understand how they feel about what is happening.*)

Focusing on Composition

Note: Through observing and evaluating children's writing in a variety of situations and at different times, you can gather data that can help you understand children's writing development. Use the *Checklist for Observing and Evaluating Writing* in the **Evaluation Resources** section of the *Teacher's Edition*.

Writing About a Celebration   Ask children to think about how they felt on their last birthday or a big holiday celebration. Have them write about the things they did, like having friends over for a cake or going to the house of a relative to exchange gifts.

Accept their writing regardless of its stage of development. Many children will draw pictures, while others scribble, write letters, or use invented spelling. Have children share their writing by reading it aloud to you, a group of classmates, or family members.

Focusing on Auditory Discrimination

Listening for Asking and Telling Sentences   Read aloud the title of the story "How Do They Feel?" Ask children if the title tells them something or asks them a question. Elicit that the title asks a question about the children in the illustrations.

Then distinguish between asking and telling sentences by orally asking a question about the first illustration and telling a statement about the same photograph. Sample sentences follow.

Stress that the words in the sentences are different and that your voice sounds different when you ask a question. Demonstrate how your voice goes up at the end of an asking sentence to suggest that something is to follow.

Focusing on Visual Discrimination

Identifying Feelings from Facial Expressions
Review with children that in "How Do They Feel?" children had different feelings because of what was happening to them. Have children "try on" characters in the story by developing facial expressions for them. Begin by having children look at the first page in the story. Ask, "How does the boy feel?" Have children show the boy's feelings by their own facial expressions.

Then continue with the next page. Discuss how different feelings make us look. Ask volunteers to make facial expressions and have classmates to identify the feelings shown by the expressions.

Focusing on Sound-Letter Correspondences

Recognizing Initial /f/f   Use **Activity Book** page 59 with children. Have them repeat the word *feels* as they finger-trace the uppercase *F* and the lowercase *f*.

Have children identify the pictures at the top of the page. As each is identified, have them find the word, run their fingers under it, and say it aloud. Explain that each word begins with the same sound they hear at the beginning of *feels.*

Ask children to identify the letter each word begins with. Tell them that the letter *f* usually stands for the sound they hear at the beginning of *feels*. Then have children listen for the /f/ sound as you say the words *fire* and *fire fighter.*

Have children name other words that begin with the same sound they hear at the beginning of *fire* and *fire fighter*. Then ask each child to draw a picture of something whose name begins with the same sound and dictate to you a word that names the picture. Write the word on the writing rule for the child. You may wish to have some children copy the word.

Activity Book: Language

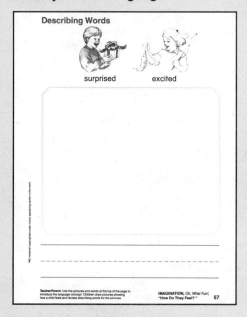

Activity Book: Language

Activity Book: Sound/Letter

Think and Extend

Cooperative Learning

Cooperative learning suggestions for *Think and Extend* appear at the beginning of the *Teacher's Edition.*

Cooperative Learning

The social studies activity can be used for coopera-tive learning. Divide children into pairs. Have the partners discuss feelings and what can cause them. Ask one child to name a feeling and dictate it to you. Write it on one side of a piece of paper. Fold the paper in half. Ask the other child to name a feeling that is the opposite and dictate the word to you. Write it on the other side of the paper. A sample follows.

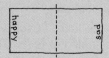

After discussing and agreeing with each other's ideas, have each child draw a picture to illustrate the word written on the partner's half of the paper. When children are finished, display papers on a windowsill or bookcase. One child in each pair can then name the words and explain the drawings.

For the Classroom

Social Studies—Identifying Changing Feelings

Remind children that they can have many different feelings throughout the day. One minute they can be very happy and then suddenly something will happen to make them sad. One minute they can feel bored and the next minute excited.

Give each child a sheet of paper. Have them fold their papers in half. On one half of each child's paper write one word that describes a feeling. Have the child dictate the describing word that means the opposite. On the second half write the word.

Read the word pair for each child and have the child repeat it. Then have children draw illustrations for the words. When they are finished, allow children to name the words and explain their drawings. Display the drawings in the classroom.

Art—Patchwork of Faces
Distribute sheets of drawing paper. Help children fold the paper into sixths. Instruct students to draw six faces, one in each box, showing different feelings. Have children color each face and decorate around the edges of the paper.

Stretch a long piece of yarn across one area of the classroom. Display children's patchwork face quilts by securing them onto the yarn with clothespins.

Notes for Cooperative Learning

Additional Classroom Activities

308

For the Home

The homework assignment that follows also appears on **Homework Notebook copying master 19.** You may wish to distribute the copying masters to the children.

Writing   Have children dictate stories about family activities that make all family members happy and excited, such as a family picnic, a family holiday, a family vacation, or visiting relatives. Encourage family members to follow this procedure after taking the child's dictation.

- Read the story to the child.
- Read the story with the child.
- Have the child read the story.
- Have the child illustrate the story.

   Suggest that children share their stories with classmates the following day.

Reading   Suggest that family members find a story in the newspaper that tells about a happy event. Have family members read and discuss with children the news story. Encourage children to share the news story with classmates the following day.

For Extended and Recreational Reading

You may wish to recommend the following books about emotions and feelings for children to share with family members. Encourage family members to visit the public library with children to select books to read.

Books About Feelings

Alexander and the Terrible, Horrible, No Good Very Bad Day by Judith Viorst. Atheneum, 1976.

Crow Boy by Taro Yashima. Puffin, 1976.

The Tenth Good Thing About Barney by Judith Viorst. Clarion, 1984.

What Mary Jo Shared by Janice M. Udry. A. Whitman, 1966.

Amifika by Lucille Clifton. Dutton, 1977.

The Quarreling Book by Charlotte Zolotow. Harper & Row, 1963.

More Books About Feelings

A Birthday for Frances by Russell Hoban. Harper & Row, 1968.

Evan's Corner by Elizabeth Starr Hill. Holt, Rinehart & Winston, 1967.

Additional Home Activities

Additional Books for Extended and Recreational Reading

Notes

Ideas for Cooperative Learning

Ideas for Meeting the Needs of Individual Students

Questioning Strategies

Focusing on "Over, Under, and Through"

While **listening** to and **reading** the selection, children will focus on everything has a place. Children will also use **writing, listening,** and **speaking** skills as they respond to the selection. They will use higher-level **thinking** skills throughout the lesson.

WRITING/THINKING

- To dictate a response to literature using the writing process.
- To write in the practical/informative domain.
- To use words that name positions.
- To write about a personal experience.

READING/THINKING

- To use position words to describe photographs.
- To recognize solutions to problems.
- To recognize the use of position words.
- To identify spacial relationships represented in photographs.
- To recognize initial correspondences. (/b/b)

SPEAKING/THINKING

- To discuss personal experiences before reading a selection.
- To participate in shared reading.
- To participate in group discussions.
- To dictate a response to literature.
- To repeat the words of a story and pantomime appropriate actions.

LISTENING/THINKING

- To listen to the oral reading of a selection.
- To listen to and analyze responses to opinions about a selection.
- To listen to and follow directions using position words.
- To listen for initial sounds. (/b/)

LEARNING STRATEGIES

- Brainstorming ideas related to children's own experiences.
- Previewing the selection and making predictions about the content.
- Completing a list to help comprehension.
- Completing a list to help organize writing.
- Analyzing the writer's use of language.

Summary

A collection of photographs labeled with position words helps children explore spatial concepts. There are ten concepts in all. The subjects of the photographs present unlimited possibilities for discussion.

INDIVIDUAL NEEDS

Suggestions for teaching children with special needs are provided on *Teacher's Edition* page 248.

- The blue objectives may require direct instruction.

PLANNING CALENDAR

		STUDENT'S EDITIONS	TEACHER'S EDITION	ACTIVITY BOOK
DAY 1 **INTO THE SELECTION**	**THINK AND READ** Preparing to Read Planning a Reading Strategy	● *pages 26–33* ■ *pages 26–33* ● *pages 26–33* ■ *pages 26–33*	*pages 313–314* *page 314*	
DAYS 2-4 **THROUGH THE SELECTION**	**THINK AND DISCUSS** Remembering the Selection Discussing the Selection	● *pages 26–33* ■ *pages 26–33* ● *pages 26–33* ■ *pages 26–33*	*page 318* *page 319*	
	THINK AND WRITE Making the Assignment Using the Writing Process **Develop Skills** Focusing on Language Focusing on Composition Focusing on Auditory Discrimination Focusing on Visual Discrimination Focusing on Sound-Letter Correspondences Focusing on the Writer's Use of Language		 *page 322* *page 323* *page 324* *page 324–325* *page 325* *page 325* *page 325* *page 324*	 *pages 60–61* *page 62*
DAY 5 **BEYOND THE SELECTION**	**THINK AND EXTEND** For the Classroom For the Home		*page 326* *page 327* ▲ Homework Notebook copying master 20	

● *Happy Times! Story Land 2*
■ *Oh, What Fun!* Storybook

▲ *Learning Resources File*

Note: Through observing and evaluating children's reading in a variety of situations and at different times, you can gather data which can help you understand and support individual children's reading development. Use the *Checklist for Observing and Evaluating Reading* in the **Evaluation Resources** section of the ***Teacher's Edition.***

Cooperative Learning

Cooperative learning suggestions for *Think and Read* appear at the beginning of the ***Teacher's Edition.***

Preparing to Read

▶**Relating to Children's Experiences**   Ask children if they have ever played "Simon Says." Ask them to tell what they did when they played the game.

After the discussion, have children play a game of "Simon Says" with you. Tell them they will follow the directions to do something only when you say "Simon Says." Have children stand and listen carefully for directions that tell them what to do. Then have them follow your actions. Try to use complete sentences and include position words such as those found in the story when giving children directions. Some examples follow.

Simon says, "Put your hands on your head."
Simon says, "Point your finger in the air."
Simon says, "Walk across the floor."

▶**Previewing and Predicting**   Point to the title of the story and read it to children. Have them think about what these three words mean to them. Then ask them what they think the story might be about. You may wish to model a response.

I can go over things like a rock. I can go under things like an umbrella. And I can go through things like a door. I think the story might be about places we go and things we can do.

Notes for Cooperative Learning

Notes for Preparing to Read

►**Setting a Purpose**   Tell children that as they listen to the words and look at the photographs in "Over, Under, and Through" they should think about where the people and things are in each picture.

Planning a Reading Strategy

Sharing Reading   Read aloud the position words, pausing after each and pointing to each corresponding photograph.

Encourage children to react spontaneously with comments and questions after you have read the story.

Reading Orally   Read aloud the story. Encourage children to join in by repeating the position words after you say them. Ask one child to point to the photograph that illustrates the meaning of the word while the others use hand motions to show the meaning of the word.

Reading Silently   Give children the opportunity to "read" the story independently. Explain that the illustrations will help them remember each word and the position it is showing.

on

in

28

29

around

across

between

30

31

beside

below

32

33

Notes

Ideas for Cooperative Learning

Ideas for Meeting the Needs of Individual Students

Questioning Strategies

Think and Discuss

Note: Through observing and evaluating children's oral language (listening and speaking) in a variety of situations and at different times, you can gather data that can help you understand and support individual children's oral development. Use the *Checklist for Observing and Evaluating Oral Language* in the **Evaluation Resources** section of the *Teacher's Edition.*

Cooperative Learning

Cooperative learning suggestions for *Think and Discuss* appear at the beginning of the *Teacher's Edition.*

Remembering the Selection

Ask children to recall the story and identify

- each position word.
- each person or thing in the photograph that shows the position.

Encourage children to look at the photographs to recall the information. Help children respond by asking "where" questions. Begin with the question "Where is the boy?" You may wish to create a class list to record children's responses. Outline each position word with crayon or colored marker. A sample chart follows.

Where Do We Find Things?
<u>over</u> the fire hydrant <u>under</u> the boy <u>through</u> the frame <u>on</u> the hand <u>in</u> the telephone booth <u>between</u> the cracks <u>around</u> the tree <u>across</u> the water <u>beside</u> the chair <u>below</u> on the street

Notes for Cooperative Learning

Notes for Remembering the Selection

318

Discussing the Selection

The following questions focus on everything having a place. As children respond to the questions, ask them to support their answers with examples from the story. Encourage children to agree or disagree with their classmates' responses and to substantiate their opinions.

Remind children to speak clearly and loudly enough so they can be heard and understood.

1. Where do you think the photographs in the story were taken? (**Possible response:** *I think they were taken in the city because some pictures show tall buildings.*) *(Interpretive)*

2. Which photographs show children having fun? (**Possible response:** *The boy jumping over a fire hydrant and children playing in a circle around a tree are having fun.*) *(Critical)*

3. Look at the photograph of the street. What position words can you use to tell where things are? (**Possible responses:** *People are walking on the sidewalk. Cars are on the road. Some cars are parked beside the sidewalk. Streetlights hang over the street. People walk in and out of stores.*) *(Literal)*

4. If you could be in one of these pictures, which one would you choose and why? (**Possible responses:** *I would like to hold the chick on my hand. I think it would feel nice. I would like to be jumping over fire hydrants. It looks like fun.*) *(Creative)*

5. Why is it important to see and know where things are and where they belong? (**Possible responses:** *I like to see where things go. I like to know where things are and how I can get to them.*) *(Critical)*

During the discussion, children will need to

- **identify** where the photographs were taken.
- **choose** photographs showing children having fun.
- **use** position words to tell where things are in one photograph.
- **decide** which photograph shows a place they would like to be.
- **evaluate** the placement of this selection in the thematic unit.

You may wish to model responses to the questions. Use the possible responses given.

Tips for Evaluating the Oral Response

- Children should speak clearly and at the appropriate volume.
- Children should respond in complete thoughts.
- Children should ask relevant questions.

Additional Discussion Questions

Notes for Evaluating the Oral Response

Think and Discuss

Talking About Stories and Poems

The children have read the stories and poems in "Oh, What Fun!" Have children compare and contrast the selections in Unit 4. Use the discussion questions and the possible responses provided.

1. If you were to paint a picture of the five little ducks, what kind of picture would it be? (**Possible responses:** *It would be a pretty picture with the ducks swimming in a blue pond. It would be a funny picture with the one duck quacking.*)
2. How would you feel if you woke up and smelled pancakes? (**Possible responses:** *I would feel happy because I like to eat pancakes. I would feel hungry if I smelled them cooking.*)
3. Which story or poem tells about a kind of fun you would like to have? (**Possible responses:** *Making pancakes would be fun. I would like to watch a magic show. I think painting a silly picture would be fun.*)
4. Which children in the stories and poems seem as happy as larks? (**Possible responses:** *the little ducks seem as happy as larks. The boy whose dog won a ribbon and the children riding bicycles look happy.*)

During the discussion children will talk about

- how it would feel to have the kinds of experiences described in the stories and poems.
- how the actions of the characters in the stories and poems relate to the unit theme.

Bookshelf

Introduce children to these and other selections that relate to the theme of the unit.

An Evening at Alfie's by Shirley Hughes. Lothrop, Lee & Shepard, 1985. There is always some excitement at Alfie's house, expecially on the night when the water pipe bursts!

Rabbits on Roller Skates by Jan Wahl. Crown, 1986. A story in verse about mischievous rabbits who skate their way to the roller rink.

Cromwell by Barney Saltzberg. Atheneum, 1986. Cromwell the dog proves to be quite different as he wears clothes, reads books, digs with a shovel, and learns to play the cello.

Jesse Bear, What Will You Wear? by Nancy White Carlstrom. Macmillan, 1986. Jesse is repeatedly asked the same question in this humorous story written in verse.

The Big Sneeze by William Van Horn. Scholastic, 1985. This collection of three funny stories centers around Burt Brontosaurus who loves flowers and never hurts anyone.

Notes

Ideas for Cooperative Learning

Ideas for Meeting the Needs of Individual Students

Questioning Strategies

Think and Write

Cooperative Learning

Cooperative learning suggestions for *Think and Write* appear at the beginning of the **Teacher's Edition.**

Making the Assignment

Review that each thing in the photographs was in its own place. Tell children that now they are going to write about the people and things they see everyday in school and places where they are found. They will make a class book of their writing.

Notes for Cooperative Learning

Notes for Making the Assignment

Using the Writing Process

Prewriting Ask children to name things in school. Have them use position words to tell where these things are found. List their responses on the chalkboard or on chart paper. Point to and read each response after you write it. A sample chart follows.

Over, Under, and Through in Our School	
chair	<u>under</u> the table
pencil	<u>on</u> the desk
books	<u>in</u> the bookcase
flag	<u>over</u> the school
bulletin boards	<u>around</u> the room
rug	<u>across</u> the floor
plant	<u>beside</u> the window

Drafting Have children dictate sentences to you that tell where things are in school. Sentences can be formed by slotting appropriate words in the following sentence.

The _____ is _____ the _____.

Begin by modeling a response and writing it on the chalkboard or on chart paper. An example follows.

The pencil is on the desk.

Write each child's sentence at the bottom of a piece of paper.
Then follow this procedure.

- Read the sentence to the child.
- Read the sentence with the child.
- Have the child read the sentence.
- Have the child illustrate the sentence.

Encourage children to dictate more than one sentence using position words.

Responding/Revising/Editing After each child has dictated sentences and illustrated them, reread the sentence you wrote. Draw attention to conventions of writing such as beginning sentences with a capital letter, leaving spaces between words, ending sentences with a period, and following left-to-right progression.

Postwriting (Sharing) Compile children's papers in a class book entitled "Over, Under, and Through in Our School." Display the book in the reading corner for children to read independently or with each other.

Notes for Using the Writing Process

Notes for Evaluating the Written Response

Develop Skills

Developing Concepts and Skills

Language:	Position Words
Composition:	Story
Auditory Discrimination:	Oral Directions
Visual Discrimination:	Spatial Relationships
Sound-Letter Correspondences:	Initial Correspondence /b/b

Focusing on Language

Using Position Words Use *Activity Book* page 60 with children. Have them identify where each person and thing is in the pictues at the top of the page. As each is identified, have them find the position word, run their fingers under it, and say it aloud. Have each child draw a picture of two things and dictate to you a position word that tells where the objects are. Write the word on the writing rule for the child. You may wish to have some children copy the word.

   Activity Book page 61 also focuses on position words. Follow the same procedure used for the previous page. Have children draw a picture of two objects or people and dictate to you a word that tells where they are.

Focusing on Composition

Note: Through observing and evaluating children's writing in a variety of situations and at different times, you can gather data which can help you understand children's writing development. Use the *Checklist for Observing and Evaluating Writing* in the **Evaluation Resources** of the *Teacher's Edition*.

Focusing on the Writer's Use of Language

   Show children the writer's name (Tana Hoban) on the first page of the story. Ask children to tell what the writer used to tell her story. *(The writer used photographs of everyday things and children.)* Then discuss why the writer used photographs. (**Possible response:** *The writer wanted to show the meaning of each word.*)
understand how these words tell where things are.)

Writing to Tell Where Things Are Located Ask children to think about things in the classroom. Talk about how each thing has a special place where it is kept. Have children write sentences telling where things are in the classroom. Encourage them to use as many position words as they can.

Accept their writing regardless of its stage of development. Many children will draw pictures, while others scribble, write letters, or use invented spelling. Have children share their writing by reading it aloud to you, a group of classmates, or family members.

Focusing on Auditory Discrimination

Listening to Oral Directions Remind children that the words in the story tell where things and people are in the photographs. Tell children you are going to read each word from the story and use it in a direction that you want them to follow. They must listen carefully to know what to do. The following are examples of directions.

on—Place a book on the floor.
over—Jump over the book.
in—Now put the book in the bookcase.
on, under—Sit on your chair and put your feet under the table.
around—Now stand up and hold hands. Circle around.
below—Stop the circle and wiggle your hands below your knees.

Focusing on Visual Discrimination

Identifying Spatial Relationships Have children look at the first photograph and review *over* and *under*.

Elicit that the boy is over the hydrant and the hydrant is under the boy. Use the same illustration to have children identify other spatial relationships. Ask what is on the boy's head, hands, and feet. *(hat, gloves, shoes)* Ask what is beside the boy. *(buildings)* Ask what is below the boy. *(street)* Ask what place the boy is in. *(city)* Continue in the same manner, using as many position words as possible to discuss each photograph.

Focusing on Sound-Letter Correspondences

Recognizing Initial /b/b Ask children to listen for the word *below* as you read aloud the writing they did for *Think and Write.* After reading, write the word *below* on the chalkboard. Follow the same procedure for the words *beside* and *between.* Then circle the first letter in all three words. Explain that the words *below, beside,* and *between* all begin with the letter *b.*

Use *Activity Book* page 62 with children. Have them repeat the words below, beside, and between as they finger-trace the uppercase *B* and the lowercase *b.*

Have children identify the pictures at the top of the page. As each is identified, have them find the word, run their fingers under it, and say it aloud. Explain that each picture begins with the same sound they hear at the beginning of *below, beside,* and *between.*

Have children name other words that begin with the same sound they hear at the beginning of *boat* and *bear.* Then ask each child to draw a picture of something whose name begins with the same sound and dictate to you a word that names the picture. Write the word on the writing rule for the child. You may wish to have some children copy the word.

Activity Book: Language

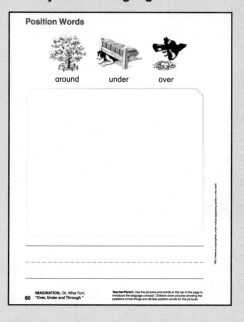

Activity Book: Language

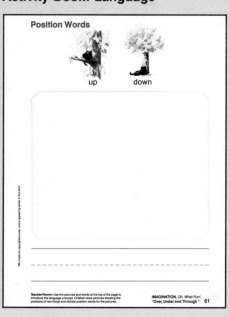

Activity Book: Sound/Letter

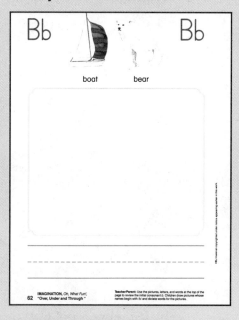

Think and Extend

For the Classroom

Social Studies—Building a City   Use hollow outdoor blocks or large cardboard boxes for children to build their own little city. Have them use the blocks or boxes to make passageways, rooms, tunnels, and mazes. Tell them to explore all the different ways they can move in relation to the structure. As children move about use a camera to photograph them. Later, discuss and label the pictures using position words.

Art—Drawing Pictures   Give children drawing paper. Help them fold the paper into sixths. Then have them listen as you ask the following questions. Have them respond by drawing one picture in each box.

1. What can go over your house?
2. What can go under a fence?
3. What can go around a package?
4. What can go through the rain?
5. What can go on a wall?
6. What can go in a refrigerator?

Have children discuss their drawings when you have finished.

Notes for Cooperative Learning   **Additional Classroom Activities**

For the Home

The homework assignment that follows also appears on **Homework Notebook copying master 20.** You may wish to distribute the copying masters to the children.

Writing Suggest that children ask their parents to spend time with them looking at family photographs. Have them discuss the photographs and describe the positions of things and people. Children should then select one favorite photograph and dictate sentences about it. Encourage family members to follow this procedure after taking the child's dictation.

- Read the sentences to the child.
- Read the sentences with the child.
- Have the child read the sentences.

Reading Suggest that family members read with children the directions for building something or for doing some other type of manipulative activity. If this is not feasible, family members can read and discuss with children stories that lend themselves to spatial concepts.

For Extended and Recreational Reading

You may wish to recommend the following books about spacial concepts for children to share with family members. Encourage family members to visit the public library with children to select books to be read.

Books About Spacial Concepts

The Little House by Virginia Burton. Houghton Mifflin, 1978.

Peter Spier's Rain by Peter Spier. Doubleday, 1982.

Simple Pictures Are Best by Nancy Willard. Harcourt Brace Jovanovich, 1978.

The Cat in the Hat by Dr. Seuss. Beginner, 1957.

There's a Nightmare in My Closet by Mercer Mayer. Dial, 1968.

More Books About Spacial Concepts

Over, Under, and All-Around by Sylvia Root Tester. Children's World, 1973.

The Discovery Book of Up and Down by Judith Conway. Raintree, 1977.

Additional Home Activities

Additional Books for Extended and Recreational Reading

Unit 5

Let's Go Outside!

Theme: The adventure of independent exploration

Reading Selections	Writing Assignments
• Coco Can't Wait	• Dictate Sentences About Things We Ride
• I Love You Mouse	• Dictate Sentences About Things We Love
• What Is Beyond the Hill?	• Dictate Asking Sentences About the World
• Connections: Water	• Dictate Descriptions About Water
• Hello and Good-bye	• Dictate Sentences About the Seasons

Unit Resources

As you work through the Integrated Instructional Plans in this unit, you may want to use the following resources included in the **Student/Teacher Resources** and **Evaluation Resources** sections of the *Teacher's Edition.*

Student/Teacher Resources

• Home Letters 6A and 6B
• Extended and Recreational Reading Ideas

Evaluation Resources

• Observation and Evaluation Guides

Students With Individual Needs

	Limited-English-Proficient Students	Less-Prepared Students	Gifted Students	Special Education Students
Think and Read	• Assist students with previewing strategies. Focus on gaining meaning from illustrations. • Use pictures and filmstrips to provide additional background information. • Use audiovisual aids to help students understand difficult concepts. • Explain the meanings of idiomatic expressions found in the selections.	• Provide additional background information when personal experiences are limited. Use pictures, magazines, and filmstrips. • Emphasize strategies included in *Setting a Purpose*. Model strategies for students. • Frequently model and review strategies for recalling and applying prior knowledge.	• After modeling effective prereading strategies, have students lead the discussions that focus on previewing and predicting. • After modeling effective thinking strategies, have students lead the discussions that focus on summarizing the reading process.	• Review individualized education programs (IEPs) with special education staff and discuss necessary modification of curriculum. • For visually-impaired students, provide specialized resources such as large print books, books in braille, or recordings.
Think and Discuss	• Model by reading aloud questions and possible responses. Have students repeat each question and add additional responses. • Provide students opportunities to listen to and repeat native-English speakers' language.	• Have students brainstorm ideas to aid them in answering creative questions. • During discussions, model strategies for asking additional questions. (See the strategies for generating questions at the front of this *Teacher's Edition*.)	• During the discussions, help students focus their abstract thoughts. Model effective strategies. • Encourage students to explain complex thoughts and ideas their classmates do not understand. Model strategies for students.	• Review lesson plans with special education staff to discuss any necessary modification of curriculum. • Develop a specialized listening program for visually-impaired students.
Think and Write	• Provide pictures to stimulate prewriting. Then help students brainstorm and list descriptive words. • During prewriting, ask students to act out words and phrases. Help students verbalize their thoughts. • Have students sketch story events and arrange the pictures in order, before they dictate stories.	• Model the use of prewriting strategies to organize ideas. • During revising, encourage students to expand one or two sentences. Model the process for students.	• During responding, revising, and editing, help students expand complex thoughts. Model effective strategies. • Have students work in cooperative learning groups. (See the suggestions at the front of this *Teacher's Edition*.)	• Review lesson plans with special education staff to discuss any necessary modification of curriculum. • For visually-impaired students, record the directions for the stages of the writing process. Have students record their compositions.
Think and Extend	• Explain vocabulary necessary to complete the activities. Integrate appropriate lessons from science and social studies textbooks. • Have students work in cooperative learning groups. (See the suggestions at the front of this *Teacher's Edition*.)	• Have students work in cooperative learning groups. (See the suggestions for cooperative learning activities at the front of the *Teacher's Edition*.) • Provide manipulatives for students to use while completing mathematics activities.	• Ask students to think of additional *Think and Extend* activities. When appropriate, assign the student-generated activities instead of the activities in the *Writer's Corner*. • Have students work in cooperative learning groups. (See the suggestions at the front of this *Teacher's Edition*.)	• For visually-impaired students, record the directions for the activities. • Review lesson plans with special education staff to discuss any necessary modification of curriculum.

Unit 5

34

Introducing the Unit

Talking About the Theme   To introduce children to the unit, point to and read aloud the title "Let's Go Outside." Ask children to look at the picture that illustrates the opening of the unit. Begin a discussion about the adventure of independent exploration by having children answer the following questions about the picture.

1. What do you see in the picture? (**Possible responses:** *I see a boy looking out the front door of his house. There is a big bird flying in the sky.*)
2. What do you think the boy will do? (**Possible response:** *I think the boy is going to play outside.*)
3. What new things might the boy in the picture discover? (**Possible responses:** *The boy will look for some new friends. The boy might find a new place to play.*)
4. What new things would you want to discover if you were the boy in the picture? (**Possible responses:** *I would like to find a pond so I could go fishing. I would like to find a tree house so my friends and I could play.*)
5. The stories and poems in this unit go together. What do you think the stories and poems will be about? (**Possible response:** *I think the stories will be about finding new things.*)

5 Let's Go Outside

35

Extending Reading   The following books extend the theme of the unit. You may want to share these books as children listen to and "read" the selections in Unit 5. Have children discuss the adventures and explorations in the stories.

The Snowy Day by Ezra Jack Keats. Viking, 1962. Making snowmen, tracks, and angels gives Peter a full but tiring day outside in the snow.

Rosie's Walk by Pat Hutchins. Macmillan, 1968. Rosie the hen is pursued by a fox as she takes a walk through her barnyard home.

Why the Sun and Moon Live in the Sky by Elphinstone Dayrell. Houghton Mifflin, 1968. This African folktale explains why the sun and moon were forced to live in the sky.

A Tree Is Nice by Janice Udry. Harper & Row, 1956. A tree is nice to have for a friend for many reasons.

Bulletin Board Suggestion

Cover the top half of a bulletin board with blue paper and the bottom half with green paper to represent sky and earth. Then ask children to help you draw and cut out outdoor things. Have children dictate naming words for their drawings. Write the names on small labels and attach to the object on the bulletin board.

When the outdoor scene is complete, make a window frame from paper to place over it. Talk about the outdoor scene when the board is finished. You may wish to include the caption, "Let's Go Outside!"

Unit 5

Unit Activities

The following optional unit activities relate to the theme of the unit. The activities may be completed during or after unit instruction. Instructions for setting up learning centers appear at the front of the *Teacher's Edition.*

LISTENING Corner

Objective: To listen to a description and respond by drawing a picture.

Materials: paper and crayons

Procedure: Read aloud a description of the outdoors. Your description may begin with a summary of the weather, such as the following:

It is a cool and windy day in the fall.

You may wish to include how it feels outside, what it looks like outside, and what people or animals are doing outside. Ask children to draw pictures and share the pictures with each other.

READING Corner

Objective: To read books about the adventure of independent exploration.

Materials: paper and crayons, books about independent exploration that may include titles from page 331 in the *Teacher's Edition.*

Procedure: Display books for children to look at. Ask children to select a book. You may wish to read it aloud to children. After you have read the story, have children draw pictures of the adventure they listened to and discuss the story and their pictures with each other.

SPEAKING Corner

Objective: To sing a song about things children can do.

Materials: "Beautiful Day" by Hap Palmer. (This song is in the front of the *Teacher's Edition.*)

Procedure: Work with children to teach them the song "Beautiful Day." Have children pantomime the actions as they sing the song.

WRITING Corner

Objective: To dictate sentences about adventures.

Materials: "Beautiful Day" by Hap Palmer. (This song is in the front of the *Teacher's Edition.*)

Procedure: Make a spinner.

- Cut a large circle from tagboard.
- Divide the circle into thirds.
- In each section draw one symbol for mountains, one for ocean, and one for jungle.
- Attach an arrow in the center using a brad.

Explain each symbol. Show children how to spin the arrow. Have each child spin the arrow and think about what they would explore in a mountain, an ocean, or a jungle. Ask children to draw a picture of their adventure. Then have them dictate sentences that tell about their adventure. Encourage children to share their pictures and sentences with each other.

Note: Some children will prefer to dictate their sentences as you write. Others will prefer to write on their own. Accept their writing regardless of its stage of development. Allow them to draw, scribble, or write using their own spelling.

Focusing on "Coco Can't Wait"

While **listening** to and **reading** the selection, children will focus on modes of transportation. Children will also use **writing, listening,** and **speaking** skills as they respond to the selection. They will use higher-level **thinking** skills throughout the lesson.

OBJECTIVES

WRITING/THINKING

- To dictate a response to literature using the writing process.
- To write in the practical/informative domain.
- To use naming words.
- To write about a personal experience.

READING/THINKING

- To interpret how characters feel.
- To evaluate the placement of a story in a thematic unit.
- To identify types of transportation.
- To recognize initial correspondences /k/c.

SPEAKING/THINKING

- To discuss personal experiences before reading a selection.
- To participate in shared reading.
- To participate in Story Theater.
- To participate in group discussions.
- To dictate a response to literature.

LISTENING/THINKING

- To listen to the oral reading of a selection.
- To listen to an analyze responses and opinions about a selection.
- To identify sounds of things people ride in.
- To listen for initial sound /k/.

LEARNING STRATEGIES

- Brainstorming ideas related to children's own experiences.
- Previewing the selection and making predictions about the content.
- Completing a chart to help comprehension.
- Completing a cluster to help organize writing.
- Analyzing the writer's use of language.

Summary

"Coco Can't Wait" is a story about a girl and her grandmother. Each set out to visit the other at the same times, and neither knows the other is coming. Coco and Grandma spend a lot of time going back and forth traveling in many different vehicles. Coco and Grandma finally meet quite unexpectedly.

INDIVIDUAL NEEDS

Suggestions for teaching children with special needs are provided on *Teacher's Edition* page 328.

- The blue objectives may require direct instruction.

PLANNING CALENDAR

		STUDENT'S EDITIONS	TEACHER'S EDITION	ACTIVITY BOOK
DAY 1 **INTO THE SELECTION**	**THINK AND READ** Preparing to Read Planning a Reading Strategy	● *pages 36–65* ■ *pages 2–31* ● *pages 36–65* ■ *pages 2–31*	*page 335* *page 336*	
DAYS 2-4 **THROUGH THE SELECTION**	**THINK AND DISCUSS** Remembering the Selection Discussing the Selection	● *pages 36–65* ■ *pages 2–31* ● *pages 36–65* ■ *pages 2–31*	*page 342* *page 343*	
	THINK AND WRITE Making the Assignment Using the Writing Process **Develop Skills** Focusing on Language Focusing on Composition Focusing on Auditory Discrimination Focusing on Visual Discrimination Focusing on Sound-Letter Correspondences Focusing on the Writer's Use of Language		 *page 344* *pages 344–345* *pages 346–347* *page 347* *page 347* *page 347* *page 347* *page 346*	 *pages 63–64* *page 65*
DAY 5 **BEYOND THE SELECTION**	**THINK AND EXTEND** For the Classroom For the Home		*page 348* *page 349* ▲ Homework Notebook copying master 21	

● ***Happy Times! Story Land 2*** ▲ ***Learning***
 ■ ***Let's Go Outside!*** Storybook ***Resources File***

Note: Through observing and evaluating children's reading in a variety of situations and at different times, you can gather data that will help you understand and support individual children's reading development. Use the *Checklist for Observing and Evaluating Reading* in the **Evaluation Resources** section of the *Teacher's Edition.*

Cooperative Learning

Cooperative learning suggestions for *Think and Read* appear at the beginning of the *Teacher's Edition.*

Preparing to Read

▶**Relating to Children's Experiences** Ask children to name the different forms of transportation they use to get from one place to another. As children name a vehicle, encourage them to tell where they went and why they use that particular form of transportation.

After the discussion, ask children if they have ever ridden in a bus other than a school bus. Have them sing "The Bus Song" with you. (The words and music can be found in the **Resource** section of the *Teacher's Edition.*) Ask children to tell what happens in the song and to compare it to a bus ride they have experienced.

▶**Previewing and Predicting** Point to the title of the story and read it to the children. Have children look at the first two pages of the selection. Ask children what they think the story will be about. You may wish to model a response.

I think the story is about someone who can't wait because the title is "Coco Can't Wait". I think the story will be about a bus ride because I see a bus.)

▶**Setting a Purpose** Tell children that as they listen to the story, they should think about how people in the story get to where they want to go.

Notes for Cooperative Learning

Notes for Preparing to Read

Planning a Reading Strategy

Sharing Reading Read aloud the story several times, sharing the illustrations and pointing to the text. Draw attention to the different modes of transportation that Coco and Grandma use throughout the story.

Encourage children to react spontaneously with comments and questions after you have read the story. Ask them to think about how Coco and Grandma must feel as they keep missing each other.

Reading Orally Read aloud the story. Encourage children to join in by saying the words that Coco and Grandma say:

"Dear me! Coco is not here!"
"Oh no! Grandma is not here!"

You may also wish to have children work in pairs to "read" the story orally. Have one child read what happens to Coco and the other read what happens to Grandma.

Children may also enjoy acting out "Coco Can't Wait." While you read aloud the selection, a group of children can act as players to perform the actions shown in the story. Refer to the techniques described in *Story Theater* at the beginning of this **Teacher's Edition.**

Reading Silently Give children the opportunity to "read" the story independently. Explain that the illustrations will help them to remember what is happening in the story and how each character feels.

Coco Can't Wait!

A story by Taro Gomi

Coco lives on top of the hill, in the house with the purple roof.

Grandma lives on the mountain, in the house with the orange roof.

2

3

One day Coco wanted to see
Grandma very much.

4

5

And Grandma wanted to see Coco
very much.

6

7

8

9

10

11

"Dear me! Coco is not here!"

"Oh no! Grandma is not here!"

12

13

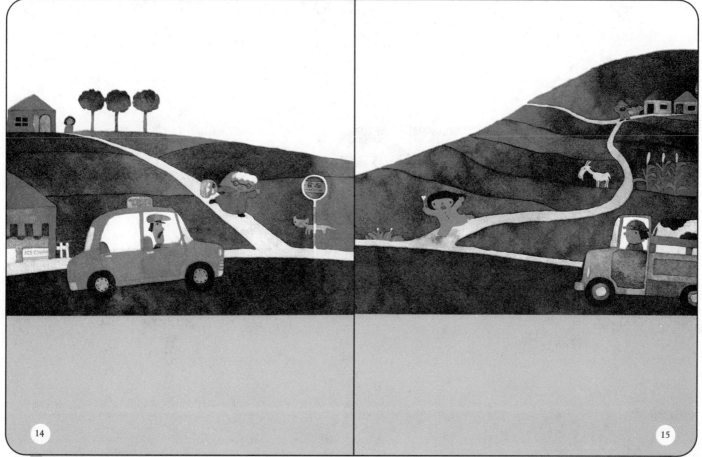

14

15

16

17

18

19

"Oh no! Grandma is not here!"

"Dear me! Coco is not here!"

"I can't wait any longer."

"There isn't a minute to lose."

"Oh, how I want to see Grandma."

"Oh, how I want to see Coco."

24

25

26

27

"Hello, Grandma!"

"Hello, Coco!"

"Next time, Grandma, let's meet in the middle, right under this tree." And Grandma and Coco ate all the apples in Grandma's basket.

28

29

30

31

Think and Discuss

Cooperative Learning

Cooperative learning suggestions for *Think and Discuss* appear at the beginning of the **Teacher's Edition.**

Remembering the Selection

Ask children to recall the story and identify the things Coco and Grandma used to travel.

Encourage children to look at the story illustrations to help themselves recall the information. You may wish to create a class chart to record children's responses. A sample chart follows.

How Coco and Grandma Travel			
Coco	bus	truck	scooter
Grandma	train	taxi	motorcycle

Notes for Cooperative Learning

Notes for Remembering the Selection

Discussing the Selection

The following questions focus on transportation. As children respond to the questions, ask them to support their answers with examples from the story. Encourage children to agree or disagree with their classmates' responses and to substantiate their opinions.

Remind children to speak clearly and loudly enough so they can be heard and understood.

1. How do Coco and Grandma travel?
   (**Possible responses:** *Coco rides in a bus, in a truck, and on a scooter. Grandma rides in a train, in a taxi, and on a motorcycle.*) *(Literal)*

2. How does Coco feel when she realizes Grandma isn't at home? How does Grandma feel when she realizes Coco isn't home? Explain.
   (**Possible response:** *Both Coco and Grandma are disappointed, sad, and a little surprised.*) *(Interpretive)*

3. Why do Coco and Grandma keep missing each other along the way?
   (**Possible responses:** *Coco and Grandma use different ways of getting to one another. They don't know that the other is coming to visit.*) *(Critical)*

4. How would you help Coco and Grandma solve the problem of missing each other along the way?
   (**Possible responses:** *Coco could call Grandma first to tell her she was coming. They could write one another a letter.*) *(Creative)*

5. What does the story of Coco and her grandma have to do with adventures?
   (**Possible responses:** *Coco and Grandma chase each other. Coco and Grandma could not find each other.*) *(Critical)*

During the discussion, children will need to

- **interpret** the characters' feelings.
- **identify** how Coco and Grandma traveled.
- **analyze** why Coco and Grandma kept missing each other and how the problem might have been solved.
- **evaluate** why the story belongs in the thematic unit.

You may wish to model responses to the questions. Use the possible responses given.

Tips for Evaluating the Oral Response

- Children should speak clearly and at the appropriate volume.
- Children should respond in complete thoughts.
- Children should ask relevant questions.

Additional Discussion Questions

Notes for Evaluating the Oral Response

Think and Write

Cooperative Learning

Cooperative learning suggestions for *Think and Write* appear at the beginning of the **Teacher's Edition.**

Making the Assignment

Review with children how Coco and Grandma travel (bus, truck, scooter, train, taxi, motorcycle). Tell children that they will write sentences about their favorite ways to ride. They will then make a picture graph to show how many children in the class like the same kinds of vehicles.

Using the Writing Process

Prewriting Ask children to name vehicles that they like to ride in. List their responses on the chalkboard or on chart paper. Point to and read each word after you write it. A sample chart follows.

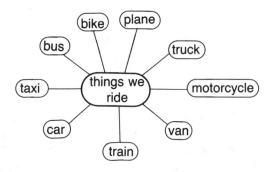

Notes for Cooperative Learning

Notes for Making the Assignment

Drafting   Have children dictate a sentence to you that names the vehicle they like to ride. Begin by modeling a response and writing it on the chalkboard or on chart paper. Examples follow.

I like to ride on a motorcycle.
I like to ride in a van.

Write each child's dictated sentence at the bottom of a sheet of paper. Then follow this procedure.

- Read the sentence to the child.
- Read the sentence with the child.
- Have the child read the sentence.
- Have the child illustrate the sentence.

You may wish to have children look through magazines and cut out pictures of the vehicles they like to ride in. Children can then paste the picture to the paper with their dictated sentences.

Responding/Revising/Editing   After each child has dictated sentences and illustrated them, reread the sentences you wrote. Draw attention to conventions of writing such as beginning sentences with a capital letter, leaving spaces between words, ending sentences with a period, and following left-to-right progression.

Postwriting (Sharing)   Have the children take turns reading aloud their writing to classmates. Then add their illustrations and sentences to a bulletin board

display entitled "Our Travels." Construct a simple graph that shows the vehicles preferred by the children. Make labels (words/pictures) for all the vehicles discussed. Ask children to draw their favorite vehicle on a 5″ × 7″ card and pin it in the appropriate column. Then discuss the results with children. A sample follows.

Our Travels								
bus								
car								
van								
train								
plane								

1 2 3 4 5 6 7 8
Number of Children

Notes for Using the Writing Process

Notes for Evaluating the Written Response

Develop Skills

Strategies for developing concepts and skills related to "Coco Can't Wait" are included in this section. Select appropriate activities to teach the whole class, small groups, or individual children.

Developing Concepts and Skills

Language:	Naming Words
Composition:	Story
Auditory Discrimination:	Sounds
Visual Discrimination:	Types of Transportation
Sound-Letter Correspondences:	Initial Correspondence /k/c

Focusing on Language

Identifying Naming Words Remind children that there are many different words that name things we ride in. Ask children to identify the vehicles they wrote about in *Think and Write*.

Use **Activity Book** page 63 with children. Have them identify the pictures. As each is identified, have them find the word, run their fingers under it, and say it aloud. Ask children to classify the type of transportation to determine if it is used on land, on sea or in air. Have children draw another kind of thing we travel in and dictate naming words. Write the naming words on the writing rules. You may wish to have some children copy the words.

Work with children to help them classify the type of transportation they have drawn. Ask them, "Does it travel on land like a bus? Does it travel in the air like a helicopter? Does it travel in the water like a boat?"

Focusing on the Writer's Use of Language

Show children the writer's name (Taro Gomi) on the first page of the story. Review the things Coco and Grandma rode in as they traveled to each other's houses. Ask children why the writer wanted them to know that Coco could not wait to see Grandma. (**Possible responses:** *It was important to know Coco couldn't wait because then we really wanted her to find Grandma. The longer it took to find Grandma, the more Coco wanted to see her and the more exciting the story got.*)

Use *Activity Book* page 64 with children. Have them identify the pictures of the vehicles at the top of the page. Ask children how they are all alike. (All three vehicles have wheels.) Ask children to draw another vehicle that has wheels and dictate the naming word(s) to you. Write the word(s) on the writing rule. You may wish to have some children copy the word(s).

Focusing on Composition

Note: Through observing and evaluating children's writing in a variety of situations and at different times, you can gather data that will help you understand and support individual children's writing development. Use the *Checklist for Observing and Evaluating Writing* in the **Evaluation Resources** section of the *Teacher's Edition*.

Writing About a Personal Experience Recall with children how much Coco wants to see Grandma. Ask children if they have ever said *"I can't wait!"* as Coco does in the story. Discuss with them that "can't wait" means that you want something very much. Have children think about a time when they had to wait for someone or something special, and have them write about it.

Accept children's writing regardless of its stage of development. Encourage children to write in the way they feel comfortable. They may draw, scribble or make attempts to write words. Have children share their writing by reading it aloud to family members.

Focusing on Auditory Discrimination

Identifying Sounds and Their Sources Review with children the different modes of transportation in "Coco Can't Wait" and in the writing completed for *Think and Write*. Encourage children to describe the possible sounds

made by each of the vehicles named. Then discuss with children how something can be identified by the sound it makes.

Focusing on Visual Discrimination

Identifying Types of Transportation Review with children that in "Coco Can't Wait" there are several types of transportation. Have children look at the pictures, identify all the vehicles, and then discuss the characteristics of each.

Focusing on Sound-Letter Correspondences

Recognizing Initial /k/c Use *Activity Book* page 65 with children. Have them repeat the word *car* as they finger-trace the uppercase *C* and the lowercase *c*.

Have children identify the pictures at the top of the page. As they identify each, have them find the word, run their fingers under it, and say it aloud. Explain that each picture name begins with the same sound they hear at the beginning of *car*.

Ask children to identify the letter each word begins with. Tell them that the letter *c* usually stands for the same sound they hear at the beginning of *car*.

Ask children to identify the letter each word begins with. Tell them that the letter *c* usually stands for the same sound they hear at the beginning of *car*. Then have children listen for the /k/ sound as you say the words *cat* and *cow*.

Have children name other words that begin with the same sound they hear at the beginning of *car*. Then ask each child to draw a picture of something whose name begins with the same sound and dictate to you a word that names the picture. Write the word on the writing rule for the child. You may wish to have some children copy the word.

Activity Book: Language

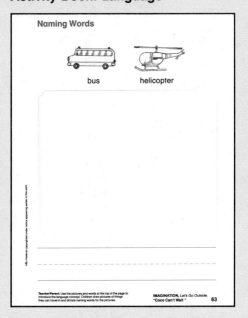

Activity Book: Language

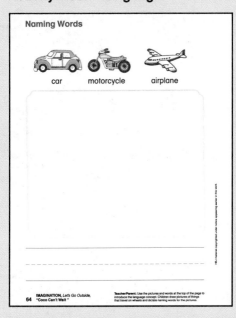

Activity Book: Sound/Letter

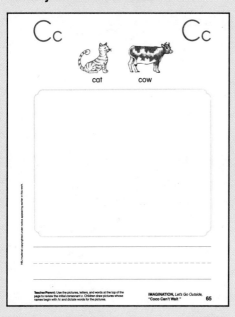

Think and Extend

Cooperative Learning

Cooperative learning suggestions for *Think and Extend* appear at the beginning of the **Teacher's Edition.**

For the Classroom

Health—Talking About Feelings   Direct children's attention to the facial expressions of Coco and Grandma in the story, particularly when they discovered that the other wasn't home (sad, upset, angry) and when they finally got to see each other (happy). Ask children to think about things that make people happy, sad, angry, and upset. Then have them draw pictures showing people when they are happy, sad, angry, and upset. You may wish to have the children dictate a sentence for each picture and then assemble the pictures into a booklet entitled "Feelings." Encourage children to share their booklets with family members.

Mathematics—Talking About Shapes   Review the illustrations of "Coco Can't Wait." Ask children to identify the shapes that the writer used to make the different kinds of vehicles. Ask them to find circles and rectangles in the illustrations.

Then have children look through magazines and newspapers to find pictures of vehicles. Have children look at some of the shapes to determine if they are the same in the story.

 Cooperative Learning

This *Think and Extend* activity can be used for cooperative learning. Have children work in pairs. Ask each child to choose a different vehicle from the story and identify the shapes that the writer used to make the vehicle. Then have each child find a picture of a real vehicle to see if the shapes are the same as in the story. Have partners share their pictures with each other. Both partners must agree on each other's work before one child shares the pictures with the class.

Notes for Cooperative Learning   **Additional Classroom Activities**

For the Home

The homework assignment that follows also appears on **Homework Notebook copying master 21.** You may wish to distribute the copying masters to the children.

Writing Have children dictate sentences to an older family member that tell about a special trip taken by the family. Children should describe how they traveled, where they went, and what they did on the trip. Encourage family members to follow this procedure after taking the child's dictation.

- Read the sentences to the child.
- Read the sentences with the child.
- Have the child read the sentences.
- Have the child illustrate the sentences.

Suggest that children share their sentences and pictures with classmates the following day. Children may also want to bring in photographs and souvenirs from the trip.

Reading Suggest that children and parents or other older family members discuss trips the family has taken. Encourage them to talk about cities or countries where relatives or friends live. If a map or globe is available, point out where relatives or friends live and how children might travel there.

For Extended and Recreational Reading

You may wish to recommend the following books about traveling and families. Encourage family members to visit the public library with children to select the books to be read.

Books About Traveling and Families

Miss Rumphius by Barbara Cooney. Viking, 1982.

Freight Train by Donald Crews. Greenwillow, 1978.

William's Doll by Charlotte Zolotow. Harper & Row, 1972.

My Grandson Lew by Charlotte Zolotwo. Harper & Row, 1974.

La expedición by Willi Baum. Baron, 1978.

More Books About Traveling and Families

Grandpa and Me Together by Susan Goldman. A Whitman, 1980.

Kevin's Grandma by Barbara Williams. Dutton, 1975.

Trucks by Anne Rockwell. E.P. Dutton, 1984.

Wheels by Byron Barton. Harper & Row, 1979.

Airplane Ride by Douglas Florian. Harper & Row, 1984.

Additional Home Activities

Additional Books for Extended and Recreational Reading

Notes

Ideas for Cooperative Learning

Ideas for Meeting the Needs of Individual Students

Questioning Strategies

Focusing on "I Love You Mouse"

While **listening** to and **reading** the selection, children will focus on feeling safe and loved. Children will also use **writing, listening,** and **speaking** skills as they respond to the selection. They will use higher-level **thinking** skills throughout the lesson.

OBJECTIVES

WRITING/THINKING

- To dictate a response to literature using the writing process.
- To write in the sensory/descriptive domain.
- To use describing words.
- To write a story extension.

READING/THINKING

- To recognize animal homes.
- To recognize behavior of animals.
- To evaluate the placement of a story in the thematic unit.
- To identify light and dark.
- To recognize initial correspondences /l// and /k/k.

SPEAKING/THINKING

- To discuss personal experiences before reading a selection.
- To participate in shared reading.
- To participate in group discussions.
- To dictate a response to literature.
- To read aloud a selection using the Story Theater technique.

LISTENING/THINKING

- To listen to the oral reading of a selection.
- To listen for details from an oral reading.
- To listen to and analyze responses to opinions about a selection.
- To listen to sounds of animals.
- To listen for initial sounds. (/l/, /k/)

LEARNING STRATEGIES

- Brainstorming ideas related to children's own experiences.
- Previewing the selection and making predictions about the content.
- Completing a chart to help comprehension.
- Completing a chart to help organize writing.
- Analyzing the writer's use of language.

Summary

A young child visits all of his animal friends and tells each one what he would do to make them feel loved if he were one of them. Finally the young boy's father tells him what he does to make the child feel loved and safe.

INDIVIDUAL NEEDS

Suggestions for teaching children with special needs are provided on *Teacher's Edition* page 328.

- The blue objectives may require direct instruction.

PLANNING CALENDAR

		STUDENT'S EDITIONS	TEACHER'S EDITION	ACTIVITY BOOK
DAY 1 INTO THE SELECTION	**THINK AND READ**			
	Preparing to Read	● *pages 66–91* ■ *pages 32–57*	*page 353*	
	Planning a Reading Strategy	● *pages 66–91* ■ *pages 32–57*	*page 354*	
DAYS 2-4 THROUGH THE SELECTION	**THINK AND DISCUSS**			
	Remembering the Selection	● *pages 66–91* ■ *pages 32–57*	*page 362*	
	Discussing the Selection	● *pages 66–91* ■ *pages 32–57*	*page 363*	
	THINK AND WRITE			
	Making the Assignment		*page 364*	
	Using the Writing Process		*pages 364–365*	
	Develop Skills			
	Focusing on Language		*page 366*	*pages 66–67*
	Focusing on Composition		*page 367*	
	Focusing on Auditory Discrimination		*page 367*	
	Focusing on Visual Discrimination		*page 367*	
	Focusing on Sound-Letter Correspondences		*page 367*	*pages 68–69*
	Focusing on the Writer's Use of Language		*page 366*	
DAY 5 BEYOND THE SELECTION	**THINK AND EXTEND**			
	For the Classroom		*page 368*	
	For the Home		*page 369*	
			▲ Homework Notebook copying master 22	

● *Happy Times! Story Land 2*
■ *Let's Go Outside!* Storybook

▲ *Learning Resources File*

Cooperative Learning

Cooperative learning suggestions for *Think and Read* appear at the beginning of the *Teacher's Edition.*

Preparing to Read

▶**Relating to Children's Experiences**   Ask children to name the kinds of pets they have. Point out that pets need special care and attention. Encourage children to discuss how they love and care for their pets.

After the discussion, have children listen as you read aloud the poem "My Dog."

My Dog
by Marchette Chute

His nose is short and scrubby;
His ears hang rather low;
And he always brings the stick back,
No matter how far you throw.

He gets spanked rather often
For things he shouldn't do,
Like lying-on-beds, and barking,
And eating up shoes when they're
new.

He always wants to be going
Where he isn't supposed to go.
He tracks up the house when it's
snowing—
Oh, puppy, I love you so.

Notes for Cooperative Learning

Notes for Preparing to Read

▶Previewing and Predicting Point to the title of the story and read it to the children. Ask them to look at the first two pictures and identify who is speaking to the mouse and what the speaker might be saying. Encourage children to give reasons for their responses. You may wish to model a response.

I think the little boy is talking to the mouse because he is the only person in the picture. I think he is telling the mouse that he loves him because the story is called "I Love You Mouse."

▶Setting a Purpose   Ask children to think about the animals the boy meets and what he says to each one as you read "I Love You Mouse."

Planning a Reading Strategy

Sharing Reading   Read aloud the story several times, sharing the illustrations and pointing to the text. Draw children's attention to the words *I love you* that are repeated throughout the story. Ask them to look at the changes in the pictures of the story.

Encourage children to react spontaneously with comments and questions after you have read the story.

Reading Orally   Read aloud the story. Invite children to join in repeating the words *I love you.*

As the story is read orally, you may wish to have a group of children perform the actions described in the reading. Refer to the techniques described in **Story Theater** at the beginning of the *Teacher's Edition.*

Reading Silently   Give children the opportunity to "read" the story independently. Explain that the illustrations will help them to remember what is happening in the story.

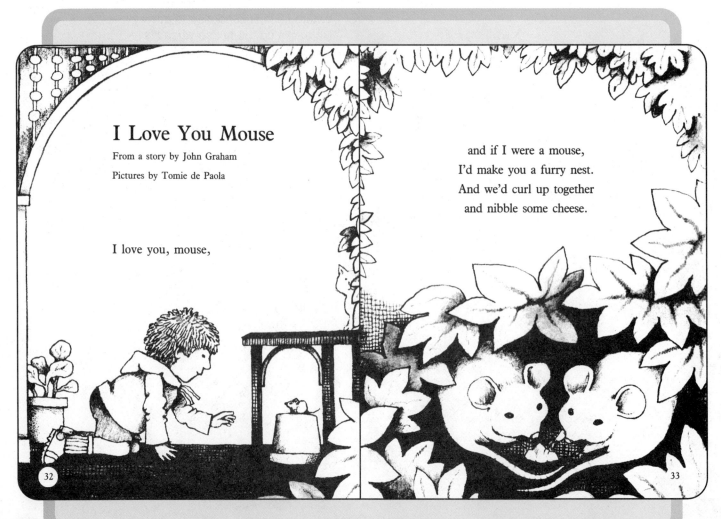

I Love You Mouse

From a story by John Graham

Pictures by Tomie de Paola

I love you, mouse,

and if I were a mouse,
I'd make you a furry nest.
And we'd curl up together
and nibble some cheese.

32

33

I love you, kitten,

and if I were a cat,
I'd make you a soft basket.
And we'd drink warm milk
and stretch ourselves.

I love you, puppy,

and if I were a dog,
I'd build you a kennel.
And we'd play tag
and, sometimes, chase a cat.

I love you, piglet,

and if I were a pig,
I'd build you a sty.
And we'd dig roots
and loaf in the mud.

38

39

I love you, chicky,

and if I were a chicken,
I'd build you a coop.
And we'd scratch for corn
and chase a butterfly.

40

41

I love you, lamb,

and if I were a sheep,
I'd build you a strong fold.
And we'd graze in the pasture
and grow wool for sweaters.

42

43

I love you, cub,

and if I were a bear,
I'd find you a cozy cave.
And we'd hunt for some honey
and watch out for bees.

44

45

I love you, tadpole,

and if I were a frog,
I'd find a quiet pond.
And we'd splash in the pond
and have races you'd win.

I love you, duckling,

and if I were a duck,
I'd find a blue lake.
And we'd swim all day long
and go "quack-quack."

I love you, gosling,

and if I were a goose,
I'd find a wide marsh.
And we'd play hide-and-seek among cattails
and go "honk-honk."

I love you, bunny,

and if I were a rabbit,
I'd find you a safe burrow.
And we'd play in the moonlight
and eat clover and carrots.

I love you, owlet,

and if I were an owl,
I'd find you a warm tree hole.
And we'd fly together, all night long,
and call out "who-who."

I love you, baby,

and since we're people,
I've built a house for you,
and given you a bed with warm quilts,
a cool drink of water,
a kiss on the nose,
and a quiet good-night.

Notes

Ideas for Cooperative Learning

Ideas for Meeting the Needs of Individual Students

Questioning Strategies

Think and Discuss

Cooperative Learning

Cooperative learning suggestions for *Think and Discuss* appear at the beginning of the **Teacher's Edition.**

Remembering the Selection

Ask children to recall the story and identify the animals the boy met and what he said to each animal.

Encourage children to look at the story illustrations to recall the information. You may wish to create a class chart to record children's responses. Some examples follow:

<u>What the Boy Said</u>

I love you, mouse.

I love you, kitten.

I love you, puppy.

Notes for Cooperative Learning

Notes for Remembering the Selection

362

Discussing the Selection

The following questions focus on feeling safe and loved. As children respond to the questions, ask them to support their answers with examples from the story. Encourage children to agree or disagree with their classmates' responses and to substantiate their opinions.

Remind children to speak clearly and loudly enough so they can be heard and understood.

1. How did the little boy feel about the animals? How do you know? (**Possible response:** *The boy loved the animals because he said, "I love you" to each one.*) *(Interpretive)*

2. The little boy said if he were a puppy, he would build a kennel, play tag and chase a cat. What would you do if you were a puppy? (**Possible response:** *If I were a puppy I would build a doghouse, play with a ball, and chew on a bone.*) *(Creative)*

3. Who loves the little boy? How do you know? (**Possible response:** *The boy's father loves him. He says so as he tucks him into bed for the night.*) *(Literal/Interpretive)*

4. How can you tell someone loves you? Give examples. (**Possible responses:** *When someone loves you, they do nice things for you. Sometimes they will take you someplace special like the zoo or the park.*) *(Critical)*

5. Why is it important to feel safe and loved? (**Possible responses:** *I am happy when someone says they love me. I feel good when I'm safe.*) *(Critical)*

During the discussion, children will need to

- **analyze** the boy's feelings about the animals.
- **imagine** the things they would do if they were an animal.
- **interpret** who loved the boy and how they know.
- **relate** who loves them and how they know.
- **evaluate** why the story belongs in the thematic unit.

You may wish to model responses to the questions. Use the possible responses given.

Tips for Evaluating the Oral Response

- Children should speak clearly and at the appropriate volume.
- Children should respond in complete thoughts.
- Children should ask relevant questions.

Additional Discussion Questions

Notes for Evaluating the Oral Response

Think and Write

Cooperative Learning

Cooperative learning suggestions for *Think and Write* appear at the beginning of the **Teacher's Edition.**

Making the Assignment

Review that the little boy in the story said *I love you* to many different animals. Tell children that now they are going to write about the things they love and tell why they love them. They will make a class book of their writing.

Using the Writing Process

Prewriting Ask children to name things they love and tell why they love them. List their responses on the chalkboard or on chart paper. Point to and read each word after you write it. A sample chart follows.

Things We Love	Why We Love Them
doll	pretty
cat	soft
gerbil	funny

Notes for Cooperative Learning

Notes for Making the Assignment

Drafting Have children dictate to you sentences similar to those of the boy in the story. Begin by modeling a response.

I love you, cat.
You are soft.

Write each child's dictated sentences at the bottom of a piece of paper. Then follow this procedure.

- Read the sentences to the child.
- Read the sentences with the child.
- Have the child read the sentences.
- Have the child illustrate the sentences.

Responding/Revising/Editing After each child has dictated sentences and illustrated them, reread the sentences you wrote. Draw attention to conventions of writing such as beginning sentences with a capital letter, leaving spaces between words, ending sentences with a period, and following left-to-right progression.

Postwriting (Sharing) Compile children's papers in a class book entitled "Things We Love." Display the book in the reading corner for children to read independently or with each other.

Notes for Using the Writing Process

Notes for Evaluating the Written Response

365

Develop Skills

Strategies for developing concepts and skills related to "I Love You Mouse" are included in this section. Select appropriate activities to teach the whole class, small groups, or individual children.

Developing Concepts and Skills

Language:	Words That Describe
Composition:	Story
Auditory Discrimination:	Animal Sounds
Visual Discrimination:	Light and Dark
Sound-Letter Correspondences:	Initial Correspondence /l/

Focusing on Language

Using Describing Words   Explain to children that there are many different kinds of words and that some words describe how things look and feel. Read and point out the describing words used in the selection and write some on chart paper or the chalkboard.

Use **Activity Book** pages 66–67 with children. Have children identify the pictures at the top of the page, and name words that describe what they see. Then have children find the word below each picture and listen as you read it aloud. Discuss how the word tells about the picture.

In the space provided, have each child draw an object and dictate to you a describing word. Write the word(s) on the writing rule for the child. You may wish to have some children copy the word.

Focusing on Composition

Note: Through observing and evaluating children's writing in a variety of situations and at different times, you can gather data that will help you understand and support individual children's writing development. Use the

Focusing on the Writer's Use of Language

Show children the writer's name (John Graham) on the first page of the story and read it aloud. Review with children the words the writer used to describe the mouse's nest and the cat's basket. *(furry, soft)* Ask children how the describing words help them picture what the little boy would make for his animal friends. (**Possible responses:** *The describing words help you know more about things the little boy would make for the animals.)*

Activity Book: Language

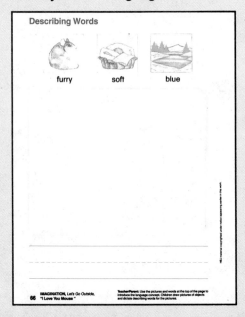

Checklist for Observing and Evaluating Writing in the Evaluation Resources section of the Teacher's Edition.

Writing a Story Extension

Reread the first two pages of "I Love You Mouse" to children. Ask what the boy would do if he were a mouse *(make a furry nest, curl up, and nibble some cheese)*. Then ask children to think about an animal they would like to be and write what they would do.

Accept their writing regardless of its stage of development. Many children will draw pictures while others scribble, write letters, and use invented spellings. Have children share their writing by reading it aloud to a group of classmates.

Focusing on Auditory Discrimination

Identifying Sounds of Animals

Ask children to demonstrate the sounds their pets or other animals make and then have the rest of the class guess what kind of animal they are imitating.

You may wish to add to the game by asking them to listen to other animal sounds. Pick animals from the story and imitate the sounds they make.

Focusing on Visual Discrimination

Identifying Light and Dark

Direct children's attention to the pictures at the beginning of "I Love You Mouse." Ask children what time of day they think it is and how they know. Discuss the fact that it is daytime because the sky is light. Then ask children to observe the remaining illustrations and discuss whether it is still daytime by the end of the story. Children should conclude that it is evening by the end of the story because the sky has grown darker and the moon is visible.

Focusing on Sound-Letter Correspondences

Recognizing Initial /l/l

Use **Activity Book** page 68 with children. Have them repeat the word *love* as they finger-trace the uppercase *L* and the lowercase *l*.

Have children identify the pictures at the top of the page. As each is identified, have them find the word, run their fingers under it, and say it aloud. Explain that each word begins with the same sound they hear at the beginning of *love*.

Have children name other words that begin with the same sound they hear at the beginning of *love*. Then ask each child to draw a picture of something whose name begins with the same sound and dictate to you a word that names the picture. Write the word on the writing rule for the child. You may wish to have some children copy the word.

Recognizing Initial /k/k

Use **Activity Book** page 69 with children. Have them repeat the word *kitten* as they finger-trace the uppercase *K* and the lowercase *k*.

Use **Activity Book** page 69 with children. Have them repeat the word *kitten* as they finger-trace the uppercase *K* and the lowercase *k*.

Have children identify the pictures at the top of the page. As each is identified, have them find the word, run their fingers under it, and say it aloud. Explain that each word begins with the same sound they hear at the beginning of *kitten*.

Follow the same procedure used for the previous **Activity Book** page and have children draw a picture of something whose name begins with the /k/ sound.

Activity Book: Language

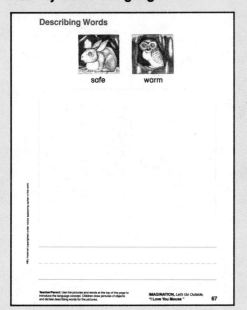

Activity Book: Sound/Letter

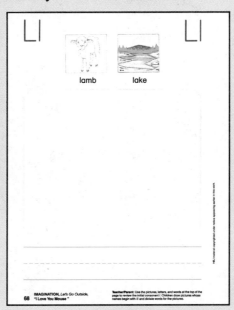

Activity Book: Sound/Letter

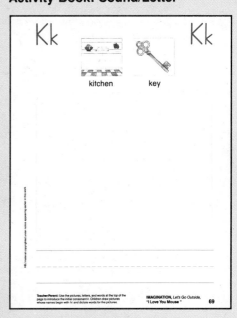

Think and Extend

Cooperative Learning

Cooperative learning suggestions for *Think and Extend* appear at the beginning of the ***Teacher's Edition.***

For the Classroom

Science—Baby Animals Show children pictures of a human baby and an adult. Ask them to compare the two. Help them understand that one is called a baby and the other is called an adult.

Show children pictures of a puppy and a mature dog. Ask them to compare the two and then ask what each is called. Explain that the puppy is a baby and the dog is older.

Have each child draw an animal and its baby and dictate the names to you. Post the drawings on a bulletin board or compile them for a class book called "Animals and Their Babies."

Physical Education—Imitating Movement Ask children to imitate the animals from the story as you ask them the following questions. You may wish to show the pictures from the selections.

Can you *stretch* like a cat?
Can you *jump* like a frog?
Can you *swim* like a duck?
Can you *fly* like an owl?
Can you *run* like a dog?

After the exercise, have volunteers imitate an animal movement and classmates guess which animal from the story is represented by the action.

Notes for Cooperative Learning

Additional Classroom Activities

For the Home

The homework assignment that follows also appears on **Homework Notebook copying master 22.** You may wish to distribute the copying masters to the children.

Writing Have children dictate sentences about someone they love to an older family member. Encourage family members to follow this procedure after taking the child's dictation.

- Read the sentences to the child.
- Read the sentences with the child.
- Have the child read the sentences.
- Have the child illustrate the sentences.

Reading Suggest that children read stories about animal friends and animal babies with parents or older family members. Encourage them to discuss the differences between animals and their babies. Children may be interested to see pictures of themselves and other family members when they were infants.

For Extended and Recreational Reading

You may wish to recommend the following books about animal friends and animal babies. Encourage family members to visit the public library with children to select the books to be read.

Stories About Animal Friends

May I Bring a Friend? by Beatrice S. DeRegniers. Macmillan, 1964.

Millions of Cats by Wanda Gag. Putnam, 1977.

Harry the Dirty Dog by Gene Zion. Harper & Row, 1956.

John Brown, Rose and the Midnight Cat by Jenny Wagner. Bradbury Press, 1978.

The Birds and the Beasts Were There by William Cole. World, 1963.

More Stories About Animal Friends and Animal Babies

The Tomten by Viktor Rydberg. Coward, McCann and Geoghegan, 1968.

Nobody Knows I Have Delicate Toes by Nancy Patz. Franklin Watts, 1980.

Friend Dog by Arnold Adoff. J.B. Lippincott, 1980.

Additional Home Activities

Additional Books for Extended and Recreational Reading

Notes

Ideas for Cooperative Learning

Ideas for Meeting the Needs of Individual Students

Questioning Strategies

Focusing on "What Is Beyond the Hill?"

While **listening** to and **reading** the selection, children will focus on the world around us. Children will also use **writing, listening,** and **speaking** skills as they respond to the selection. They will use higher-level **thinking** throughout the lesson.

OBJECTIVES

WRITING/THINKING

- To dictate a response to literature using the writing process.
- To write in the sensory/descriptive domain.
- To use naming words.
- To use asking sentences.

READING/THINKING

- To recognize questions and answers in a story.
- To gain information from questions and answers.
- To evaluate the placement of a story in a thematic unit.
- To recognize patterns in a selection.
- To identify colors.
- To recognize initial correspondences /m/m.

SPEAKING/THINKING

- To discuss personal experiences before reading a selection.
- To participate in shared reading.
- To participate in group discussions.
- To dictate a response to literature.

LISTENING/THINKING

- To listen to the oral reading of a selection.
- To listen to and analyze responses to opinions about a selection.
- To listen for asking sentences and telling sentences in a selection.
- To listen for initial sound /m/.

LEARNING STRATEGIES

- Brainstorming ideas related to children's own experiences.
- Previewing the selection and making predictions about the content.
- Completing a chart to help comprehension.
- Completing a chart to help organize writing.
- Analyzing the writer's use of language.

Summary

Two children discover the dimensions of the universe as they explore the world beyond the horizon.

INDIVIDUAL NEEDS

Suggestions for teaching children with special needs are provided on *Teacher's Edition* page 328.

- The blue objectives may require direct instruction.

PLANNING CALENDAR

		STUDENT'S EDITIONS	TEACHER'S EDITION	ACTIVITY BOOK
DAY 1 **INTO THE SELECTION**	**THINK AND READ**			
	Preparing to Read	● *pages 92–109* ■ *pages 58–75*	*page 373*	
	Planning a Reading Strategy	● *pages 92–109* ■ *pages 58–75*	*page 374*	
DAYS 2-4 **THROUGH THE SELECTION**	**THINK AND DISCUSS**			
	Remembering the Selection	● *pages 92–109* ■ *pages 58–75*	*page 380*	
	Discussing the Selection	● *pages 92–109* ■ *pages 58–75*	*page 381*	
	THINK AND WRITE			
	Making the Assignment		*page 382*	
	Using the Writing Process		*page 383*	
	Develop Skills			
	Focusing on Language		*page 384*	*pages 70–71*
	Focusing on Composition		*page 385*	
	Focusing on Auditory Discrimination		*page 385*	
	Focusing on Visual Discrimination		*page 385*	
	Focusing on Sound-Letter Correspondences		*page 385*	*page 72*
	Focusing on the Writer's Use of Language		*page 384*	
DAY 5 **BEYOND THE SELECTION**	**THINK AND EXTEND**			
	For the Classroom		*page 386*	
	For the Home		*page 387*	
			▲ Homework Notebook copying master 23	

● ***Happy Times! Story Land 2***
■ ***Let's Go Outside!*** Storybook

▲ *Learning Resources File*

Think and Read

Note: Through observing and evaluating children's reading in a variety of situations and at different times, you can gather data that will help you understand and support individual children's reading development. Use the *Checklist for Observing and Evaluating Reading* in the **Evaluation Resources** section of the ***Teacher's Edition.***

Cooperative Learning

Cooperative learning suggestions for *Think and Read* appear at the beginning of the ***Teacher's Edition.***

Preparing to Read

▶**Relating to Children's Experiences** Ask children to recall a time when they were very curious to know about something. Encourage them to discuss what they were curious about and what they did to satisfy their curiosity.

▶**Previewing and Predicting** Point to the title of the story and read it to the children. Ask them to look at the first two pictures and identify who might be asking the question "What is beyond the hill?" Then ask children what they think might be beyond the hill. Encourage children to give reasons for their responses. You may wish to model a response.

I see two children looking over a fence at a hill in the distance. I think they are asking the question because they are looking at the hill.

▶**Setting a Purpose** Tell children that as you read "What is Beyond the Hill?" they should think about the things the children in the story will find beyond the hill.

Notes for Cooperative Learning

Notes for Preparing to Read

Planning a Reading Strategy

Sharing Reading Read aloud the story several times, sharing the illustrations and pointing to the text. Draw attention to the questions that are repeated and the pattern that is used to answer the questions.

Encourage children to react spontaneously with comments and questions, after you have read the story.

Reading Orally Read aloud the story. Invite children to join in repeating the questions and the answers.

 Cooperative Learning

Have children work in pairs. Ask one child to "read" the questions and the other child to "read" the answers to the questions. Explain to children that they can follow the story by looking at the pictures.

Reading Silently Give children the opportunity to "read" the story independently. Remind them that the illustrations will help them to remember what is happening in the story.

What Is Beyond the Hill?

A story by Ernst A. Ekker

What is beyond the hill?

Does the world stop there?

58

59

374

No, the world does not stop there.

60

Beyond the hill, there is another hill.

61

Beyond that hill is another hill and
another hill and still another hill.

62

But the world does not stop there.

63

Then there is a mountain.

And what is beyond the mountain?
Does the world stop there?

64

65

Beyond that mountain is another
mountain

66

67

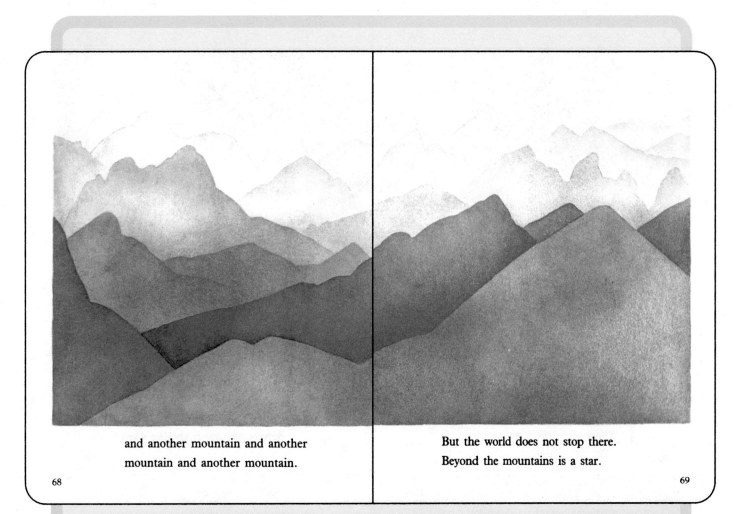

and another mountain and another
mountain and another mountain.

68

But the world does not stop there.
Beyond the mountains is a star.

69

The world does not stop there.

70

And what is beyond the star?

71

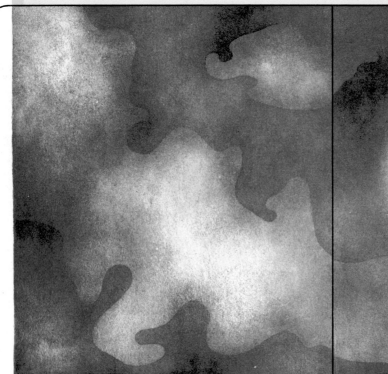

The world does not stop there.

72

Beyond the star is another star.

73

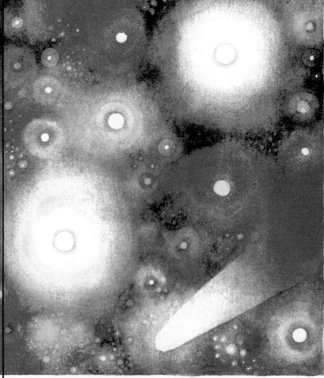

Beyond that star is another star and
another star and another star . . .

74

and another star and still another star.
And the stars go on forever.

75

Notes

Ideas for Cooperative Learning

Ideas for Meeting the Needs of Individual Students

Questioning Strategies

Think and Discuss

Cooperative Learning

Cooperative learning suggestions for *Think and Discuss* appear at the beginning of the **Teacher's Edition.**

Remembering the Selection

Ask children to recall the story and identify the questions and their answers.

Encourage children to look at the story illustrations to help themselves recall the information. You may wish to create a class chart to record children's responses.

Questions	Answers
What is beyond the ⌒〜⌒ ?	⛰
What is beyond the ⛰ ?	☆
What is beyond the ☆ ?	☆☆☆

Notes for Cooperative Learning

Notes for Remembering the Selection

380

Discussing the Selection

The following questions focus on the world around us. As children respond to the questions, ask them to support their answers with examples from the story. Encourage children to agree or disagree with their classmates' responses and to substantiate their opinions.

Remind children to speak clearly and loudly enough so they can be heard and understood.

1. What things are beyond the hill? (**Possible response:** *There are more hills with small towns and villages in between, mountains with roads and tunnels to other places, and stars that go on forever.*) *(Literal)*
2. How do you think the children felt as they discovered the world around them? (**Possible response:** *The children were probably surprised and excited to learn about things beyond the hill.*) *(Interpretive)*
3. What other things in nature would you add to the pictures in the story? (**Possible response:** *I would have added lakes, oceans, the moon, and planets.*) *(Creative)*
4. What can you say about the world after reading this story? (**Possible response:** *The world is very big and it has many, many things in it.*) *(Critical)*

During the discussion, children will need to

- **recall** the things beyond the hill.
- **interpret** how the children felt as they discovered what was beyond the hill.
- **imagine** how they would add to the story.
- **analyze** the size and scope of the world.

You may wish to model responses to the questions. Use the possible responses given.

Tips for Evaluating the Oral Response

- Children should speak clearly and at the appropriate volume.
- Children should respond in complete thoughts.
- Children should ask relevant questions.

Additional Discussion Questions

Notes for Evaluating the Oral Response

Think and Write

Cooperative Learning

Cooperative learning suggestions for *Think and Write* appear at the beginning of the *Teacher's Edition.*

Making the Assignment

Review that the children in the story wondered about the world around them. Tell children that now they are going to write questions about the world around them. They will make a class book of their writing and then talk about answers to their questions.

Notes for Cooperative Learning

Notes for Making the Assignment

Using the Writing Process

Prewriting Ask children to name some of the things they see every day that they wonder about. Cluster their responses on the chalkboard or on chart paper. Point to and read each word after you write it. A sample chart follows.

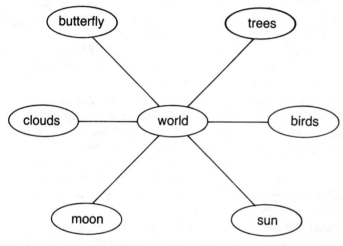

Drafting Ask children to dictate questions to you as the children did in the story. Begin by modeling responses.

Where does the sun go at night?
How do trees grow so tall?

Write each child's dictated sentence at the bottom of a piece of paper. Then follow this procedure.

- Read the question to the child.
- Read the question with the child.
- Have the child read the question.
- Have the child illustrate the question.

Responding/Revising/Editing After each child has dictated sentences and illustrated them, reread the sentences you wrote. Draw attention to conventions of writing such as beginning questions with capital letters leaving spaces between words, ending questions with question marks, and following left-to-right progression.

Postwriting (Sharing) Compile children's papers in a class book entitled "Questions for Us to Think About." Read aloud the book to children. Help to answer as many of their questions as possible. Help children use books and other resource materials to find answers as needed. Then display the class book in the reading corner for children to read independently or with each other.

Notes for Using the Writing Process

Notes for Evaluating the Written Response

Develop Skills

Strategies for developing concepts and skills related to "What Is Beyond the Hill?" are included in this section. Select appropriate activities to teach the whole class, small groups, or individual children.

Developing Concepts and Skills

Language:	Naming Words
Composition:	Story
Auditory Discrimination:	Asking and Telling Sentences
Visual Discrimination:	Colors
Sound-Letter Correspondences:	Initial Correspondence /m/m

Focusing on Language

Recognizing Naming Words   Remind children that there are many different kinds of words and that some words name things in the world around us. Then ask children to listen for words that name things in the world as you reread "What Is Beyond the Hill?"

Use *Activity Book* page 70 with children. Have children identify the pictures of things in the world at the top of the page. As each is identified, have them find the word, run their fingers under it, and say it aloud. Have each child draw a picture of something in the world and dictate to you a word that names the picture he or she drew. Write the naming word on the writing rule. You may wish to have some children copy the word.

Activity Book page 71 focuses on things we can see in the sky. Have children follow the same procedure used for the previous page, this time drawing an object they can see in the sky.

Focusing on the Writer's Use of Language

Show children and read aloud the writer's name (Ernst A. Ekker) on the first page of the story. Review with children the things the writer asked questions about (hills, mountains, stars). Point out how the writer used these words over and over again in the story.

Ask why the writer decided to repeat these words.
(**Possible response:** *The writer wanted to let the reader know that there are many, many hills in the world and that the world is a very big place.*)

Focusing on Composition

Note: Through observing and evaluating children's writing in a variety of situations and at different times, you can gather data that will help you understand and support individual children's writing development. Use the *Checklist for Observing and Evaluating Writing* in the **Evaluation Resources** section of the *Teacher's Edition.*

Writing an Imaginary Story   Have children pretend that they are climbing a mountain. Tell them that they are just about at the very top. Ask them to write about what they see beyond the mountain.

Accept their writing regardless of its stage of development. Many children will draw pictures while others scribble, write letters, and use invented spellings. Have children share their writing by reading it aloud to a group of classmates.

Focusing on Auditory Discrimination

Identify Asking and Telling Sentences   Read aloud the title of the story "What is Beyond the Hill?" Ask children if the title tells them something or asks them a question. Elicit that the title asks a question that the children in the story have.

Stress that the words in the asking sentence are different and that your voice sounds different when you ask a question. Demonstrate how your voice goes up at the end of an asking sentence to suggest that something is to follow.

Reread the story. Ask children to listen carefully and identify the asking and telling sentences in the story.

Focusing on Visual Discrimination

Identifying Colors   Display crayons in the following colors: orange, red, blue, green, white, brown, purple, and yellow. After you display and identify each color individually, ask children to find examples of objects of that color in the story. You may wish to extend the activity by pointing to various objects in the classroom and having children identify their colors.

Focusing on Sound-Letter Correspondences

Recognizing initial /m/m   Ask children to listen for the word *mountain* as you read aloud the "mountain" section of the story. After reading the sentences, write on the chalkboard the word *mountain*. Have children say the word. Then circle the first letter of *mountain* and explain that the word begins with the letter *m.*

Use *Activity Book* page 72 with children. Have them repeat the word *mountain* as they finger-trace the uppercase *M* and the lowercase *m.*

Have children identify the pictures at the top of the page. As each is identified, have them find the word, run their fingers under it, and say it aloud. Explain that each picture begins with the same sound they hear at the beginning of *mountain.*

Ask children to identify the letter each word begins with. Tell them that the letter *m* usually stands for the same sound they hear at the beginning of *mountain.* Then have children listen for the /m/ sound as you say the words *mouse* and *mitten.*

Activity Book: Language

Activity Book: Language

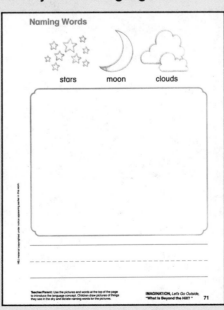

Activity Book: Sound/Letter

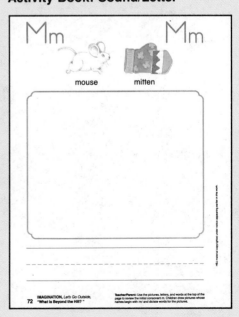

Think and Extend

Cooperative Learning

Cooperative learning suggestions for *Think and Extend* appear at the beginning of the *Teacher's Edition.*

For the Classroom

Science—Examining a Piece of the World   You will need the following materials: a small spade, a board or pie tin, paper cups, spoons, newspapers, and magnifying glasses. Tell children they will take a small piece of the world back to their classroom. Find a plot with some grass or weed growth. Remove a piece of sod and put it on the board or pie tin. Encourage children to handle, pull apart, and examine with magnifiers all the different things that make up a simple piece of sod. Then discuss their findings.

Art—Identifying Colors   Distribute a piece of colored construction paper to each child. Use as many differen' colors as possible. Ask children to look at the color of their paper and think of objects that are the same color. Have children draw pictures of these objects on the paper and discuss their drawings. You may wish to make a chart of their responses.

Red	Orange	Yellow	Blue	Green	Purple
heart rose	orange cat	banana school bus	sky water	grass coat	grapes flower

For the Home

The homework assignment that follows also appears on **Homework Notebook copying master 23.** You may wish to distribute the copying masters to the children.

Writing Have children ask a parent or an older family member to choose a household object. Then have children dictate a question about the object. Encourage family members to discuss answers to the question and then follow this procedure after taking the child's dictation.

- Read the question to the child.
- Read the question with the child.
- Have the child read the question.
- Have the child illustrate the object.

Suggest that children share their questions and pictures with classmates the following day.

Reading Suggest that children read stories with a parent or older family member about the world around them. Encourage them to discuss what is beyond the neighborhood boundaries and examine the sky and what can be seen during the day. Family members may wish to take a walk with children to explore the area.

For Extended and Recreational Reading

You may wish to recommend the following books about the world around us. Encourage family members to visit the public library with children to select books to be read.

Books About the World Around Us

A Tree is Nice by Janice Udry. Harper & Row, 1956.

The Cloud Book by Tomie dePaola. Holiday, 1975.

Rosie's Walk by Pat Hutchins, Macmillan, 1968.

Why the Sun and the Moon Live in the Sky by Elphinstone Dayrell. Houghton Mifflin, 1968.

More Books About the World Around Us

Where Does the Sun Go at Night? by Mirra Ginsburg. Greenwillow/Morrow, 1981.

Take Me to the Moon by Sal Murdocca. Lothrop, Lee & Shepard, 1976.

Little Fox Goes to the End of the World by Ann Tompert. Crown, 1976.

Toto by Marietta D. Moskin. Coward-McCann, 1972.

Additional Home Activities

Additional Books for Extended and Recreational Reading

Notes

Ideas for Cooperative Learning

Ideas for Meeting the Needs of Individual Students

Questioning Strategies

Focusing on "Water"

While **listening** to and **reading** the selection, children will focus on the uses for water. Children will also use **writing, listening,** and **speaking** skills as they respond to the selection. They will use higher-level **thinking** throughout the lesson.

OBJECTIVES

WRITING/THINKING

- To dictate a response to literature using the writing process.
- To write in the practical/informative domain.
- To use action words.
- To write about a personal experience.

READING/THINKING

- To recognize how illustrations provide information.
- To recall details in a selection.
- To evaluate the placement of a story in a thematic unit.
- To recognize water in illustrations.
- To recognize initial correspondences /w/w.

SPEAKING/THINKING

- To discuss personal experiences before reading a selection.
- To participate in shared reading.
- To participate in group discussions.
- To dictate a response to literature.

LISTENING/THINKING

- To listen to the oral reading of a selection.
- To listen to and analyze responses to opinions about a selection.
- To identify sentences.
- To listen for initial sound /w/.

LEARNING STRATEGIES

- Brainstorming ideas related to children's own experiences.
- Previewing the selection and making predictions about the content.
- Completing a cluster to help comprehension.
- Completing a cluster to help organize writing.
- Analyzing the writer's use of language.

Summary

The information story "Water" illustrates how water is used in a variety of situations. The illustrations show how people use water at home, for recreation, for transportation, and for irrigation. They also show how important water is to animals.

INDIVIDUAL NEEDS

Suggestions for teaching children with special needs are provided on *Teacher's Edition* page 328.

- The blue objectives may require direct instruction.

PLANNING CALENDAR

		STUDENT'S EDITIONS	TEACHER'S EDITION	ACTIVITY BOOK
DAY 1 **INTO THE SELECTION**	**THINK AND READ** Preparing to Read Planning a Reading Strategy	● *pages 110–114* ■ *pages 76–80* ● *pages 110–114* ■ *pages 76–80*	*pages 391–392* *page 392*	
DAYS 2-4 **THROUGH THE SELECTION**	**THINK AND DISCUSS** Remembering the Selection Discussing the Selection	● *pages 110–114* ■ *pages 76–80* ● *pages 110–114* ■ *pages 76–80*	*page 394* *page 395*	
	THINK AND WRITE Making the Assignment Using the Writing Process **Develop Skills** Focusing on Language Focusing on Composition Focusing on Auditory Discrimination Focusing on Visual Discrimination Focusing on Sound-Letter Correspondences Focusing on the Writer's Use of Language		 *page 396* *page 397* *page 398* *page 399* *page 399* *page 399* *page 399* *page 398*	 *pages 76–77* *page 78*
DAY 5 **BEYOND THE SELECTION**	**THINK AND EXTEND** For the Classroom For the Home		*page 400* *page 401* ▲ Homework Notebook copying master 24	

● ***Happy Times! Story Land 2***   ▲ *Learning*
■ ***Let's Go Outside!*** Storybook   *Resources File*

Think and Read

Note: Through observing and evaluating children's reading in a variety of situations and at different times, you can gather data that will help you understand and support individual children's reading development. Use the *Checklist for Observing and Evaluating Reading* in the **Evaluation Resources** section of the *Teacher's Edition.*

Cooperative Learning

Cooperative learning suggestions for *Think and Read* appear at the beginning of the *Teacher's Edition.*

Preparing to Read

▶**Relating to Children's Experiences** Ask children to think about how they use water every day and where they think it comes from. Then discuss the different places they can see water. Encourage children to share their ideas and experiences.

After the discussion, have children listen as you read aloud the poem "The Sea." Ask children what the poet thinks about the sea.

The Sea

Behold the wonders of the mighty
deep,
Where crabs and lobsters learn to
creep,
And little fishes learn to swim,
And clumsy sailors tumble in.

—Anonymous

▶**Previewing and Predicting** Point to the title of the story and read it to the children. Have children look at the title and the pictures to decide what the story might be about. You may wish to model a response.

The word water *is in the title of the story and there is water in each of the pictures. I think the story is about the different ways water is used.*

Notes for Cooperative Learning

Notes for Preparing to Read

Planning a Reading Strategy

Sharing Reading   Read aloud the story several times, sharing the illustrations and pointing to the text. Draw attention to the illustrations as a source of information and ask children to pantomime some of the actions that show how water is used.

Encourage children to react spontaneously with comments and questions after you have read the story.

Reading Orally   Read aloud the story. Invite children to join in by adding the word *water* in the appropriate places.

Then have children work in pairs. Encourage them to take turns "reading" a sentence and telling about the illustration.

Reading Silently   Give children the opportunity to "read" the story independently. Explain that the illustrations will help them to remember how water is used.

Connections

Water

We use water at home.

76

Water is cool on a hot day.

77

Boats help us travel on water.

Some animals live in water.

We need water to grow food.

Think and Discuss

Note: Through observing and evaluating children's oral language (listening and speaking) in a variety of situations and at different times, you can gather data that will help you understand and support individual children's oral development. Use the *Checklist for Observing and Evaluating Oral Language* in the **Evaluation Resources** section of the *Teacher's Edition.*

Cooperative Learning

Cooperative learning suggestions for *Think and Discuss* appear at the beginning of the **Teacher's Edition.**

Remembering the Selection

Ask children to recall the story and identify

- where water is used.
- how water is used.

Encourage children to look at the story illustrations to help themselves recall the information. You may wish to create a class cluster to record children's responses.

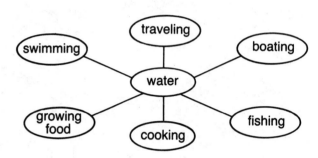

Notes for Cooperative Learning

Notes for Remembering the Selection

Discussing the Selection

The following questions focus on the uses of water. As children respond to the questions, ask them to support their answers with examples from the story. Encourage children to agree or disagree with their classmates' responses and to substantiate their opinions.

Remind children to speak clearly and loudly enough so they can be heard and understood.

1. How do people use water at home? (**Possible responses:** *People drink water. People cook with water. People wash with water. People use water to wash dishes.*) (*Literal/Interpretive*)
2. Why is water important to a farmer? (**Possible response:** *The farmer needs water to grow the corn.*) (*Interpretive*)
3. Name some other ways people have fun with water. (**Possible responses:** *Some people water ski. People use a raft. You can dive into the water.*) (*Creative*)
4. What might happen to the animals in the pond if the water dried up? (**Possible responses:** *The fish would probably die without water. The birds could fly away to another pond.*) (*Interpretive*)

5. What does water have to do with being outside? (**Possible responses:** *Most of the pictures are outside. We get water from places outside.*) (*Critical*)

During the discussion, children will need to

- **identify** how people use water in the home.
- **determine** why water is important to the farmer.
- **relate** how they would show people using water for fun.
- **analyze** what might happen to the animals if there was no water.
- **evaluate** why the story belongs in the thematic unit.

You may wish to model responses to the questions. Use the possible responses given.

Tips for Evaluating the Oral Response

- Children should speak clearly and at the appropriate volume.
- Children should respond in complete thoughts.
- Children should ask relevant questions.

Additional Discussion Questions

Notes for Evaluating the Oral Response

Think and Write

Cooperative Learning

Cooperative learning suggestions for *Think and Write* appear at the beginning of the **Teacher's Edition.**

Making the Assignment

Explain to children that water not only has many uses, but it can be described in many ways. Tell children they will write a description of water. Then they will make a bulletin board display about the ways they have described water.

Notes for Cooperative Learning

Notes for Making the Assignment

Using the Writing Process

Prewriting Talk with children about the way water looks in the illustrations of the story. You may want to bring in some ice and some warm water for children to examine. Have children touch and taste them. Record their responses in a cluster.

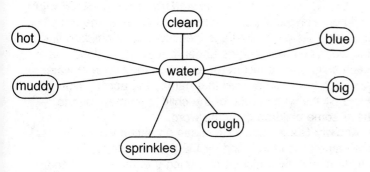

Drafting Have children dictate sentences to describe water. Begin by modeling a response and writing it on the chalkboard or on chart paper.

Water is clean and bubbly.

Write each child's dictated sentence at the bottom of a piece of paper. Then follow this procedure.

- Read the sentence to the child.
- Read the sentence with the child.
- Have the child read the sentence.
- Have the child illustrate the sentence.

Responding/Revising/Editing After each child has dictated sentences and illustrated them, reread the sentences you wrote. Draw attention to conventions of writing such as beginning sentences with a capital letter, leaving spaces between words, ending sentences with a period, and following left-to-right progression.

Postwriting (Sharing) Add children's sentences and drawings to a bulletin board display entitled "Water, Water Everywhere."

Notes for Using the Writing Process

Notes for Evaluating the Written Response

Develop Skills

Strategies for developing concepts and skills related to the information story "Water" are included in this section. Select appropriate activities to teach the whole class, small groups, or individual children.

Developing Concepts and Skills

Language:	Action Words
Composition:	Story
Auditory Discrimination:	Asking Sentences
Visual Discrimination:	Water Sources
Sound-Letter Correspondences:	Correspondence /w/w

Focusing on Language

Using Action Words Use **Activity Book** page 76 with children. Have children identify the pictures at the top of the page. As each picture is identified, have children find the word, run their fingers under it, and say it aloud. Have each child draw a picture of an action they do with water and dictate to you a word that names the action. Write the word on the writing rule for the child. You may wish to have some children copy the word.

   Activity Book page 77 focuses on action words. Follow the same procedure used for the previous page. Ask children to draw a picture of a thing that uses water and dictate naming words for the picture.

Focusing on Composition

Note: Through observing and evaluating children's writing in a variety of situations at different times, you can gather data that will help you understand and support individual children's writing development. Use the *Checklist for Observing and Evaluating Writing* in the **Evaluation Resources** section of the *Teacher's Edition.*

Focusing on the Writer's Use of Language

   Ask children to recall the uses for water in the story. Then discuss how the writer presented the uses for water in the story. (**Possible response:** *The writer used some telling sentences, but the pictures really told the story about water. It may have been easier to show more about water with pictures than to write about it.*)

Writing a Story   Ask children to review the different ways people enjoy water on a hot summer day. Have them write about what they would do if they went to the ocean, to a pool, or to a mountain lake on a hot day.

Many children will draw pictures while others will scribble, write letters, and use invented spellings. Have children share their writing by reading it aloud to you, a group of classmates, or family members.

Focusing on Auditory Discrimination

Listening for Asking Sentences   Review with children that a telling sentence tells about something and an asking sentence asks a question.

Read aloud the following poem about water one line at a time, pausing after each question. Ask children to raise their hand when they hear an asking sentence. Explain that your voice sounds different when you ask a question. Demonstrate how your voice goes up at the end of an asking sentence to suggest that something follows.

River Winding
by Charlotte Zolotow

Rain falling, what things do you grow?
Snow melting, where do you go?
Wind blowing, what trees do you know?
River winding, where do you flow?

Focusing on Visual Discrimination

Identifying Sources of Water   Ask children to identify the source of water in the first picture of the information story "Water" (faucet by the sink). Discuss the fact that the water comes through a pipe to the apartment from a well or a reservoir, and when the faucet is opened, the water comes out. Then have children look at the remaining pictures of the selection and identify each source of water (lake, river, swamp/pond, sprinkler system). You may wish to continue the discussion by asking children to think about where the water in rivers, ponds, reservoirs, and oceans comes from.

Focusing on Sound-Letter Correspondences

Recognizing Initial /w/w   Use *Activity Book* page 78 with children. Have them repeat the word *water* as they finger-trace the uppercase *W* and the lowercase *w*.

Have children identify the pictures at the top of the page. As each is identified, have them find the word, run their fingers under it, and say it aloud. Explain that each picture begins with the same sound they hear at the beginning of *water*.

Ask children to identify the letter each word begins with. Tell them that the letter *w* usually stands for the same sound they hear at the beginning of *water*. Then have children listen for the /w/ sound as you say the words *window* and *web*.

Have children name other words that begin with the same sound they hear at the beginning of *window* and *web*. Then ask each child to draw a picture of something whose name begins with the same sound and dictate to you a word that names the picture. Write the word on the writing rule for the child. You may wish to have some children copy the word.

Activity Book: Language

Activity Book: Language

Activity Book: Sound/Letter

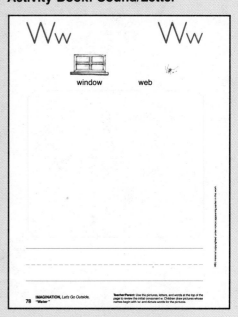

Think and Extend

Cooperative Learning

Cooperative learning suggestions for *Think and Extend* appear at the beginning of the *Teacher's Edition*.

For the Classroom

Science—Investigating How Water Helps Beans Grow Materials Needed: Styrofoam cups, cotton balls, dried beans, water.

Have children work in pairs. Give each child a cup, three beans and a cotton ball. Have one partner saturate the cotton ball with water in the cup and place the three beans on top. The other child should simply place the beans on top of a dry cotton ball in the cup. Children should add water each day to the first cup and keep the second cup dry and report the progress of the growth of the beans with and without water. Discuss with children that beans need water to develop into healthy plants and that without water, plants will die.

Science—Identifying Things That Float in Water
Demonstrate that things float or sink with a tub of water and the following objects: a cork, a sponge, a rock, an empty small plastic container. Allow children to experiment with the objects in the water. Show them that the container floats, but it sinks when the rock is placed in it. Children may want to experiment with other objects.

Notes for Cooperative Learning

Additional Classroom Activities

For the Home

The homework assignment that follows also appears on **Homework Notebook copying master page 24.** You may wish to distribute the copying masters to the children.

Writing   Ask children to discuss with family members how they use water and the importance of not wasting it. Then have children dictate rules that family members can follow to help save water. Encourage family members to follow this procedure after taking the child's dictation.

- Read the sentences to the child.
- Read the sentences with the child.
- Have the child read the sentences.
- Have the child illustrate the sentences.

Have children bring their sentences and pictures to class the following day to share with classmates.

Reading   Suggest that each child read the information story "Water" with parents or older family members. Encourage them to discuss trips or outings where water was used for transportation or recreation. Ask children to share these stories with the class the following day.

For Extended and Recreational Reading

You may wish to recommend the following books about water and its uses for children to share with family members. Encourage family members to visit the public library with children to select the books to be read.

Books About Water and Its Uses

Harry the Dirty Dog by Gene Zion. Harper & Row, 1956.

London Bridge Is Falling Down by Peter Spier. Doubleday, 1985.

The Mysterious Tadpole by Steven Kellogg. Dial, 1977.

Swimmy by Leo Lionni. Pantheon, 1963.

Umbrella by Taro Yashima. Viking, 1958.

More Books About Water

Wonders of Rivers by Rae Bains. Troll Assocs., 1981.

Benjy's Boat Trip by Margaret B. Graham, Harper & Row, 1977.

Rivers by Norman and Madelyn Carlisle. Childrens Press, 1982.

Additional Home Activities

Additional Books for Extended and Recreational Reading

Notes

Ideas for Cooperative Learning

Ideas for Meeting the Needs of Individual Students

Questioning Strategies

Focusing on "Hello and Goodbye"

While **listening** to and **reading** the selection, children will focus on the seasons. Children will also use **writing, listening,** and **speaking** skills as they respond to the selection. They will use higher-level **thinking** skills throughout the lesson.

OBJECTIVES

WRITING/THINKING

- To write a response to literature using the writing process.
- To write in the sensory/descriptive domain.
- To use naming words for things.
- To write about a personal experience.

READING/THINKING

- To compare the seasons.
- To identify the speaker of a poem.
- To make inferences from a poem and an illustration.
- To evaluate the placement of a poem in a thematic unit.
- To identify rhyming words.
- To recognize initial correspondences (/h/h)

SPEAKING/THINKING

- To discuss personal experiences before reading a selection.
- To participate in shared reading.
- To participate in group discussions.

LISTENING/THINKING

- To listen to the oral reading of a selection.
- To listen to and analyze responses to opinions about a selection.
- To listen for rhyming words.
- To listen for initial sounds. (/h/)

LEARNING STRATEGIES

- Brainstorming ideas related to children's own experiences.
- Previewing the selection and making predictions about the content.
- Completing a chart to help comprehension.
- Completing a chart to help organize writing.
- Analyzing the writer's use of language.

Summary

A child plays throughout the seasons, saying hello and goodbye to some of the things that come and go.

INDIVIDUAL NEEDS

Suggestions for teaching children with special needs are provided on *Teacher's Edition* page 328.

- The blue objectives may require direct instruction.

PLANNING CALENDAR

		STUDENT'S EDITIONS	TEACHER'S EDITION	ACTIVITY BOOK
DAY 1 INTO THE SELECTION	**THINK AND READ**			
	Preparing to Read	● *pages 115–117* ■ *pages 81–83*	*page 405*	
	Planning a Reading Strategy	● *pages 115–117* ■ *pages 81–83*	*page 406*	
DAYS 2-4 THROUGH THE SELECTION	**THINK AND DISCUSS**			
	Remembering the Selection	● *pages 115–117* ■ *pages 81–83*	*page 408*	
	Discussing the Selection	● *pages 115–117* ■ *pages 81–83*	*pages 408–409*	
	THINK AND WRITE			
	Making the Assignment		*page 412*	
	Using the Writing Process		*pages 412–413*	
	Develop Skills			
	Focusing on Language		*page 414*	*pages 73–74*
	Focusing on Composition		*page 415*	
	Focusing on Auditory Discrimination		*page 415*	
	Focusing on Visual Discrimination		*page 415*	
	Focusing on Sound-Letter Correspondences		*page 415*	*page 78*
	Focusing on the Writer's Use of Language		*page 414*	
DAY 5 BEYOND THE SELECTION	**THINK AND EXTEND**			
	For the Classroom		*page 416*	
	For the Home		*page 47*	
			▲ Homework Notebook copying master 25	

● *Happy Times! Story Land 2*
■ *Let's Go Outside!* Storybook

▲ *Learning Resources File*

Note: Through observing and evaluating children's reading in a variety of situations and at different times, you can gather data that will help you understand and support individual children's reading development. Use the *Checklist for Observing and Evaluating Reading* in the **Evaluation Resources** section of the **Teacher's Edition.**

Cooperative Learning

Cooperative learning suggestions for *Think and Read* appear at the beginning of the **Teacher's Edition.**

Preparing to Read

▶**Relating to Children's Experiences** Ask children to name the current season and to describe its characteristics in their part of the country. You may wish to take children outside to look at the playground and observe some of the characteristics of the season.

▶**Previewing and Predicting** Point to the title of the poem and read it aloud to the children. Then ask them to look at the pictures and think about the words hello and good-bye and what they might mean in the picture. Encourage children to give reasons for their answers. You may wish to model a response.

I think the girl on the swing is saying hello to a friend because she is smiling.

▶**Setting a Purpose** Tell children that as they listen to the poem, they should think about the things to which the speaker says hello and good-bye.

Notes for Cooperative Learning

Notes for Preparing to Read

Planning a Reading Strategy

Sharing Reading   Read aloud "Hello and Good-bye" several times, sharing the illustrations and pointing to the text. Draw attention to the words *hello and good-bye* that are repeated throughout the poem. You may wish to have children clap their hands each time they hear the words *hello* and *good-bye*. Also, draw their attention to the changes of seasons in the illustrations.

Encourage children to react spontaneously with comments and questions, after you have read the poem. You may wish to have children pantomime the actions and wave "hello" and "good-bye" at the appropriate times.

Reading Orally   Read aloud the poem. Encourage children to join in repeating the first two lines of the poem and the last two lines of the poem.

Reading Silently   Give children the opportunity to "read" the poem independently. Explain that the illustrations will help them remember what things the child is saying "hello" and "good-bye" to.

Hello and Good-bye

A poem by Mary Ann Hoberman

Hello and good-bye
Hello and good-bye

When I'm in a swing
Swinging low and then high
Good-bye to the ground
Hello to the sky.

Pictures by Cheryl Arnemann   81

Hello to the rain
Good-bye to the sun,
Then hello again sun
When the rain is all done.

82

In blows the winter,
Away the birds fly.
Good-bye and hello
Hello and good-bye.

83

Think and Discuss

 Cooperative Learning

Cooperative learning suggestions for *Think and Discuss* appear at the beginning of the **Teacher's Edition.**

Remembering the Selection

Ask children to recall the poem and identify the things to which the speaker says hello and good-bye. Encourage them to look at the poem's illustrations to help themselves recall the information. You may wish to create a class chart to record children's responses.

Hello	Good-bye
sky	ground
rain	sun
sun	birds
winter	leaves

Discussing the Selection

The following questions focus on the seasons. As children respond to the questions, ask them to support their answers with examples from the poem. Encourage children to agree or disagree with their classmates' responses and to substantiate their opinions.

Remind children to speak clearly and loudly enough so they can be heard and understood.

Notes for Cooperative Learning

Notes for Remembering the Selection

408

1. What things does the girl say hello and good-bye to in the poem? (**Possible response:** *The girl says hello and good-bye to the sky and the ground, the rain and the sun, winter and the birds.*) *(Literal)*

2. What season do you think it is in each picture? How do you know? (**Possible responses:** *It may be spring in the first picture because the girl is not wearing a jacket. It is fall in the second picture because the leaves have turned color. There is snow on the ground in the last picture; it must be winter.*) *(Interpretive)*

3. Why do you think the girl says good-bye to the birds? (**Possible response:** *The birds are flying south for the winter.*) *(Critical)*

4. What season is it now? What do you say hello or goodbye to? (*Encourage children to name the season and things they would say hello and goodbye to.*) *(Literal/Creative)*

5. What things do you do outside in the fall? Spring? Summer? Winter? (**Possible responses:** *I play baseball in the spring. We make a snowman in the winter. In the summer we can swim. I watch football games outside in the fall.*) *(Critical)*

During the discussion, children will need to

- **recall** the things the girl said hello and goodbye to.
- **interpret** the season of the year in each picture.

- **analyze** why the girl said good-bye to the birds.
- **select** the things they say hello and goodbye to during the year.
- **evaluate** why the poem belongs in the thematic unit.

You may wish to model responses to the questions. Use the possible responses given.

Tips for Evaluating the Oral Response

- Children should speak clearly and at the appropriate volume.
- Children should respond in complete thoughts.
- Children should ask relevant questions.

Think and Discuss

Talking About Stories and Poems

The children have read the stories and poems in "Let's Go Outside." Have children compare and contrast the selections in Unit 5. Use the discussion questions and possible responses provided.

1. What animals might the little boy find if he looks beyond the hill? (**Possible responses:** *He might find a cow eating grass on the hills. He might find an eagle flying. He might find a mountain goat.*)
2. If it were raining outdoors, do you think Coco and her grandmother would still meet under the tree? Tell why or why not. (**Possible response:** *Yes, Coco and her grandmother could wear raincoats and use umbrellas when they meet.*)
3. In what way are all the children in the stories and poems alike? (**Possible response:** *They all like to explore and go to new places.*)
4. In which place shown in the stories and poems would you like to explore? (**Possible responses:** *I would like to look for animals with the little boy. I would like to look for stars with the children.*)

During the discussion children will talk about

- new adventures for the characters in the stories.
- how the characters are alike.
- favorite places to explore.

Bookshelf

Introduce children to these and other selections that relate to the theme of the unit.

Rainy Day: Stories and Poems edited by Caroline Feller Bauer. J. B. Lippincott, 1986. Each selection gives a different viewpoint of raindrops, ranging from pesky to lovely depending on where you are standing.

Nora's Castle by Satomi Ichikawa. Philomel, 1986. Nora, along with her doll, dog, and teddy bear, set off to explore the castle she sees from her window.

Papa, Please Get the Moon for Me by Eric Carle. Picture Book Studio, 1986. Papa uses unique means to get the moon for his daughter.

The Sky Jumps Into Your Shoes at Night by Jasper Tomkins. Green Tiger, 1986. The sky is everywhere and touches everyone and everything.

Town and Country by Alice and Martin Provensen. Crown, 1985. Bustling city life is compared to quiet country life.

Notes

Ideas for Cooperative Learning

Ideas for Meeting the Needs of Individual Students

Questioning Strategies

Think and Write

Making the Assignment

Review with children that as seasons change, people say "hello" to things that the new season brings and "good-bye" to things from the old season. Tell children that now they are going to write about their favorite season of the year and tell the things that they say hello and good-bye to. They will participate in completing a graph to show the results of a class poll.

Using the Writing Process

Prewriting   Ask children to name the four seasons and to identify what is characteristic of each one. List their responses on the chalkboard or on chart paper. Point to and read each word after you write it. A sample chart follows.

Seasons

Spring	Summer	Fall	Winter
warm	hot	cool	cold
rain	sun	wind	snow
flowers grow	swim	school starts	play in snow
snow melts	no school	rake leaves	ski ice skate

Notes for Cooperative Learning

Notes for Making the Assignment

412

Drafting Have children dictate sentences that tell about the things they say "hello" and "good-bye" to during their favorite season of the year. Begin by modeling a response and writing it on the chalkboard or on chart paper. An example follows.

It is fall.
Hello, school.
Good-bye, summer sun.

Write their sentences at the bottom of a piece of paper. Then follow this procedure.

- Read the sentences to the child.
- Read the sentences with the child.
- Have the child read the sentences.
- Have the child illustrate the sentences.

Responding/Revising/Editing After chilldren have completed their illustrations, reread what you wrote. Draw attention to conventions of writing such as beginning each sentence with a capital letter, leaving spaces between words, ending each sentence with a period, and following left-to-right progression.

Postwriting (Sharing) Have children read their sentences and display their drawings. Then take a class poll to determine how many children prefer each season. Record the results on a class graph. As children state their favorite season, have them fill in a square in the appropriate column with a crayon or marker.

Seasons We Like										
Summer										
Fall										
Winter										
Spring										
	1	2	3	4	5	6	7	8	9	10

Number of Children

Discuss the results with children. Display their writing and pictures next to the graph on a bulletin board.

Notes for Using the Writing Process

Notes for Evaluating the Written Response

Develop Skills

Strategies for developing concepts and skills related to "Hello and Good-bye" are included in this section. Select appropriate activities to teach the whole class, small groups, or individual children.

Developing Concepts and Skills

Language:	Naming Words
Composition:	Story
Auditory Discrimination:	Rhyming Words
Visual Discrimination:	Seasonal Changes
Sound-Letter Correspondences:	Initial Correspondence /s/s

Focusing on Language

Using Words That Name Things   Tell children that there are many different kinds of words and that some words name things. Then ask children to listen for words that name things as you reread "Hello and Good-bye."

Use **Activity Book** page 73 with children. Have them identify the pictures showing naming words at the top of the page. As each picture is identified, have them find the word, run their fingers under it, and say it aloud. Have each child draw a picture of something from the selection. Have the child dictate the naming word to you and write it on the writing rule. You may wish to have some children copy the word.

Have children identify the pictures of the seasons at the top of **Activity Book** page 74. As each is identified, have them find the word, run their fingers under it, and say it aloud. Ask children to pick their favorite season and draw a picture of a thing they can do during that season. Follow the same procedure used for the previous page.

Focusing on the Writer's Use of Language

Show children and read aloud the writer's name (Mary Ann Hoberman) on the first page of the poem. Review with children the words the writer used to name things in "Hello and Good-bye." (*swing, ground, sky, sun, rain, winter, birds*) Ask how these words helped them understand the poem. (**Possible response:** *The words help you to understand the changes in the weather and the seasons.*)

Focusing on Composition

Note: Through observing and evaluating children's writing in a variety of situations and at different times, you can gather data that will help you understand and support individual children's writing development. Use the *Checklist for Observing and Evaluating Writing* in the **Evaluation Resources** section of the *Teacher's Edition.*

Writing About the Season Ask children to name the current season and think about things they like to do outside. Have children write a story about the activities they like to do during the season.

Accept their writing regardless of its stage of development. Encourage children to use and explore writing, drawing and invented spelling. Have children share their writing by reading it aloud to you, a group of classmates, or family members.

Focusing on Auditory Discrimination

Listening for Rhyming Words Read aloud the poem. Then repeat the words *good-bye, high, sky, fly.* Ask children to tell how the words are the same. (**Possible response:** *They all have the same ending sounds.*) Then ask children to name any other words that they can think of that have the same ending sounds they hear in *good-bye, high, sky,* and *fly.* (**Possible responses:** *eye, fry, lie, my, cry, dry, pie, sigh, tie, try, why*) Tell children that words that end with the same ending sound are called **rhyming words.**

Reread "Hello and Good-bye." Ask children to name any other rhyming words they hear. (**Possible response:** *sun/done*) Discuss why the writer used rhyming words in the poem.

Focusing on Visual Discrimination

Identifying Seasonal Changes Review with children that in "Hello and Good-bye" the girl and her friends were shown at different times of the year. Have children identify which picture illustrates fall and which picture illustrates winter. Discuss the fact that the leaves have turned color to indicate that it is fall and that there is snow on the ground to indicate that it is winter. Then ask children to identify other things in the pictures that are clues to the season.

Focusing on Sound-Letter Correspondences

Recognizing Initial /h/h Ask children to listen for the word *hello* as you read aloud the writing they did for *Think and Write.* After reading their writing, write on the chalkboard the word *hello.* Have children say the word. Then circle the first letter and explain that the word begins with the letter *h.*

Use *Activity Book* page 75 with children. Have them repeat the word *hello* as they finger-trace the uppercase *H* and the lowercase *h.*

Have children identify the pictures at the top of the page. As each is identified, have them find the word, run their fingers under it, and say it aloud. Explain that each picture begins with the same sound they hear at the beginning of *hello.*

Have children name other words that begin with the same sound they hear at the beginning of *hand* and *heart.* Then ask each child to draw a picture of something whose name begins with the same sound and dictate to you a word that names the picture. Write the word on the writing rule for the child. You may wish to have some children copy the word.

Activity Book: Language

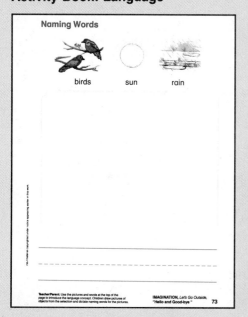

Activity Book: Language

Activity Book: Sound/Letter

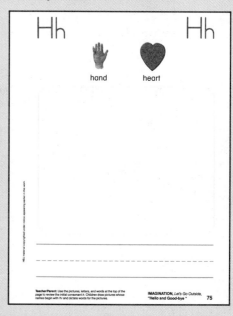

Think and Extend

Cooperative Learning

Cooperative learning suggestions for *Think and Extend* appear at the beginning of the **Teacher's Edition.**

For the Classroom

Art/Science—Making Seasonal Pictures Have children identify the current season and review its characteristics. Then take children for a walk to observe firsthand the signs of the season and to collect objects such as leaves, twigs, pebbles, moss, pine cones, and acorns.

After sharing observations, have children incorporate the objects they found into drawings, figures, or collages. Provide paste, construction paper, scissors, pipe cleaners, crayons, and paints, as needed. Display the completed projects for everyone to see.

Social Studies—Talking on the Telephone Ask children what they say when they answer the telephone or make a telephone call. Discuss telephone manners with children. Point out that when answering the phone, they should say hello and at the end of the conversation they should say good-bye. When making a call to a friend, for example, they should say hello and identify who they are. You may wish to demonstrate by using toy telephones. Then have children work in pairs to practice telephone manners.

Notes for Cooperative Learning

Additional Classroom Activities

For the Home

The homework assignment that follows also appears on **Homework Notebook copying master** page 25. You may wish to distribute the copying masters to the children.

Writing Have children talk with an older family member about some of the family customs for each season. Discussion may include seasonal holidays and family gatherings. Have children dictate a sentence or two about what they learned about a seasonal event in their family. Encourage family members to follow this procedure after taking the child's dictation.

- Read the sentences to the child.
- Read the sentences with the child.
- Have the child read the sentences.
- Have the child illustrate the sentences.

Suggest that children share their writing with classmates the following day.

Reading Have older family members read about seasonal customs and discuss with children some of the seasonal customs in the family. Suggest that parents show children things like holiday greeting cards and read or explain to children when and why they are used.

For Extended and Recreational Reading

You may wish to recommend the following books for children to share with family members.

Encourage family members to visit the public library with children to select books.

Books About the Seasons

Snowy Day by Ezra J. Keats. Viking, 1962.

The Nicest Gift by Leo Politi. Scribner, 1973.

First Snow by Helen Coutant. Knopf, 1974.

White Snow, Bright Snow by Alvin R. Tresselt. Lothrop, 1947.

More Books About the Seasons

Happy Day by Ruth Krauss. Harper & Row, 1980.

All Wet! All Wet! by James Skofield. Harper & Row, 1984.

On Sunday the Wind Came by Alan Elliot. William Morrow, 1980.

Discovering the Seasons by Louis Santrey, photos by Francene Sabin. Troll, 1980.

The Song by Charlotte Zolotow. Greenwillow Books, 1982.

Additional Home Activities

Additional Books for Extended and Recreational Reading

Unit 6

What a Funny Animal!

Theme: Entertaining characters and surprise endings

Reading Selections	Writing Assignments
• Have You Seen My Duckling?	• Dictate Sentences That Answer Mother Duck's Question
• To Market, To Market Hickory Dickory Dock Higglety, Pigglety, Pop	• Dictate a Letter
• Barnyard Song	• Create New Verses for a Song
• Connections: A Zookeeper at Work	• Dictate Sentences About Animals in the Zoo
• A Bear Went Over the Mountain Lunch for a Dinosaur	• Dictate an Invitation

Unit Resources

As you work through the Integrated Instructional Plans in this unit, you may want to use the following resources included in the **Student/Teacher Resources** and **Evaluation Resources** sections of the *Teacher's Edition.*

Student/Teacher Resources

• Home Letters 7A and 7B
• Extended and Recreational Reading Ideas

Evaluation Resources

• Observation and Evaluation Guides
• **Listening** Comprehension Evaluation

Students With Individual Needs

	Limited-English-Proficient Students	Less-Prepared Students	Gifted Students	Special Education Students
Think and Read	• Have students work in cooperative learning groups to complete the *Think and Read* chart. (See the suggestions at the front of this *Teacher's Edition.*) • Encourage students to participate in prereading activities by discussing relevant facts about their native countries. • Explain unfamiliar vocabulary. Make words concrete by using objects, pictures, and demonstrations.	• Use shared reading strategies. Discuss vocabulary and content after each selection is read. • Encourage students to talk about previous experiences related to the selections. Remind them to use *I* and *me* in their statements.	• After modeling effective prereading strategies, have students lead the discussions that focus on previewing and predicting. • After modeling effective thinking strategies, have students lead the discussions that focus on summarizing the reading process.	• Review individualized education programs (IEPs) with special education staff and discuss necessary modification of curriculum. • For visually-impaired students, provide specialized resources, such as large-print books, books in braille, or recordings.
Think and Discuss	• Pair students with native-English speakers to answer questions. • Have students work in cooperative learning groups. (See the suggestions at the front of this *Teacher's Edition.*)	• Model by reading aloud questions and possible responses. Have students add original responses. • Have students work in cooperative learning groups to answer questions. (See the suggestions at the front of this *Teacher's Edition.*)	• After modeling effective questioning strategies, have students lead the discussions that focus on the selection and its theme. • Have students work in cooperative learning groups. (See the suggestions at the front of this *Teacher's Edition.*) • Model strategies for listening tolerantly and thoughtfully to classmates' opinions.	• During discussion, have notetakers record and transmit responses for hearing-impaired students. • For hearing-impaired students, use visual aids, such as slides and overhead projectors, to reinforce learning.
Think and Write	• Have students dictate as you record their drafts. Read aloud their drafts before students read aloud what they have composed. • Have students work in cooperative learning groups. (See the suggestions at the front of this *Teacher's Edition.*) • Provide pictures to stimulate prewriting. Then help students brainstorm and list descriptive words.	• During the writing process, have students work in cooperative learning groups. (See the suggestions at the front of this *Teacher's Edition.*) • Review with students the purpose and the intended audience of each writing assignment. Remind them to consider their purpose and audience during the entire writing process.	• Encourage students to consider different ways to publish their writing for assignments in *Think and Write.* • After modeling responses for *Thinking Back,* have students lead the discussions.	• Review lesson plans with special education staff to discuss any necessary modification of curriculum. • For visually-impaired students, record the directions for the stages of the writing process. Have students record their compositions.
Think and Extend	• For social studies activities, have students share related information about their cultural experiences. • Encourage students to participate in *Think and Extend* activities that require speaking.	• Encourage students to participate in *Think and Extend* activities that require speaking. • Have students work in cooperative learning groups. (See the suggestions for cooperative learning activities at the front of the *Teacher's Edition.*)	• Have students work in cooperative learning groups. (See the suggestions at the front of this *Teacher's Edition.*) • Ask students to think of additional *Think and Extend* activities. When appropriate, assign the student-generated activities instead of the activities in the *Writer's Corner.*	• For hearing-impaired students, use visual aids, such as slides and overhead projectors, to reinforce learning. • For visually-impaired students, record the directions for the activities.

Unit 6

Introducing the Unit

Talking About the Theme   To introduce children to the unit, point to and read aloud the title "What a Funny Animal!" Ask children to look at the picture that illustrates the opening of the unit. Begin a discussion about animals by having children answer the following questions about the picture.

1. What is happening in the picture? (**Possible responses:** *There is a funny monster waving to the boy in the picture. The monster is smiling at the boy.*)
2. What is so silly about this picture? (**Possible responses:** *Monsters are make-believe. This monster looks very funny.*)
3. What would you do if you were the boy in the picture? (**Possible responses:** *I would invite the monster over to my house. I would follow the monster to his house.*)
4. The stories and poems in this unit go together. What do you think they might be about? (**Possible response:** *I think the stories might be about friendly animals.*)

6 What a Funny Animal!

119

Extending Reading   The following books extend the theme of the unit. You may want to share these books as children listen to and "read" the selections in Unit 6. Have children discuss the animals in the stories.

Little Bear by Else Holmelund Minarik. Harper & Row, 1957. A lovely story about a gentle little bear.

Mr. Rabbit and the Lovely Present by Charlotte Zolotow. Harper & Row, 1962. Mr. Rabbit helps a little girl find the best birthday present for her mother.

The Adventures of Paddy Pork by John S. Goodall. Harcourt Brace Jovanovich, 1968. Paddy gets lost when he follows a circus into the country. A wolf follows him, but he escapes just in time.

The ABC Bunny by Wanda Gag. Coward-McCann, 1933. A bunny hops away from a storm through the alphabet.

Bulletin Board Suggestion

Have children help you make an animal parade for the bulletin board. Each child will make one stand-up animal for the parade. To make the animals, fold in half a 6″ square of heavy paper for each child. Give a stand-up body to each child. On a piece of construction paper, have them draw an animal head for the body. You may wish to help them cut out the shape and glue it to the body.

Have children color the animals. Pin the animals in a row to a bulletin board called *Animal Parade.*

Unit 6

Unit Activities

The following optional unit activities relate to the theme of the unit. The activities may be completed during or after unit instruction. Instructions for setting up learning centers appear at the front of the *Teacher's Edition*.

LISTENING Corner

Objective: To listen to and learn a song about animals.

Materials: records with songs such as "Old MacDonald," "Mary Had a Little Lamb," "Monkey See, Monkey Do" and a record player

Procedure: Play a prerecorded song that features animals. Have children listen to the song and sing along. Encourage children to pantomime the actions of the animals as they sing.

SPEAKING Corner

Objective: Classify circus animals and farm animals.

Materials: cards with pictures of animals that are in the circus, such as elephants, lions, monkeys, and tigers; cards with pictures of animals that live on a farm, such as cows, horses, donkeys, sheep, ducks, hens, and goats

Procedure: Place all the animal cards in a box. Prepare a pocket chart by labeling two sections. Label one section *Circus* and draw a picture of a big top. Label the other section *Farm* and draw a picture of a barn. Show the cards to the children and ask them to name the animals.

Have children work with partners and choose an animal card. Ask them to talk about the animal and decide if it lives on a farm or if it belongs in the circus.

Then, have children put the animal card in the correct pocket chart. Allow children to take turns naming the animals and deciding where they belong.

READING Corner

Objective: To read about animals.

Materials: books about animals that may include titles from page 421 in the *Teacher's Edition*

Procedure: Display books for children to look at. Ask children to select a book. Read aloud the story to the children. Then, ask children if the animal they read about is real. Ask them how they know the animal is real or make-believe.

You may wish to have children draw a picture of the animal character they read about and have them share their drawings with each other.

WRITING Corner

Objective: To dictate sentences about animals we would like to be.

Materials: poster board, magazine pictures of animals, scissors and glue

Procedure: Assemble a collage of animal pictures for children to look at. Use the collage to help children think of an animal they might like to be for a day. Have children look at the pictures and decide which animal they would like to be for a day. Ask children to dictate a sentence about the animal they would like to be and why.

Write the children's sentences and have them draw a picture of the animal. Encourage them to share their drawings and sentences with each other.

Note: Some children will prefer to dictate their sentences as you write. Others will want to write on their own. Accept their writing regardless of its stage of development. Allow them to draw, scribble, or write using their own spelling.

Focusing on "Have You Seen My Duckling?"

While **listening** to and **reading** the selection, children will focus on exploring. Children will also use **writing, listening,** and **speaking** skills as they respond to the selection. They will use higher-level **thinking** skills throughout the lesson.

OBJECTIVES

WRITING/THINKING

- To dictate a response to literature using the writing process.
- To write in the practical/informative domain.
- To ask questions.
- To write about a personal experience.

READING/THINKING

- To answer questions about illustrations.
- To evaluate the placement of a story in a thematic unit.
- To interpret the characters' feelings.
- To distinguish animals that swim and fly.
- To recognize initial correspondences. (/y/y)

SPEAKING/THINKING

- To discuss personal experiences before reading a selection.
- To participate in shared reading.
- To participate in group discussions.
- To dictate a response to literature.

LISTENING/THINKING

- To listen to the oral reading of a selection.
- To listen to and analyze responses to opinions about a selection.
- To listen for details in asking sentences.
- To distinguish emotion in voices.
- To listen for initial sounds. (/y/)

LEARNING STRATEGIES

- Brainstorming ideas related to children's own experiences.
- Previewing the selection and making predictions about the content.
- Completing a chart to help comprehension.
- Completing a chart to help organize writing.
- Analyzing the writer's use of language.

Summary

A Mother Duck searches for its duckling, which has gone off to explore. To each animal it meets it asks, "Have you seen my duckling?"

INDIVIDUAL NEEDS

Suggestions for teaching children with special needs are provided on *Teacher's Edition* page 418.

- The blue objectives may require direct instruction.

PLANNING CALENDAR

		STUDENT'S EDITIONS	TEACHER'S EDITION	ACTIVITY BOOK
DAY 1 **INTO THE SELECTION**	**THINK AND READ** Preparing to Read Planning a Reading Strategy	● *pages 120–145* ■ *pages 2–27* ● *pages 120–145* ■ *pages 2–27*	*pages 425–426* *page 426*	
DAYS 2-4 **THROUGH THE SELECTION**	**THINK AND DISCUSS** Remembering the Selection Discussing the Selection	● *pages 120–145* ■ *pages 2–27* ● *pages 120–145* ■ *pages 2–27*	*page 434* *pages 434–435*	
	THINK AND WRITE Making the Assignment Using the Writing Process **Develop Skills** Focusing on Language Focusing on Composition Focusing on Auditory Discrimination Focusing on Visual Discrimination Focusing on Sound-Letter Correspondences Focusing on the Writer's Use of Language		 *page 436* *page 437* *page 438* *page 439* *page 439* *page 439* *page 439* *page 438*	 *pages 79–80* *page 81*
DAY 5 **BEYOND THE SELECTION**	**THINK AND EXTEND** For the Classroom For the Home		*page 440* *page 441* ▲ Homework Notebook copying master 26	

● *Happy Times! Story Land 2* ▲ *Learning*
■ *What a Funny Animal!* Storybook **Resources File**

Note: Through observing and evaluating children's reading in a variety of situations and at different times, you can gather data that will help you understand and support individual children's reading development. Use the *Checklist for Observing and Evaluating Reading* in the **Evaluation Resources** section of the *Teacher's Edition.*

Cooperative Learning

Cooperative learning suggestions for *Think and Read* appear at the beginning of the *Teacher's Edition.*

Preparing to Read

▶**Relating to Children's Experiences** Ask children if they have ever played "hide-and-seek." Discuss how the game is played. After the discussion, have children listen as you read the poem "Hiding." Ask children where they think the boy might have been hiding.

Hiding
by Dorothy Aldis

I'm hiding, I'm hiding,
And no one knows where;
For all they can see is my
Toes and my hair.

And I just heard my father
Say to my mother—
"But, darling, he must be
Somewhere or other;

"Have you looked in the inkwell?"
And Mother said, "Where?"
"In the inkwell," said Father. But
I was not there.

Then "Wait!" cried my mother—
"I think that I see
Him under the carpet." But
It was not me.

"Inside the mirror's
A pretty good place,"
Said Father and looked, but saw
Only his face.

Notes for Cooperative Learning

Notes for Preparing to Read

"We've hunted," sighed Mother,
"As hard as we could
And I am so afraid that we've
Lost him for good."

Then I laughed out aloud
And I wiggled my toes
And Father said—"Look, dear,
I wonder if those

Toes could be Benny's.
There are ten of them. See?"
And they were so surprised to find
Out it was me!

▶**Previewing and Predicting**   Point to the title of the story and read it to the children. Then have them look at the illustrations. Ask children what they think the story will be about. You may wish to model a response.

I think the story will be about a mother duck looking for her duckling because the duckling is hiding from its mother.

▶**Setting a Purpose**   Tell children that as you read the story they should think about who asks the question, "Have you seen my duckling?"

Planning a Reading Strategy

Sharing Reading   Read aloud the story several times, sharing the illustrations and pointing to the text. Draw attention to the question that is repeated to the different animals in the pond. Establish that there are eight ducklings at the beginning of the story. Have children count the number of ducklings on each spread of pictures and look for the missing duckling hidden on the page.

Encourage children to react spontaneously with comments and questions after you have read the story.

Reading Orally   Have children take turns telling "Have You Seen My Duckling?" themselves. Encourage them to build and embellish the story with details from the illustrations.

You may wish to have children take the parts of the animals in the story and have them develop or improvise their own dialogue to answer the mother duck's question. Refer to the *Creative Dramatics/Improvisation* techniques at the beginning of the **Teacher's Edition.**

Reading Silently   Give children the opportunity to "read" the story independently. Explain that the illustrations will help them to remember what is happening in the story.

Have You Seen My Duckling?
A story by Nancy Tafuri

2

3

Early one morning...

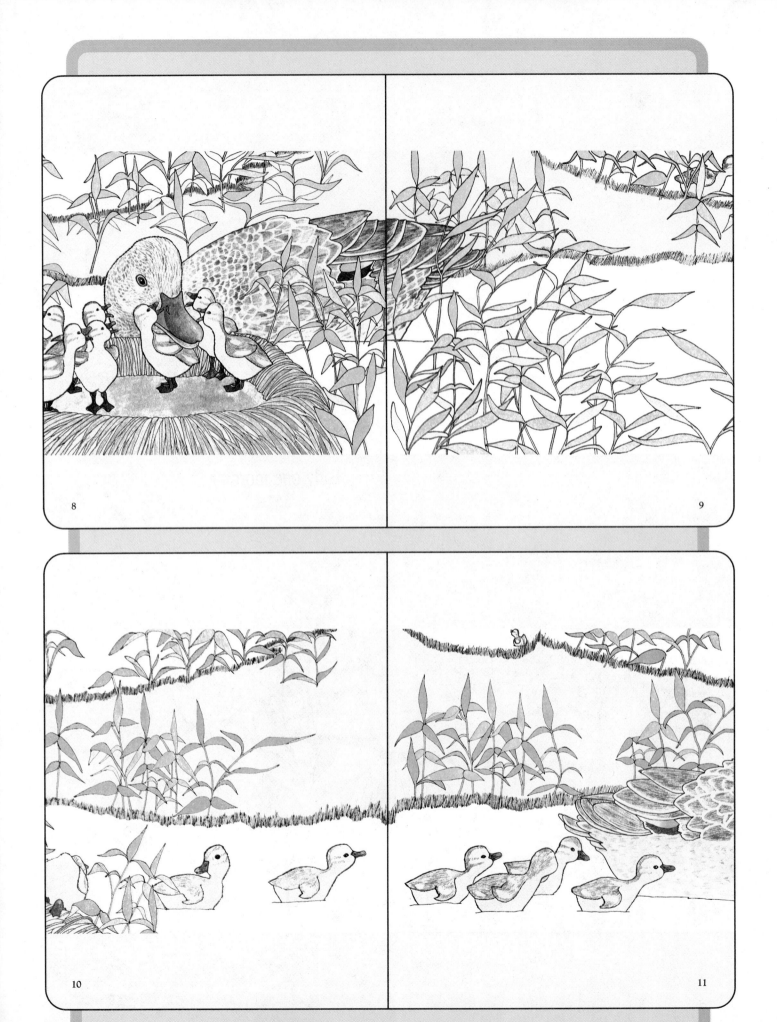

8

9

10

11

Have you seen my duckling?

Have you seen my duckling?

Have you seen my duckling?

16

17

Have you seen my duckling?

18

19

Have you seen my duckling?

20

21

22

23

24

25

26

27

Notes

Ideas for Cooperative Learning

Ideas for Meeting the Needs of Individual Students

Questioning Strategies

Think and Discuss

Cooperative Learning

Cooperative learning suggestions for *Think and Discuss* appear at the beginning of the **Teacher's Edition.**

Remembering the Selection

Ask children to recall the story and identify

- who asked, "Have you seen my duckling?"
- the animals that were asked the question.

Encourage children to look at the story illustrations to help themselves recall the information. You may wish to create a class chart to record children's responses.

Discussing the Selection

The following questions focus on exploring. As children respond to the questions, ask them to support their answers with examples from the story. Encourage children to agree or disagree with their classmates' responses and to substantiate their opinions.

Remind children to speak clearly and loudly enough so they can be heard and understood.

Notes for Cooperative Learning

Notes for Remembering the Selection

1. What does the duckling do when it paddles away from Mother Duck? (**Possible response:** *The duckling hides in the pond.*) *(Literal)*

2. Why do you think the duckling paddles off on its own? (**Possible response:** *Duckling wants to play a trick on Mother Duck. It wants to explore the pond on its own. It wants to find a friend to play with.*) *(Interpretive)*

3. How do you think Mother Duck feels when she realizes her duckling is missing? (**Possible responses:** *Mother Duck is upset. Mother Duck is worried. Mother Duck is angry.*) *(Interpretive)*

4. What would you say to the duckling if you were Mother Duck? (**Possible response:** *I would tell Duckling to let me know when he wants to go somewhere next time. I would tell Duckling not to swim away alone.*) *(Creative)*

5. Do you think it was a good idea for duckling to go off on its own? Why or why not? (**Possible response:** *It is not a good idea to go off without telling someone. Something could have happened and duckling might not have had anyone to help him.*) *(Critical)*

6. What is so funny about the story of the duckling? (**Possible response:** *The story is funny because the duckling is so close to the mother even though she doesn't see him.*) *(Critical)*

During the discussion, children will need to

- **recall** what the duckling did.
- **determine** why the duckling paddled off by himself.
- **interpret** Mother Duck's feelings.
- **judge** the duckling's behavior.
- **relate** what they would say to the duckling if they were Mother Duck.
- **evaluate** the story in the thematic unit.

You may wish to model responses to the questions. Use the possible responses given.

Tips for Evaluating the Oral Response

- Children should speak clearly and at the appropriate volume.
- Children should respond in complete thoughts.
- Children should ask relevant questions.

Additional Discussion Questions

Notes for Evaluating the Oral Response

Think and Write

Cooperative Learning

Cooperative learning suggestions for *Think and Write* appear at the beginning of the **Teacher's Edition.**

Making the Assignment

Review with children that the duckling was never really very far away from Mother Duck and that if they look carefully they can see where duckling hides. Tell children that now they are going to write sentences to answer Mother Duck's question, "Have you seen my duckling?"

Notes for Cooperative Learning

Notes for Making the Assignment

Using the Writing Process

Prewriting   Ask children to identify the places where duckling hides. List their responses on the chalkboard or on chart paper. Point to and read each word after you write it. A sample chart follows.

Places Where Duckling Hides
behind tall grass
in the flower
behind the tree
next to the rock
under the dock

Drafting   Have children complete sentences to answer Mother Duck's question. Begin by modeling a response.

Have you seen my duckling?
Yes, your duckling is under the dock.

Have each child dictate the question and his or her telling sentence, and then write them at the bottom of a piece of paper. Then follow this procedure.

- Read the sentences to the child.
- Read the sentences with the child.
- Have the child read the sentences.
- Have the child illustrate the sentences.

Responding/Revising/Editing   After each child has dictated sentences and illustrated them, reread the sentences you wrote. Draw attention to conventions of writing such as beginning each sentence with a capital letter, leaving spaces between words, ending each question with a question mark, ending each telling sentence with a period, and following left-to-right progression.

Postwriting (Sharing)   Compile children's papers in a class book entitled "Have You Seen My Duckling?" Read aloud the book to children. Then display the class book in the reading corner for children to read independently or with each other.

Notes for Using the Writing Process

Notes for Evaluating the Written Response

Develop Skills

Strategies for developing concepts and skills related to "Have You Seen My Duckling?" are included in this section. Select appropriate activities to teach the whole class, small groups, or individual children.

Developing Concepts and Skills

Language: Asking Sentences

Composition: Story

Auditory Discrimination: Emotions in Voice

Visual Discrimination: Animals

Sound-Letter Correspondences: Initial Correspondence /y/y

Focusing on Language

Asking Questions to Gain Information Explain that when people need to know something they use an asking sentence, or question. Ask children to recall the question Mother Duck asked the animals in the pond. Write on the chalkboard the sentence *Have you seen my duckling?* Draw attention to the sentence, showing children that it begins with a capital letter and ends with a question mark. Point out that by asking questions one can find out who, what, when, where, why, how, how much, and how many.

Use **Activity Book** pages 79 and 80 with children. Have them talk about the pictures at the top of the pages. Point to the asking sentences and read them aloud. Have children follow the sentences with you by finding the words and running their fingers under them.

Stress that the words in the asking sentences are different and that your voice sounds different when you ask a question. Demonstrate how your voice goes up at the end of an asking sentence to suggest that something is to follow.

Focusing on the Writer's Use of Language

Show children and read aloud the writer's name (Nancy Tafuri) on the first page of the story. Ask children to recall the question Mother Duck asks throughout the story. (*"Have you seen my duckling?"*) Discuss with children why the writer always has Mother Duck ask the same question. (**Possible response:***The writer makes the story more interesting and fun to read. It helps the reader look more closely at the pictures to find the answer because none of the animals seem to know where Duckling is.*)

438

Ask children to draw pictures and dictate asking sentences about the pictures. Write the dictated sentences on the writing rules for the child. You may wish to have some children copy the sentence.

Focusing on Composition

Note: Through observing and evaluating children's writing in a variety of situations and at different times, you can gather data that will help you understand and support individual children's writing development. Use the *Checklist for Observing and Evaluating Writing* in the **Evaluation Resources** section of the *Teacher's Edition.*

Writing About a Personal Experience   Have children think about a time when they lost or misplaced something and could not find it. Have them write about the experience.

Accept their writing regardless of its stage of development. Encourage children to draw and make attempts at writing and spelling. Have children share their writing by reading it aloud to you, a group of classmates, or family members.

Focusing on Auditory Discrimination

Distinguishing Emotion in a Character's Voice
Ask children to listen carefully as you read the asking sentence, "Have you seen my duckling?" Read aloud the sentence using different tones of voice. You may want to try using these suggested tones in your voice: frightened, upset, worried, tired, happy.

Pause after reading each sentence and ask children to determine the emotion in your voice. Ask children to repeat the sentence using the same tone you used.

Focusing on Visual Discrimination

Distinguishing Animals That Swim and Fly
Discuss with children the different ways animals move from one place to another. Point out that most of the animals in the story live in or around the water. Have children look at the pictures of the Mother duck and the ducklings. Point out that ducks can swim and fly. Have children identify the other animals in the story and determine if they swim or fly. Remind children that many animals move about in more then one way.

Focusing on Sound-Letter Correspondences

Recognizing Initial /y/y   Ask children to listen for the words *yes* and *your* as you read aloud the writing they did for *Think and Write.* After reading their class book, write on the chalkboard the words *yes* and *your.* Have children say the words. Then circle the first letter of *yes* and *your* and explain that the words begin with the letter *y.*

Use *Activity Book* page 81 with children. Have them repeat the words *yes* and *your* as they finger-trace the uppercase *Y* and the lowercase *y.*

Have children identify the pictures at the top of the page. As each is identified, have them find the word, run their fingers under it, and say it aloud. Explain that each picture begins with the same sound they hear at the beginning of *yes* and *your.*

Have children name other words that begin with the same sound they hear at the beginning of *yes* and *your.* Then ask each child to draw a picture of something whose name begins with the same sound and dictate to you a word that names the picture. Write the word on the writing rule for the child. You may wish to have some children copy the word.

Activity Book: Language

Asking Sentences

Have you seen my duckling?

Activity Book: Language

Asking Sentences

What do you do at school?

Activity Book: Sound/Letter

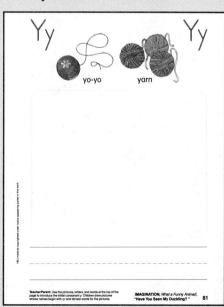

Y y   yo-yo   yarn   Y y

Think and Extend

Cooperative Learning

Cooperative learning suggestions for *Think and Extend* appear at the beginning of the *Teacher's Edition.*

For the Classroom

Social Studies—Playing "Twenty Questions" Remind children that mother duck asks one question through the story. Ask them why asking different questions can help them find the answers quickly.

Ask children if they have ever played the game "Twenty Questions". Explain that this game allows people to ask as many as twenty questions to find an object in the room. Tell them that you will write down the name of an object in the classroom on a piece of paper and cover it. They must ask questions to try and figure out which object you have chosen.

The winner of the game can choose an object and whisper the name to you so you can write it down. Show the naming word to the children after the correct answer is given.

Mathematics—Making an Animal Graph Discuss with children the different kinds of animals that are illustrated in the story. Have children count the number of each animal. Then ask children to identify the kinds of pets they have. Write the name of each kind of animal on the chalkboard. Discuss their similarities and differences. Then make a class graph to record the kinds of animals children have for pets and the total number in each group. Have each child who has a particular animal for a pet draw a picture to fit a block in the correct column.

Notes for Cooperative Learning

Additional Classroom Activities

440

For the Home

The homework assignment that follows also appears on **Homework Notebook copying master 26.** You may wish to distribute the copying masters to the children.

Writing Have children think of a place that they would like to explore. It may be real or imaginary. Have children draw a picture of the place and dictate a sentence about the place. Encourage family members to follow this procedure after taking the child's dictation.

- Read the sentence to the child.
- Read the sentence with the child.
- Have the children read the sentence.
- Read the sentences with the child.
- Have the child read the sentences.

Suggest that children share their sentences and pictures with classmates the following day.

Reading Suggest that children and parents or older family members read a story or poem about safe exploring. Encourage them to talk about times when it is safe for children to do some exploring and develop some guidelines for safe exploring.

For Extended and Recreational Reading

You may wish to recommend the following books about exploring for children to share with family members. Encourage family members to visit the public library with children to select the books to be read.

Books About Exploring

We Hide, You Seek by Jose Aruego and Ariane Dewey. Greenwillow Books, 1979.

Nothing to Do by Russell Hoban. Harper & Row, 1964.

Harry the Dirty Dog by Gene Zion. Harper & Row, 1956.

More Books About Exploring

Can You Find the Animal? by Wilda S. Ross. Coward, McCann & Geoghegan, 1974.

Hiding Game by Ben Schecter. Four Winds Press, 1977.

Joey Runs Away by Jack Kent. Prentice-Hall, 1986.

So Many Raccoons by Jan Wahl. Caedmon, 1986.

Additional Home Activities

Additional Books for Extended and Recreational Reading

Notes

Ideas for Cooperative Learning

Ideas for Meeting the Needs of Individual Students

Questioning Strategies

Focusing on "To Market, To Market," "Hickory, Dickory, Dock," and "Higglety, Pigglety, Pop"

While **listening** to and **reading** the selections, children will focus on humor and fantasy. Children will also use **writing, listening,** and **speaking** skills as they respond to the selection. They will use higher-level **thinking** skills throughout the lesson.

OBJECTIVES

WRITING/THINKING

- To dictate a response to literature using the writing process.
- To write in the sensory/descriptive domain.
- To use nonsense words.
- To write a nonsense story.

READING/THINKING

- To recognize nonsense words and humor in a rhyme.
- To identify the story in a rhyme.
- To evaluate the placement of a poem in a thematic unit.
- To distinguish between fantasy and reality in illustrations.
- To recognize initial correspondences. (/p/p)

SPEAKING/THINKING

- To discuss personal experiences before reading a selection.
- To participate in shared reading.
- To participate in group discussions.
- To dictate a response to literature.

LISTENING/THINKING

- To listen to the oral reading of a selection.
- To listen to and analyze responses to opinions about a selection.
- To listen for rhyming words.
- To listen for nonsense words.
- To listen for initial sounds. (/p/)

LEARNING STRATEGIES

- Brainstorming ideas related to children's own experiences.
- Previewing the selection and making predictions about the content.
- Completing a chart to help comprehension.
- Completing a chart to help organize writing.
- Analyzing the writer's use of language.

Summary

In three rhymes, children hear about the nonsense activities of some familiar animals.

INDIVIDUAL NEEDS

Suggestions for teaching children with special needs are provided on *Teacher's Edition* page 418.

- The blue objectives may require direct instruction.

PLANNING CALENDAR

		STUDENT'S EDITIONS	TEACHER'S EDITION	ACTIVITY BOOK
DAY 1 INTO THE SELECTION	**THINK AND READ**			
	Preparing to Read	● *pages 146–151* ■ *pages 28–33*	*page 445*	
	Planning a Reading Strategy	● *pages 146–151* ■ *pages 28–33*	*page 446*	
DAYS 2-4 THROUGH THE SELECTION	**THINK AND DISCUSS**			
	Remembering the Selection	● *pages 146–151* ■ *pages 28–33*	*page 448*	
	Discussing the Selection	● *pages 146–151* ■ *pages 28–33*	*page 449*	
	THINK AND WRITE			
	Making the Assignment		*page 450*	
	Using the Writing Process		*pages 450–451*	
	Develop Skills			
	Focusing on Language		*page 452*	*pages 82–83*
	Focusing on Composition		*page 453*	
	Focusing on Auditory Discrimination		*page 453*	
	Focusing on Visual Discrimination		*page 453*	
	Focusing on Sound-Letter Correspondences		*page 453*	*page 84*
	Focusing on the Writer's Use of Language		*page 452*	
DAY 5 BEYOND THE SELECTION	**THINK AND EXTEND**			
	For the Classroom		*page 454*	
	For the Home		*page 455*	
			▲ Homework Notebook copying master 27	

● ***Happy Times! Story Land 2***   ▲ **Learning**
■ ***What a Funny Animal!*** Storybook   **Resources File**

Note: Through observing and evaluating children's reading in a variety of situations and at different times, you can gather data that will help you understand and support individual children's reading development. Use the *Checklist for Observing and Evaluating Reading* in the **Evaluation Resources** section of the **Teacher's Edition.**

 Cooperative Learning

Cooperative learning suggestions for *Think and Read* appear at the beginning of the **Teacher's Edition.**

Preparing to Read

▶**Relating to Children's Experiences** Ask children to tell about something funny or humorous that has happened to them or that they may have seen or heard. Discuss with children what people usually do when they see something funny.

After the discussion, have children listen as you read aloud "Hey, Diddle, Diddle." Ask children to tell why the rhyme is funny.

Hey, Diddle, Diddle

Hey, diddle, diddle,
The cat and the fiddle,
The cow jumped over the moon;
The little dog laughed
To see such sport,
And the dish ran away with the spoon.

▶**Previewing and Predicting** Point to the titles of the poems and read them aloud to the children. Then ask them to look at the pictures and tell what the poems might be about. Encourage children to give reasons for their answers. You may wish to model a response:

I think the poems are about animals because there are animals in all the pictures.

▶**Setting a Purpose** Tell children that as they listen to the rhymes, they should think about what happens in each one that is unusual and funny.

Notes for Cooperative Learning

Notes for Preparing to Read

Planning a Reading Strategy

Sharing Reading   Read aloud each rhyme, sharing the illustrations and pointing to the text. Ask children to identify some of the nonsense words in each rhyme.

Encourage children to react spontaneously with comments and questions after you read the rhymes.

As you reread the rhymes, have children join you and tap out the beat of each one with rhythm sticks or clap their hands.

Reading Orally   Read aloud the rhymes. Encourage children to join in at first by repeating the nonsense words and then by reciting all three rhymes.

Call on volunteers to recite "To Market, To Market" using a clapping or galloping rhythm. Have children gallop or trot around the room while the poem is recited.

Read aloud "Higglety, Pigglety, Pop" in a rushed, excited voice. Emphasize the word *POP!* at the end. Call on volunteers to recite the rhyme making their voices sound as if this is an emergency. Have children act out the parts of the animals in the poem.

Reading Silently   Give children the opportunity to "read" the poems independently. Explain that the illustrations will help them remember what is happening in the poems.

To Market, To Market

A Mother Goose rhyme

To market, to market,
    To buy a fat pig,
Home again, home again,
    Jiggety-jig.
To market, to market,
    To buy a fat hog,
Home again, home again,
    Jiggety-jog.

28

Picture by Tony Kenyon

29

446

Hickory, Dickory, Dock

A Mother Goose Rhyme

Hickory, dickory, dock,
The mouse ran up the clock.
    The clock struck one.
    The mouse ran down,
Hickory, dickory, dock.

Picture by Sharon Harker

30

31

Higglety, Pigglety, Pop

An old rhyme

Pictures by Tony Kenyon

Higglety, pigglety, pop!
    The dog has eaten the mop;
    The pig's in a hurry,
    The cat's in a flurry,

Higglety, pigglety, POP!

32

33

Think and Discuss

Cooperative Learning

Cooperative learning suggestions for *Think and Discuss* appear at the beginning of the **Teacher's Edition.**

Remembering the Selection

Ask children to recall the rhymes and identify the characters and the funny things they do. Encourage them to look at the rhyme illustrations to help themselves recall the information. You may wish to create a class chart to record children's responses.

Animals	What They Do
horse and cow mouse dog	buy a pig and a hog runs up and down a clock eats a mop

Notes for Cooperative Learning

Notes for Remembering the Selection

Discussing the Selection

The following questions focus on the elements of humor and fantasy in each rhyme. As children respond to the questions, ask them to support their answers with examples from the rhymes. Encourage children to agree or disagree with their classmates' responses and to substantiate their opinions.

Remind children to speak clearly and loudly enough so they can be heard and understood.

1. What do the horse and cow buy at the market? (**Possible response:** *They buy a fat pig and a fat hog.*) *(Literal)*
2. Why does the mouse run down the clock? (**Possible response:** *The clock strikes one and scares the mouse.*) *(Interpretive)*
3. What make-believe things are the animals doing in the pictures? (**Possible responses:** *One animal drives a truck. One plays a guitar. One is a doctor.*) *(Interpretive)*
4. Do you know any other nonsense words? Make up some of your own. (*Encourage children to make up sounds and words.*) *(Creative)*
5. How do these rhymes make you feel? (**Possible responses:** *The rhymes make me laugh. The rhymes make me happy.*) *(Critical)*

During the discussion, children will need to

- **recall** what was bought at the market.
- **interpret** why the mouse ran down the clock.
- **judge** the make-believe things the animals did in the rhymes.
- **invent** nonsense words.
- **evaluate** why the rhymes belong in the thematic unit.

You may wish to model responses to the questions. Use the possible responses given.

Tips for Evaluating the Oral Response

- Children should speak clearly and at the appropriate volume.
- Children should respond in complete thoughts.
- Children should ask relevant questions.

Additional Discussion Questions

Notes for Evaluating the Oral Response

Think and Write

Cooperative Learning

Cooperative learning suggestions for *Think and Write* appear at the beginning of the **Teacher's Edition.**

Making the Assignment

Review with children the three rhymes. Tell children that now they are going to write a letter to another kindergarten class telling them about the rhyme they thought was best.

Using the Writing Process

Prewriting   Ask children which rhyme they liked best and why. Have children vote by raising their hands as you say the title of each rhyme. Record the numbers on a chart and the reasons why they think it is the best. Begin by modeling a response and writing it on the chalkboard or on chart paper.

I like "Hickory, Dickory, Dock" best because the mouse is so cute.

Notes for Cooperative Learning

Notes for Making the Assignment

A sample chart follows.

We like the rhyme "Hickory, Dickory, Dock."
The mouse is cute The poem is silly

Drafting   Have the class dictate a letter to another kindergarten class about the rhymes. Begin by helping children to recall the appropriate salutation of a letter. (Dear _____) Then continue to guide them by asking each child to name the rhyme they liked best and why they liked the rhyme. Have each child contribute a dictated sentence to the letter, beginning their sentence with their first name. You may wish to use the following letter as a model:

Dear Kindergarteners,
   We read three rhymes.
   Bob likes _____ because _____.
   Jessica likes _____ because _____.
   We hope you will read the rhymes and enjoy them, too.

                          Your Friends,
                          The Kindergarten class

Encourage children to respond with complete sentences. Follow this procedure after each sentence is dictated and recorded:

- Read the sentence to the individual child.
- Read the sentence with the child.
- Have the child read the sentence.

Read the completed letter to the class and make a final copy of the letter on a long "scroll-type" sheet of paper, leaving wide margins for children to draw in. Have children illustrate the borders of the letter.

Responding/Revising/Editing   Reread the letter the class wrote. Draw attention to conventions of writing a letter such as the greeting and the closing, beginning each sentence with a capital letter, leaving spaces between words, ending each sentence with a period, and following left-to-right progression.

Postwriting (Sharing)   Roll up the letter and secure with a ribbon or string. Choose a class "letter carrier" to deliver the envelope to the other class.

Notes for Using the Writing Process

Notes for Evaluating the Written Response

Develop Skills

Strategies for developing concepts and skills related to "To Market, To Market," "Hickory, Dickory, Dock," and "Higglety, Pigglety, Pop" are included in this section. Select appropriate activities to teach the whole class, small groups, or individual children.

Developing Concepts and Skills

Language:	Action Words
Composition:	Story
Auditory Discrimination:	Rhyming Words
Visual Discrimination:	Fantasy and Reality
Sound-Letter Correspondences:	Initial Correspondence /p/*p*

Focusing on Language

Using Action Words   Tell children that some of the words used in the rhymes are action words. Review the rhymes with the children, going over the action words. Explain that action words tell what someone or something is doing.

Ask children if the animals in the rhymes really can do the things the rhymes say they do. Explain that some of the actions in the rhymes are make-believe.

Use **Activity Book** page 82 with children. Have children identify the pictures at the top of the page. Ask them what makes these pictures so funny. Have children draw a picture of an animal doing something make-believe. Have them dictate an action word about the picture and write it on the writing rule.

Activity Book page 83 also focuses on action words. Have children identify the actions in the pictures. Ask children to imagine themselves doing something very silly and draw a picture of it. Follow the same procedure used for the previous **Activity Book** page.

Focusing on the Writer's Use of Language

Recall with children the nonsense words that the writers use in the three rhymes. (*jiggety-jig, jiggety-jog; hickory, dickory, dock; higglety, pigglety*) Ask why the writers use these words.
(**Possible response:** *The writers use the words to make the rhymes funny.*)

Focusing on Composition

Note: Through observing and evaluating children's writing in a variety of situations and at different times, you can gather data that will help you understand and support individual children's writing development. Use the *Checklist for Observing and Evaluating Writing* in the **Evaluation Resources** section of the *Teacher's Edition.*

Writing a Nonsense Story Ask children to think about the animals they drew for *Activity Book* page 82. Have each child write a story about the animal and what it does.

Accept their writing regardless of its stage of development. Encourage children to spell their own action words and draw pictures to illustrate their story. Have children share their writing by reading it aloud to a group of classmates or family members.

Focusing on Auditory Discrimination

Identifying Rhyming Words Read aloud the first four lines from "To Market, To Market."

Repeat the words *jig* and *pig*. Ask children to tell how the words are the same. *(They have the same ending sounds.)* Then reread the remainder of the rhyme and have children identify the other pair of rhyming words. *(hog, jog)*

Read aloud "Hickory, Dickory, Dock" and "Higglety, Pigglety, Pop" and have children identify the pairs of rhyming words in each. *(dock/clock, pop/mop, hurry/flurry)*

Focusing on Visual Discrimination

Distinguishing Between Fantasy and Reality
Have children look at the illustrations for the three rhymes. Review with them that some things in the rhymes are real because they exist. Some of the things the animals do in the rhymes are make-believe.

Focusing on Sound-Letter Correspondences

Recognizing Initial /p/p Ask children to listen for the words *pig* and *pop* as you read aloud "Higglety, Pigglety, Pop." After reading the rhyme, write on the chalkboard the words *pig* and *pop*. Have children say the words. Then circle the first letter of each and explain that the words begin with the letter *p*.

Use *Activity Book* page 84 with children. Have them repeat the word *pig* as they finger-trace the uppercase *P* and the lowercase *p*.

Have children identify the pictures at the top of the page. As each is identified, have them find the word, run their fingers under it, and say it aloud. Explain that each picture begins with the same sound they hear at the beginning of *pop*.

Have children name other words that begin with the same sound they hear at the beginning of *penny* and *peanut*. Then ask each child to draw a picture of something whose name begins with the same sound and dictate to you a word that names the picture. Write the word on the writing rule for the child. You may wish to have some children copy the word.

Activity Book: Language

Action Words

drives   dances

Activity Book: Language

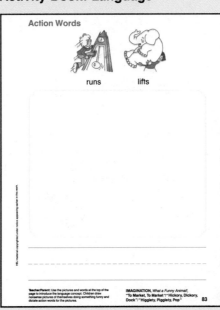

Action Words

runs   lifts

Activity Book: Sound/Letter

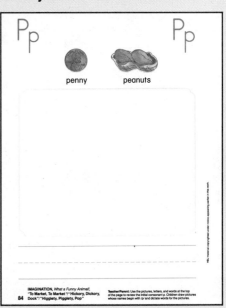

Pp   Pp

penny   peanuts

Think and Extend

Cooperative Learning

Cooperative learning suggestions for *Think and Extend* appear at the beginning of the **Teacher's Edition.**

For the Classroom

Social Studies—Playing Market Remind children that the horse and cow went to market to buy a pig. Discuss with children the importance of a market and the things that people can buy there. Then set up a market center with empty food containers and play money. Encourage children to take turns being the vendor and the shoppers. Model sentences for asking how much things cost, what kinds of foods the store has, and how much of something is needed. Ask children to bring food cans or boxes from home to add to the store.

Health—Talking About Nutrition Ask children to name foods their family buys at the supermarket. List them on the chalkboard. Ask children to decide which are eaten at breakfast, lunch, dinner, and snacktime.

Show children pictures of foods like milk, eggs, sandwiches, fruits, meats, cereal, vegetables. Set up a chart on chart paper or a chalkboard with the categories, breakfast, lunch, dinner, and snacktime. Ask children to categorize the foods. Tape the picture to the correct place on the chart, have a child dictate the name of the food, and write the response underneath.

Notes for Cooperative Learning

Additional Classroom Activities

For the Home

The homework assignment that follows also appears on **Homework Notebook copying master 27.** You may wish to distribute the copying masters to the children.

Writing Have children dictate a grocery shopping list to an older family member or parent. Encourage family members to follow this procedure after taking the child's dictation.

- Read the shopping list to the child.
- Read the shopping list with the child.
- Have the child read the shopping list.
- Have the child illustrate the shopping list.

Suggest that children share their lists with classmates the following day.

Reading Suggest that children and older family members or parents read the names on food cartons, boxes, and containers kept in the kitchen. Have them talk about when the foods are eaten or how they are prepared.

For Extended and Recreational Reading

You may wish to recommend the following books of nonsense riddles, rhymes, and stories. Encourage family members to visit the public library with children to select the books to be read.

Books About Nonsense

A Light in the Attic by Shel Silverstein. Harper and Row, 1981.

My Tang's Tungled and Other Ridiculous Situations by Sara Brewton and others. Thomas Y. Crowell, 1973.

The Mother Goose Treasury edited by Raymond Briggs. Dell, 1986.

Ganfa' Grig Had a Pig and Other Rhymes Without Reason from Mother Goose edited by Wallace Tripp. Little, Brown, 1976.

More Books About Nonsense

Nonsense Book of Riddles, Rhymes, Tongue Twisters, Puzzles, and Jokes from American Folklore collected by Duncan Emrich. Four Winds Press, 1970.

Laughing Together: Giggles and Grins From Around the Globe by Barbara Walker. Four Winds Press, 1977.

Additional Home Activities

Additional Books for Extended and Recreational Reading

Notes

Ideas for Cooperative Learning

Ideas for Meeting the Needs of Individual Students

Questioning Strategies

Focusing on "Barnyard Song"

While **listening** to and **reading** the selection, children will focus on making others happy. Children will also use **writing, listening,** and **speaking** skills as they respond to the selection. They will use higher-level **thinking** skills throughout the lesson.

WRITING/THINKING

- To dictate a response to literature using the writing process.
- To write in the sensory/descriptive domain.
- To use naming words.
- To use sound words.
- To write about a personal experience.

READING/THINKING

- To recognize sound words.
- To recognize the use of repetition.
- To evaluate the placement of a song in a thematic unit.
- To distinguish sizes.
- To recognize initial correspondences. (/g/g)

SPEAKING/THINKING

- To discuss personal experiences before reading a selection.
- To participate in shared reading.
- To participate in Creative Dramatics/Improvisation.
- To participate in group discussions.
- To dictate a response to literature.

LISTENING/THINKING

- To listen to the oral reading of a selection.
- To listen to and analyze responses to opinions about a selection.
- To identify rhyming words.
- To listen for initial sounds. (/g/)

LEARNING STRATEGIES

- Brainstorming ideas related to children's own experiences.
- Previewing the selection and making predictions about the content.
- Completing a chart to help comprehension.
- Completing a chart to help organize writing.
- Analyzing the writer's use of language.

INDIVIDUAL NEEDS

Suggestions for teaching children with special needs are provided on *Teacher's Edition* page 418.

- The blue objectives may require direct instruction.

PLANNING CALENDAR

		STUDENT'S EDITIONS	TEACHER'S EDITION	ACTIVITY BOOK
DAY 1 INTO THE SELECTION	**THINK AND READ** Preparing to Read Planning a Reading Strategy	● pages 152–157 ■ pages 34–39 ● pages 152–157 ■ pages 34–39	pages 459–460 page 460	
DAYS 2-4 THROUGH THE SELECTION	**THINK AND DISCUSS** Remembering the Selection Discussing the Selection	● pages 152–157 ■ pages 34–39 ● pages 152–157 ■ pages 34–39	page 462 page 463	
	THINK AND WRITE Making the Assignment Using the Writing Process **Develop Skills** Focusing on Language Focusing on Composition Focusing on Auditory Discrimination Focusing on Visual Discrimination Focusing on Sound-Letter Correspondences Focusing on the Writer's Use of Language		page 464 page 465 page 466 page 467 page 467 page 467 page 467 page 466	pages 85–86 page 87
DAY 5 BEYOND THE SELECTION	**THINK AND EXTEND** For the Classroom For the Home		page 468 page 469 ▲ Homework Notebook copying master 28	

● *Happy Times! Story Land 2*   ▲ *Learning*
■ *What a Funny Animal!* Storybook   *Resources File*

Cooperative Learning

Cooperative learning suggestions for *Think and Read* appear at the beginning of the **Teacher's Edition.**

Preparing to Read

▶**Relating to Children's Experiences**   Ask children to discuss how they use their voices. *(talk, sing, whisper, shout)* Then explain that animals have voices, too. Discuss how animal voices are different from human voices. You may wish to have children imitate animal sounds.

After the discussion, have children listen as you read aloud "The Barnyard."

The Barnyard
by Maude Burnham

When the Farmer's day is done,
In the barnyard, ev'ry one,
Beast and bird politely say,
"Thank you for my food today."
The cow says, "Moo!"
The pigeon, "Coo!"
The sheep says, "Baa!"
The lamb says, "Maa!"
The hen, "Cluck! Cluck!"
"Quack!" says the duck;
The dog, "Bow Wow!"
The cat, "Meow!"
The horse says, "Neigh!
I love sweet hay!'"

(poem continued on the next page)

Notes for Cooperative Learning

Notes for Preparing to Read

The pig near by,
Grunts in his sty.

When the barn is locked up tight,
Then the Farmer says, "Good night!";
Thanks his animals, ev'ry one,
For the work that has been done.

▶**Previewing and Predicting** Point to the title of the
song and read it aloud to the children. Then ask them to
look at the first two pictures to identify what is happening
and who is singing the song. Encourage children to give
reasons for their answers. You may wish to model a
response.

*There is a farm and a farmer with some animals. I think
the animals are singing the song because the cat is
playing a violin and the hen is singing.*

▶**Setting a Purpose** Ask children to listen for the
words that name animals and also for the words that are
repeated.

Planning a Reading Strategy

Sharing Reading Read aloud the song several times,
sharing the illustrations and pointing to the text. Draw
attention to the lines that are repeated throughout.

Encourage children to react spontaneously with
comments and questions, after you have read the song.

Reading Orally Teach children the music to "Barnyard
Song". (See the **Teacher's Resource** section of the
Teacher's Edition. Encourage them to join in at first by
having them repeat the sounds the animals make.

To help children learn and recall the pattern of the
song, find and cut out pictures of a cat, hen, duck, and
cow. Tape the pictures on the chalkboard in the order in
which they appear in the song. Then sing the song with
children as volunteers point to the appropriate animal
picture for each verse.

You may wish to have children sing and act out animal
parts and the farmer's part. Refer to *Creative Dramatics/
Improvisation* at the beginning of the **Teacher's Edition**
for additional suggestions.

Reading Silently Give children the opportunity to "read"
the song independently. Explain that the illustrations will
help them remember what is happening.

Barnyard Song

A Kentucky folk song

I had a cat, and the cat pleased me,
I fed my cat under yonder tree.
Cat goes fiddle dee dee.

34

Pictures by Marie-Louise Gay

I had a hen, and the hen pleased me,
I fed my hen under yonder tree.
Hen goes chimmy chuck, chimmy chuck,
Cat goes fiddle dee dee.

35

I had a duck, and the duck pleased me,
I fed my duck under yonder tree.
Duck goes quack, quack,
Hen goes chimmy chuck, chimmy chuck,
Cat goes fiddle dee dee.

36

I had a cow, and the cow pleased me,
I fed my cow under yonder tree.
Cow goes moo, moo,
Duck goes quack, quack,
Hen goes chimmy chuck, chimmy chuck,
Cat goes fiddle dee dee.

37

38

39

Think and Discuss

Note: Through observing and evaluating children's oral language (listening and speaking) in a variety of situations and at different times, you can gather data that will help you understand and support individual children's oral development. Use the *Checklist for Observing and Evaluating Oral Language* in the **Evaluation Resources** section of the *Teacher's Edition.*

Cooperative Learning

Cooperative learning suggestions for *Think and Discuss* appear at the beginning of the **Teacher's Edition.**

Remembering the Selection

Ask children to recall the song and identify what pleased the farmer. Encourage them to look at the illustrations to help themselves recall the information. You may wish to create a class chart to record children's responses.

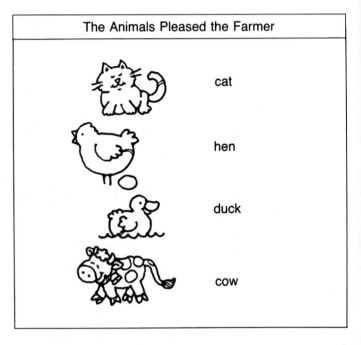

The Animals Pleased the Farmer
cat
hen
duck
cow

Notes for Cooperative Learning

Notes for Remembering the Selection

462

Discussing the Selection

The following questions focus on making others happy. As children respond to the questions, ask them to support their answers with examples from the song. Encourage children to agree or disagree with their classmates' responses and to substantiate their opinions.

Remind children to speak clearly and loudly enough so they can be heard and understood.

1. What pleases the farmer? (**Possible response:** *The cat, hen, duck, and cow please him.*) *(Literal)*
2. Why do you think the animals please the farmer? (**Possible responses:** *Maybe the cat chases away the mice. The hen lays lots of eggs. The cow gives milk. The duck has lots of ducklings.*) *(Interpretive)*
3. How do you know that the farmer is pleased? (**Possible response:** *The farmer feeds his animals under the tree.*) *(Literal)*
4. What do you do to please others? (**Possible responses:** *I help my mother and father around the house. I share my toys with my brother.*) *(Creative)*
5. How does the song please you? (**Possible responses:** *I like the song because it's about animals. The farmer is very silly.*) *(Critical)*

During the discussion, children will need to

- **identify** what pleases the farmer.
- **interpret** why the animals please the farmer.
- **determine** why the farmer is pleased.
- **relate** how they please others.
- **evaluate** why the song belongs in the thematic unit.

You may wish to model responses to the questions. Use the possible responses given.

Tips for Evaluating the Oral Response

- Children should speak clearly and at the appropriate volume.
- Children should respond in complete thoughts.
- Children should ask relevant questions.

Additional Discussion Questions

Notes for Evaluating the Oral Response

Think and Write

Cooperative Learning

Cooperative learning suggestions for *Think and Write* appear at the beginning of the **Teacher's Edition.**

Making the Assignment

Review with children the verses of "Barnyard Song." Tell children that now they are going to write their own verse to sing to classmates.

Notes for Cooperative Learning

Notes for Making the Assignment

Using the Writing Process

Prewriting   Ask children to name other animals that could live on a farm and the sounds that these animals make. List their responses on the chalkboard or on chart paper. Point to and read each word after you write it.

Barnyard Animals	Animal Sounds
horse	neigh
pig	oink
donkey	hee-haw
dog	bow wow

Drafting   Have the class choose an animal name from the list and dictate a verse to you. Begin by modeling a response using the animal chosen by the class. Write the verse on the chalkboard or on chart paper. An example follows.

I had a *(horse)*, and the *(horse)* pleased me.
I fed my *(horse)* under yonder tree.
(Horse) goes *(neigh, neigh)*.

Have each child choose another animal and dictate a verse. Write each child's dictated verse at the bottom of a piece of paper. Then follow this procedure.

- Read the verse to the child.
- Read the verse with the child.
- Have the child read the verse.
- Have the child illustrate the verse.

Responding/Revising/Editing   After each child has dictated and illustrated a verse, reread the verse you wrote. Draw attention to conventions of writing the verse, such as beginning each line with a capital letter, leaving spaces between words, ending each sentence with a period, and following left-to-right progression.

Postwriting (Sharing)   Display the children's verses on a bulletin board display entitled "Barnyard Song." Teach children the new verses they have written. Have them sing the new verses for "Barnyard Song."

Notes for Using the Writing Process

Notes for Evaluating the Written Response

Develop Skills

Strategies for developing concepts and skills related to "Barnyard Song" are included in this section. Select appropriate activities to teach the whole class, small groups, or individual children.

Developing Concepts and Skills

Language:	Sound Words
Composition:	Story
Auditory Discrimination:	Rhyming Words
Visual Discrimination:	Sizes
Sound-Letter Correspondences:	Initial Correspondence /g/g

Focusing on Language

Using Sound Words   Tell children that there are many different kinds of words and that some words name sounds. Then ask children to listen for the sound words as you reread "Barnyard Song."

After rereading the song, ask children to name the animal sound words. Write each word on the chalkboard and read it aloud. You may wish to continue the activity by rereading what children wrote for *Think and Write* and add the sound words they used in their verses.

Use **Activity Book** page 85 with children. Have children identify the pictures at the top of the page. As each is identified, have them find the word, run their fingers under it, and say the name aloud. Ask children to tell you the sounds each animal makes.

Have each child draw a picture of an animal and dictate to you a word that names the sound the animal makes. Write the word on the writing rule for the child. You may wish to have some children copy the word.

Activity Book page 86 also focuses on sound words. Follow the same procedure used for the previous page. Ask children to draw a picture of a thing that makes noise.

Focusing on the Writer's Use of Language

Ask children to recall the words for the sounds the animals made that are repeated in the song. (fiddle dee dee, chimmy chuck, quack, moo) Discuss why the writer repeated the sound words in the song. (**Possible responses:** *Saying the sound words helps you remember them. The song is fun to sing when you repeat the sounds.*)

Focusing on Composition

Note: Through observing and evaluating children's writing in a variety of situations and at different times, you can gather data that will help you understand and support individual children's writing development. Use the *Checklist for Observing and Evaluating Writing* in the **Evaluation Resources** section of the *Teacher's Edition.*

Writing About Something Happy Ask children to think about someone or something that makes them happy enough to sing. You may want to make some suggestions such as going to a baseball game, visiting a special friend or playing a favorite game. Have them write about someone or something that makes them happy.

Accept their writing regardless of its stage of development. Encourage children to draw or make attempts to write and spell. Have children share their writing by reading it aloud to family members.

Focusing on Auditory Discrimination

Identifying Rhyming Words Reread "Barnyard Song" and stress the rhyming words at the end of each line. Then repeat the words *me, tree,* and *dee.* Ask children to tell how the words are the same. (**Possible response:** *They have the same ending sounds.*) Then reread the remainder of the song and have children clap their hands each time they hear rhyming words.

Focusing on Visual Discrimination

Distinguishing Between Large and Small
Have children look at the pictures in the selection and identify the duck and ducklings. Discuss the fact that the mother duck is large and her ducklings are small. Then ask children to identify the large and small things in the remaining illustrations of "Barnyard Song."

Focusing on Sound-Letter Correspondences

Recognizing Initial /g/g Ask children to listen for the word *goes* as you read aloud the writing they did for *Think and Write.* After reading their verses, write on the chalkboard the word *goes.* Have children say the word. Then circle the first letter of *goes* and explain that the word begins with the letter *g.*

Use *Activity Book* page 87 with children. Have them repeat the word *goes* as they finger-trace the uppercase *G* and the lowercase *g.*

Have children identify the pictures at the top of the page. As each is identified, have them find the word, run their fingers under it, and say it aloud. Explain that each picture begins with the same sound they hear at the beginning of *goes.*

Have children name other words that begin with the same sound they hear at the beginning of *goes.* Then ask each child to draw a picture of something whose name begins with the same sound and dictate to you a word that names the picture. Write the word on the writing rule for the child. You may wish to have some children copy the word.

Activity Book: Language

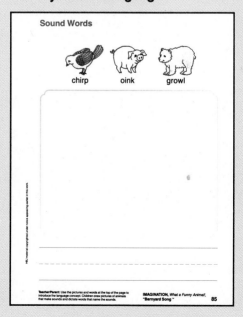

Activity Book: Language

Activity Book: Sound/Letter

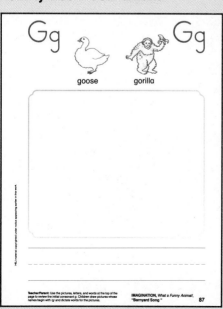

Think and Extend

Cooperative Learning

Cooperative learning suggestions for *Think and Extend* appear at the beginning of the **Teacher's Edition.**

For the Classroom

Science—Talking About Animals Look at the pictures in the selection with children and talk about where they would find the animals in the illustrations. Show children pictures of other kinds of animals such as lions, giraffes, bears, monkeys, and elephants. Ask children to name the animals and tell if they have ever seen them. Explain to children that some animals like the cow, the duck and the hen from the song live on a farm, and some animals like the lion, giraffe and elephant live in a zoo. Have children name other farm and zoo animals and write their responses on a chart. A sample follows:

Mathematics/Art—Making Animal Number Books Have children make animal number books. First, have them cut out animal pictures from old books and magazines. Cancelled stamps, picture cards, and old greeting cards with animals may also be used. After reviewing the numerals from 1–10, provide children with sheets of construction paper on which you have written the numerals one per page. Have children count out and paste the appropriate number of animals to represent the number written on each sheet. Help children compile the papers in order into a book entitled "Animal Number Book."

Cooperative Learning

This *Think and Extend* activity can be used for cooperative learning. Have children work in small groups. Each group member should choose different numbers from 1–10 and then paste the appropriate number of animals to represent the numbers they have chosen. Group members must agree on one another's work before compiling the pages into the book and sharing it with the class.

Notes for Cooperative Learning   Additional Classroom Activities

For the Home

The homework assignment that follows also appears on **Homework Notebook copying master 00.** You may wish to distribute the copying masters to the children.

Writing Have children discuss riddles with a parent or older family member. Have children make up their own riddle about a farm animal, such as: *"I say moo-moo. I give milk. What am I?" (a cow) Encourage family* members to follow this procedure after taking the child's dictation.

- Read the riddle to the child.
- Read the riddle with the child.
- Have the child read the riddle.
- Have the child draw a picture of the animal in the riddle.

Suggest the children share their riddles with classmates the following day.

Reading Suggest that each child read "Barnyard Song" with parents or older family members. Encourage them to talk about other stories and rhymes they know about animals, such as "Hey, Diddle, Diddle," "Three Blind Mice," and "The Three Bears." Have them talk about some of the silly things the animals do.

For Extended and Recreational Reading

You may wish to recommend the following books about family activities and relationships for children to share with family members. Encourage family members to visit the public library with children to select the books to be read.

Books About Animals

Little Rabbit's Loose Tooth by Lucy Bate. Crown, 1975.

Sarah's Unicorn by Bruce and Katherine Coville. Lippincott, 1979.

Winnie-the-Pooh by A. A. Milne. Dutton, 1975.

Mr. Rabbit and the Lovely Present by Charlotte Zolotow. Harper & Row, 1962.

Momo's Kitten by Taro and Mitsu Yashima. Penguin, 1977.

The Day Jimmy's Boa Ate the Wash by Trinka Noble. Dial Press, 1980.

More Stories and Rhymes About Animals

Our Animal Friends at Maple Hill Farm by Alice and Martin Provensen. Random House, 1974.

Old MacDonald Had a Farm illustrated by Robert Quackenbush. Harper & Row, 1972.

Additional Home Activities

Additional Books for Extended and Recreational Reading

Notes

Ideas for Cooperative Learning

Ideas for Meeting the Needs of Individual Students

Questioning Strategies

Focusing on "A Zookeeper at Work"

While **listening** to and **reading** the selection, children will focus on the zookeeper's job. Children will also use **writing, listening,** and **speaking** skills as they respond to the selection. They will use higher-level **thinking** skills throughout the lesson.

OBJECTIVES

WRITING/THINKING

- To dictate a response to literature using the writing process.
- To write in the practical/informative domain.
- To use telling and asking sentences.
- To write about a personal experience.

READING/THINKING

- To recognize how illustrations provide information.
- To recall details in a selection.
- To evaluate the placement of a story in a thematic unit.
- To recognize sizes.
- To recognize initial correspondences. (/z/z)

SPEAKING/THINKING

- To discuss personal experiences before reading a selection.
- To participate in shared reading.
- To participate in group discussions.
- To dictate a response to literature.

LISTENING/THINKING

- To listen to the oral reading of a selection.
- To listen to and analyze responses to opinions about a selection.
- To identify telling and asking sentences.
- To listen for initial sounds. (/z/)

LEARNING STRATEGIES

- Brainstorming ideas related to children's own experiences.
- Previewing the selection and making predictions about the content.
- Completing a chart to help comprehension.
- Completing a chart to help organize writing.
- Analyzing the writer's use of language.

Summary

The information story "A Zookeeper at Work" illustrates the variety of jobs that a zookeeper has. The illustrations show a zookeeper tending a bird pond, feeding a monkey, bathing an elephant, checking on a baby giraffe, and teaching children about animals.

INDIVIDUAL NEEDS

Suggestions for teaching children with special needs are provided on *Teacher's Edition* page 418.

- The blue objectives may require direct instruction.

PLANNING CALENDAR

		STUDENT'S EDITIONS	TEACHER'S EDITION	ACTIVITY BOOK
DAY 1 INTO THE SELECTION	**THINK AND READ**			
	Preparing to Read	● *pages 158–163* ■ *pages 40–45*	*pages 473*	
	Planning a Reading Strategy	● *pages 158–163* ■ *pages 40–45*	*page 474*	
DAYS 2-4 THROUGH THE SELECTION	**THINK AND DISCUSS**			
	Remembering the Selection	● *pages 158–163* ■ *pages 40–45*	*page 476*	
	Discussing the Selection	● *pages 158–163* ■ *pages 40–45*	*page 477*	
	THINK AND WRITE			
	Making the Assignment		*page 478*	
	Using the Writing Process		*pages 478–479*	
	Develop Skills			
	Focusing on Language		*page 480*	*pages 88–89*
	Focusing on Composition		*page 481*	
	Focusing on Auditory Discrimination		*page 481*	
	Focusing on Visual Discrimination		*page 481*	
	Focusing on Sound-Letter Correspondences		*page 481*	*page 90*
	Focusing on the Writer's Use of Language		*page 480*	
DAY 5 BEYOND THE SELECTION	**THINK AND EXTEND**			
	For the Classroom		*page 482*	
	For the Home		*page 483*	
			▲ Homework Notebook copying master 29	

● ***Happy Times! Story Land 2***
■ ***What a Funny Animal!*** Storybook

▲ *Learning Resources File*

Note: Through observing and evaluating children's reading in a variety of situations at different times, you can gather data that will help you understand and support individual children's reading development. Use the *Checklist for Observing and Evaluating Reading* in the **Evaluation Resources** section of the *Teacher's Edition.*

Cooperative Learning

Cooperative learning suggestions for *Think and Read* appear at the beginning of the *Teacher's Edition.*

Preparing to Read

▶**Relating to Children's Experiences** Ask children if they have ever visited a zoo. Encourage them to share their experiences. Discuss the many types of animals that can be seen at a zoo and the care that they need.

After the discussion, have children listen as you read aloud the poem "At the Zoo." Ask children to name the animals mentioned in the poem.

At the Zoo
by Aileen Fisher

I like the zebra
at the zoo,
his stripes are more
than just a few.
I like the stripes
on tigers, too,
and springboards
on a kangaroo.

I like the furry
black old bear,
and camel dressed
in camel's hair,
and monkeys
swinging in the air
but I am glad
I'm not so rare

Or I might be
included, too,
among the creatures
in the zoo.

Notes for Cooperative Learning

Notes for Preparing to Read

► **Previewing and Predicting** Point to the title of the story and read it to the children. Have children look at the title and the pictures to decide what the story might be about. You may wish to model a response.

I see a man doing different things with animals. I think the story is about the zookeeper because of the title and the pictures.

► **Setting a Purpose** Tell children that as you read "A zookeeper at Work" they should think about all the things a zookeeper does.

Planning a Reading Strategy

Sharing Reading Read aloud the story several times, sharing the illustrations and pointing to the text. Draw attention to the questions that are asked in the story and to the illustrations.

Encourage children to react spontaneously with comments and questions, after you have read the story.

Reading Orally Read aloud the story. Invite children to join in by saying the lines that repeat:

What does the zookeeper do?

Then have children work in pairs. Encourage one child to "read" the statement and question and the other child to answer the question by telling about the illustration.

Reading Silently Give children the opportunity to "read" the story independently. Explain that the illustrations will help them to know the answers to the question *What does the zookeeper do?*

Connections

A Zookeeper at Work

A zookeeper works in the zoo.

40

The monkeys are hungry.
What does the zookeeper do?

41

474

The elephant needs a bath.
What do the zookeepers do?

42

There is a new baby giraffe.
What does the zookeeper do?

43

Children visit the zoo.

44

What do the zookeepers do?

45

Think and Discuss

Note: Through observing and evaluating children's oral language (listening and speaking) in a variety of situations and at different times, you can gather data that will help you understand and support individual children's oral development. Use the *Checklist for Observing and Evaluating Oral Language* in the **Evaluation Resources** section of the *Teacher's Edition.*

Cooperative Learning

Cooperative learning suggestions for *Think and Discuss* appear at the beginning of the **Teacher's Edition.**

Remembering the Selection

Ask children to recall the story and identify

- the animals in the zoo.
- what the zookeeper does.

Encourage children to look at the story illustrations to help themselves recall the information. You may wish to create a class chart to record children's responses.

Discussing the Selection

The following questions focus on the jobs of a zookeeper. As children respond to the questions, ask them to support their answers with examples from the story. Encourage children to agree or disagree with their classmates' responses and to substantiate their opinions.

Remind children to speak clearly and loudly enough so they can be heard and understood.

1. How do the zookeepers care for the animals at the zoo in this story? (**Possible response:** *The zookeepers clean the bird pond, feed the monkeys, give the elephant a bath, check on the baby giraffe, and teach children visiting the zoo.*) *(Literal/ Interpretive)*

Notes for Cooperative Learning

Notes for Remembering the Selection

2. What other things do you think the zookeeper must do to care for the elephant? (**Possible response:** *The zookeeper probably has to feed the elephant, give it water, clean its cage, and keep it healthy.*) *(Critical)*

   Extend this question to the other animals in the story. Guide children to understand that all the animals have similar basic needs.

3. Why do you think a zookeeper is important to the animals? (**Possible response:** *The animals in a zoo need food and water. They need a zookeeper to do these things for them. If an animal gets sick, the zookeeper can get help for it.*) *(Critical)*

4. If you were a zookeeper, what would be your favorite job? Why? (**Possible response:** *I would like to take care of the monkeys because they are interesting to watch.*) *(Creative)*

5. Why do the animals in the zoo seem like a lot of fun? (**Possible responses:** *Animals are fun to watch. They make you laugh.*) *(Critical)*

During the discussion, children will need to

- **identify** the animals in the zoo and the jobs of the zookeeper.
- **infer** the other things the zookeeper must do for the elephant and the other animals at the zoo.

- **analyze** why a zookeeper is so important to the animals.
- **relate** their favorite job if they could be a zookeeper.
- **evaluate** why the story belongs in the thematic unit.

You may wish to model responses to the questions. Use the possible responses given.

Tips for Evaluating the Oral Response

- Children should speak clearly and at the appropriate volume.
- Children should respond in complete thoughts.
- Children should ask relevant questions.

Additional Discussion Questions

Notes for Evaluating the Oral Response

Think and Write

Cooperative Learning

Cooperative learning suggestions for *Think and Write* appear at the beginning of the *Teacher's Edition.*

Making the Assignment

Review with children the different animals in "A Zookeeper at Work." Explain that the zookeepers must know many things about the animals they care for. Tell children they will write what they know about animals in the zoo. They will make a class book of their writing.

Using the Writing Process

Prewriting   Ask children to name zoo animals and discuss the things they know about them. List their responses on the chalkboard or on chart paper. Point to and read each word after you write it. A sample chart follows.

What We Know About Animals	
monkeys	eat bananas
giraffes	have long necks
flamingoes	stand on one leg
zebras	have stripes
polar bears	live in snow
seals	have flippers

Notes for Cooperative Learning

Notes for Making the Assignment

Drafting   Have children dictate sentences that tell about animals they know. Begin by modeling a response.

Polar bears like cold weather.

Write each child's dictated sentence at the bottom of a piece of paper. Then follow this procedure.

- Read the sentence to the child.
- Read the sentence with the child.
- Have the child read the sentence.
- Have the child illustrate the sentence.

Responding/Revising/Editing   After each child has dictated sentences and illustrated them, reread the sentences you wrote. Draw attention to conventions of writing such as beginning sentences with a capital letter, ending a sentence with a period, leaving spaces between words, and following left-to-right progression.

Postwriting (Sharing)   Compile children's papers into a class book entitled "All About Animals." Display the book in the reading corner for children to read independently or with each other.

Notes for Using the Writing Process

Notes for Evaluating the Written Response

Develop Skills

Developing Concepts and Skills

Language:	Telling and Asking Sentences
Composition:	Story
Auditory Discrimination:	Details
Visual Discrimination:	Sizes
Sound-Letter Correspondences:	Initial Correspondence /z/z

Focusing on Language

Identify Asking and Telling Sentences   Tell children that there are different kinds of sentences and that some sentences tell about something and some ask a question. Ask children to listen and look as you read the following sentence from "A Zookeeper at Work." Show children the asking and telling sentences in the story.

Ask children about the sentences. After they have responded, draw their attention to the ending punctuation and explain that the period or the question mark at the end tells them the sentence is an asking sentence or a telling sentence.

Use *Activity Book* page 88 with children. Have them identify the picture at the top of the page. As it is identified, have them find the sentence, run their fingers under it, and say it aloud with you. Ask children if it is a telling sentence or an asking sentence. Have each child draw a picture of something they would like to see at the zoo and dictate to you a telling sentence that tells about the picture. Write the sentence on the writing rule for the child. You may wish to have some children copy the sentence.

Focusing on the Writer's Use of Language

Ask children to recall the kinds of sentences the writer used in "A Zookeeper at Work" *(asking and telling sentences).* Then discuss how the writer used asking and telling sentences to write the story. (**Possible responses:** *The writer wrote a telling sentence about an animal's needs. Then he wrote the question* What does the zookeeper do? *The reader than has to loik at the picture to find the answer.*)

Activity Book page 89 focuses on asking sentences. Follow the same procedure used for the previous page. Have them draw an animal at the zoo and dictate an asking sentence about the drawing.

Focusing on Composition

Note: Through observing and evaluating children's writing in a variety of situations and at different times, you can gather data that will help you understand and support individual children's writing development. Use the *Checklist for Observing and Evaluating Writing* in the **Evaluation Resources** section of the *Teacher's Edition.*

Writing About Careers   Ask children to review what zookeepers do and where they work. Have children think about other jobs that people have and then write about a job they might like to have when they grow up. Accept their writing regardless of its stage of development. Many children will draw pictures while others scribble, write letters, and use invented spellings. Have children share their writing by reading it aloud to you, a group of classmates, or family members.

Focusing on Auditory Discrimination

Listening for Details   Explain to children that they will play the game of "Twenty Questions." Tell them that you will think of a zoo animal illustrated in the story and they must ask questions to guess which one it is. They can ask up to twenty questions.

When children feel comfortable with the game, you may want to break the class into small groups and have children play the game with each other, taking turns asking and answering questions.

Focusing on Visual Discrimination

Noticing the Difference in Sizes   Have a child stand next to you. Ask children to compare your size with the size of the child standing next to you. Discuss the fact that you are taller and bigger than the child. Then have children look at the pictures of the animals in the story and compare how they differ in size.

Focusing on Sound-Letter Correspondences

Recognizing Initial /z/z   Use **Activity Book** page 90 with children. Have them repeat the word *zoo* as they finger-trace the uppercase *Z* and the lowercase *z.*

Have children identify the pictures at the top of the page. As each is identified, have them find the word, run their fingers under it, and say it aloud. Explain that each picture begins with the same sound they hear at the beginning of *zoo.*

Ask children to identify the letter each word begins with. Tell them that the letter *z* usually stands for the same sound they hear at the beginning of *zoo.* Then have children listen for the /z/ sound as you say the words *zoo* and *zebra.*

Have children name other words that begin with the same sound they hear at the beginning of *zoo* and *zebra.* Then ask each child to draw a picture of something whose name begins with the same sound and dictate to you a word that names the picture. Write the word on the writing rule for the child. You may wish to have some children copy the word.

Activity Book: Language

Telling Sentences

Animals live in the zoo.

IMAGINATION, *What a Funny Animal!,* "A Zookeeper at Work."   88   Teacher/Parent: Use the pictures and words at the top of the page to introduce the language concept. Children draw pictures of animals that live in the zoo and dictate telling sentences about the pictures.

Activity Book: Language

Asking Sentences

What do the monkeys eat?

Teacher/Parent: Use the pictures and words at the top of the page to introduce the language concept. Children draw pictures of animals and dictate telling sentences about the pictures.   IMAGINATION, *What a Funny Animal!,* "A Zookeeper at Work."   89

Activity Book: Sound/Letter

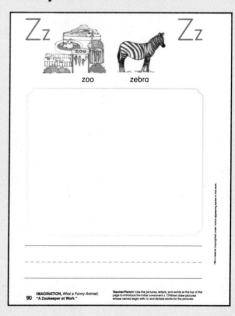

Zz   Zz

zoo   zebra

90   IMAGINATION, *What a Funny Animal!,* "A Zookeeper at Work."   Teacher/Parent: Use the pictures, letters, and words at the top of the page to introduce the initial consonant z. Children draw pictures of things whose names begin with /z/ and dictate words for the pictures.

Think and Extend

Cooperative Learning

Cooperative learning suggestions for *Think and Extend* appear at the beginning of the *Teacher's Edition.*

For the Classroom

Mathematics—Counting Animals   Have children count the number of each animal in the story. Discuss the numbers and write them in a chart on the chalkboard or on chart paper.

 ### Cooperative Learning

This *Think and Extend* activity can be used as a Cooperative learning activity. Divide class into pairs. Have children count the animals from the information story and discuss which animals each will draw on a large sheet of newsprint. After children have drawn the animals, ask them to write the correct numbers next to the drawings. Children will have created a small zoo. Ask one child to share the drawing with the class. Display drawings.

Social Studies—Learning About Community Helpers   Discuss with children that there are many people who help others, like the zookeepers. Ask children to name some helpers in the school. You may want to invite some of them into the classroom so they can tell children about their job as principal, librarian, custodian, nurse, secretary, groundskeepers, or safety patrol.

Notes for Cooperative Learning

Additional Classroom Activities

For the Home

The homework assignment that follows also appears on **Homework Notebook copying master 29.** You may wish to distribue the copying masters to the children.

Writing Ask children and family members to discuss some of the community helpers they need: family doctor, mail carrier, garbage collector, firefighter and police officer. Then have children dictate sentences about the community helpers. Encourage family members to follow this procedure after taking the child's dictation.

- Read the sentences to the child.
- Read the sentences with the child.
- Have the child read the sentences.
- Have the child illustrate the sentences.

Have children bring their sentences and pictures to class the following day to share with classmates.

Reading Suggest that each child read stories about animals. Encourage them to discuss some facts about animals.

For Extended and Recreational Reading

You may wish to recommend the following books about zoo animals and careers for children to share with family members. Encourage family members to visit the public library with children to select the books to be read.

Books About Careers and Zoo Animals

Make Way For Ducklings by Robert McCloskey. Viking, 1941.

Airport by Byron Barton. Harper & Row, 1982.

A Children's Zoo by Tana Hoban. Greenwillow, 1985.

More Books About Careers

Maybe You Should Fly a Jet! Maybe You Should Be a Vet! by Theo LeSieg. Random House, 1980.

People Working by Douglas Florian. T. Y. Crowell, 1983.

The Luckiest One of All by Bill Peet. Houghton Mifflin, 1982.

When We Grow Up by Anne Rockwell. E. P. Dutton, 1981.

Additional Home Activities

Additional Books for Extended and Recreational Reading

Notes

Ideas for Cooperative Learning

Ideas for Meeting the Needs of Individual Students

Questioning Strategies

Focusing on "A Bear Went Over the Mountain" and "Lunch for a Dinosaur"

While **listening** to and **reading** the selections, children will focus on humor. Children will also use **writing, listening,** and **speaking** skills as they respond to the selection. They will use higher-level **thinking** skills throughout the lesson.

OBJECTIVES

WRITING/THINKING

- To dictate a response to literature using the writing process.
- To write in the imaginative/narrative domain.
- To use simple sentences.
- To write about a personal experience.

READING/THINKING

- To recognize humor in a poem.
- To distinguish between reality and fantasy in a poem.
- To recognize the rhythm and pattern in a poem.
- To evaluate the placement of a poem in a thematic unit.
- To compare animals illustrated.
- To recognize initial correspondences. (b/b)

SPEAKING/THINKING

- To discuss personal experiences before reading a selection.
- To participate in shared reading.
- To participate in group discussions.
- To dictate a response to literature.

LISTENING/THINKING

- To listen to the oral reading of a selection.
- To listen to and analyze responses to opinions about a selection.
- To discriminate between questions and statements.
- To listen for initial sounds. (/b/)

LEARNING STRATEGIES

- Brainstorming ideas related to children's own experiences.
- Previewing the selection and making predictions about the content.
- Completing a chart to help comprehension.
- Completing a chart to help organize writing.
- Analyzing the writer's use of language.

Summary

In the first selection, a bear wanders over a mountain to find out what is on the other side. A little girl is prepared to wait for a dinosaur to join her for lunch in the second selection.

INDIVIDUAL NEEDS

Suggestions for teaching children with special needs are provided on *Teacher's Edition* page 418.

- The blue objectives may require direct instruction.

PLANNING CALENDAR

		STUDENT'S EDITIONS	TEACHER'S EDITION	ACTIVITY BOOK
DAY 1 INTO THE SELECTION	**THINK AND READ** Preparing to Read Planning a Reading Strategy	● pages 164–165 ■ pages 46–47 ● pages 164–165 ■ pages 46–47	pages 487–488 page 488	
DAYS 2-4 THROUGH THE SELECTION	**THINK AND DISCUSS** Remembering the Selection Discussing the Selection	● pages 164–165 ■ pages 46–47 ● pages 164–165 ■ pages 46–47	page 490 page 491	
	THINK AND WRITE Making the Assignment Using the Writing Process **Develop Skills** Focusing on Language Focusing on Composition Focusing on Auditory Discrimination Focusing on Visual Discrimination Focusing on Sound-Letter Correspondences Focusing on the Writer's Use of Language		page 494 page 495 page 496 page 497 page 497 page 497 page 497 page 496	pages 91–92 page 93
DAY 5 BEYOND THE SELECTION	**THINK AND EXTEND** For the Classroom For the Home		page 498 page 499 ▲ Homework Notebook copying master 30	

● *Happy Times! Story Land 2*   ▲ *Learning*
■ *What a Funny Animal!* Storybook   *Resources File*

Cooperative Learning

> Cooperative learning suggestions for *Think and Read* appear at the beginning of the *Teacher's Edition.*

Preparing to Read

▶**Relating to Children's Experiences**   Ask children if they have ever seen a live bear. Encourage children to discuss and describe bears. Also ask children to recall any stories they have read about bears.

Then ask children to discuss what they know about dinosaurs. Point out that we can only see dinosaur bones and footprints in museums, because there are no living dinosaurs today.

▶**Previewing and Predicting**   Point to the title of the first selection and read it aloud to children. Explain that "A Bear Went Over the Mountain" is an old song that people have sung for many years. Point to the title of the second selection "Lunch for a Dinosaur" and read it aloud to children. Then ask them to look at the pictures and tell what the selections might be about. Encourage children to give reasons for their answers. You may wish to model a response.

I think one poem is about a bear who wants to know something because there is a question mark next to his head. I think the girl in the other poem is looking for a dinosaur because she has a pair of binoculars.

Notes for Cooperative Learning

Notes for Preparing to Read

▶**Setting a Purpose**   Tell children that as they listen to the poems, they should think about what the bear and the little girl are doing.

Planning a Reading Strategy

Sharing Reading   Read aloud each poem several times, sharing the illustrations and pointing to the text. Draw attention to the lines that are repeated in "A Bear Went Over the Mountain" and to the question that is repeated in "Lunch for a Dinosaur."

Encourage children to react spontaneously with comments and questions, after you read the selections.

As you reread "A Bear Went Over the Mountain," have children join in and clap to the rhythm.

You may also wish to have children listen for and identify rhyming words as you reread "Lunch for a Dinosaur."

Reading Orally   Read aloud "A Bear Went Over the Mountain." Encourage children to join in at first by saying the lines that repeat in each verse. Then have children sing the song with you to the tune of "For He's a Jolly Good Fellow."

Have children "act out" the part of the bear as he climbs to the top of the mountain and discovers what is on the other side.

As you read "Lunch for a Dinosaur" have children join in by saying the lines that repeat.

Encourage children to pantomime the part of the little girl preparing lunch and looking for the dinosaur.

Reading Silently   Give children the opportunity to "read" the selections independently. Explain that the illustrations will help them remember what is happening in the poems.

A Bear Went Over the Mountain

An American folk rhyme

A bear went over the mountain,
A bear went over the mountain,
A bear went over the mountain
To see what he could see.

The other side of the mountain,
The other side of the mountain,
The other side of the mountain
Was all that he could see!

46

Lunch for a Dinosaur

From the poem "Company" by Bobbi Katz

I'm fixing a lunch for a dinosaur.
Who knows when one might come by?
I'm pulling up all the weeds I can find.
I'm piling them high as the sky.
I'm fixing a lunch for a dinosaur.
I hope he will stop by soon.
Maybe he'll just walk down my street
And have some lunch at noon.

Pictures by Marie-Louise Gay

47

Notes

Ideas for Cooperative Learning

Ideas for Meeting the Needs of Individual Students

Questioning Strategies

Think and Discuss

Cooperative Learning

Cooperative learning suggestions for *Think and Discuss* appear at the beginning of the **Teacher's Edition.**

Remembering the Selection

Ask children to recall the poems and identify

- what the bear wants to know.
- what the little girl wants.

Encourage children to look at the illustration for each selection to help themselves recall the information. You may wish to create a class chart to record children's responses.

Notes for Cooperative Learning

Notes for Remembering the Selection

Discussing the Selection

The following questions focus on humor. As children respond to the questions, ask them to support their answers with examples from the selections. Encourage children to agree or disagree with their classmates' responses and to substantiate their opinions.

Remind children to speak clearly and loudly enough so they can be heard and understood.

1. What does the bear want to know? Why? (**Possible responses:** *The bear wants to know what is over the mountain. The bear is curious. The bear is hungry. The bear is looking for another bear.*) *(Literal/Interpretive)*

2. What does the bear see? (**Possible response:** *The bear sees the other side of the mountain.*) *(Literal)*

3. Why is the girl looking through the binoculars? (**Possible response:** *The girl is looking for a dinosaur.*) *(Interpretive)*

4. What is the girl going to feed the dinosaur? (**Possible response:** *The girl plans to give the dinosaur weeds to eat.*) *(Literal)* What would you feed a dinosaur? (**Possible responses:** *I would share my lunch with the dinosaur. I would feed the dinosaur some leaves, grass, and flowers. I would buy him a hamburger.*) *(Creative)*

5. What is so funny about the bear and the dinosaur in these poems? (**Possible response:** *They are funny because the bear doesn't see anything but the other side of the mountain and there are no dinosaurs left in the world.*) *(Critical)*

During the discussion, children will need to

- **interpret** why the bear went over the mountain.
- **recall** what the bear saw and what the girl made for lunch.
- **analyze** why the girl is looking through binoculars.
- **relate** what they would feed a dinosaur for lunch.
- **evaluate** why the selections belong in the thematic unit.

You may wish to model responses to the questions. Use the possible responses given.

Tips for Evaluating the Oral Response

- Children should speak clearly and at the appropriate volume.
- Children should respond in complete thoughts.
- Children should ask relevant questions.

Additional Discussion Questions

Notes for Evaluating the Oral Response

Think and Discuss

Talking About Stories and Poems

The children have read the stories and poems in "What a Funny Animal!" Have children compare and contrast the selections in Unit 6. Use the discussion questions and the possible responses provided.

1. How might a zookeeper help Mother Duck find her missing duckling? (**Possible responses:** *The zookeeper would see the duckling hiding. The zookeeper would throw some food to the ducks and the duckling would come out.*)

2. What kinds of jobs do the farmer and the zookeeper do? (**Possible responses:** *The farmer and the zookeeper both take care of animals. They make sure the animals have food and stay healthy.*)

3. What other animals in the stories and poems would you like to invite for lunch? Tell why. (**Possible responses:** *I would invite the cat because she plays the fiddle. I would invite the animals from "Higglety, Pigglety, Pop" because they are silly.*)

4. Which animal do you think is the funniest? Tell why. (**Possible responses:** *I think the bear is the funniest because it is on top of the mountain and it does not see anything. I think the dog is the funniest because it has a mop in its mouth.*)

During the discussion children will talk about

- what characters from different stories do that is the same.
- what might happen if characters from different stories met each other.
- which animals are the funniest.

Bookshelf

Introduce children to these and other selections that relate to the theme of the unit.

Where Are You Going, Little Mouse? by Robert Kraus. Greenwillow, 1986. Little Mouse runs away from home because he thinks no one loves him.

Down on the Funny Farm by P.E. King. Random House, 1986. A young fellow buys a farm for only a dollar and gets a chicken that oinks, a cat that whinnies, and a horse that crows.

The Amazing, the Incredible Super Dog by Crosby Bonsall. Harper & Row, 1986. A little girl is quite excited about the tricks her wonder dog can supposedly do.

Farmer Mack Measures His Pig by Tony Johnston. Harper & Row, 1986. Farmer Mack argues that he has the fattest pig but can't prove it because Goldie won't stand still for him to measure her.

To Love a Cat by Colleen Stanley Bare. Dodd, Mead, 1986. Beautiful, colored photographs show different kinds of cats, the care they need, and the love between pet and owner.

Notes

Ideas for Cooperative Learning

Ideas for Meeting the Needs of Individual Students

Questioning Strategies

Think and Write

Cooperative Learning

Cooperative learning suggestions for *Think and Write* appear at the beginning of the *Teacher's Edition.*

Making the Assignment

Review with children what the girl had fixed for the dinosaur to eat for lunch. Tell them that now they are going to invite an imaginary friend to lunch. They will write an invitation and decide what to serve for the make-believe lunch.

Notes for Cooperative Learning

Notes for Making the Assignment

Using the Writing Process

Prewriting   Ask children to name imaginary people or animals that they would like to invite to lunch. Then have children name what they would like to have for lunch. List their responses on the chalkboard or on chart paper. Point to and read each word after you write it. A sample chart follows.

Friends	What to Make
Goldilocks	peanut butter and jelly sandwich
Three Bears	hamburgers
Coco and Grandma	spaghetti and meatballs

Drafting   Have children dictate an invitation to one of the imaginary characters on the chart. Guide the composition process by asking questions such as who and what the invitation is for and what will be served. Decide on an appropriate closing and signature. You may wish to use the following invitation as a model.

Dear Goldilocks,
    Please come for lunch tomorrow. We will have porridge and cream.

                        Love,
                        The Kindergarten Class

Have children dictate individual invitations. Then follow this procedure.

- Read the invitation to the child.
- Read the invitation with the child.
- Have the child read the invitation.
- Have the child decorate the invitation.

Responding/Revising/Editing   Reread the invitation you wrote. Draw attention to conventions of writing an invitation, such as the greeting and the closing, beginning each sentence with a capital letter, leaving spaces between words, ending each sentence with a period, and following left-to-right progression.

Postwriting (Sharing)   Display children's invitations on a bulletin board. During snack time, have children play the roles of the characters they invited to lunch.

Notes for Using the Writing Process

Notes for Evaluating the Written Response

Develop Skills

Strategies for developing concepts and skills related to "A Bear Went Over the Mountain" and "Lunch for a Dinosaur" are included in this section. Select appropriate activities to teach the whole class, small groups, or individual children.

Developing Concepts and Skills

Language:	Sentences
Composition:	Story
Auditory Discrimination:	Asking and Telling Sentences
Visual Discrimination:	Illustrated Objects
Sound-Letter Correspondences:	Initial Correspondence /b/b Initial Vowels

Focusing on Language

Identifying Simple Sentences Use **Activity Book** page 91 with children. Have them talk about the picture at the top of the page. Then have them find the sentence, run their fingers under it, and say it aloud with you. Discuss that the sentence tells about the picture. Have each child draw a picture of what might happen next to the bear in the poem and dictate to you a sentence that tells about the picture he or she drew. Write the sentence on the writing rule for the child. You may wish to have some children copy the sentence.

Discuss with children some of the possibilities for the ending of the poem "Lunch for a Dinosaur." Have children talk about the picture of the little girl and the dinosaur at the top of **Activity Book** page 92, find the sentence under it, and say it aloud. Explain that the sentence tells about the picture. Have each child draw a picture of what might happen next. Follow the same procedure used for the previous **Activity Book** page.

Focusing on the Writer's Use of Language

Review with children the lines that were repeated in "A Bear Went Over the Mountain." Discuss why the writer may have decided to repeat the lines. (**Possible responses:** *The words were used over and over to make the song sound better when it was sung.*)

Focusing on Composition

Note: Through observing and evaluating children's writing in a variety of situations and at different times, you can gather data that will help you understand and support individual children's writing development. Use the *Checklist for Observing and Evaluating Writing* in the **Evaluation Resources** section of the *Teacher's Edition.*

Writing About a Personal Experience Ask children if they have ever helped fix a meal. Have children write about their experiences.

Accept their writing regardless of its stage of development. Many children will draw pictures while others scribble, write letters, and use invented spellings. Have children share their writing by reading it aloud to you, a group of classmates, or family members.

Focusing on Auditory Discrimination

Identifying Asking Sentences and Telling Sentences Review with children that an asking sentence asks a question and telling sentence tells about something. Read aloud "Lunch for a Dinosaur" and have children identify the asking sentence and the telling sentences. Encourage children to explain how they know.

Focusing on Visual Discrimination

Comparing Illustrated Objects Have children look at the illustrations for "A Bear Went Over the Mountain" and "Lunch for a Dinosaur." Discuss with children the differences between the bear and the dinosaur. You may wish to ask children some questions to help elicit responses.

Focusing on Sound-Letter Correspondences

Recognizing Initial /b/b Use *Activity Book* page 93 with children. Have them repeat the word *bear* as they finger-trace the uppercase *B* and the lowercase *b.*

Have children identify the pictures at the top of the page. As each is identified, have them find the word, run their fingers under it, and say it aloud. Explain that each picture begins with the same sound they hear at the beginning of *bear.*

Then ask each child to draw a picture of something whose name begins with the same sound and dictate to you a word that names the picture. Write the word on the writing rule for the child. You may wish to have some children copy the word.

Recognizing Initial Vowels You may wish to use *Activity Book* pages 94–103 to introduce the initial sound-letter correspondences.

As you begin each page, set up a cluster on the chalkboard. Write the vowel in the middle and write the naming words for things that begin with the sound around the word.

Then use the *Activity Book* page with children. Have them identify the pictures at the top of the page. As each is identified, have them find the word, run their fingers under it, and say it aloud. Explain that each picture begins with the same sound-letter.

Have children name other words that begin with the same sound. Then ask each child to draw a picture of something whose name begins with the same sound and dictate to you a word that names the picture. Write the word on the writing rule for the child. You may wish to have some children copy the word.

Activity Book: Language

Telling Sentences

The bear stands on the mountain.

IMAGINATION, *What a Funny Animal!,* "A Bear Went Over the Mountain"/ "Lunch for a Dinosaur" 91

Activity Book: Language

Telling Sentences

The girl looks for the dinosaur.

92 IMAGINATION, *What a Funny Animal!,* "A Bear Went Over the Mountain"/ "Lunch for a Dinosaur"

Activity Book: Sound/Letter

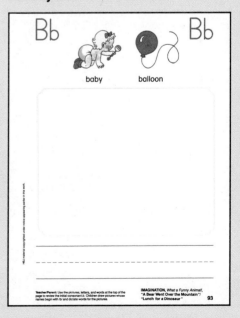

Bb   Bb

baby   balloon

IMAGINATION, *What a Funny Animal!,* "A Bear Went Over the Mountain"/ "Lunch for a Dinosaur" 93

Think and Extend

Cooperative Learning

Cooperative learning suggestions for *Think and Extend* appear at the beginning of the **Teacher's Edition.**

For the Classroom

Art/Science—Making a Model Dinosaur Display books and pictures of dinosaurs. Draw attention to the variety of dinosaurs that existed. Provide children with clay to make their own dinosaurs. When models are complete, display them for everyone to see. Have children identify the types of dinosaurs they made.

Health—Talking About A Good Lunch Explain that there are four basic food groups: milk and cheese, fruits and vegetables, meats and beans, breads and cereals. People need each kind of food every day.

Have children plan a well-balanced lunch using something from each of the four food groups. They may draw each item or cut out magazine pictures and paste them to a sheet of paper that resembles a lunch tray or plate.

Cooperative Learning

This *Think and Extend* activity can be used for cooperative learning. Have children work in groups of four to prepare a well-balanced lunch. Each group member should choose a different food group and draw or cut out a picture of something for lunch. Have children share their pictures with one another. All group members must agree on the final lunch menu before one child shares the lunch tray or plate with the class.

Notes for Cooperative Learning

Additional Classroom Activities

For the Home

The homework assignment that follows also appears on **Homework Notebook copying master 30.** You may wish to distribute the copying masters to the children.

Writing Have children talk with an older family member about imaginary friends. Children may want to talk about their imaginary friends. Then have the child dictate a story to an older family member or parent about an imaginary adventure with a dinosaur or a bear. Encourage family members to follow this procedure after taking the child's dictation.

- Read the story to the child.
- Read the story with the child.
- Have the child read the story.
- Have the child illustrate the story.

Suggest that children share their stories with classmates the following day. Classmates should then decide whether the story is real or make-believe and explain how they know.

Reading Suggest that children read a story or poem about bears or dinosaurs with an older family member. Encourage them to talk about make-believe friends and imaginary stories.

For Extended and Recreational Reading

You may wish to recommend the following books about bears and dinosaurs for children to share with family members. Encourage family members to visit the public library with children to select the books to be read.

Books About Dinosaurs and Bears

Ask Mister Bear by Marjorie Flack. Macmillan, 1986.

Little Bear by Else H. Minarik. Harper & Row, 1978.

Digging Up Dinosaurs by Aliki. Harper & Row, 1981.

Danny and the Dinosaur by Syd Hoff. Harper & Row, 1958.

More Books About Dinosaurs and Bears

Moon Bear by Frank Asch. Charles Scribner's Sons, 1978.

Supersaurus by Francine Jacobs. G. P. Putnam's Sons, 1982.

My Visit to the Dinosaurs by Aliki. Harper & Row, 1985.

Additional Home Activities

Additional Books for Extended and Recreational Reading

Notes

Notes

Student/Teacher Resources

This section of your *Teacher's Edition* includes a rich variety of resources to help you actively involve your students and their parents or guardians in the learning process.

Home Letters

Reproducible letters, in English and Spanish, with suggestions for parents to stimulate their child's interest in reading and writing. The first letter introduces parents to IMAGINATION. Subsequent letters, one for each unit, inform parents of the types of literature the children have been reading and include a list of similar literature for further reading.

(NOTE: The **Home Letters** also appear in copying-master form in the *Learning Resources File*.)

Model Plans for Extended and Recreational Reading

Two reproducible model plans—one for the classroom and one for the home—which offer tips for moving into, through, and beyond *any* literature selection.

(NOTE: The **Model Plans for Extended and Recreational Reading** also appear in copying-master form in the *Learning Resources File*.)

Bibliography for Extended and Recreational Reading

Reproducible lists of selections for extended and recreational reading—one for each unit—to share with parents and the school librarian.

(NOTE: The **Bibliography** also appears in copying-master form in the *Learning Resources File*.)

Dear _____,

I would like to introduce you to IMAGINATION, *An Odyssey Through Language,* a literature-based program that is designed to develop your child's ability to express his or her ideas effectively. The literature in this series was selected to inspire your child to think critically and creatively—to use his or her imagination. Each selection includes instructional materials designed to develop effective language concepts and skills. In addition, the selections in IMAGINATION reinforce concepts and skills taught in other subject areas such as social studies, science, and mathematics. Your child's book in the IMAGINATION series is entitled *Happy Times!*

IMAGINATION is intended to stimulate children's interest in language and its many and varied uses. You can encourage this interest in one or more of the following ways.

1. Read aloud to your child every day and encourage your child to read to, or with, you as well. Try to establish a certain time (such as bedtime) for this shared reading activity. Set a goal of about ten minutes a day or an hour a week.

2. Discuss the reading material with your child and encourage your child to express his or her feelings and opinions.

3. Encourage your child's interest in reading and writing by helping him or her learn the letters of the alphabet and words he or she may ask you about. Children will benefit from your explanations and answers to questions they have about words they want to learn.

4. Participate in your child's homework assignments. Each selection in *Happy Times!* contains writing and reading activities designed to include parents and other family members as active participants.

5. Accompany your child to the library to help select books that suit your child's interests and developmental level.

With your participation, I am looking forward to developing your child's language interests and skills with IMAGINATION.

Sincerely,

Estimado/Estimada _____,

Quiero que se familiarice con IMAGINATION, *Una aventura a través del lenguaje,* un programa basado en la literatura, el cual ha sido diseñado para que su hijo/hija desarrolle la habilidad de expresar sus ideas eficazmente. La literatura en esta serie ha sido seleccionada para motivar a su hijo/hija a investigar y pensar creativamente—para que use su imaginación. Cada selección incluye materiales de instrucción diseñados para desarrollar las destrezas y los conceptos eficaces del lenguaje. Además, las selecciones en IMAGINATION refuerzan las destrezas y los conceptos que se enseñan en otras materias, tales como Estudios Sociales, Ciencia y Matemáticas. El libro que su hijo/hija usará es parte de esta serie de IMAGINATION, y se titula *Happy Times!*

IMAGINATION tiene el propósito de interesar a su hijo/hija en el lenguaje y sus diversos usos. Usted también puede estimular este interés en una o más de las siguientes formas.

1. Léale a su hijo/hija todos los días, o permita que su hijo/hija le lea a usted, o lea con usted. Trate de establecer una hora fija para esta actividad (así como la hora de acostarse). Tenga como objetivo leer diez minutos diarios o una hora semanal.

2. Discuta la selección con su hijo/hija. Estimúlelo/la a que exprese sus sentimientos y opiniones sobre lo que ha leído.

3. Estimule el interés de su hijo/hija en la lectura y la escritura ayudándolo/la a aprender las letras del alfabeto y las palabras que no sepa. Su hijo/hija se beneficiará de su ayuda, especialmente en las palabras que les son difíciles y que quiere aprender.

4. Participe con su hijo/hija en las tareas de la escuela. Cada selección en *Happy Times!* contiene actividades de escritura y lectura diseñadas para que los padres u otros miembros de la familia participen activamente.

5. Acompañe a su hijo/hija a la biblioteca y ayúdelo/la a seleccionar libros que estén de acuerdo con sus intereses y su nivel de desarrollo.

Con su participación y con IMAGINATION, espero que su hijo/hija desarrolle el interés y las destrezas necesarias en el lenguaje.

Atentamente,

Dear _____,

Your child has just completed Unit 1 of *Happy Times!* in IMAGINATION, *An Odyssey Through Language.* The theme of this first unit is "Hello Friends." This theme runs through the literature, which focuses on the positive aspects of relationships with friends and family. The theme is also present in the activities children are working on, which include dictating thank-you notes and sentences about school and home.

The following children's books also relate to the theme of this unit. You may want to help your child find one or more of these books in your library.

May I Bring a Friend? by Beatrice Schenk De Regniers. Atheneum, 1964.
A little boy has a series of hilarious experiences when he and a friend visit the royal family.

George and Martha by James Marshall. Houghton Mifflin, 1972.
Two hippo friends, orderly Martha and bumbling, gentle George, experience quite a unique life for a hippo.

The Snowman by Raymond Briggs. Random House, 1978.
In this wordless book, a magical snowman becomes best friends with the boy who made him.

Danny's Birthday by Edith Kunhardt. Greenwillow, 1986.
Danny's father videotapes Danny's fifth birthday so he can relive the festivities again and again.

Best Friends by Steven Kellogg. Dial Books, 1986.
Kathy and Louise are best friends, but when Louise goes away for the summer, Kathy misses her terribly and begins to feel some resentment.

Lizzie and Harold by Elizabeth Winthrop. Lothrop, Lee & Shepard, 1986.
Six-year-old Lizzie wants a best girlfriend until Harold, who lives next door, proves to be a wonderful friend.

If possible, set aside time each day to read aloud to your child. Encourage your child to read to, or with, you as well. You may also wish to discuss the content of the books with your child, as well as any issues that are raised in them. Also encourage your child to continue the story or tell more about a character.

Sincerely,

Estimado/Estimada _____,

   Su hijo/hija acaba de completar la Unidad 1 de *Happy Times!*, la cual es parte de la serie de IMAGINATION, *Una aventura a través del lenguaje.* El tema de esta primera unidad es "Hola amigos". Este tema se encuentra en la literatura seleccionada, y trata de el aspecto positivo de las relaciones de amigos y de familia. El tema también se encuentra en las actividades en que los niños están trabajando, las cuales incluyen el dictar cartas de agradecimiento y oraciones sobre la escuela y la casa.

   Los siguientes libros infantiles también se refieren al tema de esta unidad. Ayude a su hijo/hija a conseguir uno o más de estos libros en la biblioteca.

   May I Bring a Friend? por Beatrice Schenk De Regniers. Atheneum, 1964.
   Un niño tiene una serie de experiencias alegres cuando él y un amigo visitan la familia real.

   George and Martha por James Marshall. Houghton Mifflin, 1972.
   Dos hipopótamos amigos, Martha la ordenada y George el amable, viven una vida única para ser hipopótamos.

   The Snowman por Raymond Briggs. Random House, 1978.
   En este libro sin palabras un hombre mágico hecho de nieve se convierte en el mejor amigo del niño que lo hizo.

   Danny's Birthday por Edith Kunhardt. Greenwillow, 1986.
   El papá de Danny le graba su quinto cumpleaños en cinta de video para que Danny pueda recordar la fiesta una y otra vez.

   Best Friends por Steven Kellogg. Dial Books, 1986.
   Kathy y Louise son íntimas amigas, pero cuando Louise se va de vacaciones, Kathy la extraña mucho y comienza a resentirse.

   Lizzie and Harold por Elizabeth Winthrop. Lothrop, Lee & Shepard, 1986.
   Lizzie, una niña de seis años, quiere tener una amiga; pero Harold el niño de al lado, le demuestra que él puede ser un buen amigo.

   Si es posible, aparte tiempo cada día para que le lea a su hijo/hija en voz alta. Anime a su hijo/hija a que le lea a usted, o junto con usted. Tal vez usted prefiera discutir el contenido de los libros, así como también cualquiera de los temas que éstos contengan. Además estimule a su hijo/hija a que continúe el cuento o añada algo más sobre los personajes.

                                        Atentamente,

Dear _____,

Your child has just completed Unit 2 of *Happy Times!* in IMAGINATION, *An Odyssey Through Language.* The theme of this second unit is "Places I Know." This theme runs through the literature, which focuses on the idea that every person, place or thing has its own place. The theme is also present in the activities children are working on, which include creating dialogue for story characters and using numbers to count.

The following children's books also relate to the theme of this unit. You may want to help your child find one or more of these books in your library.

The Biggest House in the World by Leo Lionni. Alfred A. Knopf, 1968.
A wise father snail convinces his son that a small, easy-to-carry shell is better than the biggest house in the world for a snail who wishes to have a life of travel and adventure.

Anno's Counting House by Mitsumasa Anno. Philomel, 1982.
Through the cutouts in the pages, the reader can watch young children move from house to house, page after page.

Ten, Nine, Eight by Molly Bang. Greenwillow, 1983.
A father counts backward to help his small daughter go to bed.

Oscar Mouse Finds a House by Moira Miller. Dial Books, 1985.
Oscar Mouse hunts and hunts until he finds just the right place for his new house.

This Is the Place for Me by Joanna Cole. Scholastic, 1986.
Clumsy Morty Bear makes a mess at home and searches for a better place to live, but none is quite right.

Goodbye House by Frank Asch. Prentice-Hall, 1986.
Bear experiences a painful feeling when he is faced with moving from his home.

If possible, set aside time each day to read aloud to your child. Encourage your child to read to, or with, you as well. You may also wish to discuss the content of the books with your child, as well as any issues that are raised in them. Also encourage your child to continue the story or tell more about a character.

Sincerely,

Estimado/Estimada _____,

   Su hijo/hija acaba de completar la Unidad 2 de *Happy Times!*, la cual es parte de la serie de IMAGINATION, *Una aventura a través del lenguaje.* El tema de esta segunda unidad es "Lugares que conozco". Este tema se encuentra en la literatura seleccionada, y trata de el sitio que tiene cada persona, lugar y cosa. El tema también se encuentra en las actividades en que los niños están trabajando, las cuales incluyen el crear diálogos para los personajes de los cuentos y usar los números para contar.

   Los siguientes libros infantiles también se refieren al tema de esta unidad. Ayude a su hijo/hija a conseguir uno o más de estos libros en la biblioteca.

The Biggest House in the World por Leo Lionni. Alfred A. Knopf, 1968.
Un padre caracol astutamente convence a su hijo de que una concha pequeña es mejor que la casa más grande del mundo, especialmente para un caracol que desea viajar y tener aventuras.

Anno's Counting House por Mitsumasa Anno. Philomel, 1982.
A través de los recortes en cada página, el lector puede ver a niños pequeños mudarse de casa en casa, página tras página.

Ten, Nine, Eight por Molly Bang. Greenwillow, 1983.
Un padre cuenta al revés para ayudar a su niña a irse a la cama.

Oscar Mouse Finds a Mouse por Moira Miller. Dial Books, 1985.
El ratón Oscar busca y busca hasta que encuentra el lugar ideal para su casa.

This Is the Place for Me por Joanna Cole. Scholastic, 1986.
El oso Morty, el torpe, hace un desorden en su casa y busca un mejor lugar para vivir pero nada le parece bien.

Goodbye House por Frank Asch. Prentice-Hall, 1986.
A Oso le causa un gran dolor el tener que mudarse de su casa.

   Si es posible, aparte tiempo cada día para que le lea a su hijo/hija en voz alta. Anime a su hijo/hija a que le lea a usted, o junto con usted. Tal vez usted prefiera discutir el contenido de los libros, así como también cualquiera de los temas que éstos contengan. Además estimule a su hijo/hija a que continúe el cuento o que añada algo más sobre los personajes.

                                                             Atentamente,

Dear _____,

Your child has just completed Unit 3 of *Happy Times!* in IMAGINATION, *An Odyssey Through Language.* The theme of this third unit is "Imagine That!" This theme runs through the literature, which focuses on imaginary adventures. The theme is also present in the activities children are working on, which include creating a scary poem and a weather report.

The following children's books also relate to the theme of this unit. You may want to help your child find one or more of these books in your library.

The Turnip illustrated by Janina Domansa. Macmillan, 1969.
When all the people and animals could not pull the turnip out of the ground, the magpie landed on the last one in line, and that did it.

One Fine Day by Nonny Hogrogian. Macmillan, 1971.
A fox's greed leads him to a lost tail in this cumulative tale.

The Magic Fish by Freya Littledale. Scholastic, 1986.
This is a simple version of Grimm's tale about a fisherman, his greedy wife, and a fish who grants wishes.

Pig Pig and the Magic Photo Album by David McPhail. E. P. Dutton, 1986.
Pig Pig discovers a magic photo album that takes him on exciting adventures to faraway places.

Have You Ever Seen?. . . An ABC Book by Beau Gardner. Dodd, Mead, 1986.
Comical combinations, such as an "Egg with Ears" and a "Jellybean Jump-Rope," are found in this lively ABC book.

Teeny Tiny by Jill Bennett. G. P. Putnam, 1986.
After finding a bone in a churchyard, the teeny tiny woman plans to use it for supper until a ghost begins to haunt her.

If possible, set aside time each day to read aloud to your child. Encourage your child to read to, or with, you as well. You may also wish to discuss the content of the books with your child, as well as any issues that are raised in them. Also encourage your child to continue the story or tell more about a character.

Sincerely,

Estimado/Estimada _____,

Su hijo/hija acaba de completar la Unidad 3 de *Happy Times!,* la cual es parte de la serie de IMAGINATION, *Una aventura a través del lenguaje.* El tema de esta tercera unidad es "Usa tu imaginación". Este tema se encuentra en la literatura seleccionada, y trata de las aventuras imaginarias. El tema también se encuentra en las actividades en que los niños están trabajando, las cuales incluyen el crear un poema de espantos y un informe del tiempo.

Los siguientes libros infantiles también se refieren al tema de esta unidad. Ayude a su hijo/hija a conseguir uno o más de estos libros en la biblioteca.

The Turnip ilustrado por Janina Domansa. Macmillan, 1969.
Cuando ninguna persona, ni ningún animal, pudo arrancar el nabo de la tierra, la urraca aterrizó detrás del último en la cola y lo logró.

One Fine Day por Nonny Hogrogian. Macmillan, 1971.
La avaricia de la zorra la lleva a perder su cola.

The Magic Fish por Freya Littledale. Scholastic, 1986.
Una versión simple del cuento de Grimm's sobre un pescador, su esposa avara y un pez que concede deseos.

Pig Pig and the Magic Photo Album por David McPhail. E. P. Dutton, 1986.
Pig Pig descubre un album mágico de fotos que lo lleva a lugares distantes.

Have You Ever Seen?. . . An ABC Book por Beau Gardner. Dodd, Mead, 1986.
En este libro se incluyen combinaciones chistosas tales como "Egg with Ears" y "Jellybean Jump-Rope".

Teeny Tiny por Jill Bennett. G. P. Putnam, 1986.
La mujer pequeñita encuentra un hueso en el patio de la iglesia y decide prepararlo para la cena, pero un fantasma la empieza a perturbar.

Si es posible, aparte tiempo cada día para que le lea a su hijo/hija en voz alta. Anime a su hijo/hija a que le lea a usted, o junto con usted. Tal vez usted prefiera discutir el contenido de los libros, así como también cualquiera de los temas que éstos contengan. Además estimule a su hijo/hija a que continúe el cuento o que añada algo más sobre los personajes.

Atentamente,

Dear _____,

Your child has just completed Unit 4 of *Happy Times!* in IMAGINATION, *An Odyssey Through Language.* The theme of this fourth unit is "Oh, What Fun!" This theme runs through the literature, which focuses on making new discoveries. The theme is also present in the activities children work on, which include dictating sentences about feelings and creating a recipe.

The following children's books also relate to the theme of this unit. You may want to help your child find one or more of these books in your library.

The Popcorn Book by Tomie De Paola. Harper & Row, 1978.
Tony likes to cook and Tim likes to read, but both twins like to eat . . . POPCORN!

Petunia by Roger Duvoisin. Alfred A. Knopf, 1977.
Funny and muddled Petunia always manages to solve life's problems in her own hilarious ways.

Curious George by H. A. Rey. Houghton Mifflin, 1973.
George is a funny little monkey whose curiosity always gets the best of him.

An Evening at Alfie's by Shirley Hughes. Lothrop, Lee & Shepard, 1985.
There is always excitement at Alfie's house, especially the night the water pipe bursts!

Rabbits on Roller Skates by Jan Wahl. Crown, 1986.
A story in verse about mischievous rabbits who skate their way to the roller rink.

Cromwell by Barney Saltzberg. Atheneum, 1986.
Cromwell the dog proves to be quite different as he wears clothes, reads books, digs with a shovel, and learns to play the cello.

If possible, set aside time each day to read aloud to your child. Encourage your child to read to, or with, you as well. You may also wish to discuss the content of the books with your child, as well as any issues that are raised in them. Also encourage your child to continue the story or tell more about a character.

Sincerely,

Estimado/Estimada _____,

    Su hijo/hija acaba de completar la Unidad 4 de *Happy Times!,* la cual es parte de la serie de IMAGINATION, *Una aventura a través del lenguaje.* El tema de esta cuarta unidad es "¡Qué divertido!". Este tema se encuentra en la literatura seleccionada, y trata de cómo descubrir cosas nuevas. El tema también se encuentra en las actividades en que los niños están trabajando, las cuales incluyen el dictar oraciones sobre sentimientos y crear recetas.

    Los siguientes libros infantiles también se refieren al tema de esta unidad. Ayude a su hijo/hija a conseguir uno o más de estos libros en la biblioteca.

The Popcorn Book por Tomie De Paola. Harper & Row, 1978.
A Tony le gusta cocinar y a Tim le gusta leer, pero a los dos gemelos les gusta comer. . . ROSITAS DE MAIZ.

Petunia por Roger Duvoisin. Alfred A. Knopf, 1977.
Petunia, chistosa y enlodada, siempre se las arregla para resolver los problemas de una manera alegre.

Curious George por H. A. Rey. Houghton Mifflin, 1973.
George es un mono pequeño al que su curiosidad siempre hace ver sus buenas cualidades.

An Evening at Alfie's por Shirley Hughes. Lothrop, Lee & Shepard, 1985.
En la casa de Alfie siempre pasa algo emocionante, especialmente cuando la tubería se revienta.

Rabbits on Roller Skates por Jan Wahl. Crown, 1986.
Un cuento, en forma de verso, acerca de unos conejos listos que van en patines hacia la pista de patinar.

Cromwell por Barney Saltzberg. Atheneum, 1986.
Cromwell, el perro, demuestra ser diferente al usar ropa, leer libros, cavar con una pala y aprender a tocar el cello.

    Si es posible, aparte tiempo cada día para que le lea a su hijo/hija en voz alta. Anime a su hijo/hija a que le lea a usted, o junto con usted. Tal vez usted prefiera discutir el contenido de los libros, así como también cualquiera de los temas que éstos contengan. Además estimule a su hijo/hija a que continúe el cuento o que añada algo más sobre los personajes.

                                       Atentamente,

Dear _____,

    Your child has just completed Unit 5 of *Happy Times!* in IMAGINATION, *An Odyssey Through Language.* The theme of this fifth unit is "Let's Go Outside." This theme runs through the literature, which focuses on the adventure of independent exploration. The theme is also present in the activities children are working on, which include dictating sentences about a trip and an invitation to a character in a story.

    The following children's books also relate to the theme of this unit. You may want to help your child find one or more of these books in your library.

The Snowy Day by Ezra Jack Keats. Viking, 1962.
Making snowmen, tracks, and angels gives Peter a full but tiring day outside
in the snow.

Why the Sun and the Moon Live in the Sky by Elphinstone Dayrell. Houghton
Mifflin, 1968.
This African folktale explains why the sun and the moon were forced to live
in the sky.

A Tree Is Nice by Janice Udry. Harper & Row, 1956.
A tree is nice to have for a friend for many useful reasons.

Nora's Castle by Satomi Ichikawa. Philomel, 1986.
Nora, along with her doll, dog, and teddy bear, sets off to explore the castle she
sees from her window.

Papa, Please Get the Moon for Me by Eric Carle. Picture Book Studio, 1986.
Papa uses unique means to get the moon for his daughter.

The Sky Jumps Into Your Shoes at Night by Jasper Tomkins. Green Tiger, 1986.
The sky is everywhere and touches everyone and everything.

    If possible, set aside time each day to read aloud to your child. Encourage your child to read to, or with, you as well. You may also wish to discuss the content of the books with your child, as well as any issues that are raised in them. Also encourage your child to continue the story or tell more about a character.

                      Sincerely,

Estimado/Estimada _____,

Su hijo/hija acaba de completar la Unidad 5 de *Happy Times!*, la cual es parte de la serie de IMAGINATION, *Una aventura a través del lenguaje.* El tema de esta quinta unidad es "Vamos afuera". Este tema se encuentra en la literatura seleccionada, y trata de las aventuras al explorar individualmente. El tema también se encuentra en las actividades en que los niños están trabajando, las cuales incluyen el dictar oraciones sobre un viaje y una invitación a un personaje de un cuento.

Los siguientes libros infantiles también se refieren al tema de esta unidad. Ayude a su hijo/hija a conseguir uno o más de estos libros en la biblioteca.

The Snowy Day por Ezra Jack Keats. Viking, 1962.
Peter se siente satisfecho pero muy cansado después de haber pasado todo el día haciendo muñecos de nieve, rieles y ángulos.

Why the Sun and the Moon Live in the Sky por Elphinstone Dayrell. Houghton Mifflin, 1968.
Este cuento folklórico de África explica por qué el sol y la luna tuvieron que irse a vivir al cielo.

A Tree Is Nice por Janice Udry. Harper & Row, 1956.
Por muchas razones útiles, vale la pena tener un árbol como amigo.

Nora's Castle por Satomi Ichikawa. Philomel, 1986.
Nora, junto con su muñeca, su perro, y su oso de peluche, salen a explorar el castillo que ella ve desde su ventana.

Papa, Please Get the Moon for Me por Eric Carle. Picture Book Studio, 1986.
Papá usa un método único para traerle la luna a su hija.

The Sky Jumps Into Your Shoes at Night por Jasper Tomkins. Green Tiger, 1986.
El cielo está en todas partes y toca a todas las personas y todas las cosas.

Si es posible, aparte tiempo cada día para que le lea a su hijo/hija en voz alta. Anime a su hijo/hija a que le lea a usted, o junto con usted. Tal vez usted prefiera discutir el contenido de los libros, así como también cualquiera de los temas que éstos contengan. Además estimule a su hijo/hija a que continúe el cuento o que añada algo más sobre los personajes.

Atentamente,

Dear _____,

Your child has just completed Unit 6 of *Happy Times!* in IMAGINATION, *An Odyssey Through Language.* The theme of this sixth unit is "What a Funny Animal!" This theme runs through the literature, which focuses on humorous situations involving animals. The theme is also present in the activities children work on, which include creating verses for a silly song and inviting a dinosaur to lunch.

The following children's books also relate to the theme of this unit. You may want to help your child find one or more of these books in your library.

Mr. Rabbit and the Lovely Present by Charlotte Zolotow. Harper & Row, 1962.
Mr. Rabbit helps a little girl find the best birthday present for her mother.

The Adventures of Paddy Pork by John S. Goodall. Harcourt Brace Jovanovich, 1968.
Paddy gets lost when he follows a circus into the country. A wolf follows him, but he escapes just in time.

The ABC Bunny by Wanda Gag. Coward-McCann, 1933.
A bunny hops away from a storm through the alphabet.

Down on the Funny Farm by P. E. King. Random House, 1986.
A young fellow buys a farm for only a dollar and gets a chicken who oinks, a cat who whinnies, and a horse who crows.

The Amazing the Incredible Super Dog by Crosby Bonsall. Harper & Row, 1986.
A little girl is quite excited about the tricks her wonder dog can supposedly do.

Farmer Mack Measures His Pig by Tony Johnston. Harper & Row, 1986.
Farmer Mack argues that he has the fattest pig but can't prove it because Goldie won't stand still for him to measure her.

You may wish to read these books aloud to your child or have your child read to you, or with, you as well. During the summer months, encourage your child to read these or other books for his or her enjoyment and continuing education.

Sincerely,

Estimado/Estimada _____,

    Su hijo/hija acaba de completar la Unidad 6 de *Happy Times!,* la cual es parte de la serie de IMAGINATION, *Una aventura a través del lenguaje.* El tema de esta sexta unidad es "¡Qué animal más chistoso!". Este tema se encuentra en la literatura seleccionada, y trata de situaciones chistosas que envuelven animales. El tema también se encuentra en las actividades en que los niños están trabajando, las cuales incluyen el crear versos para una canción tonta e invitar a un dinosaurio a almorzar.

    Los siguientes libros infantiles también se refieren al tema de esta unidad. Ayude a su hijo/hija a conseguir uno o más de estos libros en la biblioteca.

    Mr. Rabbit and the Lovely Present por Charlotte Zolotow. Harper & Row, 1962.
El señor Conejo ayuda a una niñita a encontrar el mejor regalo de cumpleaños para su mamá.

    The Adventures of Paddy Pork por John S. Goodall.
Harcourt Brace Jovanovich, 1968.
Paddy se pierde cuando sigue a un circo que va hacia el campo. Un lobo lo sigue, pero él logra escaparse a tiempo.

    The ABC Bunny por Wanda Gag. Coward-McCann, 1933.
Un conejito salta de una tormenta hacia el alfabeto.

    Down on the Funny Farm por P. E. King. Random House, 1986.
Un joven compra una finca por sólo un dólar, y obtiene una gallina que chilla, un gato que relincha y un caballo que croa.

    The Amazing the Incredible Super Dog por Crosby Bonsall. Harper & Row, 1986.
Una niña está muy emocionada acerca de los trucos que supuestamente su super-perro puede hacer.

    Farmer Mack Measures His Pig por Tony Johnston. Harper & Row, 1986.
El agricultor Mack alega que él tiene la puerca más gorda, pero no puede probarlo porque Goldie no se para quieta para que él la pueda medir.

    Tal vez usted prefiera leerle estos libros en voz alta a su hijo/hija, o dejar que su hijo se los lea a usted, o lo lea junto con usted. Durante los meses de verano, anime a su hijo a leer éstos u otros libros para su educación y entretenimiento.

                                          Atentamente,

Model Plan for Extended and Recreational Reading

This model plan outlines a procedure for moving into, through, and beyond *any* literature selection. It supports the Integrated Instructional Plans for the selections in IMAGINATION. The model plan is flexible: It is appropriate for use with one child, a group of children, or an entire class. The amount of time you focus on a selection depends on the length of the selection and the number of activities you want students to complete.

Before using the model plan, you may want to preview the selection to identify the theme.

Selection title: _____

Theme: _____

Into the Selection	**THINK AND READ** • Discuss background experiences that relate to the content of the selection. • Have students preview the selection and make predictions. You may suggest that they read the title and, when appropriate, look at the illustrations. Discuss what the selection may be about. • Set a purpose for reading. The purpose may relate to the theme of the selection. • Read the selection orally and/or have students read it independently.	**Notes**
Through the Selection	**THINK AND DISCUSS** • Discuss the selection, focusing on the theme. You may want to generate questions to begin the discussion; however, encourage students to ask additional questions. Ask students to support their responses with examples from the text and details from the illustrations.	**Notes**
	THINK AND WRITE • Suggest ways for students to respond in writing to the selection, focusing on the theme. *(You may want to suggest one of the assignments on the back of this model plan.)* Accept their writing regardless of its stage of development. Many students will draw pictures, while others will scribble, write letters, and use invented spellings.	**Notes**

continued

**Through the
Selection**
(continued)

THINK AND WRITE
(continued)

Notes

Ideas for Assignments

Continue the story.
Change the story ending.
Write a letter to a story character.
Pretend to be a story character; write a letter to
   another character.
Describe a character or a setting.
Give an opinion about the way a character
   solves a problem.

- Suggest that students dictate their responses.
  You may want to follow this procedure:

  1. Record each child's dictation.

  2. Read the writing to the child.

  3. Read the writing with the child.

  4. Have the child read the writing.

  5. Have the child illustrate the writing.

**Beyond the
Selection**

THINK AND EXTEND

- Consider ways to extend literature to other content
  areas. You may suggest social studies, science,
  health, mathematics, fine arts, or physical education
  activities.

Notes

Model Plan for Extended and Recreational Reading

Your child has been reading literature selections in IMAGINATION, an integrated language arts program. You may enjoy working with your child as he or she continues this reading experience. This model plan provides suggestions for sharing the joys of reading and writing.

Before using the model plan, you may want to preview the selection to identify the theme.

Selection title: _____

Theme: _____

Into the Selection	**THINK AND READ**	**Notes**
	• Discuss background experiences that relate to the content of the selection.	
	• Have your child preview the selection and make predictions. You may suggest that they read the title and, when appropriate, look at the illustrations. Discuss what the selection may be about.	
	• Set a purpose for reading. The purpose may relate to the theme of the selection.	
	• Read the selection orally and/or have your child read it independently.	
Through the Selection	**THINK AND DISCUSS**	**Notes**
	• Discuss the selection, focusing on the theme. You may want to generate questions to begin the discussion; however, encourage your child to ask additional questions. Ask him or her to support responses with examples from the text and details from the illustrations.	
	THINK AND WRITE	**Notes**
	• Suggest ways for your child to respond in writing to the selection, focusing on the theme. *(You may want to suggest one of the assignments on the back of this model plan.)*	
	Accept your child's writing regardless of its stage of development. He or she may draw pictures, scribble, write letters, and use invented spellings.	

continued

Name _____

**Through the
Selection**
(continued)

THINK AND WRITE
(continued)

Notes

Ideas for Assignments

Continue the story.
Change the story ending.
Write a letter to a story character.
Pretend to be a story character; write a letter to
  another character.
Describe a character or a setting.
Give an opinion about the way a character
  solves a problem.

- Suggest that your child dictate his or her response.
  You may want to follow this procedure.

  1. Record your child's dictation.

  2. Read the writing to your child.

  3. Read the writing with your child.

  4. Have your child read the writing.

  5. Have your child illustrate the writing.

**Beyond the
Selection**

THINK AND EXTEND

Notes

- Consider ways to extend literature to other content
  areas. You may suggest social studies, science,
  health, mathematics, fine arts, or physical education
  activities.

For Extended and Recreational Reading

Good-bye, Hello

Books About New Experiences

Madeline by Ludwig Bemmelmans. Viking, 1939.
And to Think That I Saw It on Mulberry Street by Dr. Seuss. Vanguard, 1937.
Look What I Can Do by Jose Aruego. Charles Scribner's Sons, 1971.
Mr. Grumpy's Outing by John Burningham. Henry Holt, 1971.

Poems and Rhymes About Animals

Animal Poems for Children selected by DeWitt Conyers, Childrens Press, 1982.
A Bug in a Jug and Other Funny Rhymes by Gloria Patrick. Carolrhoda Books, 1970.
Father Fox's Pennyrhymes by Clyde Watson. Scholastic, 1971, by arrangement with T. Y. Crowell Company.

Birthday Fun

Books About Families

Umbrella by Taro Yashima. Viking, 1958.
Friday Night Is Papa Night by Ruth Sonneborn. Penguin, 1987.
Ask Mister Bear by Marjorie Flack. Macmillan, 1986.
Blueberries for Sal by Robert McCloskey. Puffin, 1976.

More Books About Families

Happy Birthday, Sam by Pat Hutchins. Greenwillow, 1978.
A Birthday Wish by Ed Emberley. Little, Brown, 1977.
My Old Grandad by Wolf Harranth. Oxford, 1984.
Paul's Christmas Birthday by Carol Carrick. Greenwillow, 1978.
A Father Like That by Charlotte Zolotow. Harper & Row, 1971.

Story Time at School

Wordless Stories

The Snowman by Raymond Briggs. Random House, 1978.
Deep in the Forest by Brinton Turkle. E. P. Dutton, 1976.
Ah-Choo! by Mercer Mayer. Dial Books, 1976.
A Boy, a Dog and a Frog by Mercer Mayer. Dial Books, 1976.
Noah's Ark by Peter Spier. Doubleday, 1977.

More Stories for Children to Share

Here Comes Alex Pumpernickel by Fernando Krahn. Little, Brown, 1981.
The Knight and the Dragon by Tomie dePaola. G. P. Putnam's Sons, 1980.
Snow by Isao Sasaki. Viking, 1980.
The Story of a Little Mouse Trapped in a Book by Monique Felix. Green Tiger Press, 1980.
The Hunter and the Animals by Tomie dePaola. Holiday House, 1981.
Moonlight by Jan Ormerod. Puffin, 1983.

Silly Goose

Books About Silly Animals

Bedtime for Frances by Russell Hoban. Harper & Row, 1960.
The Tale of Peter Rabbit by Beatrix Potter in *The Complete Adventures of Peter Rabbit.* Puffin, 1984.
Amos and Boris by William Steig. Farrar, Straus & Giroux, 1971.
A Bear Called Paddington by Michael Bond. Dell, 1968.
Frog and Toad Are Friends by Arnold Lobel. Harper & Row, 1979.
The Adventures of Paddy Pork by John Goodall. Harcourt Brace Jovanovich, 1968.

More Books About Silly Animals

Paddy's New Hat by John Goodall. Atheneum, 1980.
Frederick by Leo Lionni. Pantheon, 1966.
Little Bear by Else Holmelund Minarik. Harper & Row, 1978.
Animals Should Definitely Not Act Like People by Judi Barrett. Atheneum, 1980.

Very Tall Mouse and Very Short Mouse

Books About Friends

May I Bring a Friend? by Beatrice Schenk de Regniers. Atheneum, 1964.
Corduroy by Don Freeman. Viking, 1968.
George and Martha by James Marshall. Houghton Mifflin, 1972.
The Snowman by Raymond Briggs. Random House, 1978.
Will I Have a Friend? by Miriam Cohen. Macmillan, 1967.
Mouse Tales by Arnold Lobel. Harper & Row, 1972.

More Books About Friends

Best Friends by Miriam Cohen. Macmillan, 1971.
A New Home, A New Friend by Hans Wilhelm. Random House, 1985.
Friend Dog by Arnold Doff. J. B. Lippincott, 1980.
We Are Best Friends by Aliki. Greenwillow, 1982.
Best Friends by Steven Kellogg. Dial Books, 1986.

For Extended and Recreational Reading

A House Is a House for Me
Books About Houses and Homes
The Little House by Virginia Lee Burton. Houghton Mifflin, 1978.

Listen, Children, Listen: An Anthology of Poems for the Very Young by Myra Cohn Livingston. Harcourt Brace Jovanovich, 1972.

The Biggest House in the World by Leo Lionni. Knopf, 1968.

More Books About Houses and Homes
Animals Live Here by Muriel Batherman. Greenwillow, 1979.

Tony's Hard Work Day by Alan Arkin. Harper & Row, 1972.

Benedict Finds a Home by Chris L. Demarest. Lothrop, Lee & Shepard, 1982.

Animal Houses by Aileen Fisher. Bowmar-Noble, 1978.

The Napping House by Audrey Wood. Harcourt Brace Jovanovich, 1984.

The Chick and the Duckling
Books About Animals and People
Make Way for Ducklings by Robert McCloskey. Viking, 1941.

The Ugly Duckling retold by Lorinda Bryan Cauley. Harcourt Brace Jovanovich, 1979.

Rosie's Walk by Pat Hutchins. Macmillan, 1968.

A Duckling Is Born by Hans-Heinrich Isenbart. G. P. Putnam's Sons, 1981.

The Cat in the Hat by Dr. Seuss. Beginner, 1957.

Look What I Can Do by Jose Aruego. Charles Scribner's Sons, 1971.

More Books About Animals and People
Keep Running, Allan by Clyde Bulla. Crown, 1978.

Molly's Moe by Kay Chorao. Houghton Mifflin, 1979.

The Luckiest One of All by Bill Peet. Houghton Mifflin, 1982.

I Can—Can You? by Peggy Parrish. Greenwillow, 1980.

Have You Ever Wished You Were Something Else? by Richard Armour. Childrens Press, 1983.

Count the Friends
Books About Counting
1, 2, 3 to the Zoo by Eric Carle. World, 1968.

The Very Hungry Caterpillar by Eric Carle. Puffin, 1984.

Anno's Counting Book by Mitsumasa Anno. T. Y. Crowell, 1975.

Ten, Nine, Eight by Molly Bang. Greenwillow, 1983.

Moja Means One: Swahili Counting Book by Muriel Feelings. Dial Books, 1971.

Numbers by John J. Reiss. Bradbury Press, 1971.

More Books About Counting
Don't Count Your Chicks by Ingri D'Aulaire and Edgar P. D'Aulaire. Doubleday, 1973.

The Berenstain Bear's Counting Book by Stan and Jan Berenstain. Random House, 1976.

Count and See by Tana Hoban. Macmillan, 1973.

One, Two, Three: An Animal Counting Book by Marc Brown. Little, Brown, 1976.

Uno, Dos, Tres, Cho —
One, Two, Three, Four, Five
Books About Counting
Ten, Nine, Eight by Molly Bang. Greenwillow, 1983.

Numbers by John J. Reiss. Bradbury, 1971.

Inch by Inch by Leo Lionni. Astor-Honor, 1962.

More Books About Counting
One Wide River to Cross by Barbara Emberley. Prentice-Hall, 1966.

Over in the Meadow by John Langstaff. Harcourt Brace Jovanovich, 1957.

Cat Count by Betsy Lewin. Dodd, Mead, 1981.

Harriet Goes to the Circus by Betsy Maestro and Giulio Maestro. Crown, 1977.

Over in the Meadow by Ezra Jack Keats. Four Winds, 1971.

Higher Than a House
Star Light, Star Bright
Books of Riddles
The Riddle of the Drum: A Tale from Tizapan, Mexico by Verna Aardema. Four Winds, 1979.

Sylvester and the Magic Pebble by William Steig. Windmill Books, 1969.

Why the Sun and the Moon Live in the Sky by Elphinstone Dayrell. Houghton Mifflin, 1968.

London Bridge Is Falling Down by Peter Spier. Doubleday, 1985.

Father Fox's Pennyrhymes by Clyde Watson. T. Y. Crowell, 1971.

The Cloud Book by Tomie dePaola. Holiday, 1975.

More Books of Riddles and Rhymes
The Carsick Zebra and Other Animal Riddles by David Adler. Holiday, 1983.

The Hodgepodge Book by Duncan Emrich. Four Winds, 1972.

Nailheads and Potato Eyes by Cynthia Basil. William Morrow, 1976.

The Upside Down Riddle Book by Beau Gardner. Lothrop, Lee & Shepard, 1982.

How Do You Make an Elephant Float and Other Delicious Riddles by Lee Bennett Hopkins. Albert Whitman, 1983.

For Extended and Recreational Reading

The Three Bears
Folk Tales
Little Red Riding Hood by Jacob and Wilhelm Grimm. Troll, 1981.

The Little Red Hen by Paul Galdone. Houghton Mifflin, 1973.

Snow White and the Seven Dwarfs by Jacob and Wilhelm Grimm. Translated by Randall Jarrell. Farrar, Straus & Giroux. 1973.

Marguerite De Angeli's Book of Nursery and Mother Goose Rhymes by Marguerite De Angeli. Doubleday, 1954.

The Gift of the Sacred Dog by Paul Goble. Bradbury, 1984.

More Folk Tales
Two Greedy Bears by Mirra Ginsburg. Macmillan, 1976.

The Valentine Bears by Eve Bunting, illustrated by Jan Brett. Clarion Books, 1982.

Three Friends Find Spring by Judy Delton. Crown, 1972.

Leo, Zack, and Emmie by Amy Ehrlich. Dial Books, 1981.

Three's Company by Mirra Ginsburg. Crown, 1973.

Changes, Changes
Books About Changes
Pig Pig Grows Up by David McPhail. E. P. Dutton, 1980.

There's a Nightmare in My Closet by Mercer Mayer. Dial Books, 1968.

Noah's Ark by Peter Spier. Doubleday, 1977.

The Little House by Virginia L. Burton. Houghton Mifflin, 1939.

More Books About Changes
Building a House by Byron Barton. Greenwillow, 1981.

Who Needs a Bear by Barbara Dillon. William Morrow, 1981.

The Cozy Book by Mary Ann Hoberman. Viking, 1982.

Don't Forget the Bacon by Pat Hutchins. Greenwillow, 1985.

The Secret in the Dungeon by Fernando Krahn. Clarion, 1983.

Dress for the Weather
Books About Weather and Seasons
The Cloud Book by Tomie dePaola. Holiday, 1975.

A Tree Is Nice by Janice Udry. Harper & Row, 1956.

Peter Spier's Rain by Peter Spier. Doubleday, 1982.

Katy and the Big Snow by Virginia L. Burton. Houghton Mifflin, 1943.

First Snow by Helen Coutant. Knopf, 1974.

More Books About Weather and Seasons
On the Town: A Book of Clothing Words by Betsy and Giulio Maestro. Crown, 1983.

All Wet! All Wet! by James Skofield. Harper & Row, 1984.

A January Fog Will Freeze a Hog and Other Weather Folklore by Hubert Davis. Crown, 1977.

On Sunday the Wind Came by Alan Elliot. William Morrow, 1980.

Discovering the Seasons by Louis Santrey, photos by Francene Sabin. Troll, 1980.

What Happens in Autumn by Suzanne Venio. National Geographic, 1982.

Hide and Seek Fog by Alvin R. Tresselt. Lothrop, Lee & Shepard, 1965.

The Mitten
Books About Animals
The Turnip illustrated by Janina Domanska. Macmillan, 1969.

One Fine Day by Nonny Hogrogian. Macmillan, 1971.

Corduroy by Don Freeman. Viking, 1968.

The Tale of Peter Rabbit by Beatrix Potter. Troll, 1979.

Pinkerton, Behave! by Steve Kellogg. Dial Books, 1979.

More Books About Animals and Their Adventures
The Little Girl and the Big Bear by Paul Galdone. Clarion Books, 1980.

Henny Penny by Paul Galdone. Seabury Press, 1968.

Silly Goose by Jack Kent. Prentice-Hall, 1983.

King Rooster, Queen Hen by Anita Lobel. Greenwillow, 1975.

Better Move on Frog! by Ron Maris. Franklin Watts, 1982.

Norman the Doorman by Don Freeman. Viking, 1959.

Mousekin's Golden House by Edna Miller. Prentice-Hall, 1964.

Five Little Pumpkins
Books About Imaginary Things
Strega Nona by Tomie dePaola. Prentice-Hall, 1975.

Harry and the Terrible Whatzit by Dick Gackenback. Houghton Mifflin, 1978.

The Cat in the Hat by Dr. Seuss. Beginner, 1957.

Where the Wild Things Are by Maurice Sendak. Harper & Row, 1963.

More Books About Halloween
Riddles That Rhyme for Halloween by Leonard Kessler. Gerrard, 1978.

Georgie's Halloween by Robert Bright. Doubleday, 1971.

Hey-How for Halloween! by Lee Bennett Hopkins. Harcourt Brace Jovanovich, 1974.

For Extended and Recreational Reading

Quack! Quack! Quack!

Rhymes, Poems, and Fingerplays

The Birds and the Beasts Were There by William Cole. Philomel, 1963.
Father Fox's Penny Rhymes by Clyde Watson. T. Y. Crowell, 1971.
Petunia by Roger Duvoisin. Knopf, 1962.

More Songs, Rhymes, and Fingerplays

Eye Winker, Tom Tinker, Chin Chopper: 50 Musical Fingerplays by Tom Glazer. Doubleday, 1973.
Do Your Ears Hang Low? 50 More Musical Fingerplays by Tom Glazer. Doubleday, 1980.
Out Loud by Eve Merriman. Atheneum, 1973.
Animal, Animal, Where Do You Live? by Jane Moncure. Childrens Press, 1976.
The Farmer in the Dell by Diane Zuromskis. Little, Brown, 1978.

Mix a Pancake

Singing-Time

Books About Food

The Very Hungry Caterpillar by Eric Carle. Puffin, 1984.
Bread and Jam for Frances by Russell Hoban. Harper & Row, 1964.
The Popcorn Book by Tomie dePaola. Holiday House, 1978.
The Pancake by Anita Lobel. Greenwillow, 1978.

More Books About Cooking and Food

Eats by Arnold Adoff. Lothrop, Lee & Shepard, 1979.
Cloudy with a Chance of Meatballs by Judith Barrett. Atheneum, 1978.
Pancakes for Breakfast by Tomie dePaola. Harcourt Brace Jovanovich, 1978.
Avocado Bay by John Burningham. T. Y. Crowell, 1981.
What's on Your Plate? by Norah Smaridge. Abingdon, 1982.
Kids Cooking Without a Stove: A Cookbook for Young Children by Aileen Paul. Doubleday, 1975.
The Wind in the Willows Country Cookbook by Arabella Boxer. Charles Scribner's, 1983.

Quick as a Cricket

Books About Developing a Positive Self-Image

William's Doll by Charlotte Zolotow. Harper & Row, 1985.
Look What I Can Do by Jose Aruego. Macmillan, 1971.
The Carrot Seed by Ruth Krauss. Harper & Row, 1945.
Story of Ferdinand by Munro Leaf. Penguin, 1977.
Nobody Listens to Andrew by Elizabeth Guilfoile. Modern Curriculum, 1957.

More Books About Developing a Positive Self-Image

By Myself by Lee Bennett Hopkins. Harper & Row, 1980.

Humphrey the Dancing Pig by Arthur Getz. Dial Books, 1980.
Herbert Hated Being Small by Karla Kuskin. Houghton Mifflin, 1979.
Broderick by Edward Ormondroyd. Houghton Mifflin, 1984.
When the New Baby Comes, I'm Moving Out by Martha Alexander. Dial, 1981.
P.J. the Spoiled Bunny by Marilyn Sadler. Random House, 1986.
Making the Team by Nancy Carlson. Carolrhoda, 1986.
Willy the Wimp by Anthony Browne. Knopf, 1986.

How Do They Feel?

Books About Feelings

Alexander and the Terrible, Horrible, No Good, Very Bad Day by Judith Viorst. Atheneum, 1976.
Crow Boy by Taro Yashima. Puffin, 1976.
The Tenth Good Thing About Barney by Judith Viorst. Clarion Books, 1984.
What Mary Jo Shared by Janice M. Udry. A. Whitman, 1966.
Amifika by Lucille Clifton. Dutton, 1977.
The Quarreling Book by Charlotte Zolotow. Harper & Row, 1963.

More Books About Feelings

Kate in the Morning by Crescent Dragon. Harper & Row, 1982.
The Lonely Skyscraper by Jenny Hawkesworth. Doubleday, 1980.
A Treeful of Pigs by Arnold Lobel. Greenwillow, 1979.
The Big Red Barn by Eve Bunting. Harcourt Brace Jovanovich, 1979.

Over, Under, and Through

Books About Spatial Concepts

The Little House by Virginia Burton. Houghton Mifflin, 1978.
Peter Spier's Rain by Peter Spier. Doubleday, 1982.
Simple Pictures Are Best by Nancy Willard. Harcourt Brace Jovanovich, 1978.
The Cat in the Hat by Dr. Seuss. Beginner, 1957.
There's a Nightmare in My Closet by Mercer Mayer. Dial Books, 1968.

More Books About Spatial Concepts

Over, Under, and All-Around by Sylvia Root Tester. Children's World, 1973.
The Discovery Book of Up and Down by Judith Conway. Raintree, 1977.
Goodnight, Goodnight by Eve Rice. William Morrow, 1980.
Where's Spot? by Eric Hill. G. P. Putnam's, 1980.

For Extended and Recreational Reading

Coco Can't Wait
Books About Traveling and Families
Miss Rumphius by Barbara Cooney. Viking, 1982.
Freight Train by Donald Crews. Greenwillow, 1978.
William's Doll by Charlotte Zolotow. Harper & Row, 1972.
My Grandson Lew by Charlotte Zolotow. Harper & Row, 1974.
La Expedición by Willy Baum. Baron, 1978.

More Books About Traveling and Families
Grandpa and Me Together by Susan Goldman. A. Whitman, 1978.
Kevin's Grandma by Barbara Williams. E. P. Dutton, 1975.
Trucks by Anne Rockwell. E. P. Dutton, 1984.
Wheels by Byron Barton. Harper & Row, 1979.
Airplane Ride by Douglas Florian. Harper & Row, 1984.

I Love You Mouse
Books About Animal Friends
May I Bring A Friend? by Beatrice S. DeRegniers. Macmillan, 1964.
Millions of Cats by Wanda Gag. G. P. Putnam's, 1977.
Harry the Dirty Dog by Gene Zion. Harper & Row, 1956.
John Brown, Rose and the Midnight Cat by Jenny Wagner. Bradbury, 1978.
The Birds and the Beasts Were There by William Cole. World, 1963.

More Books About Animal Friends and Animal Babies
The Tomten by Viktor Rydberg. Coward-McCann, 1968.
Nobody Knows I Have Delicate Toes by Nancy Patz. Franklin Watts, 1980.
Friend Dog by Arnold Adoff. J. B. Lippincott, 1980.
All Kinds of Babies by Millicent E. Selsam. Scholastic, 1967.
You Don't Look Like Your Mother, Said the Robin to the Fawn by Aileen Fisher. Bowmar-Noble, 1973.

What Is Beyond the Hill?
Books About the World Around Us
A Tree Is Nice by Janice Udry. Harper & Row, 1956.
The Cloud Book by Tomie dePaola. Holiday, 1975.
Rosie's Walk by Pat Hutchins, Macmillan, 1968.
Why the Sun and the Moon Live in the Sky by Elphinstone Dayrell. Houghton Mifflin, 1968.

More Books About the World Around Us
Where Does the Sun Go at Night? by Mirra Ginsburg. Greenwillow, 1981.
Take Me to the Moon by Sal Murdocca. Lothrop, Lee & Shepard, 1976.
Little Fox Goes to the End of the World by Ann Tompert. Crown, 1976.
Toto by Marietta D. Moskin. Coward-McCann, 1972.

Water
Books About Water and Its Uses
Harry the Dirty Dog by Gene Zion. Harper & Row, 1956.
London Bridge Is Falling Down by Peter Spier. Doubleday, 1985.
The Mysterious Tadpole by Steven Kellogg. Dial Books, 1977.
Swimmy by Leo Lionni. Pantheon, 1963.
Umbrella by Taro Yashima. Viking, 1958.

More Books About Water
Wonders of Rivers by Rae Bains. Troll, 1982.
Benjy's Boat Trip by Margaret Bloy. Harper & Row, 1977.
Rivers by Norman and Madelyn Carlisle. Childrens Press, 1982.
All Wet! All Wet! by James Skofield. Harper & Row, 1984.
Rain Drop Splash by Alvin R. Tresselt. Lothrop, Lee & Shepard, 1946.

Hello and Good-bye
Books About the Seasons
Snowy Day by Ezra J. Keats. Viking, 1962.
The Nicest Gift by Leo Politi. Charles Scribner's, 1973.
First Snow by Helen Coutant. Knopf, 1974.
White Snow, Bright Snow by Alvin R. Tresselt. Lothrop, Lee & Shepard, 1947.

More Books About the Seasons
Happy Day by Ruth Krauss. Harper & Row, 1980.
All Wet! All Wet! by James Skofield. Harper & Row, 1984.
On Sunday the Wind Came by Alan Elliot. William Morrow, 1980.
Discovering the Seasons by Louis Santrey, photos by Francene Sabin. Troll, 1980.
The Song by Charlotte Zolotow. Greenwillow, 1982.

For Extended and Recreational Reading

BIBLIOGRAPHY 6

Have You Seen My Duckling?
Books About Exploring
The Nicest Gift by Leo Politi. Charles Scribner's, 1973.
We Hide, You Seek by Jose Aruego and Ariane Dewey. Greenwillow, 1979.
Fox Eyes by Margaret W. Brown. Pantheon, 1977.
Nothing To Do by Russell Hoban. Harper & Row, 1964.
Harry, the Dirty Dog by Gene Zion. Harper & Row, 1956.

More Books About Exploring
Can You Find the Animal? by Wilda S. Ross. Coward-McCann, 1974.
Hiding Game by Ben Shecter. Four Winds, 1977.
Joey Runs Away by Jack Kent. Prentice-Hall, 1986.
So Many Raccoons by Jan Wahl. Caedmon, 1986.

To Market, To Market
Hickory, Dickory, Dock
Higglety, Pigglety, Pop
Books About Nonsense
A Light in the Attic by Shel Silverstein. Harper & Row, 1981.
My Tang's Tungled and Other Ridiculous Situations by Sara Brewton and others. T. Y. Crowell, 1973.
The Mother Goose Treasury edited by Raymond Briggs. Dell, 1986.
Granfa' Grig Had a Pig and Other Rhymes Without Reason from Mother Goose by Wallace Tripp. Little, Brown, 1976.
A Great Big Ugly Man Came Up and Tied His Horse to Me: A Book of Nonsense Verse by Wallace Tripp. Little, Brown, 1973.
Chinese Mother Goose Rhymes by Robert Wyndham. G. P. Putnam's, 1982.

More Books About Nonsense
There Are Rocks in My Socks! Said the Ox to the Fox by Patricia Thomas. Lothrop, Lee & Shepard, 1979.
On Market Street by Arnold Lobel and Anita Lobel. Greenwillow, 1981.
The Animals Go to the Supermarket by Alice Proudfoot. Crane, Russak, 1977.

Barnyard Song
Books About Animals
Little Rabbit's Loose Tooth by Lucy Bate. Crown, 1975.
Sarah's Unicorn by Bruce and Katherine Coville. J. B. Lippincott, 1979.
Winnie the Pooh by A. A. Milne. E. P. Dutton, 1975.
Mr. Rabbit and the Lovely Present by Charlotte Zolotow. Harper & Row, 1962.
Momo's Kitten by Taro and Mitsu Yashima. Penguin, 1977.
The Day Jimmy's Boa Ate the Wash by Trinka Noble. Dial, 1980.

More Books and Rhymes About Animals
Our Animal Friends at Maple Hill Farm by Alice and Martin Provensen. Random House, 1974.
Gobble, Growl, Grunt by Peter Spier. Doubleday, 1971.
Where's Henrietta? by Beatrice Freschet, illustrated by Lorinda Cauley. G. P. Putnam's, 1980.
Treeful of Pigs by Arnold Lobel. Greenwillow, 1979.

A Zookeeper at Work
Books About Careers and Zoo Animals
Make Way For Ducklings by Robert McCloskey. Viking, 1941.
Airport by Byron Barton. Harper & Row, 1982.
A Children's Zoo by Tana Hoban. Greenwillow, 1985.

More Books About Careers
Maybe You Should Fly a Jet! Maybe You Should Be a Vet! by Theo LeSieg. Random House, 1980.
People Working by Douglas Florian. T. Y. Crowell, 1983.
The Luckiest One of All by Bill Peet. Houghton Mifflin, 1982.
When We Grow Up by Anne Rockwell. E. P. Dutton, 1981.

A Bear Went Over a Mountain
Lunch for a Dinosaur
Books About Dinosaurs and Bears
Ask Mister Bear by Marjorie Flack. Macmillan, 1986.
Little Bear by Else H. Minarik. Harper & Row, 1978.
Bearymore by Don Freeman. Viking, 1976.
Digging Up Dinosaurs by Aliki. Harper & Row, 1981.
Danny and the Dinosaur by Syd Hoff. Harper & Row, 1958.

More Books About Dinosaurs and Bears
Moon Bear by Frank Asch. Charles Scribner's, 1978.
A First Look at Dinosaurs by Millicent E. Selsam and Joyce Hurt. Walker & Co., 1982.
Supersaurus by Francine Jacobs. G. P. Putnam's, 1982.
My Visit to the Dinosaurs by Aliki. Harper & Row, 1985.

Evaluation Resources

This section of your *Teacher's Edition* includes an assortment of valuable resources to help you monitor your students' progress.

Listening Comprehension Evaluation

Reproducible **Listening Comprehension** evaluations to assess, at midyear and end of year, your students' ability to listen for a purpose and comprehend at varying levels of thinking. For your convenience, you will also find in this section reading passages and directions for administering and evaluating the tests.

(NOTE: The **Listening Comprehension** evaluations also appear in copying-master form in the *Learning Resources File*.)

Observation and Evaluation Guides

Reproducible guidelines for observing and recording your students' development in listening, speaking, reading, and writing, with accompanying record forms.

(NOTE: The **Observation and Evaluation Guides** also appear in copying-master form in the *Learning Resources File*.)

Contents

Listening Comprehension Evaluations

The **Listening Comprehension** Evaluations are designed to assess your students' ability to listen and comprehend a story. The **Listening** Evaluations for the middle and the end of the year consist of two passages to be read to the class. The children's comprehension of the passages is assessed by having them answer five questions. Each child responds by marking the picture which best represents the answer to the question.

On the following pages you will find specific guidelines for administering each **Listening Comprehension** Evaluation. Before the children begin, make certain they have a clear understanding of the directions. Allow adequate time for the children to complete the test.

Listening Comprehension – Midyear

Directions: We are going to see how well you listen. Listen carefully to the story I am going to read. Listen to find out what made Little Rabbit afraid.

Stars

Little Rabbit ate some grass in a field. He looked up at the moon. He saw many stars.

"Look at the stars," Little Rabbit said to his father. "There are so many stars in the sky!"

Father looked up at the sky. "You can see pictures in the stars."

Little Rabbit and his father looked closely at the stars. First they saw some stars in the shape of a fish. Then they saw some stars in the shape of a house. Last they saw some stars in the shape of a carrot.

Little Rabbit smiled. "I like looking for pictures in the stars," he said.

The Little Rabbit hopped to the next field of grass. He looked at the stars and saw a fox! Little Rabbit hopped back to his father.

"Father, I see a fox in the sky! I am afraid!"

"Do not be afraid, Little Rabbit. The fox in the sky is not real. It is only a picture."

Little Rabbit felt much better. He sat close to Father and ate some grass.

Now I am going to read five questions about the story. You will see three pictures next to the number for each question. Draw a ring around the picture that shows the best answer to each question.

1. Which picture shows who looks at the sky? (*Little Rabbit and Father*) (Literal)
2. Which picture shows where Little Rabbit and Father look at the sky? (*grassy field*) (Literal)
3. Which picture shows what Little Rabbit and Father see in the sky? (*stars*) (Literal)
4. Which picture shows what Little Rabbit sees in the sky that makes him afraid? (*fox*) (Literal)
5. Which picture shows what Little Rabbit does at the end of the story? (*eats grass*) (Literal)

Name _____

Stars

1.

2.

3.

4.

  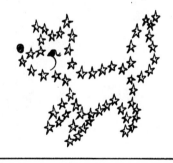

5.

IMAGINATION, *Happy Times!*

Listening Comprehension **E5**

Listening Comprehension – Midyear

Directions: We are going to see how well you listen. Listen carefully to the story I am going to read. Listen to find out about Joey's surprise.

Joey's Surprise

Joey's mother picked him up from school. She said to Joey, "There is a surprise for you at home."

Joey was curious. "What kind of surprise?"

"See if you can guess," Joey's mother said. "The surprise is small. It is grey and furry and it says 'meow,'"

"A kitten? Is it a kitten?" Joey asked. He was very excited.

"Yes, it's a kitten."

Joey could not wait to get home. He ran to the door. He jumped up and down as his mother unlocked the door.

Joey creeped slowly into the house. He did not want to scare the kitten. "Here, kitty. Hello, kitty." Joey called very softly.

Joey's mother knew where the kitten was. She went to the kitchen. The kitten was sleeping on a blanket on the floor.

"He's so little," Joey said. "Where did he come from?"

"Your grandpa found him. He thought you would like a new friend," Joey's mother said.

Joey smiled and hugged the kitten. He knew they would be best friends.

Now I am going to read five questions about the story. You will see three pictures next to the number for each question. Draw a ring around the picture that shows the best answer to each question.

1. Which picture shows who has a surprise for Joey? (*Mother*) (Literal)
2. Which picture shows Joey's surprise? (*kitten*) (Literal)
3. Which picture shows where the kitten is sleeping? (*on a blanket*) (Literal)
4. Which picture shows who brings home the kitten for Joey? (*Grandpa*) (Literal)
5. Which picture shows how Joey feels at the end of the story? (*Joey is happy*) (Interpretive)

Joey's Surprise

1.

2.

3.

4.

5.

Listening Comprehension – End-of-Year

Directions: We are going to see how well you listen. Listen carefully to the story I am going to read. Listen to find out a girl named Annalee.

Waiting
by Nicki Weiss

Early one sunny summer morning Annalee walked to the gate with her mother.

"I will be back before you know it," Mama said. She kissed Annalee and pulled the gate shut behind her. Mama walked down the road until all Annalee could see was a spot.

"I hope she comes back soon," Annalee thought, and she sat down to wait. Somewhere a voice started singing. "She's back!" Annalee said. But it was only a bird, chirping in a tree. "She said she'd come back soon," Annalee thought and she shut her eyes.

Suddenly she smelled something good. "She's here!" Annalee said. But when she opened her eyes, all she saw were the roses growing on the fence.

"Soon. She'll come back soon," Annalee thought. The grass rustled, and Annalee said, "Is that you, Mama?" But it was only the wind blowing across the hill.

"I know she'll come back soon," Annalee thought. She flopped back in the grass and waited. Something tickled her and she giggled, "Stop it, Mama." But it was only a ladybug crawling on her leg.

She looked up at the sky and waited. And when she heard a noise at the gate, she didn't turn around. "I bet you didn't even know I was gone," a voice said. Mama was standing there, and they walked up the path together.

Now I am going to read five questions about the story. You will see three pictures next to the number for each question. Draw a ring around the picture that shows the best answer to each question.

1. Which picture shows who Annalee waits for? (*Mother*) (Literal)
2. Which picture shows where Annalee waits? (*gate*) (Literal)
3. Annalee smells something good. She thinks it is her mother. Which picture shows what she smells? (*roses*) (Literal)
4. Annalee thinks her mother tickles her leg. Which picture shows what tickles her leg? (*ladybug*) (Literal)
5. Which picture shows where Annalee and her mother walk after her mother returns? (*path*) (Literal)

Name _____

Waiting

1.

2.

3.

4.

5.

Listening Comprehension – End-of-Year

Directions: We are going to see how well you listen. Listen carefully to the story I am going to read. Listen to find out two friends.

A Lily Pad Day

Peter and Douglas were frogs. They sat on a lily pad in a pond. They loved to look up at the beautiful clouds in the sky. It was a beautiful day to be a frog.

Suddenly a cricket jumped onto the lily pad. He made a chirping noise. Douglas was frightened. He jumped off the lily pad and swam away.

Peter said to the cricket, "My friend is afraid of you. You better leave or he won't come out of the water."

"I like this lily pad," said the cricket. "It is sunny here. It is warm here."

"If you do not leave," said Peter, "I will eat you!"

"I do not believe you. You are not brave enough to do that!"

Suddenly Douglas jumped out of the water. He swallowed the cricket.

"Why Douglas," said Peter. "I am surprised! You are very brave."

"Thank you," Douglas replied. And the two frogs sat on the lily pad all day long.

Now I am going to read five questions about the story. You will see three pictures next to the number for each question. Draw a ring around the picture that shows the best answer to each question.

1. Which picture shows the two friends in the story? (*Two frogs*) (Literal)
2. Which picture shows where the friends sit? (*lily pad*) (Literal)
3. Which picture shows why one friend is frightened? (*cricket*) (Literal)
4. Which picture shows how Douglas feels at the end of the story? (*Douglas is happy*) (Interpretive)
5. Which picture shows what Douglas will do the next time he sees a cricket? (*Douglas eats the cricket*) (Interpretive)

Name _____

A Lily Pad Day

1.

2.

3.

4.

5.

IMAGINATION, *Happy Times!*

Listening Comprehension **E11**

Observation and Evaluation Guides

In this section you will find copying masters for observing and recording your students' development in listening, speaking, reading, and writing.

Listening and Speaking Evaluation Guides: These reproducible forms are to be used with students throughout the year to record developmental growth in listening and speaking.

Reading Evaluation Guide: This reproducible form is to be used with students throughout the year to record developmental growth in reading.

Writing Evaluation Guide: This reproducible form is to be used with students throughout the year to record developmental growth in writing.

Name

RATING **N:** no behavior **B:** beginning behavior **D:** developing behavior **S:** secure behavior

OBSERVATION GUIDE

LISTENING

	Aug.	Sept.	Oct.	Nov.	Dec.	Jan.	Feb.	Mar.	Apr.	May	June	July	Comments
• Distinguishes sounds in the environment													
• Listens to stories from books, records, films													
• Listens to new ideas													
• Listens to peers													
• Appreciates prose, poetry, rhyme													
• Listens for information													
• Comprehends facts, main ideas in discussion													

IMAGINATION, *Happy Times!*

Name

OBSERVATION GUIDE

SPEAKING

	Aug.	Sept.	Oct.	Nov.	Dec.	Jan.	Feb.	Mar.	Apr.	May	June	July	Comments
• Uses language to satisfy personal needs, give instructions, imagine, predict, project													
• Talks to the teacher													
• Uses social language (greetings)													
• Talks to peers													
• Describes objects and pictures													
• Narrates personal stories													
• Tells complete story about one topic													
• Retells stories from literature													
• Sequence events in stories													
• Tells stories with expression													
• Uses sound effects in story telling													
• Uses dialogue in story telling													
• Dictates personal stories													

IMAGINATION, *Happy Times!*

continued

Name

RATING   **N:** no behavior   **B:** beginning behavior   **D:** developing behavior   **S:** secure behavior

SPEAKING (continued)

	Aug.	Sept.	Oct.	Nov.	Dec.	Jan.	Feb.	Mar.	Apr.	May	June	July	Comments
• Role plays in a variety of situations (alone or with others)													
• Participates in dramatizations													
• Uses telephone with familiar or imaginary person													
• Dictates information													
• Shares facts and information													
• Predicts outcomes of stories													
• Asks relevant questions in a variety of situations													
• Is aware of appropriate speaking behavior (being polite, listening to peers, taking turns)													
• Participates in small group discussions													
• Speaks clearly with appropriate volume													

IMAGINATION, *Happy Times!*

Name

OBSERVATION GUIDE

READING

Beginning Reader	Aug.	Sept.	Oct.	Nov.	Dec.	Jan.	Feb.	Mar.	Apr.	May	June	July	Comments
• Recognizes environmental print													
• Enjoys listening to stories													
• Participates in shared reading activities													
• Looks at books as a self-initiated activity													
• Holds books right side up													
• Turns pages from front to back of the book													
• Examines pictures in a book													
• Recalls the main idea of familiar story													
• Recalls details from familiar story													
• Names events in familiar story													
• Understands cause and effect in familiar story													
• Predicts new endings to familiar story													

continued

IMAGINATION, *Happy Times!*

Observation Guide • **E18**

Name

OBSERVATION GUIDE

READING (continued)

Beginning Reader (continued)	Aug.	Sept.	Oct.	Nov.	Dec.	Jan.	Feb.	Mar.	Apr.	May	June	July	Comments
• Uses pictures to gain meaning from text													
• Interprets stories through interpretive activities (art, drama, construction)													
• Holds books and tells a story as though reading													
• Tells an appropriate story to match main idea of the book													
• Tells an appropriate story to match a picture in a familiar book													
• Reconstructs holistically a whole story to match a familiar story (story may not match exact text)													
• Retells a refrain from a familiar story													
• Retells with accuracy a repeated pattern in a book													
• Attends to lines of print when attempting to reconstruct the story													

continued

IMAGINATION, *Happy Times!*

Name _____

RATING   **N:** no behavior   **B:** beginning behavior   **D:** developing behavior   **S:** secure behavior

READING (continued)

Beginning Reader (continued)	Aug.	Sept.	Oct.	Nov.	Dec.	Jan.	Feb.	Mar.	Apr.	May	June	July	Comments
• Retells a dictated story maintaining main idea													
• Turns pages consistently from right to left													
• Attempts to match an oral story with each page of print as pages are turned													
• Recognizes where print begins on a page													
• Recognizes where print ends on a page													
• Begins to move his/her eyes and finger left to right across the print while attempting to read (finger does not stop at individual words)													
• Develops awareness of line directionality (child's finger moves left to right across line of print and then moves to the far left of the page and down to track the next line of print)													

IMAGINATION, *Happy Times!*

continued

Observation Guide • **E20**

Name _____

OBSERVATION GUIDE

READING (continued)

Developing Reader	Aug.	Sept.	Oct.	Nov.	Dec.	Jan.	Feb.	Mar.	Apr.	May	June	July	Comments
• Begins to point to groups of letters and assigns an oral response (each oral response may not accurately match the text)													
• Reads a page in a familiar pattern book													
• Tracks accurately words in a familiar sentence													
• Tracks to find a specific words													
• Uses pictures, patterns, semantics, and syntax to gain meaning													
• Recognizes common words in stories													
• Tracks accurately several sentences in a familiar story													
• Tracks accurately two or more sentences in a dictated story immediately after dictation													
• Reads any page in a familiar book													

IMAGINATION, *Happy Times!*

Name _____

OBSERVATION GUIDE

RATING   **N:** no behavior   **B:** beginning behavior   **D:** developing behavior   **S:** secure behavior

READING (continued)

Developing Reader (continued)	Aug.	Sept.	Oct.	Nov.	Dec.	Jan.	Feb.	Mar.	Apr.	May	June	July	Comments
• Uses memory and pictures to gain meaning from familiar text													
• Uses memory, pictures, syntax, and pattern to gain meaning from a familiar text													
• Uses memory, pictures, pattern, and tracking to gain meaning from the familiar text													
• Reads for meaning													
• Reads accurately familiar pattern books													
• Tracks current dictated story with accurate word matching													
• Reads familiar charts													
• Tracks old dictated stories with accuracy													
• Becomes aware of sound-letter correspondences													

continued

IMAGINATION, *Happy Times!*

Observation Guide • **E22**

Name _____

OBSERVATION GUIDE

READING (continued)

Developing Reader (continued)	Aug.	Sept.	Oct.	Nov.	Dec.	Jan.	Feb.	Mar.	Apr.	May	June	July	Comments
• Uses phonetic cues with familiar material													
• Reads numerous familiar pattern texts with accuracy													
• Begins to read new predictable pattern books with accuracy													
• Uses picture clues, syntax, tracking, memory, and semantics to gain meaning													
• Uses picture clues, syntax, tracking, memory, semantics, and phonics to gain meaning from new predictable pattern books													
• Makes meaningful substitutions in reading													
Independent Reader • Begins to self-correct reading													
• Reads new pattern literature with ease													

IMAGINATION, *Happy Times!*

Name

RATING **N:** no behavior   **B:** beginning behavior   **D:** developing behavior   **S:** secure behavior

READING (continued)

Independent Reader (continued)	Aug.	Sept.	Oct.	Nov.	Dec.	Jan.	Feb.	Mar.	Apr.	May	June	July	Comments
• Reads current dictated stories (5 to 10 sentences)													
• Reads own published dictated stories													
• Appreciates favorite authors													
• Reads grade level text													
• Becomes aware of information in a book (title, author, illustrator, pages)													

IMAGINATION, *Happy Times!*

Name _____

RATING **N:** no behavior **B:** beginning behavior **D:** developing behavior **S:** secure behavior

OBSERVATION GUIDE

WRITING

Composition	Aug.	Sept.	Oct.	Nov.	Dec.	Jan.	Feb.	Mar.	Apr.	May	June	July	Comments
• Communicates through talk													
• Communicates through drama and picture making													
• Communicates through invented symbols (scribble, invented letters)													
• Dictates stories on one topic													
• Composes narrative through scribble or invented letters													
• Composes narrative using conventional letters													
• Dictates poetry, stories, letters, and lists													
• Writes from model sentence patterns													
• Labels with words													
• Writes series of pattern sentences													
• Participates in group writing of poetry, letters, lists, pattern stories, and reports													

IMAGINATION, *Happy Times!*

Name

RATING   N: no behavior   B: beginning behavior   D: developing behavior   S: secure behavior

WRITING (continued)

	Aug.	Sept.	Oct.	Nov.	Dec.	Jan.	Feb.	Mar.	Apr.	May	June	July	Comments
Composition (continued)													
• Writes according to model given by teacher													
• Dictates stories with series of events													
• Dictates fantasy stories													
Prewriting													
• Uses a variety of prewriting strategies													
Responding/Revising													
• Shares stories with an adult													
• Shares stories with peers													
• Uses conference techniques with self and peers													
• Considers minor additions to dictated stories providing an adult makes the changes													
• Suggests minor additions to stories													
• Deletes or reorganizes information													

continued

IMAGINATION, *Happy Times!*

Name

RATING   **N:** no behavior   **B:** beginning behavior   **D:** developing behavior   **S:** secure behavior

WRITING (continued)

	Aug.	Sept.	Oct.	Nov.	Dec.	Jan.	Feb.	Mar.	Apr.	May	June	July	Comments
Editing													
• Prefers stories with nonstandard spellings to remain unedited													
• Allows changes to written stories													
Publishing													
• Shares final copy with teacher, peers, class													
Symbolic Representation													
• Symbolizes stories through talk													
• Symbolizes stories through drama													
• Symbolizes stories through picture making													
• Symbolizes stories through dictation													
• Symbolizes stories through random scribble													
• Symbolizes stories through horizontal scribble													
• Uses sentence scribble (one line of scribble represents a sentence)													

IMAGINATION, *Happy Times!*

continued

Observation Guide • **E27**

RATING **N:** no behavior   **B:** beginning behavior   **D:** developing behavior   **S:** secure behavior

WRITING (continued)

	Aug.	Sept.	Oct.	Nov.	Dec.	Jan.	Feb.	Mar.	Apr.	May	June	July	Comments
Symbolic Representation (continued)													
• Uses word scribble (scribble is broken into segments to represent words)													
• Uses invented letters (*N* for *H*)													
• Uses uppercase letters													
• Integrates scribble symbols with conventional letters													
• Uses predominance of conventional letters													
Spelling													
• Uses scribble to represent spelling													
• Uses random letters to represent words													
• Uses conventional letters but no sound-letter correspondences													
• Uses letter name spelling (*m* for *am*, *n* for *and*)													
• Uses initial consonant spelling (*i w s l n* for *I went skating last night*)													

IMAGINATION, *Happy Times!*

OBSERVATION GUIDE

Name _____

RATING **N:** no behavior   **B:** beginning behavior   **D:** developing behavior   **S:** secure behavior

WRITING (continued)

	Aug.	Sept.	Oct.	Nov.	Dec.	Jan.	Feb.	Mar.	Apr.	May	June	July	Comments
Spelling (continued)													
• Uses vowels in spelling													
• Uses invented spelling (*I wnt sktg lst nit*)													
• Spells high-frequency words conventionally (*name, to, a, and, the*)													
• Begins to make the transition from invented to standard spelling (*w, wt, wnt, went*)													
• Writes one-quarter of a story using standard spelling													
Conventions													
• Prints scribble or letters horizontally left to right across the page													
• Leaves spaces between words													
• Uses punctuation occasionally													
• Begins to use punctuation at the ends of lines													
• Uses random punctuation													

IMAGINATION, *Happy Times!*

continued

OBSERVATION GUIDE

Name _____

RATING **N:** no behavior **B:** beginning behavior **D:** developing behavior **S:** secure behavior

WRITING (continued)

Conventions (continued)	Aug.	Sept.	Oct.	Nov.	Dec.	Jan.	Feb.	Mar.	Apr.	May	June	July	Comments
• Uses uppercase and lower case letters indiscriminately													
• Uses uppercase letters for beginning of own name													
• Uses uppercase letters for the beginning of names of friends													

IMAGINATION, *Happy Times!*

Notes

Notes

Notes

Notes

Notes

Notes

Notes

Notes

Notes

Notes

Notes

Notes

Notes

Notes